The Library of Scandinavian Literature

FIVE MODERN SCANDINAVIAN PLAYS

FIVE MODERN SCANDINAVIAN PLAYS

CARL ERIK SOYA

WALENTIN CHORELL

DAVIÐ STEFÁNSSON

NORDAHL GRIEG

PÄR LAGERKVIST

TWAYNE PUBLISHERS, INC., NEW YORK
&
THE AMERICAN-SCANDINAVIAN FOUNDATION

The Library of Scandinavian Literature
Erik J. Friis, *General Editor*

Volume 11

Five Modern Scandinavian Plays

MANUFACTURED IN THE UNITED STATES OF AMERICA

CONTENTS

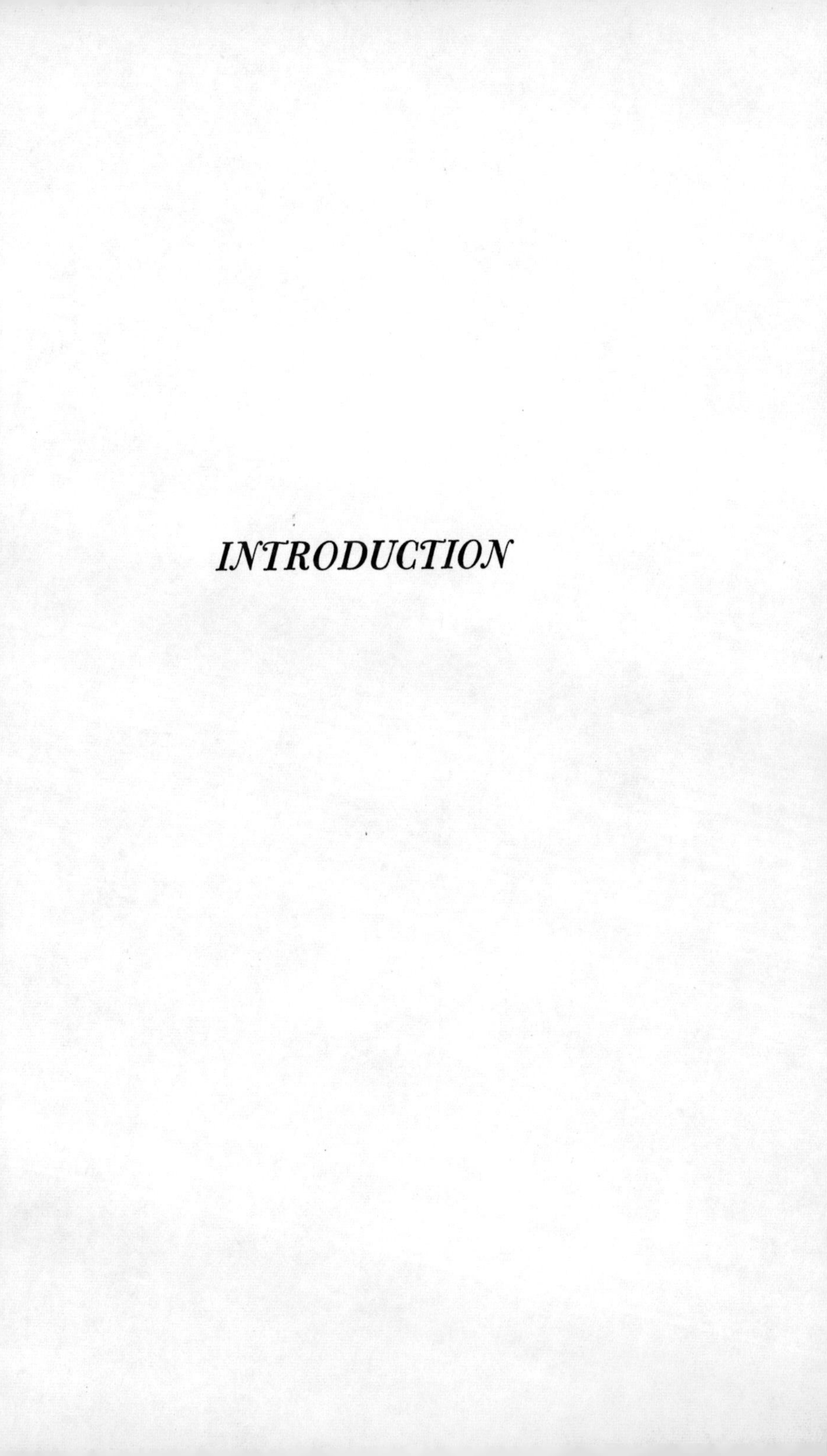

INTRODUCTION

THE rapid pace at which historical time in the present century advances accustoms the mind's eye to wide panoramas resembling views in aerial photography. These camera shots are both inescapable and inescapably alluring, not in themselves directly inspired by imagination, as panoramic painting a millennium ago in China, but none the less arresting. The more our world contracts, the more our bird's-eye view of it expands. This sense of largeness in both physical and mental space which Walt Whitman prophetically foresaw grows upon us. It is with the aim of viewing such an extended horizon that this brief introduction to a collection of five Scandinavian plays in English is conceived, for such a book obviously invites the outlook of comparative literature.

The plays themselves are selected from four languages, each spoken over a relatively small area, but in this volume they appear in the language most widely spoken today throughout the world. The book is thus in more respects than one an adventure in what might be called trans-nationalism. Each of the five plays, as it happens, shows uncommonly well the qualities typical of the country of its origin. Moreover, each is prefaced by an introduction devoted to some of the peculiar problems surrounding it. Hence this foreword to the collection as a whole assumes a collative and an inclusive view. What, it may be asked, are the special qualities rendering these plays and works like them attractive in their own sections of the world and, more important here, their qualities motivating translation into languages of still other lands and at times even inviting their appearance on what we have come of late to call the world theater? How generously do these and similar plays carry whatever meaning thought and expression in Scandinavia may have for the world at large?

Geography is the prior condition of a culture or a civilization, as the instances of these countries most strikingly show. The

Scandinavian peninsula lies at what we instinctively regard as the top of Europe, for half the year a snowy mountain land with peaks from which, on intervals when the sky is clear, views are peculiarly expansive. Geographically considered, Denmark is its vestibule, a small, low-lying, green land spread before its door; Norway is a narrow fringe of rocky coast; Iceland an icy jewel crowning the Atlantic; Finland that extraordinary conjunction of forest and clear lakes reflecting the northern sky; Sweden and Finland together seem leaning to the East, even suggesting a figure with eyes bent toward Asia. In these cases we have sub-arctic lands, imaginatively considered, both more and less European than the main parts of that continent, for here, as will presently be observed, Western man seems both more and less Western than elsewhere. Slenderly attached to Europe, Scandinavia provides an ideal observation post for the study of Europe. With its degree of isolation, least notable in Denmark, most conspicuous in Iceland, the most remarkable of all provincial lands, it favors not only self-examination but a review of other cultures, holding aloft a glass that might be likened to an ice-crystal before mankind. Scandinavian thought is both unique and synthetic. It enjoys a favorable vantage point to survey and triangulate the map of the world—always with that humorous reservation that its summits may be veiled in fog.

For an initial view it may be helpful to take one or two extreme instances in Scandinavian experience expressing the peculiar relationships considered here. It comes first to my thought that with no slight emotion one takes in hand the first book printed in Iceland, belonging to the period designated in European terms the Renaissance. This is a collection of Icelandic sagas, its handsomely engraved title page adorned with figures of Neptune and other watery deities of the Classical world. The suggestion is at once of a proud provincialism and a virtually heroic eclecticism. For the second instance I note that the author of the Icelandic play contained in this volume after a childhood on a farm in the northern part of his beloved island received a fellowship to study in Italy. Pausing for a moment's thought on these two widely spaced incidents, our minds may be the better prepared for more serious reflections.

Relative to Europe itself Classical culture came late to Scandinavia and Roman Catholicism built itself less deeply into the national minds, so that Protestantism on its arrival found its most secure home. This, however, signified for the most part not the fanatical and searing Protestantism of Calvin or Jonathan Edwards but a renaissance of an individualism apparently native to the cultures of the North. Mysticism, with its familiar tendency to individualism, thrived far more than ecclesiasticism. Yet the spiritual climate was no gentler than the physical climate. Life in Italy has always rested more or less upon smoothly accepted assumptions, never quite so serenely conceived as life in classical India but none the less an experience whose boundaries are surveyed and known. Virgil surveyed the ancient world and found it good; Dante surveyed the Christian world and at least found it strictly in accord with Christian theology. In the North a quite different condition has prevailed and one which early manifested itself as charged with dramatic potentialities. Its best symbol is, perhaps, the title of a poem by an American, E. A. Robinson, "The Man Against the Sky." Life became not only a problem but to some extent a fresh problem as each individual experienced it. So "A" confronted "B" and thus a social problem presented itself for which no ready solution stood at hand. Drama is never completely dramatic without the confrontation of a problem. All great plays, in fact, symbolize thought and imply a problem. It was highly natural, therefore, that a type of play which presented a somewhat dubious orientation to esthetics but a highly rational and pragmatic orientation to life should arise with peculiar vigor in Scandinavia. The Scandinavian countries became the cradle of the so-called "problem play."

These thoughts themselves present, of course, virtually inexhaustible problems. As the Orient envisages the stage it is by tradition a semi-religious dance; as the West envisages the stage it presents an "agon," or contest between individuals, an arena favoring the presentation of "characters." And what characters they are! Ibsen has been violently attacked and nowhere more virulently than by his fellow Scandinavians. But Western actors prize "character parts" the most highly and what dramatist presents these so vividly as the great Norwegian? The condition lies deep in the experience and tradition of the Scandinavian people. It explains, especially in Western eyes, an extremely important factor in the vitality of the Scandinavian drama as a whole.

Where the East has arranged its mental and emotional affairs with greater smoothness, the West has managed its own in a disturbing fashion highly agreeable to serious and moving drama. A Chinese sage made the stipulation that when his body received its final honors he should wear Confucian shoes, a Buddhist robe, and a Taoist hat. There have been terrifying wars in China but none have been wars of thought or religion. Europe and above all the Scandinavians have, on the contrary, found small room for such genial adjudication of spiritual, intellectual, and ethical problems. They live in a climate of debate, whether of sword or pen. Also, the very severities of their physical climate have assisted in Scandinavia in creating a correspondingly strong sense of mutual association and coopera-tion, living together, and hence have induced various forms of socialism that have invariably been willed and not presumed. The claims of society in the Northern cultures are impressed on students of English literature through familiarity with *Beowulf*. Thus side by side with clannishness or the communal ties stand in their hearts the dignity and rights of the individual. Scandi-navia is the land of both freedom and parliaments. A peculiarly high tension is at once established. Tension is the cord upon which our drama ever since Aeschylus has hung its robes. Here lies obviously one of the basic themes of the Scandinavian theater and one of its main sources of power. In contrast with Europe, dramatic sentiment in Scandinavia is expressed less by gestures of the body, more by gestures of the mind.

It is, or at least should be, a commonplace that Ibsen and Strindberg are the two outstanding forces revitalizing and freshly defining drama in the modern world. Each was certainly an individual, an "original" in the European sense, a "character" in the dramatic sense; each lived dramatically. Each stood alone. But each reached out with gestures felt throughout the entire world and significant for it. Each touched to the quick the complicated soul of modern man in both his social and private capacity. Yet it equally follows that each is representative of his own country and in a much more important respect of Scandinavia as a whole. They are only the highest parts of a mountain range.

Scandinavia is known for lonely lives but not for isolated mountain peaks and, similarly, on any close inspection it becomes clear that the preeminent Scandinavians are by no means historically eccentric, either as persons or as artists. On the contrary, they are highly representative and only when so considered are they properly understood. Genius is, of course, the supreme witness of the inequality of men but is more a matter of degrees than of essential qualities. This alone makes genius significant for us. Our democracy declares men to be born with equal rights but Thomas Jefferson would have been first to assert that they are by no means born with equal gifts. The degree to which the two giants of the Scandinavian theater rise above their neighbors is clear and it is equally clear that in relation to other native playwrights this stature is commonly much exaggerated. No others, to be sure, give us products transported with anything approaching the success attending the transportation of theirs. But as both the libraries and the stages of the world witness, these fellow playwrights have produced works that can be found and have been found of cosmopolitan value. I think it hardly extravagant to assert that even without Ibsen and Strindberg the spirit of Western man, both in its limitations and its grandeur, is as amply expressed by the remaining Scandinavian dramatists as by any single body of writing in the literature of the last one or two centuries.

This is not to presume that such talented playwrights as represented in this volume will at any foreseeable time be familiar names to a large proportion of the peoples outside their own regions. For this there are many causes. The world's classics are always decidedly limited in number. Especially in the rendering of dramatic dialogue the gifted translator is not easily found. These plays often have a great deal of local color. It would be over-optimistic to suppose that such plays will provide food for "the general reader" or under our present circumstances for our typical commercial theaters. But especially for the more thoughtful readers they will be eminently alive, as this book goes far to prove.

For the virtues of an artful drama close in spirit to folk drama the Icelandic Davið Stefánsson is, I believe, the equal of Yeats or Synge; for an exposure of the nervosities of modern idealism, commonly more or less adolescent, no dramatist can be more revealing than the Norwegian Nordahl Grieg; for the metaphysical imagination that brings into vital relationships the sensuous world with the spiritual consciousness few equal Pär Lagerkvist; for that most precious of civilized qualities, a keen-probing wit, few rival the Danish Carl Erik Soya; for a clear view of the modern consciousness few surpass the representative of the youngest and least tradition-ridden Scandinavian nation, the Finnish Walentin Chorell; such playwrights not only show with exceptional clarity the special contributions of their own lands; they hold before the world's eye a singularly revealing mirror of Western man, with his triumphs and his delinquencies alike italicized for all who comprehend to read. Moreover, in the beauty of their insights and the finesse of their art they may confidently be said to light modest candles hinting at pathways out of one of man's Darkest Ages, the twentieth century.

There are, of course, further convolutions to these problems. Although it is, or at least recently was, a common observation that few persons can on the whole be more traditionally minded than Scandinavian fishermen or farmers, at least in recent generations few persons have been more emancipated from confining conventions than Scandinavian intellectuals and, above all, those among them having incontestable genius. There is and long has been a bracing, pioneering temper in the Scandinavian air. Scandinavians may travel light but travel fast and far. It seems equally natural that Ibsen and Strindberg should have quarreled with the general public while few men have stood so much in advance of it or ultimately occupied such conspicuous positions of leadership. Scandinavia provides a point of vantage not only to observe past but future. In the arts and above all in the drama this inventiveness has appeared. Scandinavia has proved the laboratory of Europe. A certain reciprocity has been evidenced between lands bordering the Mediterranean and those facing the Baltic and the North Sea. Although it is obviously true that many special ideas and esthetic outlooks have reached the North belatedly, it is equally true that Northern lands have been nurseries of creativity and laboratories of invention, freeing themselves from the Classical regimentations of the South. The explorative work of Edvard Munch in the field of modern painting is conspicuous. Ibsen, when at Bergen, learned much of his basic techniques from dramatists writing in the capitals to the south but in the end gave vastly more than he received, creating far more than he borrowed. Scandinavia has been the home of independent-minded men, giving conspicuously more than might seem their share to the restless development of modern thought and creative art.

In conclusion, a word should be said here on the role of the Scandinavian playwrights strictly as men of the theater. All five dramatists presented in this book are poetic in the sense that they are strongly imaginative and it is significant that most have won considerable reputation in pure poetry itself—not to mention work in fiction and other literary fields. Indeed, it is significant that the typical Scandinavian playwright has never been narrowly and exclusively a playwright. Moreover, they have at times written plays which have failed in actual production, occasionally because of offenses against any conceivable stage technique but in many more cases because the technique demanded by their plays was not at the moment to be had in the existing theater. Scandinavians have moved forward in stage technology hardly less strikingly than in dramatic literature. Their works are on the whole conspicuously theatrical, even when in certain aspects they may theoretically appear not to be so. A conspicuous instance may be found outside the contents of this book. The overwhelmingly didactic and moral elements in almost any play by Kaj Munk might at first sight be supposed inimical to theatrical success but in the face of established fact no conclusions could be more erroneous. The basic explanation for the dramatic and theatrical force of this body of playwriting as a whole can be found, I believe, in such reflections as presented in the earlier pages of this foreword. To recapitulate: all serious art is a way of envisaging life. The tensions drawn to a peculiar rigor in Scandinavian experience have favored drama that becomes dramatic not only for the European or the Western mind as a whole but for the world. Would that the well-conceived and well-written plays in this book would be more widely read than probability suggests! But at least it can with some confidence be held that wherever they are understandingly read they will be found significant, equally rewarding in their stimulus for philosophical thought and for esthetic enjoyment, on or off the stage. Occasionally a sober Scandinavian play has a way of looking more profound than it really is. But such a play may well enjoy a longer life as pure theater than as dramatic literature. First and last, Scandinavians are playwrights.

HENRY W. WELLS

Columbia University

LION WITH CORSET
A PLAY
By *CARL ERIK SOYA*

TRANSLATED FROM THE DANISH BY
BARBARA KNUDSEN

INTRODUCTION BY
P. M. MITCHELL

INTRODUCTION

Carl Erik Soya is a dramatist who has something to say. The ideas which imbue his works are as irritating—and as valid—to the liberal as to the conservative, neither of whom Soya is specifically addressing. Soya is no partisan. He is a playwright—and a novelist, short-story writer, and aphorist as well—who can speak to the general public and be understood. While he is able to utilize a variety of dramatic devices with such cleverness and originality that the reader or spectator is impressed by his technical virtuosity, Soya remains a neo-naturalist for whom ideas are more important than techniques.

From his earliest to his latest works, Carl Erik Soya has been concerned in a philosophical but at the same time a profane way with the search for a pattern in human existence. This concern is reflected in the titles of several of his twenty-odd plays, such as *Pieces of a Pattern (Brudstykker af et Mönster*, 1940), *Thirty Years' Reprieve (30 Aars Henstand*, 1944), and *Free Choice (Frit Valg*, 1948) . Moreover, the possibility of more than one solution to a problematical human situation intrigues him. Notably in *Free Choice* he has written a humorous, carricature-like drama with two endings; the reader may choose between them. The much earlier *Who Am I (Hvem er jeg*, 1931, publ. 1932) also had a double ending, one a dream and the other a reality. This earlier drama depicted allegorically a number of forces which act within the individual and which constitute the *ego* that the individual himself is unable to identify or describe. *Who Am I* foreshadowed techniques as well as ideas which have found more refined application in some of the later dramas.

The unity of thought which pervades Soya's dramas is demonstrable by a comparison of *Who Am I* and *Lion with Corset*

(*Löve med Korset*, 1950), plays written about twenty years apart. Abstractly considered, both present several characters who are in disagreement about a fundamental ethical problem, and who are permitted to have their say. There is no clear-cut solution, although the reader or the audience finds some reason to be optimistic at the end of each play. No remedy suggested is perfect, but there is at least a way out which will relieve the dilemma that confronts the central character—and man.

In an apology for his work published in the Copenhagen newspaper *Berlingske Tidende* in 1935, Soya made several statements of principle which still serve to elucidate his plays. In view of his continual concern with the possibility of a pattern in life, one sentence is of signal importance: "I am completely ignorant of the goal of life." Soya thus identified himself as a nonbeliever; but his plays testify that he constantly has debated the problem of order vs. chaos and faith vs. nihilism. While Soya may not accept any religious dogma, he unwittingly holds tenets that may be called religious, or if one will, ethical. They are simple tenets: first, that one should practice goodness toward one's neighbor; and second, that one should strive for truth. From these tenets he deduces two practical corollaries: that every act of goodness should silence satire; and that everything which clearly is untrue should be ridiculed. Soya is not unaware of the difficulties in defining the terms "goodness" and "truth," but he believes that a subjective judgment is better than no judgment.

Soya may be ignorant of any ontological goal in human life, but he is conscious of a personal goal: He is suggesting the better world that might be. Imaginative writer that he is, Soya knows that the most effective way of making one's point is not by enunciating principles. "Personally, I do not like the theme in a literary work to be expressed directly; I want to put my mind to work whenever I read a book or see a play . . . in the same way, I prefer to hold the soup spoon rather than to be fed," Soya wrote in 1935. As he lets the nominally central character complain in *Who Am I,* the action on stage is symbolic—the playwright is saying something more than he seems to be saying; but Soya does not write so obliquely as to be unintelligible.

Since Soya is in essence dealing with recurrent, basic problems of self-recognition and meaning in life, his success cannot be attributed to either a choice of subject matter or the idea projected by a play. It must, rather, be ascribed to his geniality, to his clever juxtaposition of situations, persons, and events, and to the easy comprehensibility of his dialogue. The effective elements of Soya's plays derive in part from the traditional naturalistic drama, in part from some expressionistic drama influenced by Freudian thought, and in part from the cinema. The relation with the cinema is pronounced, especially in Soya's use of the flashback. For example, *Thirty Years' Reprieve* consists of an introductory drama followed by a series of other short plays which in a somewhat impressionistic fashion reveal the background from which the situation shown in the first play evolved. Not only has the cinema affected Soya's drama in general, but at times he makes use of actual cinematic production —slides and moving pictures—and nowhere more freely than in *Lion with Corset.* This technique, which adds variety to the stage presentation, is one of several which Soya employs to insure that the audience is attentive.

Incidentally, Soya writes an idosyncratic Danish. The propensity toward a phonetic reproduction of daily speech is evident in most of his works. His disregard for the niceties of standard Danish orthography often adds a note of humor or indeed levity to Soya's language. The Copenhagen *patois* coupled with willful anachronisms, such as those evident in *Lion with Corset,* and an admixture of English and French loanwords increase the amusing—or annoying—quality of Soya's language and suggest the technique of sudden disillusionment which critics associate with the term "Verfremdungstechnik."

Not only does Soya splinter the mirror of illusion from time to time in the dialogue of his plays, he intersperses comments in his stage directions which are both interpretive and narrative, and which cannot be communicated from the stage—as for example the fantastic and ironic similes upon the appearance of the three diagnosticians of war in *Lion with Corset*. This type of stage direction, a grotesque extension of the detailed notes of naturalistic dramatists at the end of the nineteenth century, indicates that Soya has willfully written closet drama quite as much as drama for the stage.

Satire and irony are present throughout Soya's work, but the frankness which makes the angel of peace blush in *Lion with Corset* is, oddly enough, characteristic of the older Soya. While Soya may also have come to realize the drawing power of uninhibited naturalism in matters pertaining to sex, his commitment to truth probably led him to disregard genteel and bourgeois taboos. His retrospective and doubtless partially autobiographical novel of adolescence, *Seventeen (Sytten,* 1954), was something of a shock to readers who expected a continuation of Soya's amusing autobiographical picture of Copenhagen at the turn of the century, *My Grandmother's House (Min Farmors Hus,* 1943). On second thought, however, even Soya's adverse critics have come to realize that, unlike certain modern writers who have speculated in sex, Soya simply recognizes the important role which sex plays in human life and, with a smile, accords to it a comparable, although not necessarily a predominant, role. If the truth is to make us free, we must seek more than selected truths.

Because of his concern with contemporary problems and because of his frankness, Soya's later production has a youthful air; it is a bit difficult to accept the fact that he turns 75 in 1971. One might expect to categorize him with Kaj Munk (1898–1944) and Kjeld Abell (1901–1961), the other two leading Danish dramatists of the 1930s and 1940s, but Soya is still part of the contemporary scene. And *Lion with Corset* speaks more forcefully in 1971 than it did when it was first published in 1950, for the threats to peace and the possibility of more war hysteria have increased rather than diminished in recent years. In *Lion with Corset,* Soya depicts a number of the manifold causes for the continued belligerency of the human race. As example follows example in the play, one is perhaps a bit chagrined to find that these causes are not always as impersonal and distant as Everyman might wish to believe. Soya intimates that, if ecstasy and excitement are not provided by mob action and war, they must then be furnished from other sources. The lion may be subdued, but he does not cease to exist.

P. M. MITCHELL

University of Illinois

LION WITH CORSET

Note to the Stage Director

The play is performed without intermission or similar break.
The "setting" is a white backdrop. On this curtain, scene
pictures are cast by means of lantern slide and movie projectors.
The lantern slide projector is employed when the picture is
stationary; the movie projector, when motion is required. The
scene pictures ought—like all other stage settings—to be in full
color. Most of the changes are effected through fading, a few
occur abruptly. Whichever procedure is to be used will, I believe, be evident from the dramatic situation. In several cases,
the setting ought to precede—and, as it were, augur—the scene
to which it belongs.

Side flats, or tormentors, may be utilized to hide the backstage.
In such event these flats—which are not to be moved—must be
stylized and neutral.

Furniture and other objects slide out and in, or ascend and
descend.

In the scene in front of the royal castle in Mycenae, Agamemnon steps onto the apron, facing the audience. The voices from
the crowd are broadcast from the rear of the house.

The tempo is variable, but the general impression: *pre-
cipitando*.

THE AUTHOR

(A lion's roar.
Pause.
A lion's roar.
Pause.
Another lion's roar.
And then the curtain rises.)
(Fanfare of trumpets.
An anatomy arena. Waiting students. Murmuring. Two order-
lies with a stretcher; on the stretcher a woman patient. The
professor is suddenly elevated from below stage, standing on his
rostrum. Silence.)

PROFESSOR: Ladies and gentlemen—.

(Takes off his glasses.)

To combat a sickness, it is as a rule not a bad expedient: to look for the cause. *(Pours water.)*

(Fanfare of trumpets. The Professor disappears from sight.)

ASST. DIRECTOR *(Entering with a manuscript):* Here's an essay from School Principal P. H. D. Jensen.

(The arena fades. The students vanish.)

CHIEF EDITOR *(Behind his desk):* An essay?

(A room in a newspaper office—the innermost sanctum.)

ASST. EDITOR *(Nods):* Well, you might call it an editorial.

CHIEF EDITOR *(Reads):* "To combat war, it is undoubtedly wise, first, to seek out the cause."

PATIENT *(Sitting up):* Or the cau*s*es.

CHIEF EDITOR: And who, may I ask, are you?

PATIENT *(Sitting up):* Or the cau*s*es.

ASST. EDITOR: You'll find the political cartoonist third door on the right—*(Gestures with thumb)*—on the other side of the hall—

ANGEL OF PEACE *(Shakes her head):* I know him—he can caricature me in his sleep—with white robe and broken palm reed—but cure me—he can't do that.

CHIEF EDITOR *(Politely):* Are you sick?

ANGEL OF PEACE: I thought the news had leaked out.

CHIEF EDITOR: Well, yes, of course—But—May I be so bold as to inquire what ails the lady?

ANGEL OF PEACE: War.

CHIEF EDITOR: Yes, yes, naturally, that's clear—war. But then war is a name, a label—just like—cancer and—schizophrenia—We know it's something unpleasant—a sickness—but the cause of the sickness, no one knows. So I thought—now that we have the little lady right here—I believe it would please the newspaper's great reading public—*(Gesture toward the audience)*—tremendously—if you would tell us, what is the true cause of war?

ANGEL OF PEACE *(Shakes her head):* Your guess is as good as mine. *(Peevishly)* Anyhow, a patient isn't normally called upon to make his own diagnosis. I should think that's what we have doctors for!

CHIEF EDITOR: In that case, it's up to the philosophers. Eventually, the sociologists and the national economists.

ASST. EDITOR *(Eagerly):* Or the editorial writers and journalists!

CHIEF EDITOR: Yes, obviously—the ideal solution. *(Grabs the manuscript)* What's he say here?

ASST. EDITOR: Absolutely nothing.

ANGEL OF PEACE *(Sighs):* Of course—no one ever does.

ASST. EDITOR: Much less editorial writers.

CHIEF EDITOR: If he said anything, he'd be a genius.

ASST. EDITOR *(Nods):* And geniuses don't write for newspapers.

CHIEF EDITOR *(Hefting manuscript):* But surely there must be something in it—so many expertly typewritten pages—?

ASST. EDITOR: He examines the question historically. He propounds three theories about war which have prevailed, one after the other, during the past 150 years.

CHIEF EDITOR: The historical approach, huh?—appeals to many readers. *(Leafs lightly through the manuscript.)* Okay. Let's see what causes wars, according to these three theories—

(Fanfare of trumpets.)

(Music. "Malbrough s'en va-t-en guerre."

Three gentlemen—with signs—dance in, single file. The foremost has a high forehead, honest eyes, brave nose, and noble full beard. He makes one think of a St. Bernard dog, which has, on a magic carpet, rescued a little Savoyard from freezing to death in the Alps. Costume: around 1800. The placard on the standard bears the words: "ROMANTICIST."

Gentleman No. 2 is a troll and a dwarf rolled into one person. It would take twelve Einsteins to match him for hair. He reminds one of a staircase up to a printing office in a backyard in Germany. Costume: around 1875. On the placard: "MATERIALIST."

No. 3 bears a certain resemblance to Freud. But he is younger than the Freud of the photographs, he is not Jewish, and he is not quite so eccentric or distinguished. Costume: ordinary suit from around 1950. The manner of dress is a bit too casual, but presumably this is intentional. Placard: "PSYCHOLOGIST."

The three gentlemen stop in front of the Angel of Peace in an informal group. Simultaneously the music stops.)

CHIEF EDITOR: Let's get right down to cases. Which of you gentlemen can explain the cause of war?

ROMANTICIST *(Raising his hand):* I!

MATERIALIST *(Raising his hand):* I can do it better!

PSYCHOLOGIST *(Raising his hand):* I can do it best!

(A deserted beach with snail shells. A couple of these shells are the size of castles, and there is a gradation of all sizes and shapes down to the most minute. Many are strange, mysteriously convoluted, bizarre; no two are alike. Some individual ones seem unaffected by wind and weather; most of them, however, are disintegrating, and many must be presumed to be—sand.)

CHIEF EDITOR: Who's first?

ALL THREE *(Raising hands):* I!

ASST. EDITOR: Wouldn't it be most reasonable to take the gentlemen in chronological order? That's what they do in school.

ANGEL OF PEACE: Absolutely. Chronological order and alphabetical order are the most splendid inventions I know of. Think how much mankind—thanks to these—has been spared of wrangling and dissension!

ROMANTICIST: Then I'm the one to begin.

(Three chairs shoot up from the floor.)

CHIEF EDITOR *(Nervously):* Nothing elaborate now. I haven't the time. *(To Asst. Editor)* Is there anything in it that can offend anybody?

ASST. EDITOR: No.

CHIEF EDITOR: Then, let's use it. *(Hands him the manuscript. Hurries out.) (The writing desk exits right behind him.)*

ASST. EDITOR: *(Hands the manuscript on to the prompter):* Go ahead, in eight-point—five-line head.

(Exit on opposite side from Chief Editor.)

(The three gentlemen seat themselves. They have stuck the placards in the floor behind the chairs. The Angel of Peace lies down on the stretcher.)

(Fanfare of trumpets.)

(Hall in a royal palace. Columns and lions. Lions are affixed over the doors—in pairs, facing each other.

Agamemnon, followed by three counsellors, enters from one side; a servant, from the other.)

SERVANT: Forgive me, Agamemnon. A runner from Sparta has just arrived. He brings a message from your brother Menelaus—personal and confidential. He says it's most urgent!

AGAMEMNON: Here then! And quickly!

(Exit servant. Counsellors turn to leave.)

AGAMEMNON: Wait! Gentlemen. When I have heard the message from my brother, I shall surely have need of your advice—your wise counsel.

1ST COUNSELLOR: Our advice is unfortunately somewhat conflicting. I don't see how it can be of any possible use to you.

3RD COUNSELLOR: A king must hear many divergent opinions. His art is to sink a lion's claw into the best of them.

(Servant returns with messenger.)

MESSENGER *(Prostrate):* Evil tidings, O King! Your brother has been struck by the wrath of the gods. Now he storms about in a fury, roaring like a lion, now he casts himself upon a couch, overcome with agony and shame. And all Lacedaemon is plunged in sorrow.

AGAMEMNON: Rise. And deliver your address with calm and dignity.

MESSENGER: A fortnight ago, we were visited by a Trojan prince. A son of Priam—by name, Paris. But one day he vanished—without a trace! And not *he alone*—but also Helen, the queen. We searched the palace and the whole city. I believe we searched all of a day and a night. We searched until the peasants from the environs of the city solved the riddle. They had seen them flee from Lacedaemon—in the same carriage!

AGAMEMNON: Did he carry her off by force?

MESSENGER: They said her hands were tied behind her back, and that she wept and cried out incessantly.

AGAMEMNON: A shameful deed! Unfortunately Paris will be in Troy before our people could swing themselves into the saddle. I fear my brother must resign himself to Destiny. I see no possibility of help or revenge.

MESSENGER: Forgive my boldness, Agamemnon, but your brother thinks otherwise.

AGAMEMNON: What does he think then?

MESSENGER: He feels that if Paris had been hard up for a woman, he might have said so. The King would gladly have presented him with as many slave girls as he wished. But to carry off Helen was an outrage against the queen, a mockery against Menelaus, an infringement upon domestic authority, and a Trojan insult to Hellas.

2ND COUNSELLOR: Do not be angry, Agamemnon, but it is my opinion that your brother is right.

AGAMEMNON: Perhaps. But then what does Menelaus wish?

MESSENGER: That you and the other kings of Hellas prevail

upon King Priam to surrender the queen.

AGAMEMNON: And if Troy is defiant?

MESSENGER: Then you must use force.

AGAMEMNON: By "force" you mean "war"?

MESSENGER: Precisely. Your brother favors war with Troy.

(A faint pause.)

AGAMEMNON: I hate war, I dread war, I would go to great lengths to avoid war. But even peace can be bought too dearly. And righteousness and honor must be valued more highly than the stuffy complacence of peace. My brother's claim is in accord with law and justice. My brother's claim concerns Helen's honor. My brother's claim is not just his own claim, but the claim of every Greek. And therefore I shall support his claim— as far as my power and my abilities extend.

(To the servant.) Let half of the palace guard spread out through the city. Let them inform the citizenry that the king will make an important announcement. Those who would hear this news must appear immediately in the market-place. There the king will step forth from his palace and, in his own person, address his beloved people. *(Exit servant.)*

AGAMEMNON *(To Messenger):* You follow behind me. And take careful note of all I say. When you return to Sparta, you must faithfully report my speech and the people's answer.

(Murmur of a crowd.

Steps and pillars. On one of the steps stands a pink corset. Agamemnon advances, followed by the counsellors and the messenger from Sparta.

The shouting mounts at his appearance. The people do homage to their king.

Then he raises an arm—and all is still.)

AGAMEMNON: Friends. Citizens. Greeks. A grave message has been brought to us from Lacedaemon. Prince Paris of Troy was recently the guest of my brother, Menelaus. But he has ill repaid the king's hospitality. One night he fled like a thief, without warning or thanks. Yes, a thief he is, and a thief's deed he has done. He has stolen and taken with him that which was dearest to the king's heart. Helen—Helen, of whose beauty every Greek speaks with reverence and pride—was also gone on that luckless morn, gone like Prince Paris, gone *with* Prince Paris—

(*Silence. Here and there a titter.*)

ROMANTICIST: Where did that idiotic corset come from?

PSYCHOLOGIST: Excuse me—I brought it. If it offends, I'll take it away.

(*The corset fades away.*)

AGAMEMNON (*Raising his voice*): This stranger, this barbarian, has carried her off—*by force!*

Do you comprehend the enormity of Paris's misdeed? First, it is an abuse of the unwritten laws of hospitality. Next a transgression against the sanctity of the home. But it is still more than that. To carry off by force a free-born woman is a violation against her freedom. And if that woman is a Greek, then the brute has trodden Hellenic freedom under foot. The brute has wronged not only *her,* but each one of us! *Every single Greek!* Free men and women! Do you realize what has happened? *A Trojan has sullied our honor!* (*Many shouts.* "Agamemnon is right!" "Long live Agamemnon!" "Revenge upon Paris!")

AGAMEMNON: You men who love your wives, think, if it had been in your house that the outrage had taken place. Think, if you woke up some morning and found your wife's bed empty. Empty because a barbarian had dragged her away, a barbarian, who, in barbaric fashion, had taken advantage of the night and man's superior strength.

Think of your rage—your impotent rage! Think of your sorrow. Your sorrow and despair.—And think of your children. Can you see them running about the rooms and calling for their mother! Can you see them casting themselves upon her bed and whimpering, "Mother! Mother!" But no mother answers them—and no mother ever *will* answer them—And then try to imagine the existence that awaits *her*. That woman who loves you, only you, must now helplessly endure a man she detests, suffocating her with slimy sensuality. But even with that degradation, her suffering has not reached its culmination. One day the wretch will tire of her—she is no longer a novelty, no longer young—and then! Out with her! A farewell kick! Out with her—on the *slave market*. And then you know the story. She will toil on: lonely, sick, treated like a dog by all alike—and with a heart that, day in and day out, weeps for those she loves. But never! never! She will never know the joy of reunion. One day she will sink down in the dirt—tortured to death with drudgery and grief, consumed by lice and longing.

(The women weep.)

MEN: After Paris! Death to Paris! Torture him!

ONE VOICE *(Prevailing)*:: We must set out after Paris and free Helen!

(Agamemnon lifts his arm. Silence.)

AGAMEMNON: Unfortunately I fear that Paris has too great a head start. We will hardly catch up with him before—Troy—

STRONG SHOUTING: To Troy! To Troy!

(The Materialist writhes in his chair. It is clearly hard for him to remain silent.)

AGAMEMNON *(In a subdued tone. Artlessly and simply)*: I am king. And you believe that a king is a powerful man, who can do just as he pleases. But a *good* king—and I try to be a good king—has only one aim—to serve his people. To fulfill his people's wishes—when they wish wisely and rightly.

And therefore I ask you now:

Shall we help my poor brother and his ill-starred queen? Shall we show the barbarians that he who abuses the freedom of one Greek, abuses us all? Shall we erase the stain which Troy has cast upon the honor of Hellas?

In short, citizens and countrymen: What do you want? What is your will?

VIOLENT SHOUTS: War!! War!!

(And suddenly silence.)

AGAMEMNON: You have spoken. Your wish is my command. Go to your homes, wipe the rust from your swords and spears—and await my orders! *(Exit.)*

(Counsellors and messenger follow him.)

SHOUTS: Long live Agamemnon! Long live Agamemnon!

(The shouting dies down; the people disperse.)

MATERIALIST: And you want us to believe that? *(He is very excited.)*

ROMANTICIST: Believe what?

MATERIALIST: That an entire people would go to war for a married woman who has run away with her lover!

PSYCHOLOGIST: Wars are often fought—perhaps not over *one* woman—but over *women*.

(Two fighting harts are seen in a clearing in a beech forest. A little distance away, a flock of hinds await the victor.)

MATERIALIST: Not within my experience, I'm sure.

PSYCHOLOGIST: You never heard of the Roman theft of the Sabine women?

MATERIALIST: Pure nursery tale!

ANGEL OF PEACE: What kind of war was that? I'm afraid I don't know about that one.

ROMANTICIST: How peculiar! It's a very romantic incident—much exploited by both painters and sculptors.

ANGEL OF PEACE: No doubt before my time. Remember, I'm of quite recent vintage.

PSYCHOLOGIST: The story runs like this: Shortly after the founding of Rome, the Romans discovered that there was a shortage of women. Fortunately, the wily Romulus found a solution. He invited a neighboring tribe—the Sabines—to a luxurious feast. But this was only a ruse: in the middle of the feast, the Romans carried off the young Sabine women by force. But the Sabines would not stand for this—and so the war began. Luckily it ended pretty quickly. The young Sabine women sent word to their fathers and brothers, asking them not to take any action. The stolen women did not in the least wish to be liberated. The way the Romans treated them satisfied them completely.

MATERIALIST: It's beneath the dignity of a man of science to dish out a story like that.

PSYCHOLOGIST: Naturally it's a myth, but I shouldn't be surprised if it had some foundation in fact. Sex is usually mixed up in the warfaring impulse.

MATERIALIST: A postulate—demanding proof!

(Psychologist is about to answer. But—)

ROMANTICIST *(Injects, in offended tones):* Remember, I was the one who was talking! It was my turn!

PSYCHOLOGIST: You're right. Excuse me.

(The beech forest fades in the meantime into a camp of tents among green hills. Northern landscape. In the distance: turmoil of war, about the year 1200. The King, the Bishop, and the Chaplain enter from one side; Marshal from the other.

The King and the Marshal are in armor. On the King's shield: a lion.)

KING *(Opens visor):* How goes the battle, Marshal?

MARSHAL: Nothing in this world goes so badly as one fears, nor so well as one hopes.

KING: It's the facts I want. No pious platitudes. Are we winning or losing?

MARSHAL: It rests with God.

KING: Everything rests with God.

BISHOP: Amen.

CHAPLAIN: Amen.

KING: But what do you think is God's will?

MARSHAL: We are hard pressed on the left flank.

KING: If it goes badly, I shall throw myself into the combat; it will inspire our people.

MARSHAL: Do not be angry, Sire—but neither the Bishop nor I would permit that. As long as we have you, we have hope; should you fall, or be taken captive, all would be lost.

(Voices and shouting.)

MARSHAL (*Shading eyes with hand*): Something must have happened. They're our people, the group that's coming this way.

KING: They are leading two men with them. Two prisoners.

BISHOP: From their appearance, freeborn men of power and authority.

(*Enter three or four knights with their attendants. Two prisoners, hands tied behind their backs.*)

KING: Whom do you bring?

ONE KNIGHT: The chieftain. And his son.

KING: The chieftain? The leader of the enemy?

KNIGHT: Yes, Sire.

KING: How did you get your hands on him?

KNIGHT: He and his son were in the front ranks. They are courageous people—that much praise is due them. All at once it occurred to me who they were. Then I said to my kinsmen and servants: "If we can take those two alive, we'll have made a good haul! A capture that perhaps can change the course of the battle!" For, if I may say so, it is not proceeding entirely according to plan. We drew back—as if we were afraid of them—whereupon they became even more foolhardy, and ventured out in front of their own people. But then all at once, we stormed forth, surrounded them, and hurled ourselves upon them. And while the servants and those two there lay and struggled in the grass, my kinsmen and I held off their people. And the servants were clever: they did not kill them, they bound them instead—as I had instructed. And then we withdrew hastily from the field of battle.

KING: Cleverly planned. Skillfully executed. I shall remember you and your kinsmen in the hour of victory. (*To the chieftain.*) Are you the king of the heathens?

CHIEFTAIN: I am a chieftain, like you.

KING: And this is your son?

CHIEFTAIN: I don't know him. Never saw him before.

KNIGHT: Don't believe him! He lies! To save his son's life.

MARSHAL: I shall instruct our warriors. They are to shout

joyously: "The chieftain and his son are captured!" Then I think the enemy will surrender—or flee! *(Exit.)*

KING: Why do you defy me?

CHIEFTAIN: Wouldn't you defy *me*—if I came to seize your land?

KING: Yes. But I have not come to seize your land.

CHIEFTAIN: Why have you come then?

KING: To convert you and your people to Christianity.

CHIEFTAIN: A fat lie, if I ever heard one!

KING: My faith forbids me to tell a lie.

CHIEFTAIN: Why should we swallow Christ's flesh and blood instead of sacrificing to Svantevit!? What's the advantage?

KING: I was born in a Christian land, I have grown up in a Christian land—but to tell the truth, in my younger days, I was no more Christian than you and yours. I loved the pagan virtues: courage, strength, ability to bear pain without complaint, nobility of spirit—I love them still, but—one day, one of my servants was found in a great wood, his hands bound behind his back. He had been robbed by bandits—and they had not only robbed him, they had also blinded him! I had the wood surrounded, and my servants succeeded in capturing the bandits. Then I caused the bandits to be led forth before the blinded man, and bade him pass sentence upon them. I expected that he would repay their crime with gruesome tortures, or at least have them blinded. But he was a Christian. He knelt down—and asked God to forgive them their atrocity. And thereupon he decreed that the bandits should be set free, if only they promised to give up their evil ways. The bandits fell to their knees and cried. I wept also—and in that moment I perceived that high above all the pagan virtues, shine the Christian virtues; helpfulness, mercy, the spirit of forgiveness. Then I saw that high above all the other gods, shines the god of gentleness: Christ—with arms extended. And I had to steady myself against a tree—so as not to fall headlong—so great was that vision.

BISHOP: God's grace often falls like a hammerblow.

KING: The bandits became part of my bodyguard. They have served their God and their king zealously ever since. Do you believe me now?

CHIEFTAIN: I believe you. But I don't see what bearing your religious hallucinations has upon me and my country.

BISHOP: Christ has said: "Go ye into all the world and teach all nations to be my disciples."

CHAPLAIN: The man who has discovered that love for one's neighbor is the greatest love to be found, that man longs to share his discovery with all of mankind.

CHIEFTAIN: And in order to tell me that love for one's neighbor is the greatest to be found, you have strewn the hills with death and mutilation?

CHAPLAIN: First we sent you unarmed monks. You put them to death!

CHIEFTAIN: Yes, thank you. I know those gentlemen of the fifth column.

KING: We have a saying in my country, that of two evils one chooses the lesser. It is a great evil to take up the sword, but it is an even greater evil if you and your people remain heathens.

BISHOP: Well spoken, Sire! If the heathens will not of their own free will accept God's Word, we shall have to bind them, stick funnels in their ears, and pour in buckets of salvation through Jesus Christ.

CHIEFTAIN: In my country, we scorn superfluous words. Kill me now, without further nonsense.

KING: I shall not kill you.

CHIEFTAIN: Too bad. I'd rather die than be locked up for life.

KING: Neither shall I lock you up.

CHIEFTAIN: So I am to be blinded, or mutilated?

KING: None of these.

CHIEFTAIN: Then what are you going to do with me?

KING: I will loosen your bonds and make you king.

CHIEFTAIN: A king? A puppet king?

KING (*With a little smile*): Naturally you will not be entirely independent of me. But I shall interfere as little as possible with your royal duties. You will be able to rule your country and your kingdom in almost the same manner as heretofore.

CHIEFTAIN: If only I pay tribute!

KING: I promise you that the tax which will be levied upon you and your country will be so light that it will not burden you.

CHIEFTAIN: But there must be something you demand. Every victor does. You must impose some condition or other—in return for my freedom.

KING: Yes, there is one condition.

CHIEFTAIN: I knew it!

KING: That condition: that you and your people allow yourselves to be baptized.

CHIEFTAIN: That I and my people—?! Is that all?

KING: That's all.

SON: Father! Don't do it! Svantevit will never forgive it!

CHIEFTAIN: Silence, boy! *(To the king.)* I agree to your condition.

MARSHAL *(Returns):* The battle is at an end. Our adversaries have laid down their weapons, and only await your command.

KING: Good. Release all captives. And lead them down to the sea. Prepare everything needful for a great mass baptism. That sweet hour is upon us, when my weak hand will guide a heathen people before the throne of Almighty God.

BISHOP: Amen.

CHAPLAIN: Amen.

KING: I shall divest myself of my armor, as a sign that the war is ended. Wait for me down by the sea. I desire to witness that blessed sight, thousands upon thousands immersing themselves in the waters of baptism.

(Exit.)

(Exeunt others on opposite side.)

ROMANTICIST: Well, do the gentlemen desire further examples?

MATERIALIST *(Who has been suffering for a long time):* God

forbid!!!

PSYCHOLOGIST: I believe the reading public would understand you best if you were to omit the examples, and instead give a resumé—an abstract—of what you consider to be the causes of war.

ROMANTICIST: Yes, perhaps. People go to war for their faith and their fatherland, for freedom, honor, and justice.

MATERIALIST: Justice!!! (*Clasps hands together and casts his eyes heavenward.*)

ROMANTICIST: As a beautiful instance of a battle for justice, I could mention the struggle of the Northern States against the Southern States, 1861–65. The purpose of the North was to make the South give up Negro slavery.

MATERIALIST: Don't you know anything about economic motives?

ROMANTICIST: Oh, yes! When the Southern States defended slavery, it was precisely a question of money. And then there are also the condottieri and the mercenaries.

PSYCHOLOGIST: Pardon me for asking—but is there, to put it in plain language, not a single "scoundrel" in your world history?

ROMANTICIST: Oh, yes,—many.

PSYCHOLOGIST: Who, for example?

ROMANTICIST: Judas, Nero, and Louis XI.

MATERIALIST (*In falsetto*): O-o-oh (*Slouches down.*) Judas, Nero, and Louis XI! You're worse than Walter Scott, Daddy Dumas, and Fenimore Cooper, all rolled into one.

Have the gentlemen any objection now if science takes over?

(*Room in a palace. Pillars and lions. The lions are arranged over the doors, in pairs, and facing each other.*)

PSYCHOLOGIST: I disagree that you are more of a scientist than my friend, the Romanticist. But, naturally, we will be glad to yield you the floor—if the Romanticist has quite finished.

ROMANTICIST: I have finished.

(*Fanfare of trumpets.*)

(Enter Agamemnon. From the opposite side: three gentlemen of the council.)

AGAMEMNON: Well met, my counsellors!

FIRST COUNSELLOR: You bade us meet hastily, Agamemnon?

AGAMEMNON: My informers and spies have recently come in with highly unpleasant reports. All Argolis is seething and bubbling. Dissatisfaction is spreading like a cancer. And this dissatisfaction is directed against us Atriedae. Sickness, death, crop failure, famine,—everything that is bad issues from me, Agamemnon. One of my most accomplished informers even claims that *revolt* is in the air, that the revolt will occur the moment the people find someone they can rally around, a *leader.* Should he appear, then it will be my death knell,—and not only mine; the infuriated mob will not spare Clytemnestra, Orestes, Electra, Iphigenia—It is on account of this news that I have sent for you. What does one pay counsellors for, if it is not to get counsel? Consequently: Is it true what the Secret Police report?

FIRST COUNSELLOR: I have heard nothing. There is always unrest. Unrest, gossip, grumbling. It was so in the times of Atreus, and it will be so when Orestes some day—may it be a long time hence—succeeds his father. I believe Mycenae's Secret Police are exaggerating. Of course they have an economic interest in unrest. No unrest would mean that the police were superfluous.

SECOND COUNSELLOR: It is true that there is unrest. But it is not a desire for revolt that fills the people. It is fear and terror. They are huddled together like beasts in the forest, in fear of the divine wrath.

THIRD COUNSELLOR: There is unrest. Although your policemen exaggerate, still you can believe them this time. There is unrest, and if a misfortune should occur, the unrest could very well end in a bloody revolt.

AGAMEMNON: Well, that much is established. Next question: Why is the wrath turned upon us Atriedae?

First Counsellor: Envy. It is always the lot of the great to be envied by the little people. If you and I, Sire, belonged among the little people, then we, too, would hate the great.

Second Counsellor: You must not be angry, Agamemnon, but the cause is your own carelessness. Your lack of veneration for the gods. The people know how you—intoxicated with the joy of hunting—pressed on into the holy grove of Artemis and killed a deer. And now the people think that the famine, which just at present prevails in Argolis, is a punishment for your sacrilege.

Third Counsellor: Famine always causes unrest.

Agamemnon: We have a famine then?

Third Counsellor: A bit of one. And I am afraid we are just at the beginning. If you could go about in Argolis, as I have, then you would get first-hand proof instead of reports. Then you would see old people collapsing for lack of vitamins, and children who have stomachs like footballs—from eating earth and bark. If you could go into the houses, you would discover that jars and vats echo hollowly when one knocks on them. You would see dishes with the glaze gone. They were *scraped* so, the last time there was food in them. And what is worst of all: You would encounter one untended field after another. Not because the people are lazy or shortsighted, but because the men do not have strength enough to lift hoe and spade; nor the oxen, strength enough to pull a plow.

Agamemnon: But am I somehow to blame for this famine?

Third Counsellor: Not in the least. But a people that are plagued with famine, epidemic, or war crave a cause. And the cause must not lie with the people themselves, and preferably it should be visible. The best is a living entity, a person—or many persons. In the case of war, it is easy to find the guilty party—right there, always the enemy. With famine, and sickness, it is immediately more complex. And yet! And yet! The guilty ones must be those who rule and decide, those who are in power. When things go so badly, it must be the king and his advisors who have managed matters so injudiciously.

Therefore, Agamemnon, the people's wrath over the people's misfortune falls—upon *you*.

AGAMEMNON: Ah, well. I understand that. I'd reason the same way, if I were one of the people. But where does this famine come from?

FIRST COUNSELLOR: Famine is all too big a word. The common man is always semi-starved. It can't be otherwise; it is one of life's laws. Back home where I come from—and, generally speaking, in those circles in which I move—famine does not affect us in the least.

SECOND COUNSELLOR: You must not be angry, Agamemnon, but I confess that I share the opinion of the people. The famine is a punishment for your sacrilege against Artemis.

THIRD COUNSELLOR: The famine comes because, for a long time, we have had the opposite. When a population lives in prosperity and abundance, it multiplies vigorously. So vigorously, that one fine day there are more people living on the land than the land can support. That, in all simplicity, is what has happened here in Argolis—and in the rest of Greece, too, for the most part.

AGAMEMNON: But now the most serious matter of all! Advice, my counsellors! What shall I do to win back the people's respect and love?

FIRST COUNSELLOR: Nothing. Popularity rises and falls like the price of hides. One fine day you will again be the "dearly beloved." A wise sovereign rules without regard for his commodity rating.

SECOND COUNSELLOR: Make a sacrifice to Artemis. Sacrifice what is dearest of all to you: your daughter Iphigenia.

AGAMEMNON: Iphigenia! The light of my life! My favorite child!!! Artemis can get a hundred deer in place of the one I slaughtered—by accident, I might add. But my deer that bounds about here in the palace—with ball and skipping-rope—never! *never!!!*

(Turns to the Third Counsellor.)

THIRD COUNSELLOR: There are two ways. The first: to shift the blame over onto someone else.

AGAMEMNON: On whom?

THIRD COUNSELLOR: Well, there is always the classic scapegoat—although it is somewhat unimaginative—

AGAMEMNON: What sort of scapegoat is that?

THIRD COUNSELLOR: The Jews.

AGAMEMNON: We haven't any Jews in this country!

THIRD COUNSELLOR: We have one—a poor, blind cobbler.

AGAMEMNON: Do you really think one could convince the people that he is to blame for the famine?

THIRD COUNSELLOR: It would be difficult—

AGAMEMNON: The other way?

THIRD COUNSELLOR: Yes, it's better. That is to do away with the famine.

AGAMEMNON: A beautiful bit of advice! A nice bit of advice! My, isn't that ingenious! What intelligence I have in my privy council! Ha! *(Changes tone.)* But even if I were to distribute the entire palace supply, it would amount to no more than a sparrow in the dragon's mouth. And to buy it in other states— they have famine there, just like ourselves! Gold is a good commodity for daily use, but not when the world lacks meat and bread!

THIRD COUNSELLOR: One can abolish famine in other ways than with food!

AGAMEMNON: I'd like to have the recipe for that miraculous cure!

THIRD COUNSELLOR: One abolishes famine when one abolishes overpopulation.

AGAMEMNON *(Starts):* Yes, one does indeed—But how does one abolish overpopulation?

THIRD COUNSELLOR: Through war.

AGAMEMNON *(Starts again):* Through war!

THIRD COUNSELLOR *(Nods):* War is an absolutely infallible

remedy for overpopulation. If you win the war, you get more land. If you lose the war, you get fewer people.

(Pause.)

AGAMEMNON *(Looking at him):* Give me time to think it over.

(Enter a servant hastily.)

SERVANT: Excuse me, Agamemnon. But a runner has just come from Sparta. He brings a report from your brother Menelaus—personal and confidential. He says it's urgent!

ROMANTICIST: This is where I came in. Now you're back to my account.

MATERIALIST: Naturally. But the backgrounds are totally different—Anyhow, if you want we'll cut to the crowd scene—

(Murmur of a crowd. Agamemnon steps forward and the noise mounts. There are cries of allegiance, but some boos and taunts. On one of the steps, the pink corset is seen again.)

MATERIALIST *(To Psychologist—ready to burst):* Now, get that thing out of here!

PSYCHOLOGIST: Okay, okay. Pardon me. *(Corset quickly vanishes.)*

MATERIALIST: I fail to understand what these schoolboy jokes are all about. If there was any possible meaning to that corset!

PSYCHOLOGIST: Well, the intention was that there should be some meaning to it.

MATERIALIST: I don't see it.

ROMANTICIST: I don't either, but—*(Bows before the Materialist and lays a hand on his arm.)* It's probably a touch of—surrealism!

MATERIALIST: Better call it—*(Points to his forehead.)* BLUR-realism! Utter madness, I say.

AGAMEMNON: Friends. Citizens. Greeks.

ROMANTICIST: Oh, God! Must we sit through this again?

MATERIALIST: Okay. Okay. Agamemnon, cut to the peroration.

AGAMEMNON *(In a subdued tone. Artlessly and simply):* I am king. And you believe that a king is a powerful man who can do just as he pleases. But a king in a democracy—and I try to be a good democratic king—has only one aim—to serve the people. In all things—to fulfill the people's wishes.

And therefore I ask you now: Shall we do something to help my poor brother and his ill-starred queen? Shall we show the barbarians that a Greek is a free man? Shall we show the barbarians that he who abuses the freedom of one Greek, abuses us all? Shall we erase the stain which Troy has cast upon the honor of Hellas? In short, comrades and countrymen: What do you want? What is your will?

VIOLENT SHOUTING: War! War!

(And then sudden silence.)

AGAMEMNON: You have spoken. Your wish is my command. Go to your homes, polish your helmets, wipe the rust from your swords and spears—and await my orders! *(Exit.)*

(The messenger follows him.)

SHOUTS: Long live Agamemnon! Long live Agamemnon!

(Shouting dies down. The people quickly disperse.)

THIRD COUNSELLOR: Troy is an important vantage point for trade with the barbarians.

SECOND COUNSELLOR: Now there'll be busy days at my forge!

FIRST COUNSELLOR: Two years back, I bought a big shipment of hides. I haven't been able to sell them since. But now they'll start moving, all right, as if they had legs—war legs!

(Exit counsellors, pleased and smiling.)

MATERIALIST *(Rubbing his hands. Speaks triumphantly to the Romanticist)*: Wasn't that a different story though?

ROMANTICIST: Undeniably. But where is the guarantee that your version is more correct than mine?

MATERIALIST: In my sound argument!

ROMANTICIST: Your argument is altogether unsound. It is infused with proletarian envy.

ANGEL OF PEACE *(Raising her hand)*: Now, now, now, now!

PSYCHOLOGIST: May I suggest an experiment. Let us for the moment suppose that the Trojan War did begin just as the

Materialist represented it.

MATERIALIST: We don't need to "suppose" it. It *did* begin that way.

ROMANTICIST *(Speaking at the same time):* I don't see what use an experiment can possibly be.

PSYCHOLOGIST: Let us suppose we accept the Materialist's version as historically correct. Then we notice that on one point the Materialist is in agreement with the Romanticist—

MATERIALIST *(Explodes):* I!?! As a matter of principle, I don't agree with the Romanticist on anything whatsoever!

ROMANTICIST *(Speaking at the same time):* This sounds interesting.

PSYCHOLOGIST: Namely, on this point: that many people go to war for idealistic reasons.

MATERIALIST *(Boiling):* I never said that! *Never!* On the contrary, I maintain that it is exclusively economic interest that motivates the people.

PSYCHOLOGIST: Agamemnon and his three advisors plainly enough desire war in their own interest. But when the king appealed to his people, he didn't say a word about economic considerations. He mentioned neither famine, nor overpopulation, nor that Troy is vantage point for trade. No! He appealed to his subjects' *sympathy, sense of honor, sense of justice, love of freedom.* And I should like to know if that doesn't mean that the great majority go to war for ideas—often even lofty ideas—and out of emotion, but almost never for economic gain—be it trade, oil wells, or manganese deposits.

(A rice paddy. A dark cloud descends over it. The cloud is made up of locusts.)

MATERIALIST: An entirely superficial point of view. When Greece expanded, it was simply from famine—due to overpopulation. Precisely the same cause that produces swarms of locusts, beech-spinner plagues, and epidemic cycles. All the idealistic notions that people swallow, at the outbreak of war, are fraud and self-deception.

PSYCHOLOGIST: I have every respect for self-deception. It unmistakably exists. But to deceive oneself and others would be unnecessary if there weren't so many who believed in high-minded ideas. Could wars start, if these ideas were pure deception?

MATERIALIST: I'm doing the talking just now.

PSYCHOLOGIST: I wasn't the one who interrupted you.

ROMANTICIST (*Gloating*): No—he interrupted himself!

MATERIALIST (*Explodes*): Pssjjj !!!

(*The swarm of locusts has meanwhile transformed itself into a camp of tents among green hills.*

Northern landscape. In the distance: turmoil of war, about the year 1200.

The King, the Bishop, and the Chaplain enter from one side; the Marshal from the other. The King and the Marshal are in armor. On the King's shield: a lion.)

KING (*Opens visor*): How is the battle proceeding, Marshal?

MARSHAL: Nothing in this world goes so badly as one fears, nor so well as one hopes.

KING: It's the *facts* that interest me. Not aphorisms. Besides, I think I've heard that before. Are we winning or losing?

MARSHAL: The course of battle rests with God.

KING: Everything rests with God.

BISHOP: Amen.

CHAPLAIN: Amen.

KING: But what is God's will, in your opinion?

MARSHAL: We are hard pressed on the left flank.

KING: If it goes badly, I shall fling myself into the combat; it will inspire our people.

MARSHAL: Do not be angry, Sire—but neither the Bishop nor I would permit that. As long as we have you, we have hope. Should you fall, or be taken captive, we would be checkmated.

(*Voices and shouting.*)

MARSHAL (*Shading his eyes with his hand*): Something must have happened. Those are some of our own people, the group coming this way.

KING: They have two men with them. Two prisoners.

BISHOP: Judging by their clothing and bearing, they are high-ranking folk with influence and position.

(Enter three or four knights with their attendants; two prisoners, hands bound behind their backs.)

KING: Whom do you bring?

KNIGHT: The chieftain. And his son.

ROMANTICIST: Now, really! You are stealing my material again.

MATERIALIST: Only to show you how things *really* happen. So we'll skip the conversion scene and see what follows.

(Green slopes. The Bishop and the Chaplain, on their way down to the sea.)

BISHOP: A great victory for God's kingdom!

CHAPLAIN: And the holy universal Church!

BISHOP: Amen.

CHAPLAIN: Amen.

BISHOP *(Stops. Gazes over the landscape):* I see that lovely, luxurious land closely dotted with steeples and cloisters.

CHAPLAIN: And this lovely luxurious land belonging to the Holy Church.

BISHOP: Partly, my son—partly. The king and the men of secular power will take their share.

CHAPLAIN: And the greater part! The way they always do!

BISHOP: Beware of greediness, my son. Greed generates envy, and envy is the axe that fells great men.

CHAPLAIN: But it should be *we,* God's representatives, who own the land, who rule the land, who decide what all the others may do and may not do!

BISHOP: Naturally, my boy. That is the goal, naturally. But remember: the more quietly a man works toward his goal, the greater his hope of achieving it. If other people get to know what we are aiming at, they will work against us. God's kingdom on earth is best advanced through silence and stratagem.

(They move on.)

(A green meadow. The Marshal with his followers.)

MARSHAL: Listen carefully to what I say. Now they're all going to baptize the heathens. While that nonsense is going on, comb the battlefield and collect everything you find of any value. No clothes, no shoes—such junk has no value. But all the metal you find on the dead and wounded. If any of the wounded offer resistance, then just bash their heads in. Put the loot in a good hiding-place. Then, when you've covered the territory, slip quietly onboard my ship and stow the stuff into my empty chest. Any man caught holding out on me will be hanged. Those who inform on thieves will get half the loot. D'you understand me?

PEOPLE: Yes, Sir Marshal.

MARSHAL: One more thing. If you're caught, remember you're plundering for yourselves. D'you understand?

PEOPLE: Yes, Sir Marshal.

(Exit Marshal. The people scatter.)

(Inside the royal tent. Enter the King, followed by two merchants. The King is in armor. The merchants are richly attired in furs.)

FIRST MERCHANT: We congratulate Your Majesty on this honorable victory—

SECOND MERCHANT:—although naturally it was just what we expected.

(Servant helps the King out of his armor.)

KING: Well, we came very close to defeat. If it hadn't been for the miraculous capture of the chieftain and his son, why, I would hardly have this opportunity now of negotiating with you gentlemen.

FIRST MERCHANT: God sustains a worthy cause.

SECOND MERCHANT: Amen.

KING: Not always! And I think you gentlemen should be glad of that.

FIRST MERCHANT *(Laughs)*: Very witty, Your Majesty.

SECOND MERCHANT: Yes, it is rare to encounter such irony.

FIRST MERCHANT: Business! Let's get down to business!

KING: Yes. Let's get out the rake.

SECOND MERCHANT: One part of the contract we agreed upon—

FIRST MERCHANT: —that which concerns Your Majesty's obligations—

KING *(Nods):* I cede to you two gentlemen the exclusive right in this country to all import and export; I am supporting the development of trade with countries further inland—

SECOND MERCHANT: —and protecting our rivers, our warehouses, our caravans, and our travelers if necessary, with armed force.

KING *(Nods):* If necessary, with armed force. Thus far we are in agreement.

(Exit Servant with the armor.)

FIRST MERCHANT: And for this we offer a compensation of 10 per cent on all the trade over which Your Majesty has granted us a monopoly, and which Your Majesty protects.

KING: I've told you I won't go below 15. You've got me down from 25, that should be sufficient.

SECOND MERCHANT: Your Majesty overrates the profit we have on our merchandise. If we are to yield 15 per cent to Your Majesty, there'll be nothing left for us.

KING: You must be happy that the Church has invented the concept of remission of sins.

SECOND MERCHANT: Why, Your Majesty?

KING: Otherwise, you'd be roasting—thanks to your lies— down in the sub-basement. *(Points.)*

FIRST MERCHANT: Don't let's quarrel. We offer eleven per cent. But no more than that.

KING: If you can go *up* one per cent, why, I can go down one. Fourteen.

SECOND MERCHANT: Perhaps I might remind Your Majesty that we are in possession of several promissory notes signed by Your Majesty.

KING: Don't remind me. That was for the outrageous fee my advisors charged me, when they recommended this—this "Crusade." A crusade most profitable for those in the background.

SECOND MERCHANT: I must draw Your Majesty's attention to the fact that these observations are only partially correct. Part of the debt is from Your Majesty's younger days, and one might venture to point out, without being unjust, that this money went for amusements—liquor, women, and luxury.

FIRST MERCHANT: Of the remainder, there is nothing in the promissory notes to indicate what the money was used for. It just says that Your Majesty owes us such and such a figure.

KING (*Paces to one end of the tent; paces back again. Stops in front of the merchants*): These notes are worthless. Or rather, it rests with my good grace whether I pay them or not. Merchants without army and navy can scarcely collect debts from a king who *has* an army and a navy.

FIRST MERCHANT: His Majesty, the German Kaiser, has offered to buy the notes—

SECOND MERCHANT: And he will certainly be able to collect on them.

(Pause.)

KING: Thirteen.

SECOND MERCHANT: Eleven. And not a jot more.

KING: Now then, twelve, damn it!

FIRST MERCHANT: Shall we be generous, dear brother, and say eleven and a half?

SECOND MERCHANT (*Sighing*): Well, then, 11½, for God's sake!

KING: Good. Then it's a bargain. My clerk will draw up the document—(*Raises his hand, when the merchants try to protest.*) *My* clerk! I don't care to be fleeced any further!

SECOND MERCHANT: One thing more, Your Majesty. Before we pay out the percentages, Your Majesty's debt will be paid off in installments.

KING: Pay off the debt first!! Impossible!!

FIRST MERCHANT: Then, most unfortunately, in the absence of liquid assets, we'll be obliged to dispose of the notes to the Kaiser.

KING *(Desperately):* Installments, then! Damn it! And to hell with all crusades! *(Strides out, raging, followed by merchants.)*

ROMANTICIST: This new-fangled way of writing history is quite simple: all people are made out to be hypocrites. But I can't see that there is more science in ascribing to people motives other than those they ascribe to themselves.

PSYCHOLOGIST: For once I agree with the Materialist. In the first place, I believe in what I like to call "multiple motivation." That is to say: as a rule there must be several motives in order for an action to take place. When a man describes his own motives, he leaves out a number of secondary ones; and I think it may be assumed that the motives he mentions will be the ones that present him in the most favorable light. Next: Man knows very little about this motivation. That applies to us and to other people as well. We can safely take it for granted that when we assume motives for our own actions and those of others, we are very often mistaken. But I'll grant that the Romanticist is right on one point: there are hardly as many acknowledged hypocrites in the world as the Materialist would have us believe. People are seldom hypocrites; but they are masters of self-deception.

(During the Psychologist's account, the tent is slowly transformed into a large, well-appointed office, vintage 1914.)

MATERIALIST *(Furiously):* I was doing the talking—and I hadn't finished!

OTHER TWO: Excuse us please.

(A writing desk shoots up from the floor. At the desk, a businessman, obviously a top executive. Knocking. The man says, "Come in!" A secretary appears.)

SECRETARY: Excuse me, sir, but Director Schmidt has arrived.

DIRECTOR: Show him in.

SECRETARY: Right away?

DIRECTOR: Hm.

SECRETARY: Shouldn't he wait a little?

DIRECTOR: When the owner of the world's largest munitions factory visits the owner of the world's next largest munitions factory, he gets in right away.

SECRETARY: Quite so, sir.

DIRECTOR: It's only cabinet ministers—and other inferior personages—that we keep waiting.

SECRETARY: Yes, sir. (*Exit.*)

DIRECTOR (*Takes one of the 37 telephones*): I'm not to be disturbed—no matter who it is. (*Replaces receiver.*)

SECRETARY: If you please, this way, Mr. Director.

SCHMIDT: Sank you. Sank you (*Speaks with slight foreign accent.*)

DIRECTOR (*Rises*): Welcome, my dear sir. (*Secretary disappears discreetly.*)

SCHMIDT: Sank you, sank you, dear Mr. Smith. And sank you for your pleasant reception of a competitor.

SMITH: You're always welcome, my good sir. Please have a seat.

SCHMIDT: Sank you. Sank you.

(*They sit down.*)

SMITH: Well now, how is everything going?

SCHMIDT: Bad. Bad. It's many years since we haff had such peaceful times as we haff now.

SMITH: Yes, I'm not complaining.

SCHMIDT: Oh, dear, dear Mr. Smith—let's not pretend vid each odder. I have my scouts out, just as you haff yours. I know vell you face a major setback if someding gratifying doesn't happen soon.

SMITH: A major setback! That's going a bit far. But I do concede that the situation is disturbing. Not even Uruguay and Paraguay are at war.

SCHMIDT: What do you intend to do, Mr. Smith?

Smith *(All business):* What had you yourself in mind?

Schmidt *(Smiles):* I can let you in on a secret. I haff already done someding!

Smith: And what is that?—if I am not being indiscreet—

Schmidt: I haff looked *you* up, dear Mr. Smith!

Smith: Ah! I see! You mean we should undertake a little something together?

Schmidt *(Rubs his hands):* Guessed right! Absolutely guessed right!

Smith: Say, a modest little conflict?

Schmidt: I admire your intuition!

Smith: As a matter of fact, I have been thinking along those very lines myself. But where should it be? Paraguay and Uruguay are a poor credit risk at the moment. There's always the Balkans: and China, or Turkey—

Schmidt: Chicken-feed! Doesn't pay off!

Smith: Are you aiming as high as Germany and France?

Schmidt: I am aiming even higher—

Smith: Even higher! You want England in it too?

Schmidt: I am aiming at a WORLD WAR!

Smith: A—a world war? A war in which every country on earth is involved?

Schmidt: Exactly. A cosmic conflict.

Smith: But you can't mean it!

Schmidt: The day the first locomotive stood on rails, it had never been heard of before either.

Smith: But you are ingenious! A Stephenson, an Edison, a—a Nobel!

Schmidt: I pride myself that it is a great, a truly great idea.

Smith: That will bring untold profits to the munitions industry!

Schmidt: To all industries. And to all people. The workers will also have a share in it. A world war means full employment and higher wages.

Smith: You are not only ingenious, but a true benefactor of

mankind!

SCHMIDT *(Deprecates modestly):* Let's not exaggerate. Many will suffer greatly. Many will die—

SMITH: In olden days, doctors went in for bloodletting. Mankind has got away from that, but I have been told that the patients afterwards felt singularly relieved. Freed of headache, melancholia, shortness of breath. I should imagine that a war might have much the same effect. And then we would also avoid that gross overpopulation which so many economists foresee.

SCHMIDT: Absolutely my sentiment.

SMITH: The question is simply: how do we bring about such a world chaos?

SCHMIDT: My dear Smith, you have an excellent propaganda organization. You own two newspapers, three cabinet ministers, and no end of politicians, to say nothing of the thousands of intellectual subordinates who are ready to carry out their orders. In fact, your propaganda machinery is almost as good as mine.

SMITH: But the pretext?

SCHMIDT: Pretext! Doesn't someding happen every year that we can use as a pretext? An officer in a border country creates provocation. A member of a royal house visiting in a foreign country is the victim of an assassination attempt. And there are other "incidents," equally easy to arrange. We let one of our people trample on the banner of a neighboring state, or overturn a patriotic statue—

SMITH: Yes, but that kind of thing is always smoothed over by the diplomats—

SCHMIDT: Because they have instructions to smooth it over. But if they don't have orders to patch it up, then they won't patch it up. *(Confidentially)* And besides, these gentlemen are not swayed by their governments alone; there are also, thank God, many of them whose requirements exceed their incomes, or who have to maintain mistresses.

SMITH *(Gets up):* I suggest that we discuss the matter in detail at a private luncheon. Will you do me the honor?

SCHMIDT *(Gets up):* With pleasure.

SMITH: There's still one thing: Our countries are bound to confront one another.

SCHMIDT: Unfortunately—we can scarcely avoid that. But in spite of that, my dear Director, you and I can be just as good friends.

SMITH: Naturally. Capital is the only true "International." But—let's face it—one of us will wind up on the losing side.

SCHMIDT: Unfortunately, that cannot be helped. But, notwithstanding, we'll both emerge from it with a thumping profit.

SMITH: I would hope so. But—certain problems arise after a war. Economic depression. Bankruptcies. Revolutions that deprive owners of their rightful property—

SCHMIDT: I've thought of all that, too. We can protect ourselves by investing capital in each other's operations.

SMITH: Just what I was about to suggest. And then I think we should assure each other of full protection. That is to say, if there should be a revolution here, then one of your castles would be a safe refuge for me and mine, *and* vice versa.

SCHMIDT *(Delighted):* An excellent suggestion! Excellent! I subscribe to it fully.

SMITH *(Takes Schmidt by the arm, and guides him out):* This way, dear brother—

PSYCHOLOGIST: That was poetry, not science.

ROMANTICIST: And bad poetry at that!

MATERIALIST: Will you deny it was the munitions industry that brought about World War I?

PSYCHOLOGIST: I won't deny that arms manufacturers, in the course of time, have done their bit in creating wars.

MATERIALIST *(Interrupting):* An understatement!

PSYCHOLOGIST *(Without pause):* It strikes me, though, as completely incredible that millions upon millions of people would go to war—against their wishes, against their interests—just because two cynical capitalists have agreed upon it.

MATERIALIST: Naturally I offered you only the barest sketch. There are, of course, more than two playing at this game.

PSYCHOLOGIST: Well, then, 200 or 2,000. But the capitalists will always be a vanishing minority in proportion to the "have-nots." And when these "have-nots" have nothing to gain economically from war—usually it's just the opposite—then I can't understand why they should allow themselves to be drafted into war by a small diminishing minority.

MATERIALIST: The power of money! The capitalists corrupt those in the government who carry any weight, and thus capital gains a strangle-hold over a group of petty officials—clergymen, teachers, professors, officers. For this whole category, then, livelihood depends upon preaching faith in God, king and country, in liberty, honor, holy matrimony—ideals worth dying for, if necessary—all that which can make the average man march enthusiastically off to war, without his knowing that he is the tool of capitalism. In addition, the capitalists have "whips," "whips" who are economically dependent on them, "whips" in the form of editors, journalists, politicians, public speakers, authors, bank directors, etc., etc.

(The office appears slowly in the same space, but upside down.)

PSYCHOLOGIST: An old story. Popular among intellectuals and communists in the years following World War I. And what happened? People who believed in that idea became leaders in their countries. They nationalized the munitions industries. And, all the same, along comes World War II.

MATERIALIST: That was because the states nationalized only the munitions industries. Men forgot that other capitalistic enterprises also profit by war, and are therefore just as interested in bringing about a state of war.

PSYCHOLOGIST: Damned if I know what they are. To be sure, there are capitalists who profit by war, but the question is, whether they wouldn't be better off, materially speaking, if no war developed. The general impoverishment that follows a war strikes at capitalists as well—among other things, in the form of taxes.

MATERIALIST: The deciding factor for the capitalists is not what is actually to their best interest, but what they *think* is to their best interest.

PSYCHOLOGIST: And although people look contemptuously upon the capitalists, they must not under-estimate them, either. Among other things, they are hardly so stupid that they can't see that each war means a step to the left.

MATERIALIST: But they also know that after the war, reaction sets in just as regularly, and that means two steps to the right.

PSYCHOLOGIST: If you are through, I'd like to contrive a little sequel to your sketch—

ROMANTICIST: Bravo! Ha!

MATERIALIST: Are you about to distort historical fact? I think that you, too, are serving capitalistic ends!

PSYCHOLOGIST: What I propose to do is no more nor less than what you did for our honored colleague, the Romanticist.

MATERIALIST: Very well, I *am* through. But I reserve the right to comment on the commentary.

PSYCHOLOGIST: Naturally.

(Fanfare of trumpets. The office again, but right side up this time. Director Smith comes in and sits down. At the same moment, one of the 37 telephones rings.)

DIRECTOR *(Picks up phone)*: Yes? *(Pauses to listen. His face lights up.)* Let him come in! *(Replaces receiver.)*

(Short pause. Young man enters.)

YOUNG MAN: Hello, Dad.

DIRECTOR *(Happily):* Hello, my boy. It's certainly good to see you. You're an infrequent guest.

SON: I hate to disturb you. I know how busy you are.

DIRECTOR: Sit down, Johnny. For you and your mother, I can always spare a few minutes. It must be something important you have on your mind, I should imagine, since you invade the inner sanctum.

SON: Both yes and no. It's about a very big matter. Dad, they say down at the Club that we are about to go to war. Probably a worldwide war involving us all.

DIRECTOR: Do you think I have some gift of prophecy?

SON: Not exactly a gift of prophecy. But perhaps some inside information.

DIRECTOR: Can I trust you to be discreet?

SON: I hope so.

DIRECTOR: No, you're not. No one is. Why should you be, more so than the others? But talk as much as you want. Only I rely upon you to give out your observations as your opinion, and not as inside information from me.

SON (With a little smile): Trust me.

DIRECTOR: Yes. We shall have war. The unimportant assassination of an inconsequential grand-duke will in no time at all flare up into a worldwide conflagration. If you have been wanting a new car, new shirts, or socks; or if you must have your own wine cellar, then I advise you to get it now. In a short while, all of that will be more expensive, and before long it will be unobtainable.

SON: That wasn't why I asked. They said down at the Club— (Hesitates.)

DIRECTOR: What do they say?

SON: Well, there was only one who said it. He's sort of a radical. I don't like to accuse him of being an out-and-out Communist, but—

DIRECTOR: And what did he say?

SON: Even though he is sort of a sneak, he is often surprisingly well informed—

DIRECTOR: But what did he say?

SON: He said you are arranging the war.

DIRECTOR: I'm not *that* powerful.

SON: No, but he said, too, that you weren't alone in it. You were working hand in glove with Schmidt & Sohne, Inc.

(*The Director rises, walks about, turns back to the desk, and stands facing his son. Pause.*)

DIRECTOR: What I am about to tell you, I have never told you before. What you hear now, you have never heard. And what you find out about world politics, you'll do well to keep to yourself.

Yes, it is correct that the directors of the world's largest munitions interests have put their heads together and agreed that there is to be a war.

SON (*Rises slowly as if hypnotized*): Father! Father! Yes, but, Father—But that's a crime! A crime against your own country, a crime against mankind!

DIRECTOR: Sit down, Johnny.

SON (*Still standing*): And this crime, this gigantic crime, you plan coldly and soberly with only one end in view—to make even more money.

DIRECTOR: Sit down, my boy.

SON: You must be out of your mind. Obsessed! That's the only excuse I can find for you. Perhaps you can't see what suffering war brings in its wake. Perhaps you can't see that the thing you have least use for in all the world is money. Would your life be any different, even if you do soak up a few more billions? You can't eat more than you do now. Nor can you eat better. You have twelve automobiles, but even if you got 1,200, you still couldn't drive in more than one at a time. We can't live more pleasantly than we do. And even if we acquired more palaces and estates and villas and apartments, we can still only live in one place at a time. We can't actually improve on our present way of life in the smallest degree, even though your fortune were to grow ever so enormous, on paper.

DIRECTOR: Sit down, my boy. And let me have a chance to say something to defend myself.

SON (*Sitting down*): I don't see how any defense is possible.

DIRECTOR (*Sits down. Looks at his son. Pause*): Actually, I am a pacifist.

MATERIALIST (*Explodes*): Ha! Pacifist! That's crazy! If ever there was a lousy judge of people, it's a psychologist.

PSYCHOLOGIST: Be good enough to hold your peace while I have the floor.

SON: The owner of the world's second largest munitions plant, a pacifist. If I didn't feel so wretched, I'd have to laugh.

DIRECTOR: You know I was in the Franco-Prussian War—as a volunteer?

SON: Yes, I know that.

DIRECTOR: I joined up on the French side, to defend the cause of justice. For no one could have any doubt that it was Germany who attacked France. You see, it was youthful idealism that decided it, the same youthful idealism that you express when you reproach your father for his "criminal greed."

SON: I wonder if all men are idealists when they're young, and cynics when they're old!

DIRECTOR: When the war was over, I was a lover of peace. What I had seen of mutilation had filled me with horror and despair. Remarkably enough, it was the *horses,* the wounded and dying *horses,* that had made the most profound impression on me. Perhaps because a man can say to other men: "It was your own fault. You could have refrained from this." To a horse, on the other hand, a horse, who looks at one with great sad eyes, one can only say, "Yes, we men are to blame for your sufferings. I am ashamed."

SON: So off you went and became a munitions manufacturer.

DIRECTOR: I fell in love, my boy. Truly in love. Without reason. Without the slightest thought of the girl's economic connections. I saw her on board a ship—she stood by the rail— and she looked like an angel—in the latest Parisian style. Love hit me like a straight right to the jaw. So I began moving heaven and earth to get introduced to her. I was successful. And it was not until two weeks later that I found out she was one of the world's richest girls, daughter of an arms manufacturer. And then we were married. And I did *not* become an arms manufacturer. I started a refrigerator plant—to be sure, with the economic support of your mother's father. But when we had been married a couple of years, he died—of a heart attack—and his enterprises were administered by a lawyer and a banker—two vultures. After they had plundered and neglected everything so completely that your grandmother was on the brink of ruin, I took over the directorship, to save the rest for her, if possible. And once there, well— (*shrugs his shoulders.*)

SON: And now, in other words, you're a Dr. Jekyll and Mr. Hyde. A pacifist, who, out of a primitive hunger for profit, arranges wars.

DIRECTOR: You're still wrong. I work only toward world peace. But I work farsightedly. And in a way which I have never confided to anyone—until now.

SON: And you—are confiding in me, then?

DIRECTOR (*Nods*): Peace, you see, world peace, will never be achieved as long as there are many nations, many states, here on the surface of the earth. More than one state will mean chronic unrest, chronic insecurity, intervals of war—war that will be more and more atrocious. But one state, one realm— that we shall never attain through peaceful means. For that, men are too small and vain, too quarrelsome, too belligerent. (*Rises.*) *The united states of the world will only be attained when one country—by force—engulfs all the others.*

(*Walks about. Stops.*) Alexander the Great was on the way to the creation of a united world. The Roman state likewise. Unfortunately it broke up from within, due to unknown causes. In our time, there is only one country that has the possibility of swallowing up all the others—and that is ours. It is also the only one that is worthy of it—especially since we are the most enlightened nation, the most humane people to be found; we have the best system of justice, and are the only people who will not exploit the conquered, or tread upon them. **Now do you understand my master plan?**

(*Half seats himself on the desk.*) On those grounds, and not on any other, I went along with Dr. Schmidt's proposal, when he came here and suggested that we munitions manufacturers should arrange a total war. He did it for profit, or from a simple instinct of self-preservation—for Schmidt & Sohne, Inc., are hard hit by the long-lasting peace—but I acted from an entirely different motive, one I have never talked about to him, or to any other person, with the exception of you. *(Goes over to his son, lays his hands on the boy's shoulders.)*

Understand, my boy, from the coming war we shall emerge victorious. Anything else is unthinkable. And *then we will be the world's richest state, the world's strongest nation, and the country which can unite all the other lands into one single realm.*

Son *(Rising):* Father, I understand you. It is a great concept. An ingenious plan. Some day, you will be reckoned as mankind's greatest benefactor. As soon as the war breaks out, I shall join as a volunteer.

Director *(Pauses in front of his son, face to face):* My boy, nothing would be easier for me than to arrange for you to be exempted from military service, although there will be a strict draft system here. But I tell you: I'm glad of your resolution. It would be an unbearable loss for your mother and me, if you, our only child, should die on the battlefield. And yet—and yet I won't advise you to stay home. Without idealism, without men willing to sacrifice themselves, mankind will never forge ahead, never conquer war. *(Takes him by the shoulders, playfully.)* In any case, I can tell you that just the other day I applied as a volunteer. Unfortunately they say up at the War Ministry that men over sixty are more of a handicap than an asset. *(As he speaks, he leaves the office, taking his son with him.)*

Materialist: That's a very unlikely story you served up there! For example—

Psychologist *(Interrupting):* Just wait a minute. There's still one more sketch.

(Library in a millionaire's home. 1918.)

Angel of Peace: If this is the way I'm to be made well, I

think the cure is worse than the sickness!

(*Director Smith enters from one side. From the other, Mrs. Smith and the General. Mrs. Smith trembles, weeps, sniffs. She behaves as if she had just been hit with a sledgehammer—that sledgehammer to which life now and then treats its little creatures. The General, a white-haired staff officer, steadies her in a gentlemanly fashion.*)

DIRECTOR (*Hurries in*): The General wanted to— (*Stops. Pause. Looks at the two others.*) So— So— It's happened. (*Sits down.*)

GENERAL: Yes. It's— (*By fits and starts.*) It was my secretary who—came and told me that—he had seen your son's name— on the new—list of missing persons. "See to it that this is kept quiet," I said, "see first and foremost that the Director and his wife don't get to know about it." You understand, I wanted personally—to break the bad news to you. And at the same time to express to you my deepest sympathy for your terrible loss.

DIRECTOR: It was nice of you, General, it was—

GENERAL: Your son fell on the field of honor. He fell during a commando attack—with a bullet in his breast.

DIRECTOR: Yes—that's what they usually tell the bereaved family—even if the death struggle lasted for hours and even if the bullet in the breast was a bayonet in the abdomen.

GENERAL: In this case, it—

DIRECTOR (*Raises hand to ward him off*): Now at any rate, he does not suffer. (*Pause.*) He was the only one we had.

GENERAL: I know.

DIRECTOR: And even though he died for a cause I believed in—and still believe in—still, it hurts me deeply.

GENERAL: I understand that.

MRS. SMITH: I also understand very well that it hurts you. Because you are responsible for his death! (*Suddenly wildly and shrilly.*) You!

(*The Director rises, stooped, moving with difficulty.*)

GENERAL: Your husband can have no responsibility whatsoever for that particular enemy bullet—

MRS. SMITH: My husband talked him into going!

GENERAL: We have a compulsory draft.

MRS. SMITH: You know as well as I do that nothing would have been easier for my husband than to station him where there was no danger. For instance, one of his directors, who is a general, could have used his influence.

DIRECTOR: It was Johnny himself who wanted to go to the front.

MRS. SMITH: But why! Why! Because you thought he should act like a hero. Because you, irresponsible, hard-hearted, without thought for me, instilled in him an idiotic idealism—

DIRECTOR: Johnny was an idealist *anyway*.

MRS. SMITH: You know how he looked up to you, admired you—

GENERAL: Your husband is a great man, who deserves admiration from all of us. It is only anarchists and their ilk who cannot see your husband's services to mankind.

MRS. SMITH: A great man? A miserable, befuddled, confused creature! A man who one minute is a patriot; the next, an idealistic peace-lover; now, a cynical businessman.

GENERAL: That last, I object to.

MRS. SMITH: A cynical businessman—who plans wars along with other cynical businessmen. They are right, those you call "anarchists." It's the big munitions manufacturers who have wanted this war, wanted it to pile up still greater wealth than they have already.

GENERAL: This argument is entirely new to me. Usually we officers get blamed for creating wars.

MRS. SMITH: Why should officers start wars? To get shot?

GENERAL: People say that when we have played at war on a map for so many years, one fine day we want to try it in reality. People also say that we want war for the sake of prestige, and a somewhat neglected class suddenly becomes the darling of society. They also say that especially the younger officers are anxious for war to promote their careers. Advancement is pretty slow in peacetime.

DIRECTOR: If it is the military who have created the war, it's on the opposing side. According to the White Papers we have issued, there is no doubt that it is the Kaiser and his General Staff and the top politicians who wanted this war.

GENERAL: The other side maintains that we are to blame, and their Yellow, Blue, Green, and Orange pamphlets are not without certain accusations. No, the truth about war is that no one is responsible. It is a natural catastrophe, like earthquakes, tornadoes, floods. And it wouldn't help if we abolished the military. People would fight anyway—with knives, axes, scythes, pitchforks, bare fists—

DIRECTOR: That's a pessimistic viewpoint, which I hope is wrong. But it brings to my mind an idea I have long entertained, and my son's death provides the occasion. I will endow a peace prize—a price of a couple of hundred thousand—which is to be awarded each year to that man or woman who has done the most for world peace.

MRS. SMITH: And you think that will soothe your conscience, and your loneliness!

GENERAL: A nice thought, a *very* nice thought. I'd be happy to serve on the committee that administers it.

DIRECTOR: And I'll name it after my son, "The John Smith Peace Prize." If this prize can accomplish anything, then he will not have died in vain.

MRS. SMITH: Ten thousand peace prizes are no comfort to me. I want my son. If I can't have my son back, there's no happiness left in my life—*(Leaves in tears.)*

GENERAL: Excuse me for interfering, but you should hardly allow your wife to be alone in such an emotional state.

DIRECTOR: No. You're right. *(Continues, chiefly to himself.)* Perhaps I have sacrificed too much for an ideal—And what if that ideal, after all, turned out to be a mistaken one—

(Exeunt both. Mr. Smith walks like a very old man.)

MATERIALIST: Your addition to the story has made my portrayal of the arms manufacturer both blurred and inconsistent.

PSYCHOLOGIST: Indisputably! And that's how he comes to resemble a human being. Believe me, however much you may object to them, capitalists are also human beings.

(Bubbling fountains, mud volcanoes, bubbling sulfur pools, smoking crevices—all located, close together, helter-skelter, upon a rocky plain. The water in the fountains is of different colors.)

ROMANTICIST: I watched your sketch with genuine pleasure— I might even say, with sympathy. But you still haven't told us what, in your opinion, are the causes of war.

MATERIALIST: He has no opinion. He's just obtuse—

(Fanfare of trumpets. The prompter sticks a pointer up in the air. Psychologist takes it. During the ensuing conversation, he struts up and down, like a somewhat dogmatic schoolteacher who has stepped down from the rostrum.)

PSYCHOLOGIST: In my opinion, both the gentlemen are right. *(Astonished outbreak from his two colleagues.)*

PSYCHOLOGIST: I believe that people go to war for all the reasons you have named, Mr. Romanticist. There are indeed men to be found who are ready to offer life and limb for country, liberty, honor, justice, etc., etc.

ROMANTICIST: Thank you.

PSYCHOLOGIST: But it is obvious that one ought also to consider the economic forces, from the very simplest—hunger, brought about through overpopulation—to the one that vulgar Marxism is always so absorbed with: capitalistic greed.

MATERIALIST: You haven't understood one word I've said. There are only material causes.

(Fashionable restaurant)

PSYCHOLOGIST: But in addition to all these motives—patriotism, religious fervor, sense of justice, avarice, (which is either a mania for hoarding, or a compensation for a feeling of inferiority), hunger, desire for a change of scene, etc., etc., then there's a long list of other motives—

ANGEL OF PEACE: For instance?

PSYCHOLOGIST: Motives which I shall now attempt to demonstrate.

(Two chess players, seated on either side of a table, rise up from the floor. One is dressed entirely in black; the other, entirely in white. They sit a long time in silence, with long pauses between moves.)

PSYCHOLOGIST: Chess players—

MATERIALIST: You don't say!

PSYCHOLOGIST: They are in the middle of a war. Not a bloody war, but nevertheless a war. A war they take so seriously that they expend more energy upon it than upon their daily tasks. A war in which they are so absorbed that they don't hear our conversation. And yet they have not the slightest economic interest in this war. They aren't playing for money. The winner will not get any extra food, power, or income. What impels them is the longing for excitement, joy in solving a problem— (each new move means a new problem) —*and*—vanity, vanity. The two chess players prove, in other words, that my colleague, the Materialist, is wrong when he maintains that all wars have an economic cause.

(Short pause.)

ROMANTICIST *(Looking askance at the Materialist)*: Have you nothing to say, sir?

MATERIALIST: Pshaw! That—that's no war. That's—monkey business!

THE WHITE CLAD *(Triumphantly)*: Checkmate!

THE BLACK CLAD *(Protests heatedly)*: Nah, what d'you mean! You can't do that! *(Begins to fumble with the pieces.)*

WHITE: Why not?

BLACK: What the hell! I didn't notice you'd moved your king. I took it for granted that you'd left your king open to a check, if you—Damn it! That's annoying! I thought I had you!

WHITE: Have me? *(Grins mercilessly)* You must have a hole in the head.

BLACK: I've got one more pawn than you.

WHITE: Yes, but with that unprotected flank there, you'd have been checkmated in a few moves.

BLACK: I'm not so sure of that—*(Annoyed)* It was because someone was talking then! *(Looks around)* Must have been that party over there—*(The "party" consists of the three historians and the Angel of Peace.)* It always distracts me when people jammer. *(Suddenly)* I want a return match!

WHITE *(Looks at his watch)*: It's pretty late—

BLACK: I can't sleep anyway. I always lie there and get more and more annoyed when I've lost. All night long I keep on playing the game over, and the next day, I'm tired and depressed.

WHITE *(Somewhat arrogantly)*: Well, I can rest easy! And the little woman is waiting for me too.

BLACK *(Shrilly, almost hysterically)*: You can't refuse me! *(Bangs the table at the word "never." Turns the chessboard.)*

(Black is suddenly clad in white; and White is suddenly clad in black.)

WHITECLAD *(Continuing)*: It's a point of honor for me to show you that my playing is not inferior to yours.

(Begins to set up the pieces.)

BLACKCLAD *(Somewhat crest-fallen at having to start in again)*: I suppose so. It's for you to decide the moment of revenge. *(Begins to set up pieces.) (The two chess players sink into the floor.)*

PSYCHOLOGIST *(Indicates with pointer)*: That little scene illustrated one of war's causes—the feeling of inferiority—the outcome of defeat. This painful sense of inferiority, which can only be relieved by a victorious return match.

ANGEL OF PEACE *(Lifts head)*: Do you really think a sense of inferiority plays any part?

PSYCHOLOGIST *(Nods)*: Yes, even a major role. It was one of the main reasons the Germans began World War II.

ROMANTICIST: Just think. Such a cause of war was not even

thought of in my time.

(Hitler. A glimpse. And a fragment of a speech. "Early this morning our troops broke across the border." *The audience breaks out in a lengthy earsplitting roar of applause. Crazed enthusiasm, uninhibited jubilation. The Psychologist goes on lecturing, every time the noise permits.)*

PSYCHOLOGIST *(Pointing):* Here, we see ecstasy. The highest pleasure known to mankind. Or in any case, a pleasure scarcely less than sensual rapture. Isn't this ecstasy worth all a war's sufferings?

ANGEL OF PEACE *(Sharply):* NO!

(A young man's room. Bed, chair, table, books, some sport trophies.)

PSYCHOLOGIST: I didn't really mean that. But who thinks about the hangover in the hour of intoxication! In his sad, tedious, humdrum existence, Mr. Average Man sits and longs unconsciously for the great, uninhibited ecstasy. But there is also something else he longs for—

(Mr. Average Son comes in with a suitcase. Begins to pack. Someone knocks.)

AVERAGE SON: Yes.

(Mr. Average Friend hurries in.)

AVERAGE FRIEND: Hi! You packing already?

AVERAGE SON: I'm leaving tonight. I got a telegram that I'm to report tomorrow morning by eight at the latest.

AVERAGE FRIEND: How do you feel about it, really?

AVERAGE SON: I'm glad.

AVERAGE FRIEND: You're glad? Do you mean it seriously?

AVERAGE SON: Yep.

AVERAGE FRIEND: You're not a little—uh—not a little nervous?

AVERAGE SON: Nope.

AVERAGE FRIEND: After all, it's not entirely—without danger. According to statistics, eight to nine million were killed and nineteen million wounded.

AVERAGE SON: To hell with the danger, if I can just get out

of this stink-hole.

AVERAGE FRIEND: D'you really think it's so bad?

AVERAGE SON: I think this town is hell!

AVERAGE FRIEND: You mean this inoffensive little village?

AVERAGE SON: Yes, hell! There are no women here.

AVERAGE FRIEND: No women! But—

AVERAGE SON: You know what I mean. No women a man can have a little fun with. They're all so proper, and come from such nice families that a guy has to marry one if he wants to ——, and you know I can't support a wife for the next five years. Okay, there's one prostitute, but I can't afford her on my pocket money. And then you know how the town is. Everybody spying on each other. If I say two words to a girl on the street, they know it at home in half an hour! Mother gets upset, Father roars like a sea lion—and what's the result? A guy goes around and thinks of nothing but women, women, women! And every now and then he plays with himself to get some peace.

AVERAGE FRIEND: Wow! You do?

AVERAGE SON: Don't be a fool! Just because you're a year younger doesn't mean you're any different from me.

(Average Friend looks away.)

AVERAGE SON *(Triumphantly):* But now I'll be getting away from this town—away where nobody watches over me—no one to tell tales—and I get a uniform and pocket money—*(Flings clothes into the suitcase)*—then you'll see!! Then you'll see!!

(Average Man enters, without knocking.)

AVERAGE MAN: So you're packing. That's good, my boy.

AVERAGE FRIEND *(Bows a little too politely):* Hello, sir.

AVERAGE MAN: How do you do, young man, how do you do? Oh, I almost envy you, my boy! It sounds strange, but—I remember from the last war—all the pretty girls we ran across— and had fun with. And they weren't even American girls. I'll tell you, those foreign girls, they can't resist a foreign soldier. There were houses, too. Splendid, orderly bordellos, with anything you happened to want. In that respect, I must say the army was well organized. Well, those places didn't interest me. I always preferred girls who do it out of friendliness and affection. And I must say, I had no trouble. I was pretty handsome in those days. Lean, curly hair, and so forth. I knew what I wanted, boys. I don't think about those things any more. Now I'm past that age, and enjoy happy married life—I said all this to you just to cheer you up—so you won't think that war and soldiering are nothing but misery.

AVERAGE FRIEND: This time I guess you won't be called up, Mr. Average.

AVERAGE MAN: No, I guess not. Men of my age won't be drafted. But still I'm wondering whether or not I ought to enlist—for the sake of my country. You come down when you're ready, and have a cup of coffee. Both of you. *(Exit.)*

AVERAGE FRIEND *(Bowing in a servile manner)*: Thank you, sir.

AVERAGE SON: I wonder if the old man doesn't have in mind —playing around a little.

AVERAGE FRIEND: Do you really think so?

AVERAGE SON: Sounded like it. *(Shuts suitcase)* Now I'm ready.

(Average Son goes out with suitcase; Average Friend follows.)

ANGEL OF PEACE: That was a rather crude scene, I must say —and in the presence of a lady.

ROMANTICIST: An Angel, at that!

PSYCHOLOGIST: Wait. You haven't seen anything yet.

ANGEL OF PEACE: But is all this really necessary?

PSYCHOLOGIST: We have set out to find the causes of an illness, and it can't be done without a look at naked humanity, however revolting the sight may be.

(A sidewalk cafe in a large city. Two gentlemen, sitting close together, rise up through the floor. One is young, the other older. They sit at a round marble-topped table, on lions' feet. On it are two glasses containing a shining liquid, rich green in color.)

YOUNG MAN: I can't understand why you enlist. War is so

vile—ugh!

OLDER MAN: A man owes everything to his country, my dear.

YOUNG MAN: Imagine your using such a phrase! You don't mean it, either. You and I are above that sort of vulgar brawling. You and I, Charlie Boy, we're internationals.

OLDER MAN: We might as well join up first as last. We'd soon be drafted.

YOUNG MAN: But let's wait, then, until we *are!*

OLDER MAN: It looks more noble to volunteer.

YOUNGER MAN: Know what I think? I believe you're tired of me!

OLDER MAN: I fail to see the connection.

YOUNGER MAN: You'll go out where there are young men. Soldiers. A happy hunting ground. I'm not enough any longer. You want to make little Fritz unhappy.

OLDER MAN: I don't want to make you unhappy, but—you're so moral! And that gets a little monotonous in the long run.

YOUNGER MAN: You admit, then, that you want to break it off.

OLDER MAN: Yes, little Fritz, yes. I admit it. I admit that that's why I want to enlist.

YOUNGER MAN: And I'll be miserable—I, who love you.

OLDER MAN: You know I was in World War I. I'll never forget those days. They were the happiest years of my life. Then, everything was very different for us—we were persecuted, despised, sent to jail, had a hard time finding one another—and then suddenly Paradise opened up for me! Mohammed's Paradise—full of young, succulent men. At the front, you understand, in the trenches, where the boys don't have access to women. I'll tell you, I've seldom been so devastatingly thrilled as when I heard war had started. It's as if my youth had been awakened anew. For years I've dreamed we might have a war again. And here it is.

YOUNGER MAN: I'll never be happy again.

OLDER MAN: Nonsense, Fritzy, you can go too!

(Table sinks down again—into flames.)

ANGEL OF PEACE: What an absolutely disgusting scene!

ROMANTICIST: We didn't have that type in my day.

PSYCHOLOGIST *(Laughs loudly)*: Haw! We've always had that type. They were under cover, that's all.

(A farm. Early evening. Muffled sounds of cannon. In the distance, glow of light from the front. A soldier enters, buttoning his clothing. A comrade joins him.)

COMRADE: Where've you been?

FIRST SOLDIER: In there.

SECOND SOLDIER: In there? What'd you do in there?

FIRST SOLDIER: Had a little fun with the woman of the farm.

(The two soldiers begin to walk along. They walk away, side by side. Their way lies along a rough country road. The landscape, which rolls past them, consists of fields. Here and there are stretches wasted by war.)

SECOND SOLDIER: I thought they hated us here in these parts. That's what the lieutenant says.

FIRST SOLDIER: It's the truth.

SECOND SOLDIER: If they hate us, you don't get the women to—

FIRST SOLDIER: Who said it was voluntary?

SECOND SOLDIER: You took her—by force?

FIRST SOLDIER: You said it.

SECOND SOLDIER: I thought a woman couldn't be raped. Seems to me you'd be short a couple of hands.

FIRST SOLDIER: It's not easy. You've got to keep at it, you see, until they get tired. And if you have a hard time, hit 'em one over the head.

SECOND SOLDIER: That's damn dangerous, what you did.

FIRST SOLDIER: How come? The woman was alone. We shot the husband the other day, as a spy.

SECOND SOLDIER: That's not what I mean. If your superiors learn about it, you risk being shot.

FIRST SOLDIER: We don't exactly have an excess of man power.

SECOND SOLDIER: In the Twelfth Battalion, they had one guy who got hanged.

FIRST SOLDIER: Yeah—that one! But he'd strangled the girl, you see. He was a killer. Get it?

SECOND SOLDIER: All the same, it's pretty gruesome to think that there are people who love to kill.

FIRST SOLDIER: There's lots like that! Sure! But they don't get the opportunity every day. They can hardly do anything in peacetime. But when war comes, then they have a ball! And are praised to boot. The more they pick off, the more they rip open, the more confetti they get, and medals and decorations. In war, a killer is not a killer. He's a hero, and gets his name in all the newspapers.

SECOND SOLDIER: I guess it'll rain tomorrow.

FIRST SOLDIER: Looks like it.

SECOND SOLDIER: Honestly, it can't be much fun to take a girl by force. I feel this way; to have a good time, we ought to like each other—

FIRST SOLDIER: Sure, sure, but with me it's just the opposite. I don't like it unless she fights like a cat, bawls me out, cries and screams, hating me all the time, and then finally has to give in! But that kind of kicks a man doesn't have every day. Then he goes to jail for it. In wartime it's different. You know what? I've been hoping all along we'd have a war!

(*Stops.*) Now, I'm heading that way.

SECOND SOLDIER: So long then. (*Starts in a different direction*) See ya.

FIRST SOLDIER: I'm gonna get some shuteye, you can bet your life! God, how I'm gonna sleep! I'll sleep as sound as a baby that's just been given the birthday present he wanted more than anything else in the world!

(*Their paths separate, like the ends of a bow. They vanish in the dusk. The scene shifts slowly to a dark cellar.*)

ANGEL OF PEACE: You know, I really don't think I can stand any more scenes like that.

PSYCHOLOGIST *(Amiably):* So, we'll have something more cheerful.

(A vat, a wine-vat, shoots up in the air. Under it, a couple of crude jugs. Behind: long rows of vats, losing themselves in the darkness of the cellar. Two Vikings come noisily in. One is a grown man, the other a young fellow. Height: about five feet tall, full beards—massive red beards.)

FIRST VIKING: Hojotoho! Hajahoha! Hooloohoohoo!

(Aside) R. Wagner.

SECOND VIKING *(Looking around):* So that's how they look —their famous wine-cellars!

FIRST VIKING: *One* of them. *One* of them! There are hundreds like this. The whole of France is full of them. Every cloister has its own; every landowner has one.

SECOND VIKING: What strange kind of boats are those?

FIRST VIKING: Boats! Those are vats, you idiot. They're full of wine.

(Hands him a jug.)

(Second Viking grabs it with both hands.)

FIRST VIKING: That arm on the side is to hold with. *(Helps him.)* That way.

(Squats on the floor beside the vat.) See? *(Holds his jug under the tap and opens.)*

(Second Viking is seized with a fit of laughter.)

FIRST VIKING: What the hell are you laughing at?

SECOND VIKING: It looks like a fat man pissing.

FIRST VIKING: He's more practically equipped than us. You should have such a faucet on you! You'd smell better!

(They draw wine a while in silence.)

ANGEL OF PEACE *(During this interval):* Aren't they small though?

PSYCHOLOGIST: Who? What? Where?

ANGEL OF PEACE: The Vikings.

PSYCHOLOGIST: That is historically correct. We know it from archeological findings.

ANGEL OF PEACE: How could they have been so feared all over Europe?

PSYCHOLOGIST: The people they attacked were even smaller.

MATERIALIST: The whole world was undernourished. It was lack of food in those days that caused all the wars, all the migrations, and all the forays of the Vikings.

PSYCHOLOGIST: Sh-h-h-h!

FIRST VIKING: One for the gods. Don't hold back—there's plenty more. And so—(*Touches jugs with his companion*) Here's to you and here's to me and here's to the Nornie girls! (*They drink.*)

FIRST VIKING: Ah! A-aw! Oh!

SECOND VIKING (*Smacks his lips—slowly and appreciatively*): It tastes kind of queer.

FIRST VIKING: It tastes just divine. And the effect is even better. But I remember the first time, when I thought it smacked of decadent bourgeoisie. Once you acquire a taste for it, though, it's like the bear who's sampled human flesh. You've gotta have *more!* Skoal!

SECOND VIKING: Skoal!

FIRST VIKING: At home they're always talking about heroism and self-sacrifice, that war is the only sport fit for a man. Especially when a chieftain is recruiting for a raid. The others, they mumble about all the gold and silver, and all the safety pins and razor blades you can take home under the thwarts. But what do I want with heroism, gold, rape, and razor blades? Give me good Bordeaux and Burgundy until it comes out of my ears. Skoal, man!

SECOND VIKING: Skoal. (*Drinks up. Suddenly reaches out his jug.*) More! (*Laughs.*) I'm beginning to like it.

FIRST VIKING: And it's beginning to like you. As soon as you get back home, you'll be yearning for the next little Viking excursion!

Yes, you'll like it all right, better than mother's milk!

All you'll be able to think of is to drink—drink and drink and drink—drink until you topple over and dream you're in Valhalla. Knocking Thor about and making a play for Freya!

FIRST VIKING (*Waves his jug*): More!!!

FIRST VIKING (*Pushes it aside*): Wait! We'd better go upstairs first, to see that the dead are plenty dead. Then we can come back, barricade the door, and get down to serious drinking. Before you know it we'll be on the trolley to Valhalla.

(*Exeunt.*)

MATERIALIST: I protest! Thirst is, like hunger, an economic cause.

PSYCHOLOGIST: But this isn't ordinary thirst; this is more of a *luxury* pursuit.

MATERIALIST: Whether people crave food in excess, or simply as a means of sustaining life, does not alter the fact that the craving is a link in the human economy. Capitalists are people who amass a supply far larger than their need, far larger than they can ever use up, and yet their motive is also economic.

PSYCHOLOGIST: Would you call the craving for morphine an economic motive too?

MATERIALIST: Everything man does to satisfy a material need is of an economic order. (*Maliciously*) And those who send opium to China are clever economists all the same.

PSYCHOLOGIST: Very well. We won't quarrel over a trifle. I'll accept your genuine Vikings and their luxury thirst.

(*Materialist swells with pride.*)

(*The scene changes to Place de l'Etoile in Paris. In the background: The Arch of Triumph. Spring, in the early '40s. A German soldier marches in, backwards. Another follows after, forwards, holding a camera against his stomach.*)

PHOTOGRAPHER: *Halt! Gut! Lächeln!* (*As the other cracks a broad smile, he snaps the shutter.*) *Danke.*

COMPANION: *Bitte.*

FIRST SOLDIER: War is a wonderful invention.

SECOND SOLDIER:* Do you mean that—seriously?

---

*The following episode is completely in German in the original.

FIRST SOLDIER: But certainly. I love to travel and see new surroundings, and talk with foreigners. But with my income, travel is out of the question. And furthermore, my vacation lasts only two weeks. *(Sighs.)* I have always suffered a terrible longing for faraway places. *(Brightens up.)* But then the war came! And nobody is happier about it than I.

And even before this, it was also wonderful! I've seen the Acropolis, the Cathedral in Milan, the Chapel of the Medici in Florence, St. Peter's in Rome, the Sistine Chapel, Napoleon's Tomb, the Eiffel Tower—and now even the Arch of Triumph!

SECOND SOLDIER: But this kind of travel is not without its risks.

FIRST SOLDIER: There's risk in any travel. And our Army is so well-organized. And then the trip is free, free accommodation, free food—and on top of all that, pay! Any other travel agency hands you a bill.

SECOND SOLDIER: Well, I'd enjoy it too, if there wasn't all this damned shooting!

FIRST SOLDIER: Come here a moment! I want to snap the Arch of Triumph from the other side. Gretchen collects photographs of famous buildings. *(They move on.)*

ANGEL OF PEACE: You take all kinds of motives into account, I must say.

PSYCHOLOGIST: Even so, I do not claim that my enumeration is complete. Rather, the contrary. It is impossible to draw up an exhaustive list.

(A street in a provincial town. The houses are burning. Red light shines from both sides. The glow waxes and wanes. Sound of fire: roaring, seething, crackling. Two soldiers. One with a burning stick of wood. Both blackened and perspiring.)

FIRST SOLDIER: You! Why have we done all this? Did we have orders to burn the town?

(A thought has obviously struck him—now, when it is too late!)

SECOND SOLDIER *(The one with the brand):* No—*(Appears a*

little absent-minded.)

FIRST SOLDIER: Why the hell did we do it?

SECOND SOLDIER: Look how it glows! Hear how it roars!

FIRST SOLDIER: This was your idea!

SECOND SOLDIER *(Listening, as to music):* Listen to the sound of burning!

FIRST SOLDIER: Why the hell did you think this up?

(Pause.)

SECOND SOLDIER: I love to watch things burn.

(His eyes shine—or is it only the reflection?)

FIRST SOLDIER *(Horrified):* Are you—are you—serious?

SECOND SOLDIER: FIRE! It's better than laying a girl.

FIRST SOLDIER: You're—you're a psycho!

SECOND SOLDIER: Everybody's crazy.

FIRST SOLDIER: Yeah, perhaps. But some people are crazier than others.

I get a charge out of seeing a factory chimney get hit, and ever so slowly topple over. But to go and set fire to just anything and everything—It ain't right.

SECOND SOLDIER: Huh! In war, a guy's allowed to do it! Come on! There's one over there that's not burning!

(Rushes out.)

(Companion follows.)

MATERIALIST *(Who recently has been yawning a good deal):* It's getting a bit tiresome, this rigmarole!

PSYCHOLOGIST: Good! Then I'll finish up. Last example.

(An opening in a forest. A bush comes crawling in. The bush is a soldier with green branches in his shoulder straps and helmet net. He worms himself forward, gun in hand—extremely slowly and extremely carefully. The soldier takes aim, but does not fire. He waits. Long pause. A comrade enters, walking backwards, suspecting nothing.)

No. TWO: What gives? *(Stops in the middle of the sentence. Bullets begin to whistle around him.)*

THE FIRST ONE: Duck, for God's sake! On your belly! *(The*

other is down, before the first one has finished speaking.)

SECOND: What the hell is this? I thought the area was cleared?

(Crawls, flat as a flounder, over to the side of No. 1.)

FIRST: Somebody's on the other side of the bog, over there among the rushes. We've been having a little target practice with each other the last half hour.

SECOND: Is that why you didn't show up for chow?

FIRST: Right.

(During the whole conversation, his eyes are fixed on a distant point.)

SECOND: Why stick it alone? Report it! Then a patrol will be sent out—and you probably wouldn't even be one of them—

(Little pause.)

FIRST: I like it this way.

SECOND *(Taken aback):* You like it!

FIRST: I dig it.

SECOND: The hell you say!

(A couple of shots from the opponent.)

FIRST: He's shooting blind, the dope. That means he doesn't know where I am. Now it's just a test of patience. The first one to move—finished! *(Pause.)*

Hunting's always been my meat—and shooting competitions. I'm not a bad shot, if I do say so myself. But most hunting really isn't much. It's kind of good to hunt deer—but too unequal, too safe. Better, lions—that could tear a man apart if he missed; or hippos—that trample a man. Now this kind of hunting is the real thing. This kind, where the game can shoot back, where a man's both hunter and hunted. Weren't you bored at home— every day?

SECOND: Maybe. Everybody is—

FIRST: People got to have a certain amount of—

(Shoots 3 or 4 shots.)

(Pause.)

There! I got him!

That is, I think so. You see, he could be play-acting, just

to make me expose myself. (*Pause.*) People got to have a certain amount of excitement. Otherwise it's too damn dull. (*Moves a little to reconnoitre.*)

(*Shot.*)

FIRST (*Collapses*): He got *me*. But it was fair play. He was smarter, that's all.

(*The other slips back. Takes the first one by the legs, and drags him away. The whole maneuver takes place flat on the stomach.*)

PSYCHOLOGIST: Finis! (*Sits down.*)

(*Interlude of kettle-drums.*)

ANGEL OF PEACE: Well, you gentlemen have all described, in your various ways, the causes of my sickness—(*Quickly*) and it was most interesting, it was indeed—but it would be far better if you also prescribed a remedy.

PROFESSOR (*Suddenly propelled up from below, standing on his rostrum*): After the diagnosis come the therapeutic considerations. (*Down again.*)

ANGEL OF PEACE: Just so. In other words, do any of you gentlemen know how wars can be prevented?

ROMANTICIST: I do!

MATERIALIST: I do!

PSYCHOLOGIST: I do!

(*A staircase, an endless marble staircase, that leads up among clouds and stars. On each side, and on each step: a harp. Every other harp has blue strings; alternate, red. The strings shine from within. Neon and argon. Sound of harps.*)

ANGEL OF PEACE (*Sits up, with happy expression*): That sounds like heavenly music! (*Sound of harp ceases.*)

ANGEL OF PEACE: I suppose we will observe the usual order?

(*The gentlemen nod.*)

(*Fanfare of trumpets. Beautiful imaginary garden. Marble busts. Pines and cypresses.*)

ROMANTICIST (*Rises*): The human race must better itself— be more noble, more unselfish—

(Materialist and Psychologist break out into ribald laughter.)

ROMANTICIST *(Indignantly)*: I can't understand why you gentlemen laugh. It is certainly self-evident that if people were better—that is, gentler, kinder, more tolerant and understanding—then war would be unknown!

MATERIALIST: Man's behavior hinges upon material circumstances, and the material circumstances are in turn dependent upon accepted social standards. Without a change in the social structure, there can be no change in human behavior.

PSYCHOLOGIST: Man can no more change his instincts, than Munchhausen can pull himself up out of the lake by his own pigtail. Yes, some day, when we can experiment with our own inherited talents, make artificial mutations in a favorable direction—then perhaps! But that's a long way off, and possibly the atom bomb will come first.

ANGEL OF PEACE: How had you thought people could become better?

ROMANTICIST: By having poets and priests, philosophers, and storytellers, make mankind understand that they must better themselves.

ANGEL OF PEACE: Is that all?

ROMANTICIST: That's it.

ANGEL OF PEACE *(Distressed)*: Alas, I am a skeptic. I've heard so many words—gentle words, beautiful words, wise words, exalted words, exhorting words—and a lot of help they are. Next gentleman.

(Romanticist sits down sorrowfully.)

(Fanfare of trumpets. A pattern factory. But it is so ideal and clean and well-ordered that it is depressing.)

MATERIALIST *(Rises):* Mankind is by nature peaceful—

(Psychologist laughs explosively. And it isn't admiration that makes him laugh.)

MATERIALIST *(Sends him an angry glance, but continues)*: People don't hate, unless they are poisoned by propaganda; the average man would rather sit in his comfortable parlor than go to war, with its danger to life and limb. The worker has international sympathies, and doesn't understand why one nation should struggle against another; and the worker's common sense tells him that his economic condition is improved through peaceful cooperation, and worsened by war. Those who want war are just a little circle of capitalists. They profit by war, they alone, and that's why they want it. But the very moment that we abolish private ownership—naturally, not in one country, but in all countries—at that very moment, when we all share joint ownership of the social wealth, no one will be interested in war—which is saying, once more, that war is unthinkable.

ANGEL OF PEACE: If only I could believe in that—

PSYCHOLOGIST: No! You must not! That reasoning is as rash as a drunken debutante.

MATERIALIST (*With a voice of thunder*) : Proof!

(*Psychologist rises.*)

PSYCHOLOGIST (*Friendly*) : Gladly.
(*Like a sergeant.*) Sit down!

(*Materialist sits down, disconcerted. Fanfare of trumpets.*)

PSYCHOLOGIST: The Materialist asserts that mankind is by nature peaceful. This is a postulate, and an erroneous one. The truth is that part of mankind is peaceloving—namely, the women. (Although they certainly do their bit for war, the way they prefer men in uniform!) It is true that men become more peaceful with age—due, I believe, to a degeneration of the male sex hormones. The young man, on the other hand, and the mature man are the warriors; that is to say, they have a need for war, if their glands function normally. Men love peace only when they have war. In peacetime, they wander around with an unspoken dream of a nice, healthy little war—at the very least, in the form of a fist fight, a football game, or a chess match.

(*Steaming springs, and volcanoes, bubbling sulfur pools, smoking crevices—all located, close together, helter-skelter, on a stony plain. The water in the springs is of different colors.*)

PSYCHOLOGIST: The Materialist has argued that it's the capitalists who start wars. But is it possible that hundreds or even thousands of capitalists should get *millions* of people to go to war, if these millons are not willing? I don't see how hundreds can force hundreds of millions! No, the truth is that the millions are sometimes, quite of their own volition, in the spirit for war!

ANGEL OF PEACE (*Holds her forehead*): I think I am going to be sick— (*Lies down.*) (*Romanticist helps her.*)

PSYCHOLOGIST: And as to this preposterous theory that communist states will not start a war! You can be sure that if the world were full of communist states, we'd really have a war in earnest. Wars as evil and hateful as civil wars.

MATERIALIST (*Heatedly*): Postulate! Postulate! Postulate!

PSYCHOLOGIST: Naturally. But your contention to the contrary was also a postulate. The difference is that my theory is psychologically probable, and yours is not.

ANGEL OF PEACE (*Looks up, with a litttle hope*): But, so far, you have said nothing about how you would cure me?

(*Fanfare of trumpets.*)

(*Mr. Average Man's living room. Ordinary furniture, ordinary paintings, ordinary potted plants.*)

(*Psychologist lifts his index finger. A light from above shines on it.*)

(*Around a round table, sit Mr. Average Man, Mrs. Average Wife, Mr. Average Son, and Miss Average Daughter. Mr. Average Man sits in the best chair, a wicker chair with embroidered pillows. He is also the one who has the newspaper, haha! Mrs. Average Wife is doing embroidery, Mr. Average Son is reading a school textbook, Miss Average Daughter is mending a nylon stocking. On the wall is an embroidered motto in a frame. The motto reads: "What is a cage without a father!"*)

PSYCHOLOGIST (*Points with index finger*): Mr. Average Man, Mrs. Average Wife, Mr. Average Son, Miss Average Daughter.

(*Sits down.*)

(*The roar of a lion.*)

MRS. AVERAGE (*Sweetly*) : Your stomach is rumbling, Father.

(*Mr. Average growls. The meaning is uncertain, but the sound is reminiscent of an old lion's growl.*)

(*New roaring of lion. This time nearer. Average Son sticks his fingers in his ears.*)

MRS. AVERAGE (*Sweetly*): Don't you think you should take a little soda, Father?

(*Mr. Average does not reply, not even with a growling sound.*)

(*Third lion's roar. Very close this time. MY! Mrs. Average sighs, but now she, too, says nothing. She merely assumes a suffering and abused look.*)

(*Then in comes the lion, dressed in a pink corset. The lion seats himself at Mr. Average's feet, nice and quiet. Then it lays a paw on his knee—like a sweet little dog calling attention to itself.*)

MR. AVERAGE: Again! Well, it's all right with me. Thank God others can't see you. Or hear what we talk about, either. Thoughts have no sound!

(*Lion growls. The sound rises and falls, as if the beast were saying something.*)

MR. AVERAGE: You're absolutely right. This situation is not to be tolerated. God knows how many thousand times I've sat here in the same room, beside the same table, with the same tablecloth (with the same spot on it!)—together with the same three people! The only thing that varies a little bit, is the newspaper,—and not even *that* very much.

Yes, naturally—my three cohabiters also change. The children, in the course of time, have grown older and more impudent, and my wife older and fatter. But the changes from day to day are so small that they offer no entertainment. There's a piece in the paper here about a man who killed his entire family. I don't know why I don't do the same! The truth is really that I almost hate them. If they died, I'd cry for a day or two, and miss them for a fortnight, and at the same time I'd feel as if I'd laid aside a corset that was seven sizes too small. I don't do away with them only because of the consequences to me. Prison isn't quite as comfy as the present arrangement. My daughter. Does she love me? Not as much as I love her—and my feelings are 99 per cent disgust. She has only one idea in her head: to get a man. But be sure, a man whose position is so important that she can feel superior to her girl friends! She won't do it. Not with her looks. In a year's time she'll be ready to marry a bank teller, with a pittance of a salary, and in five years, a postman. And if not even the postman shows up, she'll be ready and willing to be seduced. She doesn't know what love is, and she'll never find out. All she has to furnish in that direction is a little sultry warmth.

People say my son is like me. I can't see it. He's a bum. He'll never be more than mediocre. How industrious you look over there, M'sieu, with all those books, but I'll bet you aren't even reading! You're just sitting and dreaming—of motorcycles, or some little obscenity. God knows why you've got such dark circles under your eyes? And always looking as if you had a bad conscience! I have my own opinion, undeniably! But to talk over something like that together? No! There isn't the least bit of confidence between us. Or love, or affection. Only hate. And fear. We are afraid of each other. We know that if we strike up a conversation, it will always wind up as a furious argument. And that's too hard on the nerves. A grown son living at home—phew! And then that fat pig I'm married to. Just think, I was once in love with her! How crazy young men are. For two weeks' honeymoon, they take it upon themselves to provide for a stranger the rest of their lives. I hardly ever sleep with her any more—every third week maybe—but that's just because I don't care—or can't—find somebody else. It's a wonder I don't strangle her—the way she sits there—stupid, ugly, fat, boring! She never cared for me. When she talks to me, it's as if she had a cherry in her mouth, only because she, like me, hasn't the strength any more for arguments and fights. My life is hell. A hell of disgust, monotony, melancholy. And

I can't get out of it before the Garbageman picks me up.

(Lion growls.)

MR. AVERAGE: You're right—there is a possibility of laying aside the corset—and that's a nice little war. Imagine, if a world war came about, so that I'd get away from it all! So that I'd see other rooms, other streets, other landscapes—just something different from what I stare at every day! Imagine, if something happened in my existence! Just imagine, if, for a change, I got a little excitement, a little experience! Imagine, if I had a motorcycle to drive! Imagine, if I were decorated, and got headlines in the papers! Imagine, in some ruined city, if I were to find a gold ring with diamonds, worth 5,000 dollars!

(Lion growls.)

MR. AVERAGE: You're right. I'd almost forgotten the most important thing. Think, if I, just once— (*Whistles, a couple of capricious trills—it seems to trill out of the air.*)

MR. AVERAGE:—with some woman other than my wife!!!

(Lion growls.)

MR. AVERAGE: Yes, that's clear enough. If General Miles Gloriosus gets into power in this country, there'll be a war. He hasn't promised it directly, but he has spoken out as clearly as it is possible for any politician to do: that our latest defeat must be avenged! That's why I vote for him every time, you understand. But hush, hush! I should never have told anyone that I'm not a pacifist!

(Someone knocks.)

MR. AVERAGE: Hmph.

(Enter Mr. Average Suitor.)

PSYCHOLOGIST (*At the same moment*): This is Mr. Average Suitor.

SUITOR: G'd evening. Excuse me for disturbing you, but—

AVERAGE FAMILY: Good evening. Good evening.

SUITOR: I wanted to ask Miss Average if she would do me the honor to go to the movies—now, that is—to the nine o'clock show?

Miss Average (*Rises hurriedly*) : Oh yes, indeed. (*Changes tone.*) I mean—just by luck I happen to be free to-night.

Suitor: There's a wonderful picture playing—"Heroism and Love," at the Arena. The action's in India and Africa, so for once we'll get to see some places other than what we're used to. John Heman's in it—

Miss Average: Ooooh! He's so gorgeous!

Mr. Average: If I were a young man, I wouldn't invite a girl to see that—Mr. Heman!

Suitor (*Astonished*) : Why not?

Mr. Average (*Shrugs*) : Well, for goodness' sake! I'd be jealous! Suppose the girl starts comparing—

Suitor: That comparison doesn't scare me. I'm flesh and blood; he's merely a strip of canvas with a little light on it!

Miss Average: Anyhow, there's more reason for the woman to be jealous! Mind you, I don't think Rita Box is nearly so luscious as people say. But she exhibits both this and that—and, well, you know how men are!

(*Solo laughter.*)

Suitor: I never think of the hero on the screen as a stranger—or a rival. It may sound childish, but to tell the truth, I feel that it's myself. When he lies and shoots with a machine gun—(*Imitates noise*) behind a cactus, it's me shooting. When he's wounded in the shoulder, it's myself that's wounded. And when he comes to the hospital and falls in love with the pretty nurse, it's me coming to the hospital and falling in love. And when, at the last moment, he rescues her from a big buck nigger, it's me who rescues her. (*Laughs shyly.*) Yes, I know I sound like a kid, but I actually believe that it's that way with many people in the audience.

Mrs. Average: Yes, I always feel like the sweet young thing—

Suitor: But excuse me, we better be going. It starts in ten minutes. Bye. (*Bows.*)

Miss Average (*Triumphantly*): So long.

(Murmurs of "Good-bye" and "Have a good time" around the table.)

(Exeunt Average Suitor and Average Daughter.)

MR. AVERAGE *(To the lion)*: I'll go to the Arena tomorrow and see that picture myself. It sounds good. I can slip out of the office two hours earlier—but I won't say anything about it to the others—No!

(Knocking.)

MR. AVERAGE: Hm.

PSYCHOLOGIST: Average Friend. We saw him earlier.

AVERAGE FRIEND *(Enters)*: Good evening. *(Bows politely.)*

(Average Son jumps up, delighted at the interruption.)

AVERAGE FAMILY *(In varying degrees of friendliness)*: Good evening.

AVERAGE FRIEND: I've come to see if you'd go to the football game with me on Sunday.

AVERAGE SON: Have you got tickets?

AVERAGE FRIEND: The old man has outdone himself. He gave me two.

AVERAGE SON: Great! And I'm glad that you thought of me. *(Enthusiastically)* What a tremendous dad you've got!

MR. AVERAGE *(Irritated)*: Have you got time for this kind of nonsense?

AVERAGE SON *(Raging—almost hysterical)*: It's mean of you to say such a thing! There's no one who does more than I do! I work from morning till night, and the minute I've had a mouthful of food, I'm off to a lecture, or to read! If I can't have a couple of hours free on Sunday, then you can bury me pretty soon!—From overwork! But then you'll be rid of me, and that's what you want most! *(At the end, his voice breaks.)*

MRS. AVERAGE: Now, now, my boy—now, now, now.

MR. AVERAGE *(Calms down)*: I'd prefer that you were free both in the evening and on Sunday. But you've got to get a degree if you're to amount to anything. And you owe your parents some good grades—it's costing us enough.

(*He takes pains to seem calm and collected, but he is shaking.*)

Average Friend (*Politely, almost too politely*) : Your son will survive all right, Mr. Average. He just mustn't overdo it, or his nerves will give way. Everyone has to relax now and then—

Mr. Average (*Finishing the sentence for him*) :—the best way to do it is to go to a football game?

Average Friend (*Still proper*) : Football is excellent diversion. Something is happening all the time. There's nothing so exciting, so nerve-shattering as a football match. It's almost as exciting as a real war. And this one on Sunday will be especially exciting. We're going to battle against our born enemies, the Neighborians. So it's a point of honor for us to win.

Mr. Average: Hm—Neighborians—then I myself would be tempted to—er—d'you think it's difficult to get tickets?

Average Friend: The game's going to be a sell-out. But if you ordered them first thing tomorrow morning—

Average Son (*Hurriedly*): Hey, I'll walk part way home with you. I need a little fresh air, before I study any more. (*To his parents*) So long.

Average Friend (*Bows politely*): Good-bye.

Parents: Good-bye.

(*Mr. Average's voice sounds neither friendly nor sympathetic.*)

(*The two young men hurry out.*)

Mr. Average (*Down to the lion*) : I'll go and see that football game. If we can beat the Neighborians in football, then we don't really need that war of revenge that General Miles Gloriosus dreams so much about. Seems to me you're shrinking. You're not sick, I hope?

(*Lion growls miserably.*)

Mrs. Average: Daddy dear—

Mr. Average: Mm.

Mrs. Average: Now that everyone else is going out, I'd kind of like to go out too.

Mr. Average: Where do you want to go?

MRS. AVERAGE: To the theater.

MR. AVERAGE: To the theater! With the price of tickets what they are!

MRS. AVERAGE: Well, what of it? It's been such a long time.

MR. AVERAGE: Is it the Revue Theater you want to go to, or the State?

MRS. AVERAGE: Well, revues really are the most fun—

MR. AVERAGE: Revues are rubbish.

MRS. AVERAGE: They might appeal to you, Father—what with all those naked girls—

MR. AVERAGE: Me? I couldn't be bothered looking at them.

MRS. AVERAGE: Go on! You're no eunuch, I know that.

MR. AVERAGE: I tell you: I usually shut my eyes! However, I don't understand why you're so intent on my seeing something like that. Don't you get a bit jealous?

MRS. AVERAGE: Oh, no. You only have your enjoyment at a distance—I know that. And you're most always so lively and—attentive when you come home from a revue.

MR. AVERAGE (*Whistles*): It's as if you wanted to work me up to eat fried herring by tempting me with boiled turbot and oyster sauce!

MRS. AVERAGE: I'd just as soon go to the State. So many of our friends go there—and it's so annoying, at a party, not to be able to discuss a play. What's on there now?

MR. AVERAGE: It's a Greek tragedy.

MRS. AVERAGE (*A little crestfallen*): Do you suppose it would be *very* dull?

MR. AVERAGE: Well—

MRS. AVERAGE: What's it about?

MR. AVERAGE (*Rises*): A king—a king of ancient Greece, you know—he had first murdered his father, and then afterwards he commits incest with, and marries, his own mother. (*Stalks up and down the carpet, rattling his key-chain and his newspaper learning.*) That is to say, he didn't really know they were his father and mother. But then it's found out, and in his despair, he tears out his own eyes. You see him come in, with empty bloody eye-sockets and the blood seeping down his cheeks—

MRS. AVERAGE: Oh my! (*She shivers with pleasure.*)

MR. AVERAGE (*Continuing*) : It's a horror play—purest sadism in reality—(*Parenthetically*)—that's what they said in the morning paper— (*Assumes more reverent tone of voice*) but naturally it is a classic, a famous play. It is more than two thousand years old.

MRS. AVERAGE: Just think, that people wrote such amusing plays in those days!

MR. AVERAGE: It must deal with certain eternal emotions— (*Morning paper?*)—since it can be played today—even with success!

MRS. AVERAGE: I think it sounds good! I'd love to go and see it.

MR. AVERAGE (*A little surprised*) : As a matter of fact, I would too.

MRS. AVERAGE (*Rises*) : Now I'll make a little tea, Daddy. And first thing in the morning, I'll call up for tickets. (*As she goes out*) Do you think it's real blood?

MR. AVERAGE: Probably not.

(*Exit Mrs. Average Wife.*)

MR. AVERAGE: To tell you the truth, little lion— (*Stands up, discovers it has gone*) Well, now, he's gone. (*Mumbles*) I never even noticed— (*Sighs softly*) Anyhow, we'll have peace for a while. (*Sits down, rustling his newspaper.*)

(*And Mr. Average Man vanishes, with room and furniture.*)

(*Fanfare of trumpets. A stadium, a Greek stadium, appears.*)

ANGEL OF PEACE (*Sitting up*) : I think I understand your reasoning. You mean—

PSYCHOLOGIST (*Jumps up, unable to keep silent*): I mean that neither lecturing nor economic improvement can change the deep-lying instincts of mankind. But those instincts that lead me into war can be sublimated so that they are satisfied

in a harmless way. We can sublimate them with the help of
play and *fantasy*—which is to say: *sports, movies, plays,* and
novels.

(*The sports arena has slowly changed into a theater of the
time of Sophocles.*)

PSYCHOLOGIST (*Without pause*): Analyze a tragedy of Sophocles, or a tragedy of Shakespeare, and you will see that they
are as colorful as comic strips. And what effect do they have?
When the spectators leave the theater, they find that they are
pleasantly tired, perhaps also a little worked up, as when one
has satisfied an impulse long repressed. The spectators are
washed clean—as Aristotle says. For the time being they do
not need action, excitement, war, sadism.

(*The Globe Theatre appears, almost imperceptibly.*)

MATERIALIST: You'll never get any theater or movie censor
to endorse that viewpoint. He'll maintain just the opposite, and
rightly, too! That all this violence begets immorality, that it
induces people, especially children, to go out and do likewise.
And as far as international sports contests are concerned—

PSYCHOLOGIST (*Interjects presto*): I know. They bolster the
national vanity and competitive spirit.

(*Football field. With two kinds of flags.*)

MATERIALIST: Yes, or stirs them up! We have cases where the
angry public rioted after football games. No, these competitions
in sports and these Olympic Games, they deepen the rift between nations. They make it even easier for the rulers to get
the man-in-the-street to go to war. I wonder if it isn't Capital
that arranges international sports contests!

(*A field of poppies.*)

PSYCHOLOGIST: Sport and art are, in this connection, a sort
of medicine. And what matters here, as with all medicine, is
that the result depends on the dosage. Underdose, and the
medicine doesn't work; overdose, and it's *poison.*

ROMANTICIST (*Rises*): If I may make a remark, I think that
these instincts you are always trafficking in, are somewhat neb-

ulous. In any case, you haven't given us any proof of their existence.

MATERIALIST: Bravo! Bravo! *(Despite the approbation, the admiration is not entirely unmixed with wonder; "Just think, that even you can say something sensible!")*

ROMANTICIST *(Continuing, without pause)* : Actually, I think your psychology is just as romantic as mine—except for your transcendent love of the ugly, the demoniacal, and the perverse—

(A giant beetle appears, rolling a cannon-ball.)

MATERIALIST *(Nods in agreement)*: Romanticist in a minor key!

(All three gentlemen speak hurriedly, and vehemently. They find words without stammering or hesitation—skilled debaters, who are discussing their specialty.)

PSYCHOLOGIST: Neither instinct, nor inclination, nor need is an especially good term—admitted! They are all too vague, too abstract, and they can be defined in far too many ways. Nonetheless, you can get any biologist to swear—by all that's holy to him—that every animal, man not excepted, follows instinctive behavior patterns.

(A bird builds nest.)

PSYCHOLOGIST *(Continuing without pause)* : If, in passing, I should define instinctive behavior, it would sound something like this: A chain of actions, directed toward a positive goal, founded in heredity, unreflecting, and not governed by reason, the same for all or many individuals of the same species. *(Bows lightly.)* It's yours, without obligation.

(Street in a Chinese city. Long rows of people dead of hunger, or well on the way to it.)

MATERIALIST *(Rises. More conciliatory than before)*: It is quite possible that I and those who agree with me, have laid too much stress on "hunger" *(Pronounced as in German)* and too little on "liebe." This is perhaps a reaction against the Romanticist's all too visionary, all too ethereal, view of things. *(Struts back and forth.)* But you, Mr. Psychologist, lay far too little emphasis on hunger. For two reasons. First, you've reacted against me, as I previously reacted against the Romanticist; second, you have grown up in a time and in a place where famine is entirely unknown. But that famine has existed, due to overpopulation, and that famine still exists—from the same cause—I believe you will not deny. But this is what I'd like to know: *How do you propose to prevent war brought about by famine?* You surely haven't planned to sublimate *real, physical hunger,* with sports, movies, and plays?

(A street in a large city. Houses of the kind that are found in large cities the world over. Pedestrians, cars, buses, streetcars, railroad trains—the street overcrowded to the point of impossibility. A sandwich man steps slowly along the sidewalk. On the placard, at the top, is a picture of a nurse, with noble features, dressed in a Red Cross uniform, and underneath:

Always use SANA rubber!

The best protection
against
Venereal Disease
and

OVERPOPULATION

Good Fit
Recommended by Doctors

(Angel of Peace turns her head away, blushing.)
(The three gentlemen have meanwhile seated themselves.)
PSYCHOLOGIST: There certainly ought to be remedies against overpopulation. I wonder if a little education about—*(Wave of the hand toward the placard bearer.)*
MATERIALIST: Well, so you, too, also assume certain materialistic views!
ROMANTICIST *(Happy):* Perhaps we're not so much in disagreement as we first thought!
MATERIALIST: But I give you my support, all the same. And

admiration. There are real possibilities for world peace in your proposal.

(Romanticist claps.)

(A long wall grows up out of the earth. A long, formal wall, with a shining gold door. Over the door, shine the words:

HERE DWELLS HOPE

Above and beyond the wall can be seen the tops of mild trees, and a Heaven, mystic blue as eternity.)

(Music—as it sounds in Paradise.)

ANGEL OF PEACE *(Rises): I'm walking! I'm walking!* With crutches, to be sure. But it's been many years since I (poor little me) could walk so well. Thank you, my friends, my brave, learned friends—thank you for my new hope!

(The three gentlemen rise and bow.)

(The golden door opens by itself. And while the music mounts to a crescendo, the Angel of Peace hobbles on her crutches into Hope's Paradise. The door closes. Paradise vanishes. The music fades away.)

ASSISTANT EDITOR *(Enters, breathless, with proof sheets and manuscript):* Excuse me. So I can make up the cover, I'd like to know what it really is the gentlemen have been arguing about—

ROMANTICIST: Ideas.

MATERIALIST: That vacant professorship in history.

PSYCHOLOGIST: In truth, we've been fighting out of pure vanity—and because it's such damn good fun.

ASSISTANT EDITOR: Thank you. *(Hurries out.)*

(Music, "Malbrough s'en va-t-en guerre." The three gentlemen have taken their standards, and dance out in a row, just as they came in. Thereafter three cannon shots are heard. The three cannon shots that bring to a close every well-organized fireworks display. And then the lights are lowered on the stage.)

THE END

THE SISTERS

A PLAY IN THREE ACTS BY
WALENTIN CHORELL

TRANLATED FROM THE SWEDISH BY
TINA MORDUCH

INTRODUCTION BY
GEORGE C. SCHOOLFIELD

INTRODUCTION

The main strength of Finno-Swedish literature—that is, literature written by members of Finland's Swedish-speaking minority
—has been in the lyric. But the Finno-Swedish drama has also
had its memorable plays and even its masterpieces. The single
play of Josef Julius Wecksell, *Daniel Hjort* (1863), puts its
pioneering finger on several chronic and artistically profitable
disorders of Finnish culture: 1) treachery for the nation's greater
good (Hjort betrays Åbo Castle to Duke Carl of Södermanland,
soon to be king of Sweden); 2) the struggle between classes
(the action takes place during the "Club War," a civil war with
distinctly social overtones which rent western Finland in the
last decade of the sixteenth century); 3) the isolation of the
individual (Hjort is an outsider in the castle's wealthy Swedish
society, because he is poor and a Finn: by the time Wecksell
wrote *Hjort,* the Swedish speaker had begun to regard himself
as the outcast in Finnish society). *Daniel Hjort* has been called
the best play written in the Swedish language before Strindberg's *Mäster Olof.* As a theater piece it is surely much more
alive than *Kungarne på Salamis* (1863), the closet-drama by
the supreme figure of Finno-Swedish letters, Johan Ludvig
Runeberg (1804–1877). And, as literature, it stands head and
shoulders above the historical dramas, likewise dealing with the
"Club War," of Runeberg's friend, Fredrik Cygnæus (1807–
1881); neither can the once so popular *Regina von Emmeritz*
(1853), a melodrama by Zachris Topelius (1818–1898) about
the Thirty Years' War, bear comparison with *Hjort,* which
Wecksell (1838–1907) completed on the eve of the madness
that destroyed him.

Finno-Swedish literature lay dormant until the debuts of
Karl August Tavaststjerna (1860–1898) and Mikael Lybeck

(1864–1925); it was to be expected that Tavaststjerna and Lybeck, thinking to emulate Ibsen, would try their hand at the drama, Lybeck more frequently and with considerably more success than his early-dead contemporary. The best of Lybeck's plays, *Ödlan* (1908) and *Broder och syster* (1915), have to do once again—Wecksell's precedent is slowly transformed into a tradition—with outsiders: in the former drama the weakling Alban and his cousin Adla, who does her best, and worst, to possess him, in the latter the brother Per and the sister Johanna, who are held together, and cut off from the rest of the world, by not altogether healthy bonds. Runar Schildt (1888–1925), during that brief dramatic flowering which came between the end of his career as a novella writer and his death by suicide, walked still further along the road Lybeck had taken, and, in doing so, won a reputation outside Finland. His play, *Den stora rollen* (1923) about an old theatrical hanger-on (actor would be too flattering a word) who is killed in the Finnish Civil War of 1918, was given all over Scandinavia; for Schildt, in his anti-hero Armas Fager (a figure he had borrowed from his novella of that name), had created a Finnish equivalent of Sean O'Casey's Captain Jack Boyle, a braggart whose dreams destroy him—but who could not have lived without those dreams. Of Schildt's other two plays, the one, *Lyckoriddaren,* was a failure; but its small companion, *Galgmannen,* a one-act play about an old and lonely man, terrified of death, won favorable attention of James Joyce in its Parisian production, and appeared in English translation as well.[1]

Schildt's place as Swedish Finland's leading dramatist was taken by Hagar Olsson (b. 1893), a critic of the first water and a prolific although not always satisfying novelist. As a dramatist, she depended heavily, at first, on what she had learned from German expressionism—her *S.O.S.* (1928), for ex-

---

[1] *Scandinavian Plays of the Twentieth Century: First Series* (The American-Scandinavian Foundation and Princeton University Press: New York and Princeton, 1944).

ample, reads like Georg Kaiser's *Gas;* still, she did not move away from those painfully isolated and painfully intimate domestic situations which Lybeck and Schildt had used, even when she dealt with political questions, as in *Det blåa undret* (1932), where the quasi-Fascist brother and the quasi-Communist sister are joined by ties of incestuous affection. Also, she never failed to let some carefully measured light pierce whatever darkness it was she had placed before her audience; that was strikingly the case with *Rövaren och jungfrun* (1944), a play about the Finnish famines of the 1860s, which ends with a miracle. Only the wretched inhabitants of her shabby hotel in *Kärlekens död* (1952) have come to the conclusion that "we are utterly alone"; and even here, at play's end, we hear a canary singing happily off-stage.

Walentin Chorell (b. 1912) began his literary career in a characteristically Finno-Swedish way, with the publication of two volumes of poetry, *Vinet och lägeln* (1941) and *Spegling* (1943). What he wrote in those days seems to be epigonic modernism and nothing more, a composite of Edith Södergran, Rabbe Enckell, and Elmer Diktonius (no doubt the "E.D." in the dedication of one of the poems). But, in a handful of lyrics, something fresh is to be found: in "Den poetiska poliskonstapeln," for example, there is an awareness of the dramas (seen by a friendly but hardly sentimental eye) which take place in a back street, and in "Röd planet" a character is drawn swiftly, the young soldier who has been a romantic, like most little boys from happy homes. "Röd planet" was written just after the Winter War of 1939–40, and on the eve of its continuation.

When Chorell returned to literary production in 1947, he was determined to live by his pen, that most difficult of accomplishments for a Finno-Swedish author; he made his second debut with a detective novel, *Lektion för döden,* and a psychological study, *Jörgen Hemmelinks stora augusti.* Hemmelink was the first specimen in what was to be a very extensive collection of peculiar folk; the son of a Polish-Jewish musician and a Finno-Swedish mother, Hemmelink has had a pleasant childhood, the serenity of which has been broken only by a severe sexual shock. As an adult, however, both the happy past (his father swaddled him in dreams) and its single interruption make it impossible for him to lead a "normal" life: he exists in phantasies, he cannot accept the women—the one good, the other bad—who would release him from his magic circle. At the conclusion, nevertheless, the reader is made to believe that Hemmelink's "great August," a month when events have contrived to turn his existence upside down, has led him into a new life after all.

In *Calibans dag* (1948), Chorell crowded the avalanche of terrifying novelties into a single day, the last in the life of the owner of a third-rate restaurant. A practical man in his attitudes toward both his business and his erotic activity, Justus seems to be Hemmelink's opposite. But, for all his heartiness and hardness, Justus is as much out of things, as "strange," as Hemmelink in his second-hand bookstore. The customers of Justus have left him, and he has left his wife's bed, these many years since, to content himself with the regular visits of a prostitute to the storage room of his café. The prostitute is always the same one, "Sjuan" ("Number Seven," after the city ward from which she gets her pass); she and Justus spend their happy moments on a shaky pile of kegs—it has never occurred to Justus to fix up anything better. He dies, of a stroke, and has not lived; the son who could have carried on his name does not exist. There is more than a touch of Bloom in Justus.

Blindtrappan, the next year's novel (1949), is a book about not one stunted case but several. Of its isolated beings, the first, a man blinded in an accident, will never escape the half-life into which he has been thrust, unlike the blind hero of Ingmar Bergman's early film *Musik i mörker* (1947), who is saved by love. Another, Jerine, repatriated to Finland after following a Nazi officer to Germany, seems unable and unwilling to rid herself of sadism's infection; her new lover, the talka-tive student Seth Övergård—a forerunner of Maximilian in the play *Systrarna*—may thank his lucky stars that he escapes from her with minor damages. Or will they turn out to be major ones in time? Only the married couple, Eemes and Katzi, he a worker in a hospital morgue, she a retired prostitute, may be able to find a little happiness, Eemes because he is willing to forget Katzi's last desperate fling, Katzi because she has accepted the fact that she has lost her teeth, if not her figure, and is growing old. *Intim journal* (1951), however, finds not even the most pathetic balm in Gilead. Martin has been reared by his sister Marta, a woman almost old enough to be his mother. Somewhere her affection has slid over into perversity (the worst expressions of which are left to the imagination by Chorell, a writer of admirable and old-fashioned discretion); it smothers Martin, cuts him off from normal love, and eventually makes him plot her murder. He is killed instead, in the apparent accident which he has planned, and the grieving Martha is left behind. Who is the murderer here, and who the victim?

After *Intim journal*, Chorell began to write novels which were at once somewhat less penetrating and somewhat more hopeful. The hero of *Sträv gryning* (1952) has been reared by a devoted grandmother, has killed a man in a fit of rage, has served his sentence, and is about to succumb to the new loneli-ness to which society has condemned him when he assists, quite accidentally, at the birth of a baby, and so wins a ticket of entry into the community. The heroine of the trilogy *Miriam* (1954), *Främlingen* (1956), and *Kvinnan* (1958), has been brought up by a more or less maiden aunt; after the aunt's death, she tries to get affection from a frightened boy and a well-to-do university student, only to receive it—when she does not really want it—from a factory worker, a widower and so a victim of loneliness himself. At last, Miriam decides that she will live for the sake of the baby which she is about to bear; she refuses, however, to marry its well-intentioned father. The trilogy's conclusion would put Miriam into that long line of women who, particularly in Scandinavian literature, have decided to stand on their own feet; it would seem to say, as well, that isolation can be broken, if one has the prerequisite hardness to break it. Yet, the thought crosses the reader's mind that Miriam's child will be reared in very much the same way that Miriam was (and as Lo Simsal of *Sträv gryning* and Jörgen Hemmelink and even Martin were) : with a great and estranging affection. Isolation will breed isolation.

The five novels produced during the 1960s deal, like all their predecessors, with the world of those who either are already alone, or in training for a career of loneliness. Stig Sundkvist, the boy whose theft of a wallet comprises the main event of *Stölden* (1960), has been the charge of a kindly grandmother, and, by his theft, almost cuts the few ties he has to life. The seaman Ivar Aalto, in *De barmhärtiga* (1962), is an alcoholic and a coward, who moves in with a widow and her crippled daughter and, eventually, moves out again, into an institution. Selim Karle of *Saltkaret* (1964) is a veteran of the Russian wars and a successful salesman, whose mind begins to decay. He plans a giant practical joke on the church (the "salt shaker" of the title) which is being built opposite his apartment, misuses the trust and financial need of a simple-minded former comrade in order to carry out the plan, and eventually, without intending to do it, kills the semi-prostitute Anli with whom he once shared his rooms. All these things happen because of Selim's fear that the church will capture him—a fear that once beset, and almost consoled, poor Justus on his Caliban's day, the last day of his life. In *Grodan* (1966) the eventide falls faster and the darkness deepens. Called "the frog" of the title by her fellow orphans because she has a membrane between her toes, Hanna is sheltered by a weakling schoolteacher (a descendant of the Topelius-enthusiast who succored young Miriam) and his wife, dying of cancer. The girl then takes particularly nasty advantage of the childless couple. But can we condemn

Hanna for puffing herself up with a frog's apparent vanity, and for viewing life with a frog's eye?

Physical flaw and human kindness, mixed differently, are also destructive forces in *Agneta och lumpsamlaren* (1968), a title paraphrasing that of Hans Christian Andersen's dramatic poem, *Agnete og Havmanden*. Viktor, a junkdealer frequenting the Swedish-speaking regions of Finland's southern coast, comes across a family whose life is poisoned by a wretched secret: the wife is allergic to the husband, or to the lime with which his skin gets impregnated at his place of work. Stubborn and a little stupid, Harald cannot find other employment in the neighborhood; he is also obsessively faithful to his Agnes. Filled with pity for Agnes and genuinely devoted to Agneta, the family's nine-year-old daughter, Viktor kills Harald in a feigned accident, and gets away with it. "Everything was all right again." But the savior must live with the knowledge of what he has done; a desperately lonely man even before the murder, good-natured Viktor has experienced fits of weeping he attributed to his "climax," his climacteric. Medical jargon comes naturally to him: he has been something of a shaman-physician to his rural customers. His "magic," however, isolates him still more, cutting him off forever, like Andersen's merman who loves Agnete, from the human beings resident on the shores of the sea. In the sequel, *Sista leken* (1970), Viktor drowns himself.

It is not difficult to discern the ways in which the novels of Chorell resemble one another. They take place in back lots or bad housing, and their characters come, for the most part, from the lower middle-class and the poor; Lars Hamberg has called attention to the importance of Nummisbacken, a rundown section of Chorell's home city of Åbo (Turku), for his literary production.[2] Those somewhat more optimistic narratives of the 1950s, *Sträv gryning* and the Miriam trilogy, have their setting in the skerries; yet the cottages of this better ventilated milieu

---

[2] Lars Hamberg, "Chorell och Backens värld." *Nya Argus* (1963), 205-207.

can also be filled with stagnant air, as the latest novels, *Grodan, Agneta och lumpsamlaren,* and *Sista leken* richly show. The people in Chorell's novellistic world do not want money, save when they think it can buy a little happiness (witness the case of the pathetic adolescent Stig Sundkvist), and they do not want to rise in the world, or to change its social and economic order. What they want from life is love; but life itself has frozen them into such odd postures, or locked them into prisons with such high walls, that they cannot have love—or, if they find love, they do not know what to do with it, and misuse it. In much of Chorell's work there is a Christian implication; one of his earliest prose narratives was the religious novel *Ensam sökan* (1948), published, unlike all the rest of his work, by a church-sponsored house, and the main figure of his latest novel, the blasphemer Selim (why does this "persecutor" of Christianity bear the name of a Turkish sultan?), is straight from Graham Greene and Francis Thompson; the hound of heaven, which once apeared to him in the form of a pious soul named Märta, will not let him go. For all the meanness of their lives, the majority of Chorell's characters are genuinely kind and well-intentioned; they try, without thinking of it, to be "good Christians," while Selim, who *does* think of it, turns his thoughts into hatred—love is again misunderstood and abused.

The characters in Chorell's unusually large gallery may look alike, but the careful reader will see that they are different enough from one another to be memorable as separate entities: Justus, Ivar Aalto, and Selim Karle are all men in rapid decay, Lorna (Hemmelink's prostitute), Sjuan, Katzi, and Anli are all filled (as one customer of Katzi poetically puts is) with life's wine—but none is quite like the other. The same is true of the dramas of Chorell; he has written a great many plays (Lars Hamberg lists 53 in an accounting from 1963;[3] thirteen

---

[3] Lars Hamberg, "Walentin Chorells dramatiska produktion." *Historiska och litteraturhistoriska studier,* No. 38 (Helsingfors, 1963), 81-96. *Skrifter utgivna av Svenska Litteratursällskapet i Finland,* No. 399.

have appeared in print), studded with characters his audiences will not forget. As a matter of fact, Chorell has used several of his character creations for both narrative and dramatic purposes. Fru Santig, a sometime colleague of Katzi in *Blindtrappan*, becomes the main figure in the radio play *Tomflaskan* (1949). Miriam, the heroine of the trilogy, turns up in a radio play (1953) which bears her name. In the stage play *Kattorna* (1961), the women who inhabited the tenement in the trilogy's last part reappear, extensively transformed but still recognizable. The radio play *Stölden* (1959) has its characters in common with the novel of the same name. The novel *De barmhärtiga* has a stage equivalent in *Nässlorna* (1961).

From the above it will be seen that Chorell's dramatic production has not been limited to the stage. His first radio drama is from 1946, and since then he has composed some thirty works in the genre. Nine of the earlier plays were printed in the volume *Åtta radiopjäser. Haman* (1952: *Haman*, intended as a stage play, was also given on the radio); from them, some idea can be had of Chorell's qualities in this field. A main theme, loneliness, is familiar to us from the novels. *Tomflaskan* is about a prostitute, too old for the trade, who ekes out a living by counting bottles; she gets a gift of money from a young woman—her daughter, evidently, but ashamed to admit the relationship—and is left still more the "empty bottle," her nickname, than before. In *Dialog vid ett fönster*, a bedridden old man in a hospital allows his roommate to die in order to get the latter's place by the window; he learns that the roommate made up his tales of what he saw outside: the window faces a wall. *Andrea Sölfverne* (who comes from a higher social level than is customary in Chorell) is an aging old maid, slowly destroying herself; the women of *Kvinnors hus,* three lonely sisters, destroy a young man who stumbles into their midst. It is Chorell's world at its darkest; the possibility of redemption which we saw or sensed in the novels has been removed—isolated, as it were, in other radio plays where it comes about too hastily to be convincing. In the collection's earliest work, *Dockhand-laren och den sköna Lilith,* an innocent youth (not very different from Seth Övergård of *Blindtrappan*) is saved by the love of a not-so-good woman; his Greek counterpart in the comedy *Den höga damen sover* is saved by earthly passion too, assisted by a handy miracle. In the legend play *Kristoffer Tjänaren,* Kristoffer has to go through some constructive suffering before he realizes the nature of God's intentions for him; the passengers in the rowboat of *Vår herres roddare* (a pocket-size *Outward Bound?*) readily become convinced that Paradise awaits them on the other shore. In *Haman,* a good deal has been changed from the Book of Esther, but not the chief minister's evil ways; he gets his comeuppance fifty cubits high, while his master, the emperor, gets the honest love of Haman's former fiancée, here named Ruth.

Fem spel (1967) continues the broadcast line: four of the plays herein presented had their premières on Finlands Rundradio between 1959 and 1965; the fifth was awarded a prize and a performance by the anemic Swedish service of Finland's television. *Voces intimae* and *Auktionen* make happy use of their medium, capturing respectively the shifting atmosphere of a seedy apartment house and a snobbish auction audience; the listener hears fleeting snatches of conversation from various rooms, from various bidders. *Den nakna över Vitebsk* (the title is from Chagall) and *Grå Eros* have detailed plots whose exposition is crowded with some difficulty into the confines of a radio play. An old man and his young housekeeper murder the old man's son, who has confessed his phantasies of the housekeeper as Chagall's nude giantess, hovering over a Russian town; an aged schoolteacher, his face contorted and his speech thickened by a stroke, pays a visit to his mistress of fifty years ago, now the victim of paralysis. In the one instance the characters do not understand their emotions well enough, in the other they understand them too well, although they are prevented (physical flaws again) from expressing them. Fascinated by the heart's intricacies, Chorell gives the maze a quasi-emblematic representation in *Ariadne*, his television comedy-of-love. The offices and corridors of a firm are emptied for the night; only a small population remains: a band of charwomen, an effeminate watchman, a man and a woman putting in overtime, and the woman's jealous husband, who makes his Chaplinesque way through the labyrinth.

The fault of Chorell's plays for mass media (and perhaps of such plays as a whole) is that they are better at creating moods than at presenting arguments or analyses. The evidently manifold reasons for Andrea Sölfverne's predicament are overshadowed (or, more accurately, outvoiced) by the verbal formulae employed to hammer the *fact* of Andrea's collapse into the audience's ear; the mumbles and splashes accompanying the bath which Nils-Johan administers to Helga in *Grå Eros* are effective, but they make the listener think too much about the grotesqueness of the event, too little about its other implications. The stage plays of Chorell share the radio play's ability to conjure up an atmosphere; but, affording the playwright more space for work, they allow him to use other skills than hynosis. Only five of Chorell's stage plays are available in print: three relatively early ones, *Madame* (1951), *Vandringsman* (1954), and *Systrarna* (1955), were printed together as *Tre skådespel* in 1956; *Gräset* (produced in 1958) was published in Finnish translation *(Ruoho)* in 1959, and most recently (1961), *Kattorna* was published in a separate volume. (In connection with *Gräset/Ruoho*, it should be mentioned that Chorell has found his way quite easily into the Finnish consciousness and onto the Finnish-language stage; his radio plays have frequently been broadcast in Finnish translation, and some of his stage plays have been given, thus far, *only* before Finnish-speaking audiences.)

The earliest and shortest of the printed stage plays, *Madame*, takes up where Runar Schildt's *Den stora rollen* left off. In Schildt, the shield-carrier Armas Fager dies because the single "great role" of his life—his membership in the Red Guard—is too much for him; and the last great role (or, perhaps, the only great role) of the forgotten and aged actress, Madame, is too much for her. Like the Actor in the "apocalyptic comedy" of Danish Romanticism, Johan Ludvig Heiberg's *En Sjæl efter Døden,* she has acted so many roles that she cannot be herself, and thus, in the last moments of life, she can only fumble desperately through her collection of other selves, trying to find the part to fit the occasion. It is left up to the audience to decide whether her choice has been the right one—she plays her great role before God, like the Jongleur de Notre Dame. Much depends, in stage performance, on the manner in which Madame's faithful servant, the pious Boubou, carries out the final stage directions. Shall her applause, "hard and quick," simply be her trained reaction, the reaction she has given, as part of her job, to so many other private performances of the lonely old woman? Or shall she show approval, and, through her, the approval of the God whom Madame has addressed in her last speech?

The other, supernatural world, which Madame's worn-out words perhaps have reached, invades the stage in *Vandringsman;* but this bolder supernatural world does not give consolation, however momentary; it takes revenge instead. Twenty years ago, Irene was in love with Jörgen Trane, the "wanderer" of the title, but she rejected him—he was ill and somehow an outsider—for the solid Bengt, with the result that Trane committed suicide. The life of Irene and Bengt has been poisoned by Jörgen's ghostly presence, and when Stig, their son—or is he the son of Irene and Jörgen?—falls in love with Stella, a young woman who is a guest in their house, the shade of Jörgen takes her away too. The outsider, whom life apparently defeated, is the winner. Runar Schildt has an early novella, *En sparv i trane-dans* (the title is taken from J. Chr. Hostrup's mid-nineteenth century Danish comedy), in which a poor boy learns that he is only a sparrow in the elegant and formalized dance of the cranes, his rich friends. Jörgen Trane—whose last name means "crane"—would have seemed to be the sparrow, too; but he has made Bengt and Irene, Stig and Stella dance to *his* pattern.

The family life of Bengt, Irene, and Stig has been distorted, during twenty years, by Jörgen's shadow; the family in *Gräset* has been destroyed by the war, leaving the Mother and her daughter, Judith, as survivors—Judith's elder brother, it is assumed, has been killed in an air raid. Years later, Judith becomes engaged to a shy young man named Simeon; and true love's course runs smooth until they go to visit Judith's home; then the Mother and Simeon—but not Judith—realize that the family has been reunited. Simeon kills himself, and (as we learn from an epilogue) Judith will go on living in her mother's house. Chorell asks his audience to accept one of those coincidences which were beloved of the fate drama (see Schiller's *Braut von Messina*) once upon a time; and the audience may hesitate to do so, unless it keeps in mind the play's setting in postwar Germany and the immeasurable human dislocations the war had brought about. What is more important about the play, however, is that Chorell has made *his* customary war—between society and the outsider—go in the former's favor this time, in contrast to *Vandringsman*. The Mother, Judith, and Simeon are all lonely, and, in their efforts to escape the magic ring, the two women see the ring strengthened instead, the man is thrust into the final loneliness of death. Yet, had the Mother and Simeon smothered their suspicions about Simeon's identity, had Simeon married Judith, then we should have been confronted with an incestuous ménage in technical fact.

There is no answer: the "normal" world is forced to reject the outsider, the outsider is forced to fight back. Lo Simsal in *Sträv gryning* "talked differently from the other boys" and eventually became a murderer, Miriam in *Kvinnan* succeeded in being more independent than the other women in the apartment house and saw them turn against her. That is what Chorell's tour-de-force, *Kattorna*, is about: the women workers in a factory rebel against their chief, Marta Porsche, and almost murder her in a dressing room (the play's only setting), because

she is different from them—they accuse her of Lesbian inclina-
tions—and a little better off. The play consists of the mounting
and falling tide of their hatred; Marta leaves her job at the
end, caught forever in that "borderland which is a desert, a
lifeless, soundless desert." Were the accusations true? It does
not matter: Marta cannot help being whatever she is, and the
world cannot help tormenting her—and, in its way, the world
is right. The women in the gang love men and bear children
and have homes, the necessary tasks of existence which Marta
can never perform.

Until the production of *Kattorna,* it would have been generally agreed that *Systrarna* was Chorell's best work for the
stage. The two plays do not, it appears, have very much in
common. *Kattorna* takes place in the workers' world where
Chorell is plainly quite at home; *Systrarna* takes place in a
more refined milieu, in which emotions are effectively covered
over. *Kattorna* uses the mass, the "cats"; *Systrarna* concentrates
on the sisters of its title. Yet both plays take place in a limited
and over-heated space, the factory's dressing room and the father-
less home; both have to do with a "house of women," to borrow
the title of Chorell's radio play. (Chorell's latest stage play,
Lavendel [1971], uses a related situation: here, three sisters,
aging and eccentric, return—or rather, try to return—to the sweetly innocent world of their childhood.) In *Systrarna* there are
male intruders, of course, Marcus Trastheim and Maximilian; but
Marcus is simply an old maid in trousers, and is not Maximilian
more a pipe-smoking instigator of the tragedy than a part of
it? Finally, and obviously, both plays deal with loneliness: the
sisters, Jennifer and Camilla, have been cut off from the world
as Marta Porsche has. In their adolescence, it appears, the girls
have conducted a guerrilla war against their little community,
very much—it is a handsome feint on Chorell's part—like Finno-
Swedish belles of St. Trinian's. We would smile if we did not
sense the hatred between the allies. At last, in marriage, the
one sister has the chance to flee her isolation; it is a chance

the other sister would like to take, too. Yet, by her suicide, Camilla would seem generously to have opened the door to freedom for Jennifer, or, at any rate, to a better sort of existence than that which they have known, shot through as it has been with false gossip and still falser piety. But "Where is Camilla?" is the play's last line; and we must conclude that, like Jörgen Trane, the dead Camilla will be everywhere now: in Jennifer and Maximilian and even, perhaps, in the uncomprehending heart of Mrs. Behrens.

It might be stretching a point to say that Chorell's outsiders represent the Finno-Swedish element in a hostile and vital, a "normal" Finnish world. Certainly, Chorell himself moves easily between the two language realms; and he can claim, as well, a much larger validity, reaching far beyond Finland's limits, for what he says about the fate of those who do not fit in. Nevertheless, a century and more of cultural development and cultural discord cannot be denied. Chorell's characters come from tight, ingrown, and defensive milieus; many try to flee from their differentness, others maintain it and use it as a punitive means. However, another national trait should be remembered: Chorell, with his genuine affection for humanity, even a dwarfed humanity which indulges in hatefulness and counter-hatefulness, is very Finnish. For the best that Finnish literature has to offer in both its languages, from Kivi to Linna, from Runeberg to Chorell, is its humble and quite untheoretical humanity.[4]

GEORGE C. SCHOOLFIELD

Yale University

---

[4] For another view of Chorell, see the essay of Johannes Salminen, "Walentin Chorell: An Appreciation." *The American-Scandinavian Review* (1968), 136-139. Cf. Salminen's Swedish essay on Chorell, "I strandlinjen," in Salminen's *Levande och död tradition* (Helsingfors, 1963), 147-52. The essay was originally published in the Helsingfors newspaper *Hufvudstadsbladet* (December 3, 1961).

THE SISTERS

THE CHARACTERS

MARTHA BEHRENS
JENNIFER ⎱ Her daughters
CAMILLA ⎰
MAXIMILIAN
MRS. DOLLY LIEN
MRS. VIVEKA HAAG-SEGLIDKIN
MARCUS TRASTHEIM

The action of the play takes place in Mrs. Behrens's villa which is situated in a small village some way from the town.

The time: Saturday morning till Monday evening in September.

ACT ONE

Scene One

Eleven o'clock Saturday morning.

The hall-living room of Mrs. Behrens's house is a large room—with a wonderful view through French windows on to a well-kept garden. Various doors leading to the rest of the house lead into the room.

The room is beautiful, but somewhat overfurnished in conventional taste, with bric-a-brac all over the place. An overwhelmingly feminine room, which in the long run would probably prove most irritating to anyone paying a visit to the house.

The three friends are approaching the house from the garden as the curtain rises; Mrs. Lien, Mrs. Haag-Seglidkin and Mr. Trastheim enter the living room. They are the three representatives of the village community. They approach hesitantly—open the door. Stand still on the threshold.

MARCUS: Where is Camilla? Where can Camilla have got to?

DOLLY: We were supposed to have met her at 11 o'clock—by the large stone.

MARCUS: Eleven fifteen to be precise. And by the path to the bridge.

DOLLY: But we can't wait any longer. As you say it looks like rain.

VIVEKA: We've had a wonderful September. . . .

DOLLY: Enchanting, Viveka—a real Indian Summer. No rain for a month.

MARCUS: Nineteen days to be precise.

VIVEKA: I don't like waiting. But young people nowadays. . . .

DOLLY: We might just as well go on—perhaps we'll even catch a look at Jennifer's fiancé. Didn't dear Martha say he's called

Maximilian? And isn't he an engineer or something?

MARCUS: He's an up and coming man—a man with a future, Aunt Dolly.

DOLLY: Actually I caught sight of them yesterday—Jennifer and her fiancé. I think they came to pay me a visit, but I couldn't welcome them. Oh no, not yesterday. I was busy all day.

VIVEKA: You're wearing a new dress.

DOLLY (*In a loud whisper*): It's my old one dyed, dear. At the Hall. . . .

MARCUS: Where can Camilla be dawdling. If she doesn't put in an appearance soon all our plans will be upset. It hasn't been easy to arrange for each group to pay their respects to the Pastor. The choir is scheduled to start at twelve o'clock, the community center at one o'clock, and the funeral committee at two o'clock.

VIVEKA: You know I only said to the Pastor yesterday what a great pity it is that Jennifer's fiancé had to come on a visit just now. Jennifer is so much more practical and capable than Camilla. She could have been of such help to us.

DOLLY: But we are not going to part a pair of lovers. They're expecting a baby up at the Hall.

VIVEKA (*Very interested*): Ah—a baby. Are you certain about that? (*Dolly sniggering.*) Ah well! They've been married for over a year. (*Losing all interest in the news.*) I must say I think its unforgivable of Camilla to keep us waiting. Just like her of course. Indifferent and lacking all sense of responsibility. Without any feeling—any feeling at all for the occasion. I mean that suggestion of hers—to put a shepherd and sixteen sheep on the cake—in icing and ice cream. For the Pastor's sixtieth birthday!

DOLLY: Camilla always was a bit of a mad one.

VIVEKA: She's eighteen—she ought to be more settled by now. Dear Marcus, won't you go and see if you can find her. I don't think anyone has noticed our arrival. Surely we deserve just a little attention. Go and call them, Marcus.

Marcus: Hrm. Hrm. Hallo! Good morning!

Dolly: Hoo—oo. We're here, Camilla. Martha. Jennifer.

Marcus: It's eleven thirty and ten, no five seconds, exactly.

Viveka: Perhaps the arrival of the male fiancé has deranged this female household. Or else. . . .

(But Mrs. Martha Behrens enters the room, from the house, and stops further conversation.)

Martha: Dear friends. You've come here after all! I thought it was probably Jenn and Maxi back from their morning walk. Good morning, Viveka dear. Good morning, dear Dolly. Good morning, Marcus dear. How nice to see you all.

Dolly: Such a wonderful September, dear Martha! But it does look like rain today, and up at the Hall they're expecting a . . .

Viveka: Where is Camilla?

Marcus: Dear Aunt Martha. Camilla must hurry up! We've got to run through those songs again before we sing to the Pastor.

Dolly: I can never manage "Oh for the Wings of a Dove." There's a B that just escapes me.

Marcus: A then C to—. Aunt Martha, the choir is waiting for Camilla.

Martha: Camilla. Camilla. Where is Camilla?

Viveka: That is what we would like to know.

Dolly: If a mountain doesn't give birth to a mouse—I mean, if Mahomet . . . Oh you know what I mean. . . .

Marcus: Aunt Martha. Where is Camilla? She's promised to play the piano for us.

Martha: You'll see—she's just overslept. She sleeps like a a dead man sometimes. I'll go and wake her at once. Please do sit down for a little while. Help yourselves to a chocolate. There's hardly time for anything else. I'll go upstairs at once. (Calling out as she leaves the room.) Camilla. Camilla. The choir is waiting.

Viveka: Asleep. At eleven o'clock. Our dear Martha never

did know how to bring up children. I flatly refuse to sit down. I'm going on.

DOLLY: I remember when they were eight and nine—Camilla and Jennifer I mean. They stood and waited for the school bus every morning. They were all eyes and pigtails. Such darling little angels. But far too thin.

VIVEKA (*Drily*): That didn't stop them from pushing the doctor's daughter into a muddy ditch. Or denying it. Even though there were witnesses.

DOLLY: Jen and Maxi—she calls him Maxi—out for a morning walk. A September morning with spiders' webs and falling leaves. Everything so damp and so wonderful. . . . To love and be loved. . . .

VIVEKA: Thank you. No chocolate for me. Come with me, Dolly.

MARCUS: If you ladies will forgive me—I must make certain that we have our pianist with us.

(*Viveka and Dolly exchange meaningful looks.*)

VIVEKA: Of course you must stay here. We'll find the way alright.

DOLLY: We understand perfectly. You are going to wait for the little sleeping beauty.

MARCUS: Thank you. Anyway we'll run round by the short cut—and get to the Community Center before you. Au revoir—mesdames.

DOLLY (*Very playfully*): Even a chilly September is spring for youth. We'll see you later.

(*Before the two older ladies have a chance to make their way, Jennifer and Maximilian can be seen approaching through the garden.*)

VIVEKA: Here comes Jennifer with her fiancé. Now we'll have to stay and greet them.

DOLLY: So that's him. How distinguished. . . .

MARCUS: He should never walk two paces ahead like that. It doesn't look proper.

VIVEKA: That young man strikes me as being somewhat sullen.

DOLLY: Virile, dear Viveka. Virile and austere. . . .

MARCUS: Highbrow—and cynical. The first impression isn't entirely favorable.

(*The two young people have arrived at the French windows and enter the room rather shyly.*)

JENNIFER: Good morning.

MARCUS: } Good morning.
DOLLY: } Good morning, Jen.
VIVEKA: } Good morning, Jennifer.

(*Pause.*)

JENNIFER: May I introduce my fiancé. Maxi—these are our friends. You must all call him Maxi. Mrs. Haag-Seglidkin, Mrs. Lien, Mr. Trastheim.

VIVEKA: I'm delighted to meet you.

DOLLY: I'm so happy, so very happy. You must call me Aunt Dolly.

MARCUS: Hallo Maxi. I am really just like a brother to the girls. We've collected flowers—and insects—swum together. Done everything together. But—but—Honi soit qui mal y pense.

JENNIFER: Marcus has been dreaming about Camilla—platonically—for ten years.

MARCUS: My dear Jennifer, one shouldn't say such things.

VIVEKA: Hrm. Hrm. Maximilian—are you going to be able to stay with us for long?

MAXI: Only a week, Mrs. Haag-Seglidkin.

DOLLY: Dear boy. You have found yourself a jewel of a woman. You must do your duty by her. Jennifer is an angel. I am not exaggerating, my dear child. She is an angel.

MAXI: Yes, of course, yes. She is an angel.

MARCUS: A cigarette, Maxi?

MAXI: No thanks. I'm a pipe smoker.

JENNIFER: Why are we all standing about in here?

VIVEKA: We are waiting for your dear sister, Jennifer.

DOLLY: The whole choir is in an uproar. We've got to rehearse the songs we're going to sing to the Pastor, and it's so late already.

MARCUS: Have you seen Camilla, Jen?

JENNIFER: Not since last night. Where is she?

(*Mrs. Behrens rushes in.*)

MARTHA: She's not in her room, but her bed is made.

JENNIFER: Where are you going, Mother?

MARTHA: She must be on the beach. She's probably gone for a swim and forgotten all about the time.

MAXI: Let me go—I'll find her. (*He leaves through the French windows.*)

DOLLY: Such a nice young man, Jen. You must be very, very happy.

JENNIFER: I certainly am! We get on so well together.

MARTHA: I never dreamt that Jennifer would surprise us like this. I've often said to myself: Jennifer is independent. She doesn't need anyone to look after her. And then one fine day—there she stands saying—this is Maxi, Mother. We're going to get married. I must take an aspirin.

VIVEKA: And when will the wedding take place?

JENNIFER: Maxi hopes to finish his thesis by Christmas—we'll be married then.

MARTHA: And then they're going to France. My prospective son-in-law has been awarded a grant, a very generous scholarship.

DOLLY: Oh, how romantic. That's what young people do these days. They use their scholarships for honeymoons.

MARCUS: I've a feeling that we've met before. Does Maxi play bridge?

VIVEKA: I'd be so delighted if your fiancé would call. Shall we say Tuesday? Three o'clock on Tuesday?

DOLLY: And you must find the time to visit my little cottage. Just come along whenever you like. Just whenever you like.

JENNIFER: Maxi is only here for such a very few days. Thank you—both of you. We'll try to drop in for a moment before he goes back. Mother—you must get changed.

MARTHA: But we're not expected at the Pastor's till four o'clock. I promise you I'll be dressed by then. You'll see, you'll be very pleased with me. I must tell you, one of Maxi's professors said that—

JENNIFER: Maxi's coming back—alone.

MARTHA: Where is Camilla?

(A sudden silence.)

MAXI (Rushing in): Camilla is not in the bathing hut—or on the beach. Where can she have got to?

MARCUS: But we've got to sing. Who's going to play for us?

VIVEKA: This is unforgivable. To leave us stranded like this.

JENNIFER: She's probably gone on to the Parish Hall alone.

MARTHA: Why doesn't she tell us where she's going? It's always the same—never shows any consideration. Never dreams how she upsets me.

MARCUS: We must be off now. Dear Jen—would you perhaps accompany us?

DOLLY: But we can't possibly take Jen away from Maxi. Especially seeing he's only staying a few days.

JENNIFER: Of course I'll do it. Please telephone me—if Camilla isn't there.

VIVEKA: We must fly now. Thank you, dear Martha. Good-by, little Jen. My warmest wishes.

DOLLY: God bless you, my dear child.

MARCUS: We'll have to cut one song out of the program now. Otherwise we'll never get through. 'By, Jen. Maxi, welcome to our happy circle. We'll see you later, Aunt Martha.

MARTHA: Good-by to you all. We meet here at three, don't we—and then we all go to the party together.

(The three friends leave the way they arrived, via the French windows. During the last interchange Maxi has been standing to one side, lighting his pipe.)

JENNIFER: Maxi—Maxi.

MAXI: What's the matter, darling?

JENNIFER: You weren't scared by them, were you? They are—very well-meaning. All the three Aunties. You're a great experience for them.

MAXI: I'd recognize them anywhere! People are the same all over the world.

MARTHA: Where on earth is Camilla? Didn't you see here?

JENNIFER: We went out at seven o'clock. Everyone in the house was asleep. We only got back a few minutes ago. No, we haven't seen her.

MARTHA: She mustn't do these things. They'll all be so cross with her. She has the most astonishing ability to hurt—It's about time you had something to eat.

(*Mrs. Behrens leaves the room in despair.*)

JENNIFER (*After a pause*): What are you looking at?

MAXI: At this portrait. It's your Father, isn't it?

JENNIFER: Yes. And that's Grandfather above. And that's Granny. She used to run the local dramatic society. That's Thomas—he died when he was twelve.

MAXI: Did your Father die a long time ago?

JENNIFER: Ten years . . . he committed suicide.

MAXI: I'm sorry. I didn't know.

JENNIFER: But you had to know sooner or later. You're one of the family now. Father fell ill. Mother says they behaved very badly to him at the Ministry where he worked. Father brought a lawsuit against his boss. It's not a pleasant memory.

MAXI: And isn't this you, Jennifer, as a little girl? And Camilla? Jen—what sort of a person is Camilla really?

JENNIFER: She's just like Mother—always acting—never natural. She wants to create the right impression—she wants to react the way she believes that each situation demands. You'll have to make allowances for her—and for Mother. She's not herself at all. Perhaps we're all a bit upset because of you. There hasn't been a man in the family for so long—not since Father died.

MAXI: You've all been wonderful to me. . . . Camilla does love teasing though, doesn't she? And making people sit up with surprise?

JENNIFER: Oh yes. She just loves to shock. Once she cycled through the village wearing only a bathing suit, and Mother received an anonymous letter as a result. We thought it was Aunt Haag-Seglidkin and dear Marcus.

MAXI: Don't believe everything she says.

JENNIFER: You find my sister interesting?

MAXI: Where do you think she's hiding now?

JENNIFER: She's probably lying in the wood with a book of poetry. She'll go tripping into the Pastor's house—well after everyone else has got there and she'll say, "I was reading poetry, time flew by so quickly." And no one will believe her. She's well aware of that fact. And Mother will have a migraine over what they're all saying in the village—again.

MAXI: Jennifer dear—last night—Oh Lord! It's not easy to explain. . . . I express myself so badly and I'm only going to make a mess of things.

JENNIFER: But Maxi dear, don't start preaching! What's worrying you?

MAXI: We parted on the stairs last night—and I went up to my room. And when I got upstairs . . . I was wearing my pajamas, brushing my teeth, so . . . It's all so utterly stupid.

JENNIFER: And then, Maxi—

MAXI: Suddenly Camilla stood there—she'd opened the door so quietly I hadn't heard a sound—she stood there, in her night-gown with a lighted candle in her hand—why in God's name did she have a lighted candle? You've got electricity. She came right up to me, and only stared.

(*Jennifer bursting into laughter.*)

It wasn't at all funny. She behaved most strangely. She was so very solemn, and she looked rather ill.

JENNIFER: She's a very talented actress. Inherited the gift from Granny.

MAXI: I don't think she was acting—not entirely, that is.

JENNIFER: And so—she made a ghostlike and silent entrance—

and an equally silent exit.

Maxi: No. We stood there looking at each other and I felt so stupid. I said, "What's the matter? Are you ill? Is there anything I can do for you?"

Jennifer: You're making a real tragedy out of it.

Maxi: And she answered very slowly and clearly. "I want to know what you look like, and then I can say good-by. That's all."

Jennifer (*Laughing heartily*): That must have been one of her most successful improvisations. And you, poor thing, you were scared to death.

Maxi: Please don't jest about it—it was most unpleasant. And then she took my hand and kissed it.

Jennifer: Took your hand and kissed it. Magnificent!

Maxi: Then she left me.

Jennifer: With her candle—highly delighted with her successful scene. You'd taken her seriously.

Maxi: Oh well. If that was a hoax it was most beautifully done. I really thought the poor girl had gone mad.

Jennifer: I must tell you what she did to Marcus. She sent him a telegram from the station, and he rushed off, half out of his mind. She had a splinter in her finger.

Maxi: She's a troublemaker alright. We won't give this episode any further thought.

(*Mrs. Behrens appears in the door—she is a little more articulate and less hysterical.*)

Martha: Jennifer, Maxi. Camilla went into town last night.

Jennifer: That's not true.

Martha: The girl says so. The milk boy saw her. She caught the late bus down by the bridge.

Maxi: We can check on that.

Martha: Her hat and coat have gone—and her handbag.

Jennifer: What a damned silly thing to do.

Martha: No adult would behave the way she does. She had nothing to do in town.

JENNIFER: When Maxi was going to bed last night, she went into his room and treated him to some melodrama. She said good-by.

MARTHA: She said good-by? Did she say that she was going to go—so late?

JENNIFER: In her nightdress with a lighted candle in her hand! How she must have reveled in that scene—so pretty and so theatrical.

MAXI: I don't think it's right to treat this episode quite so lightly. The fact is she wasn't quite herself when she came into my room last night. She must have gone back to her own room, got dressed, and gone on her way. If that's Camilla's idea of a joke then she must be told that it's not ours. That it's totally unappreciated.

MARTHA: I can't help it. I'm afraid.

JENNIFER: Camilla isn't even thinking of the pain she's caus-ing me. She's ruining the very few days Maxi and I were going to spend here.

(*The telephone rings, Jennifer, who stands nearest it, an-swers.*)

Hello. Yes. I see. I'll be along then. No, Aunt Viveka. It's not such a great sacrifice. I'll come back home as soon as the choir has finished singing. (*Putting down the receiver.*) The whole Parish is buzzing with rumors already.

MAXI: I'll come with you, darling. We're going to laugh and go our own way. If Camilla must amuse herself by putting on a performance—it's not going to be at our expense.

JENNIFER: You're right. And you're a darling to come with me. Aunt Dolly will let you share her hymn book—and you'll stand beside her and sing—that'll make her a slave of yours for life! You must ask Marcus all about his art. He writes short precious pieces for the local papers. You will let Aunt Viveka know that your mother's maiden name was Von Boldt—then you'll have an ally on every front.

MARTHA: Don't be spiteful, Jennifer. They've all been very

generous to us. When Father died. . . .

JENNIFER: I am going to forget "when Father died." I am going to forget Camilla and her crazy ways. I shall play hymns in waltz time and kiss Maxi right in front of their eyes. Maxi is my life now, Maxi and no one else.

MARTHA: Don't you think we ought to contact somebody. Perhaps she's gone to stay with Aunt Alice.

(*Maxi puts his arm around Jennifer and whispers something to her. They both start to laugh, and make ready to leave, when the telephone rings again. Several short, sharp intense rings before Mrs. Behrens answers.*)

MARTHA: Off with you both then—alright, I'll take it. (*She goes to the phone, lifts the receiver, and shouts into it*) Yes. It's a long distance call. Wait, Jen, Maxi. Yes, yes.

(*The two have listened to the conversation between Mrs. Behrens and the operator—now Mrs. Behrens is silent, and her expression indicates that she is hearing some frightful and totally unexpected news.*)

Good God!

JENNIFER: What is it, Mother? What's the matter? Is it—is it Camilla?

(*Mrs. Behrens has subsided onto the chair beside the phone, she sits very still and answers in monosyllables. When the conversation is finished, she slowly replaces the receiver. Jen and Maxi wait for the explanation.*)

MARTHA: That was from—from the—police. They've found her in a third-rate boarding house.

MAXI: Then it wasn't a joke.

JENNIFER: But Mother, what's happened? Where is Camilla?

MARTHA: Camilla tried to commit suicide during the night—but they got to her in time. She is in the hospital now. Out of danger.

MAXI: How simply—ghastly.

JENNIFER: What luck—what astonishing luck our dear Camilla always has!

CURTAIN

Scene Two

The same evening.

As the curtain rises, the clock can be heard striking seven o'clock. Mrs. Behrens enters from the garden. It is very dusky and the long-awaited rain has begun to fall. It is also a little cooler. Mrs. Behrens is in a highly nervous state, she was the only member of her family present at the Pastor's sixtieth birthday celebrations, and the strain has told on her. She takes off her coat and throws it in a heap on one of the chairs. She lights a lamp, sits down, then gets up again and draws the curtains, lights another lamp, then puts it out. She goes over to the French windows, opens them and looks out, listening. An idea strikes her, and she leaves the room suddenly on an impulse.

Marcus Trastheim enters from the garden as she leaves by the door into the rest of the house, he knocks very gently on the half-opened door, and whispers "Aunt Martha" and again "Aunt Martha." He takes a step inside and clumsily and quietly finds himself in the middle of the room. Mrs. Behrens finds him standing like this when she returns.

MARCUS: Dear Aunt Martha.

MARTHA: Oh—how you frightened me.

MARCUS: Dear Aunt Martha. I simply had to come. I couldn't let you wait here all alone. . . .

MARTHA: How very good of you.

MARCUS: No—no. I'm not good at all, but I just couldn't help noticing that you weren't feeling too well, Aunt Martha. *(Suddenly.)* Aren't Jen and Maxi with you here?

MARTHA: They are—they aren't at home.

MARCUS: Aunt Martha—please understand. I don't want to seem pushing and heartless; to be precise: impertinent, but after having run in and out of this house for many years, as I have done, been like a son, now don't deny that, Aunt Martha. You yourself said, "You are almost my son." Then surely one can, then one *must* have certain rights, I mean I just had to come to help and comfort you.

MARTHA: Why should *you* want to come and comfort *me?*

MARCUS: Where is Camilla? What has happened to her? Something is wrong. Aunt Martha, Aunt Martha, you know what I feel for her. And in any case you are in a bad state. I don't think that anyone else at the Pastor's party noticed it. But you can't pull the wool over my eyes.

MARTHA: Marcus—don't you think they may be missing you?

MARCUS: Not in the least. I told Aunt Viveka where I was going. I whispered to her.

MARTHA: Marcus—I would like to be left by myself.

MARCUS: No. Certainly not. Something is wrong. What has happened to Camilla, Aunt Martha?

MARTHA: Please, please, leave me.

MARCUS: No. It wouldn't be right for me to obey you on this occasion. Why don't you sit down. Let me bring you something—how about a glass of wine—or one of your pills? Please— just sit down quietly. I know where to find everything. I'll bring you a glass of madeira.

(*Mrs. Behrens sits helplessly in a chair while Marcus fusses around her. He goes out to the kitchen, and returns almost immediately with a bottle and two glasses. He fills the glasses from the bottle, and then pulls up a chair to be nearer Mrs. Behrens.*)

MARCUS: Well, Aunt Martha. Isn't that better? Just lie back— try and relax. I'll stay here until you feel better, or at least till Jen and Maxi get back. Have they—have they gone to fetch Camilla?

(*For a moment Mrs. Behrens loses her self-control. She starts to sniffle and puts her head between her hands.*)

MARCUS (*His eyes light up*): Are things that bad for Camilla?

MARTHA (*Pulling herself together, taking a drink from the glass—then staring hard at Marcus*): Why aren't you a man, Marcus?

MARCUS: What!

MARTHA: If you'd been a real man, Marcus—you'd have gone to fetch Camilla. *And* none of this would have happened.

MARCUS: But Aunt Martha—I don't really think I deserve to be so insulted.

MARTHA: Forgive me—I wasn't really thinking of what I was saying. I mustn't be spiteful. You are such a good boy—in your own way.

MARCUS: I always try to do what I regard as my duty.

MARTHA: And sometimes you even exceed the bounds of duty. Now you must go back to the party.

MARCUS: No—I am not leaving you alone in this house.

MARTHA: I beg you to leave now. Camilla is in trouble. Jen and Maxi have gone to fetch her. I don't feel any too well myself. Please try and understand—I must lie down for a while.

MARCUS: Will she—will they soon be back?

MARTHA: I don't know. O God—I've no idea.

MARCUS: Camilla did go into town—didn't she?

MARTHA: Yes. . . .

MARCUS: She must have gone in last night then—I happened to see the morning bus and she wasn't on that. So she went in last night.

MARTHA: Yes, yes.

MARCUS: But she did leave a message for you. She was running away. Why?

MARTHA: Can't you stop talking. Don't you understand anything at all? I have two daughters whom I now no longer know, I can't reach them. They've shut themselves behind a wall and they can't even hear my voice. They're strangers to me.

MARCUS: Why did Camilla run away?

MARTHA: Camilla went into town last night because she had a perfectly unbearable toothache and didn't want to alarm us. She spent the night with Aunt Alice. This morning, when she was on the way back, she had an accident. She was knocked down by a bus at the terminal. Her leg is badly cut and she has a very mild concussion. They took her to the hospital—but they're allowing her to come home this evening.

MARCUS: How simply terrible. (*He is not completely con-*

vinced by this story, but he does get up and make a move to go—then) Which dentist does she go to—Never mind— (*He is extremely inquisitive and insensitive.*) Well then, nothing dangerous, perhaps? No broken bones, or. . . . Was she run over by a bus?

MARTHA: I can assure you—she's not in any danger.

MARCUS (*Standing rather uncertainly—of two minds whether to stay to hear the rest, or to rush off to spread the gossip*) : Did the hospital telephone you or. . . ?

MARTHA: The hospital.

MARCUS: So she was run over at the bus terminal and taken off to the hospital. And they're letting her come home this evening.

MARTHA: Yes. But why don't you go now. Go and tell Viveka and Dolly and all the others what has happened. And don't forget to let them know that Camilla is in no danger.

MARCUS: I really don't know what to do. You aren't making a fool of me are you, Aunt Martha? Somehow I don't believe the story you've just told me. Camilla hasn't been in a car accident, has she? I can see it on your face. You don't deceive Marcus Trastheim so easily.

MARTHA: In heaven's name boy—go home—leave me in peace.

MARCUS: I am going. I am going at once. You completely misinterpret my intentions. I only wanted to show you how much, how much you all mean to me.

(*As Marcus approaches the French windows, two figures can be seen emerging from the dark garden. Mrs. Haag-Seglidkin and Mrs. Lien.*)

MARTHA: Get out! Get out!

MARCUS: Aunt Martha, you mustn't allow yourself to get so worked up. (*Noticing the two ladies approaching.*) Well I can't leave now. My departure at this stage would be the cause of such painful comment. Good day. . . .

(*The two ladies have reached the door on this last speech and entered the room.*)

Viveka:
Dolly: } Dear Martha, dear, dear Martha.

(*Mrs. Behrens does not return their greeting, but moves further down the room—the two ladies are astounded into speechlessness.*)

Marcus: Aunt Martha is in an extremely nervous state—to be precise, hysterical.

Viveka: I knew you wouldn't be of much help. Men are always so clumsy and unfeeling. Dear Martha—we think. . . .

Dolly: Dear darling Martha—we did so terribly want to know how you are.

Marcus: Sh, sh. Aunt Viveka, Aunt Dolly. This is a terrible business. Camilla has been in a car accident.

Viveka: My goodness, Martha! What's all this about?

Dolly: You need your friends about you at a moment like this.

Marcus: Only I don't believe this story. I believe that it's something worse, far, far worse. Something that Aunt Martha cannot bring herself to tell us.

(*The two ladies approach Mrs. Behrens, but even this gesture evokes no response at all.*)

Viveka: Martha dear. We felt that something was amiss, and we couldn't just leave you here alone without seeing if there is anything at all we can do to help you.

Marcus: Jen and Maxi have gone into town—to fetch Camilla.

Viveka: For your own sake—for everyone's sake, you must have faith. Dear, dear Martha, what has happened?

Dolly: Dear Martha—has Camilla been badly hurt?

Marcus: Careful, careful. Aunt Martha behaves as though she were paralysed. Yes, *paralysed*. I've never known anything like it.

Viveka (*Moving nearer, and taking Mrs. Behrens by the shoulders*): You must relax—try to weep—it's the most wonderful relief.

Dolly: Perhaps you should take some medicine. Twenty drops of Cowslip wine would work wonders. (*She moves over *to face the two ladies.*)

Marcus: I managed to get her to drink a glass of wine.

Viveka: Come and sit down, dear. Sit here. Come, tell us exactly what's happened.

Dolly: You'll find it such a relief to tell us all about it.

Marcus: But tell us the truth—it's only the truth that brings an easing of the burden.

(*They all wait, all three of them with gaping mouths—their heads cocked to one side, like three eager vultures, anxious not to miss a single word.*

Mrs. Behrens looks at them with fear, hearing all the rumors that will soon be circulating in her small world, which is tumbling rapidly round her ears.)

Martha: Why must you plague me so? Why did you come here?

Viveka: Then it's not true about Camilla's accident?

Dolly: You needn't give us all the details.

Viveka: There are only the three of us here. Your nearest and dearest friends. Whatever you tell us will stay within these four walls. We promise you that.

Marcus: The honor of your family is my honor too.

Viveka: Dear Martha. Your attitude is most strange, honestly, it's almost hurtful. Tell us—our dear Camilla must. . . .

Dolly: We didn't breathe a word at the Pastor's house. We just left the meeting and came straight here.

Marcus: Perhaps each second counts. Think of that, Aunt Martha.

Dolly: A shared burden is a double joy.

Viveka: Children are impossible.

Dolly: They never understand a mother's feelings.

Martha (*In great anguish*): But you won't tell anyone else? You must know how I feel—you've got to help me. You'll have to shield me. . . .

Dolly (*Spontaneously*): But tell us about it, Martha dear.

Viveka: Camilla?

DOLLY: Camilla?

MARCUS: Camilla?

MARTHA: I had a phone call—from the police. Camilla tried to commit suicide last night. In a third-rate boarding house.

(A long intense pause follows.)

VIVEKA: A third-rate. . . .

DOLLY: Last night. . . .

MARCUS: Suicide?

MARTHA *(Suddenly becoming aware of their dreadful inquisitiveness and realizing what she has told them)* : No—that's not the truth, either. Don't ask me any more questions. Just go away—go home and leave me in peace.

VIVEKA: Was she temporarily out of her mind?

DOLLY: Is she pregnant?

MARCUS: Did she take poison—or use a gun—or. . .

MARTHA: Don't stand there staring at me. Do something—help me. Tell me why—. It's my daughter who's done this terrible thing. Can't you understand how I feel—and I don't know anything, anything at all. Why did she do it?

(But there is no time for any further speculation. Jen and Maxi—between them Camilla—stand in the doorway. Camilla can barely support herself, and she is being propped up by the other two. There is silence while they all stare at her—bewitched.)

MARTHA: Camilla—Camilla—what have you done?

(They lead Camilla off past the door, but Jennifer turns, comes back and pauses for a moment.)

JENNIFER: Mother, please see that we're left alone. Alone, do you understand.

(On a sudden impulse the three friends leave the room—leaving Mrs. Behrens standing alone, hopeless and helpless in the middle of the room.)

CURTAIN

ACT TWO

Scene One

Sunday Morning.

Jennifer and Maxi have obviously been talking over the problem of Camilla for a very long time. When the curtain rises Jennifer is standing by the window, looking out, unhappy and moody. Maxi is smoking his pipe, furiously—feeling miserable and inadequate in the face of a problem which he has never confronted before. The church bells can be heard chiming in the silence.

MAXI: But Jen. I don't think you're being very kind to your sister. Good grief! I don't set myself up to be an expert on female psychology—but no woman, no woman behaves like she did without some reason. (*Pause.*) I just don't understand you. This is a ghastly business, and believe me I'm extremely unhappy, it's cast its shadow over the little time we have together—but it's our duty. It's our duty as human beings to help her out of her depression. You don't seem to realize what Camilla did—she could have succeeded.

JENNIFER: Well, she didn't succeed. It was never her intention to actually commit suicide.

MAXI: You yourself heard what the housekeeper said. It was only because she heard the noise of the jug falling to the floor that she went into Camilla's room at all.

JENNIFER: But you don't know all the tricks my dear little sister gets up to. It's easy to drop a jug on the floor, and to make absolutely certain that someone will hear the noise.

MAXI: Jen—you seem to have changed . . . Jen, Jen.

JENNIFER: Forgive me, Maxi—it all seems so impossible this morning. We should have gone for a long walk—we should have been happy—and now, now nothing has any significance unless it involves the two of us. So we have to stand here, listening to the church bells, waiting for Camilla to wake up and for Mother to calm down. This is one Sunday that's ruined, thanks to a girl who refuses to grow up.

MAXI: We can't just do as we please.

JENNIFER: I tell you—Camilla's making trouble just for the hell of it. It's her favorite game. She's always got to play a part that will be noticed. Mother's taken in—she always is, always has been since the days when Camilla used to play at being sick when we were at school. Now you've appeared—a new, unexpected and grateful public—

MAXI: I don't believe you.

JENNIFER: It doesn't take any great intelligence to do what she did. Steal Mother's medicine, leave on the last bus, take a room in some third-rate hotel, and make absolutely sure of rousing someone's suspicions. If she had really wanted to die— why didn't she make her attempt at night, in silence. Then no one could have stopped her. Oh God—how evil it all is. Forgive me, Maxi. Forgive me. I don't know what I'm saying. Oh Maxi—let's get out of here. Let's go and take a good long walk in the fresh air. Can't you feel the autumn? Let's escape where no one can find us.

MAXI: We can't leave your mother alone with Camilla.

JENNIFER: We'll forget Mother's existence. We'll forget all about Camilla. Out there—in the fresh air—there's only you and I, Maxi. Please, Maxi—let's get out of here.

MAXI: One day you'd despise me were I to obey you now.

JENNIFER: Well then I shall go alone. I do not want to be here to applaud Camilla's entrance.

MAXI: You can't do it—for God's sake, Jen. Aren't you aware of the fact that there are certain times when there are certain obligations to fulfill. You can't run away when everything seems impossible and terrible.

JENNIFER: I didn't ask for these obligations. I asked for you. Are you coming with me?

MAXI: No. I can't, I can't walk out.

JENNIFER: Good-by, Maxi. There's some fishing gear on the beach, or the lawn mower, and lots of books. When you tire of your bedside vigil.

MAXI: Wait, Jen. You can't do this. Wait, my darling.

(*But Jennifer walks out of the door into the garden, leaving him alone, uncertain, troubled and upset. He looks out after her retreating figure, and lights his pipe. He wants to follow her, go with her on the much talked about walk. He is already in the doorway when he stops. The first early visitor is approaching. Mrs. Haag-Seglidkin arrives, wearing half-mourning. She greets him in a clear whisper.*)

VIVEKA: Good morning, Maximilian.

MAXI: Good morning.

VIVEKA: I'm on my way to church, but I just had to drop in to hear how that poor child is this morning. Is she really out of danger?

MAXI: Yes, thank you.

VIVEKA: She's being allowed to sleep surely? I always say a good night's sleep can work miracles.

MAXI: We hope so.

VIVEKA: How—how is she? Does one know. . . . I mean has Camilla said anything?

MAXI: She has not yet woken up. So we haven't spoken to her. At all.

VIVEKA: Haven't any of you found out anything?

MAXI: No, Aunt Dolly.

VIVEKA: Dolly? I am Aunt Viveka, dear Maximilian. Aunt Viveka Haag-Seglidkin. My husband was a Justice of the Peace. Aunt Viveka, dear boy.

MAXI: I'm so sorry.

VIVEKA: You've probably been watching by her bedside all night, haven't you? I'm very willing to do all I can. We must all do what we can to help that poor child.

MAXI: We will do our best.

VIVEKA: And Martha? Can I speak to her?

(*She tries to force her way further into the room, but Maxi bars her progress.*)

MAXI: I don't think Aunt Martha can see anyone just now.

VIVEKA (*Disappointed and crestfallen*): Naturally I don't want to disturb her. What a day—with such misfortune in the house. I only looked in on the way to church. Perhaps you'll give Camilla this book when she can find enough strength to read. It is called "Words on the Way." It's a book that gives such comfort—it's been such a help to me. Such a great help.

MAXI: I shall certainly leave it for her. Thank you, Aunt Dolly, thank you so much.

VIVEKA: Aunt Viveka, Aunt Viveka Seglidkin. Good-by.

MAXI: Please forgive me. Good-by.

VIVEKA: And if Martha wishes to see me—tell her that I'll come at once. Don't forget to tell her that, will you?

MAXI: Thank you—I'll let her know immediately.

(*He follows Mrs. Haag-Seglidkin to the door, his eyes blazing. Puts the book down with marked distaste. Then he stands there, not knowing what to do next. Mrs. Behrens is calling as she comes into the room.*)

MARTHA: Jennifer—I think Camilla will soon be waking up. Good morning, Maxi! Je-en.

MAXI: Good morning. Jen isn't here.

MARTHA: But I need her help. Camilla is sleeping very restlessly just now. Je-en.

MAXI: Jen isn't here. She went out for a walk.

MARTHA: How stupid of her. And how utterly heartless. She must have realized that Camilla would need something nourishing when she wakes up. And the girl is slow. I'll have to do it myself, Maxi—do you think a cup of soup or an omelette? Dear Maxi—I'm so glad that you are here. I'm so completely alone in the middle of all these trials and tribulations. You'll have to talk to Camilla. I don't think, I don't think she'd tell me, tell me why she did what she did. Not me—or Jen. They never became the good friends I'd hoped they would.

MAXI: I can't do much. Jen didn't understand my attitude, I can't understand hers. She thinks that Camilla's just playing a part—that nothing really took place—Oh God! It's all such a mess.

MARTHA: But Camilla will listen to you, I know that.

MAXI: I'll—talk to her. There is perhaps something. I can't tell you about it—or Jen. It's something that concerns only Camilla and me.

MARTHA *(Surprised and frightened)*: Camilla and you?

MAXI: I think I can almost promise you that everything will be alright again—I think I have a way of influencing Camilla.

MARTHA: It makes me so happy to hear you say that. I knew you'd put everything right. For Jen, for Camilla, for me. I ask for so little. Only that my girls should be happy.

MAXI *(With difficulty)*: Camilla wrote a letter—the doctor at the hospital gave it to me. It was found in that hotel room. She gave the reason for her ghastly action in her letter. But I mustn't reveal its contents. That's her secret; now you understand, and because I know more than all of you, I can help to solve the problem.

MARTHA: You will do it, you can do it. We're all going to be happy again. A harmonious, happy family. Thank you, Maxi. You are the boy I never watched grow up, you are my son.

(She is about to go off to the kitchen to prepare something for Camilla when Mrs. Lien arrives.)

DOLLY *(In a choked whisper)*: Good morning. Good morning dear, dear Martha. Dear boy. How is everything?

MARTHA: Camilla has slept well all night. We are just waiting for her to wake up—I was just on the way to prepare a snack for her.

DOLLY: If there is anything at all that I can do—I'll sacrifice my visit to God's house. An action of love is surely more rewarding than listening to a sermon, isn't it? Don't you think so, dear boy?

MAXI: Oh yes. You're absolutely right. But we don't need

any help, we can look after Camilla alone, Aunt Viveka.

DOLLY: I am Dolly—you must be about the first person to have confused us. I am Aunt Dolly, my friend. Dolly Lien.

MAXI: Please forgive me.

DOLLY: It doesn't matter, Maxi—Aunt Viveka, Aunt Dolly. Perhaps one—perhaps it is possible to make a mistake between us, sometimes. But I would stay, so willingly. I am not as powerful as Viveka, but I am tough. Very tough. (*Whispering again.*) Hasn't Camilla said anything at all yet?

MAXI: She hasn't said anything. We haven't asked any questions. And Camilla is still asleep.

DOLLY: Oh—I do shout! You must excuse me. Dear Martha, can't I do anything at all? Anyway, I've brought her a few plums. Plums are always so good for depression—it's such fun to lie in bed and spit out the stones. It's an action that's so fraught with meaning in some way. . . .

MARTHA: Thank you, dear. You mean so very well.

MAXI: Aunt—Viveka was here a minute ago. She left a book for Camilla.

DOLLY: But books are not at all good—not in her state—religious reading—oh no, not now. I mean she must get well first. I find there's so much about punishment. Sometimes—and human beings are frail. (*Looking sideways at them.*) If Camilla has sinned. . . .

MAXI: What the hell. What do you mean, Aunt Dolly?

MARTHA: Dolly never means ill—she is goodness personified.

DOLLY: If in my small way there is anything, I. . . .

MAXI: The bells for morning service rang some time ago.

MARTHA: Thank you for coming.

DOLLY: You know I'd do anything for you—for all of you.

(*She makes for the door, disappointed with her visit. But then what they've all been waiting for happens: Camilla has woken up, and come downstairs, stands motionless in the door, looking at them with uncertain, searching glances, and yet she seems a long way away. She wears a dressing gown, thrown over her pajamas, she walks unsteadily over the floor, supporting her way with a table, a chair, saying nothing. Like a sleepwalker, she makes for a small table to take a cigarette which she picks up with slow deliberate gestures.*

Camilla is by far the prettier of the two sisters, but she lacks Jennifer's calm and self-control. She will make a gesture, but stop before it is completed. She begins an accusation, but never substantiates it. She laughs at her own seriousness, and yet takes her own jokes very seriously. She belongs to that type of person who do not dare to take themselves seriously, who dare not believe in their own power, or their own future.

Now that she stands in front of us for the first time, completely aware of the overwhelming interest she has aroused— "She has tried to commit suicide"—we cannot rid ourselves of the impression that this is fraud, a pose. Camilla must act now— she is altogether too uncertain of the reactions of those around her. Her public all react in totally different fashion. Her mother tries to hide her shame and sorrow with exaggerated and misplaced solicitude. Maxi is ill at ease and he tries to withdraw— and remains a stranger standing at one side, outside. He would prefer to leave, but his strong sense of duty, and his love, keep him there. Mrs. Lien is deeply touched. She wipes her eyes with her handkerchief. Touched, but also extracting every single bit of enjoyment from this thrilling situation.)

CAMILLA: Oh, here you are, Mother. Little Aunt Dolly, and Maxi!

MARTHA: You shouldn't have come down. And really you ought not to smoke so early.

DOLLY: You must look after yourself now.

CAMILLA: Maxi dear—be an angel and give me a light. I left my matches on my bedside table.

(He gives her a light quickly—too quickly—and withdraws like a soldier on guard duty.)

CAMILLA: Thank you, Maxi—thank you.

MARTHA: Why don't you go back to bed. Would you like

some flowers by your bed—would you like the radio on?

DOLLY: Oh no, Martha—don't do that—not for all the tea in China. I always cry when I hear music.

CAMILLA: Maxi, please stand to one side so that the sun can warm *me*.

MARTHA: Would you like a rug for your shoulders, dear?

DOLLY: You aren't in a draft, are you?

CAMILLA: You are all so kind and good to me. I haven't thanked you for everything, all of you, for everything you've done for me. Mother, Maxi, dear Aunt Dolly. Where is Jen, Maxi dear? Can't you ask her to come in so that I can thank her too?

MARTHA: She—she isn't at home just now. She had to go out on an errand.

CAMILLA: I see, I understand.

MAXI: I am absolutely certain that's the last thing you do.

DOLLY: Have you any pains, child?

CAMILLA: I beg your pardon, Aunt Dolly?

DOLLY: I asked you if you were in pain, child?

CAMILLA: I have no pain, Aunt Dolly.

DOLLY: I've brought you some plums.

MAXI: And Aunt Viveka left you a book. Mr. Trastheim still hasn't found the time to bring you anything.

CAMILLA: I expect he's going to bring me some flowers. He is so very romantic.

MARTHA: Camilla, you must have something to eat. I'll go and see to a snack for you myself. You must have something to nibble, an omelette, or some of the meat we had last night. You're going to listen to me now, you've got to understand that I want to help you.

DOLLY: We all want to help you to get over this. (*Very pathetic and a little illogical.*) To the other shore, Camilla, to the other shore. The shore of good hope.

CAMILLA: And what do you say, Maxi? Do you think it is imperative for me to eat now.

MAXI: How should I know what you need just now?

(*And he glares at her with hate, for all her words, her actions have roused in him the thought that perhaps Jen is right, she is only playing a part.*)

CAMILLA: Maxi, reach me the ashtray. Thank you.

(*Maxi is still polite and correct, but he cannot meet her gaze, which she never takes away from him. He opens the door and goes out on the verandah.*)

DOLLY: Camilla, Camilla dear child. You don't know how we're all thinking about you now. We understand. We were all young once, you mustn't forget that. We've all been in love.

CAMILLA (*Disturbed*): What did you say, Aunt Dolly?

DOLLY: I just said that we have *all* been in love.

CAMILLA: Aunt Dolly—have you been in love often?

DOLLY: I was married once—but he died so soon after.

CAMILLA: From mumps.

DOLLY: It was his heart. His heart. I used to say to him— no. We're not going to discuss my problems now. I shall try to understand you, dear child. It must be dreadful to be alone. (*Whispering.*) But why can't you get married?

CAMILLA: What are you talking about. Jen is going to get married, not I.

DOLLY: Camilla! Is the child—his?

CAMILLA: Child? Child? What child?

DOLLY: The child you are carrying.

CAMILLA: I'm expecting a baby? Is that what Mother thinks?

DOLLY: Oh no. That's what I've gathered, Camilla. I realized at once, when your Mother told us about, about your terrible accident. I immediately said she's pregnant. I've read about these things.

CAMILLA: Do they all think that's the case?

DOLLY: No—they never listen to me. But I'm right, aren't I? Tell me I'm right about it.

CAMILLA (*Evil and insinuatingly*): Of course you're right, Aunt Dolly. I am pregnant—his child. And I'm alone, so alone.

What's left when your sister steals your lover, only—the dark water in the harbor, the racing express train, the small white tablets. You, Aunt Dolly, can understand the terrible plight of the unmarried mother, can't you?

DOLLY (*Moved as she's never been moved in her life before*) : Oh yes . . . yes . . . the water—the train—the tablets. And no one else knows all this. Only I, Dolly Lien. Not even Viveka Haag-Seglidkin.

CAMILLA: Only you know this. Mother is so impractical. And Maxi, you can't go and tell a man these things.

DOLLY: No—that's not possible, is it? Men—are men. But I will do something for you. You shall come and live with me. All the time you're carrying the child, you shall make your home with me. You, and the baby.

CAMILLA: Oh thank you, Aunt Dolly. You are so generous, so very generous.

DOLLY: We'll have to take a bed down from the loft. Two beds. Oh God. I'm so happy. I'm so happy. I shall have you to look after.

CAMILLA (*A little frightened of what she has brought upon herself*) : But I must talk to Mother first. And I think it would be as well, Aunt Dolly, if you were to leave us now. We need so much rest, I and the baby.

DOLLY: Of course. I'm so selfish, such an egotist. I'll be on my way at once. I've really got so much to do now that you're coming. I'll telephone you—no, I'd better write. We don't want anyone else to overhear our little secret, do we?

(*While she is waiting for an answer Mrs. Dehrens comes back with a tray for Camilla.*)

MARTHA: These maids are always so difficult. I don't want to be spiteful or too free with my accusations, but I don't think we can trust her any longer. In fact I know we can't. There were three meat balls left over last night—and there isn't a single one today.

CAMILLA: Darling Mother—I woke up at six this morning,

and I was hungry. I ate them.

MARTHA: They were most certainly very good for you. (*Obviously disbelieving this story.*) Well, I only slept for a very short while.

CAMILLA: Mother, go to church with Aunt Dolly. Don't worry about me, I'd like to be alone with Maxi for a while—there's something we have to discuss.

MARTHA: Is Maxi allowed to tell me what it's about?

CAMILLA: I'll tell him to tell you what you need to know. Mother, you aren't cross with me are you? You have forgiven me, haven't you? I beg of you, please forgive me. I don't always know what's right—or what to think or what to do. . . .

MARTHA: Darling baby. You've grown so far away from me. I know so little about you, but I am your Mother and I do my best to understand you. I only want your happiness.

CAMILLA: I will be happy. Very soon, Mother, I'll be happy.

MARTHA: Well, I think I'll go to church with Aunt Dolly— I'm trusting you my darling, I trust you.

(*Mrs. Lien takes her farewell with mysterious signs to Camilla. Mrs. Behrens also leaves the room—hesitatingly, and the scene is quiet. As soon as she is left alone, Camilla drops the pose and shows herself to be a gauche overgrown school girl, terrified of the awful situation she has created. She rushes to the verandah doors and calls for Maxi in a low voice. Then she shouts again, and again. Maxi has been standing in the shadows of the room—looking at her. As she becomes aware of him she moves slowly into the room.*)

CAMILLA: Maxi—Maxi—Maxi. I didn't see you. I thought I'd been left here all alone.

(*She goes back to the sofa and starts to nibble from the tray of food, looks at him, waiting for him to start speaking. Finally, her impatience gets the better of her.*)

CAMILLA: I've behaved like a fool. Give me back that letter. (*Pause.*) Please don't stand there looking at me like that. Give me back the letter. Say you forgive me. Say something—or get out. (*Hysterically.*) Say that you see through me.

MAXI (*With difficulty*): I find it hard to understand you. I've got nothing against you. What is it all about?

CAMILLA: Then you aren't cross with me?

MAXI: It's hard to be cross with a child—or a fool.

CAMILLA: So that's how you see me. As a child or a fool. Give me back my letter.

MAXI: Oh for God's sake. I don't want to hurt you. Camilla. I'm sorry for you in a way, really sorry. But I don't understand a damn thing. Can't you see how things stand? I love Jen. I came here to learn more about her home—her mother, and you. But the second night under your roof you went away and. . . .

CAMILLA: And took an overdose of sleeping tablets so that I passed out—and then Maxi—

MAXI: I maintain it was never your intention to commit— to take—

CAMILLA: Is that what Jen thinks. In fact she said "Don't believe Camilla—she's a child. She gets up to all sorts of tricks to arouse interest—she's always got to be the center of attention." Did you laugh together at my farewell lines?

MAXI: Perhaps I should have given Jen the letter. Perhaps that would have been the right thing to do—but I couldn't do it.

CAMILLA: Carry on with your detailed account of my downfall! I went my own way—made a childish attempt—a rotten miserable attempt at—and you came into town to fetch me back. Do you remember how I kissed your throat as you carried me down to the car?

MAXI: Just you keep quiet about that.

CAMILLA: I am sorry, Maxi. I'm very spiteful.

MAXI: Are you just only spiteful—a ghastly child who wants to create confusion. I'm trying to say something else—what you did, you did quite deliberately.

CAMILLA: You know the truth. Won't you believe it?

MAXI: It's not done to behave as you do. You don't write letters to your sister's fiancé, letters like that. You wouldn't throw yourself at me—if you were a woman with any pride, with a trace of modesty, don't you feel any shame—haven't you any normal instincts?

CAMILLA: What did I say to offend your modesty? That I love you, desire you—that I can't live without possessing you—that I am malicious and full of evil intentions—that I hurt people—that they all hate me. That's true, Maxi. Mother is scared of me, and you hate me now.

MAXI: Good God! What can I do with you? What can I do to help you?

CAMILLA: Kiss me. We'll go our own way. At least you realize there's no more room for Camilla here. You two will get married, Mother will wander around in a blissful state of granny-hood. Where would I fit in—can you see me washing out your eldest's dirty diapers—. . .

MAXI (*Screaming at her, temporarily losing all self-control*): You are out of your mind!

CAMILLA: I am crazy about a stupid, clumsy, conceited man who is like a red rag to a bull for me. You heard what I suggested. We'll go our own ways. I'll go away—to town—I shall live in a room near you.

MAXI: I shall never be at home to you.

CAMILLA: I shall sit and wait for you on the stairs of your flat. I shall follow you. I shall wait for you to come home. People will ask—who is Camilla waiting for? Why does she stand there every day? In sunshine, in rain. And I shall answer—I am waiting for my beloved, and he doesn't want to know me.

MAXI: You're nothing but a devil!

CAMILLA: Won't you hit me again—I like it. Will you have a whiskey—that's the right thing to do in your situation. What all men do.

MAXI: Men? What do you know about men?

CAMILLA: If you ask me if men have wanted me—I'll answer

yes. If you like I'll even count them for you. Marcus, the baker's boy, the bookseller at the station, all the local clergymen, the English teacher, two hundred bus travelers. But if you mean anything else—no one has slept with me.

MAXI: Look at me. There is something I must ask you—when you went into town—did you really wish to commit suicide—or was that gesture just an act.

CAMILLA: I read how many pills were needed for sleep—and how many for death. I made quite certain that the housekeeper knew I wasn't too happy—I shrieked and I broke the jug as noisily as I could to make a hundred per cent certain that they'd get to me on time. Why should I want to die? I want to live so that I can learn the taste of your kisses, feel your arms around me, my beloved. Why should I want to die when I love you?

MAXI: Then you admit it was never your intention? What on earth do you hope to gain from your lies?

CAMILLA: Would you have paid me any attention otherwise? Would you have believed in me without—? I'm just a shadow, good little Jen's shadow, my stable and strong sister wins out every time. Oh no. . . .

MAXI: I don't believe you—your letter—your senseless words—nothing has any meaning—

CAMILLA: I've shot an arrow, my darling, and it found its mark. It pierced the wound, and rests there, trembling, painful. Maxi—I know that you are in love with me. Doesn't that hurt just a little bit—only for my sake?

MAXI: I've just about had enough of you. Please keep quiet.

CAMILLA: You will never know what it is to kiss me—you will never feel my weight in your arms—you will never respond when I call—never answer my questions. If you love me. . . .

MAXI: For God's sake—shut up.

(*Camilla approaches him, Maxi in panic leaves the room, leaving Camilla standing there looking out at him as he flees down into the garden.*)

CAMILLA (*Very slowly*) : Forgive me for hurting Mother, and for causing Jen such pain. Give me Maxi. Let him be my husband.

(*She goes back to the sofa, lies down, yawns, and forgetting where she is, falls asleep.*)

CURTAIN

Scene Two

Sunday evening.

Marcus Trastheim is standing in the room with his overcoat still round his shoulders. He has obviously just arrived and is hiding something behind his back, he addresses his remarks to Mrs. Behrens but is continually looking at Camilla with great curiosity.

MARCUS: You know I wasn't quite sure whether I ought to come or not. I went down to the stile, you know the one at the bottom of the hill, and I argued with myself. Should I disturb you, or should I not—a real conflict of conscience to be precise. I thought I ought not to come here—but I—. Well I honestly did decide not to come this evening. I thought I'd let you enjoy a peaceful Sunday evening without Marcus. But I ran into Aunt Dolly. (*Pause*) To be precise, Aunt Dolly paid me a visit. I've picked a few flowers, I wanted you to have them. (*A little stiffly*) Please, Camilla. I hope your ill-health will soon—I mean —in its own time. . . .

CAMILLA: Thank you, Marcus dear, I do understand what you mean.

MARTHA: I think it's very kind of you not to forget us. Camilla has such need of an old and faithful friend. Come and sit down, Marcus.

MARCUS: No thanks. I really can't. I decided just to drop in, see how you all are, leave my flowers, and go home.

CAMILLA: Take your coat off, Marcus. Come and sit beside me. We'll sit here in the dusk and talk about our childhood, our long, happy childhood . . . remember how we used to kiss one another down by the beach hut?

MARTHA: You were always such a charming child. So good and so helpful.

MARCUS: I've never been of any help to anyone. People laugh at me. I've never been any good at all—no, don't protest. I could run for the doctor, hold the skeins of wool. I was even kissed behind the beach hut—but no one has ever taken me seriously, anywhere. If I'm not careful I'll end up as a baby-sitter, an unpaid baby-sitter, to be precise.

CAMILLA: You'll get married, Marcus. You'll make an ideal husband.

MARCUS: I wouldn't dare. . . .

MARTHA: I think you underestimate yourself—there's always been one person who's had faith in you, liked you, and yet hasn't found a way of letting you know. You must look to the future, Marcus.

MARCUS: Aunt Martha—you know what I've felt for Camilla. Camilla has never bothered about me. I've suffered—at least I used to suffer. Now I've learnt how to master my suffering.

CAMILLA: Marcus—you are quite different today. You've become so determined, so decisive, I don't recognize you.

MARCUS: I've learnt my lesson well.

MARTHA: Please sit down, Marcus. You'll get tired from standing so long.

MARCUS: I won't get tired, thank you. I have perfectly good supports in my shoes.

CAMILLA: Why did you want to see me this evening particularly? Was it something Aunt Dolly told you? Something that made you feel you absolutely had to come this evening?

MARTHA: But Camilla, Marcus wants to know how you feel—you mustn't be so short with him.

CAMILLA: I feel wonderful, Marcus. I don't feel in the least bit unwell. I shall take long walks—I shall be careful to do my exercises—in fact I shall do all the things I ought to do now.

MARTHA: Marcus, you like walking don't you? You'll go, won't you, with Camilla?

CAMILLA: I'm going to let Marcus look after me altogether.

MARCUS: I don't know about that——I'll be terribly busy. You're forgetting about the Bazaar in aid of the Old People's Home—the choir, and the scouts. Will you carry on as you have done up to now with everything?

MARTHA: Of course. She must. I've always said that these social interests are useful. We forget ourselves. I'd be most disappointed if Camilla no longer played her part in the parish.

CAMILLA: Mother dear—we must ask Marcus what he thinks? What is your opinion, Marcus? After all—I won't be able to appear very much longer. Well?

MARCUS (*Standing against the wall—very agitated*) : Well, I really don't know. That's something, something only you yourself can decide. As Aunt Martha says, social work is a wonderful outlet, but we have our responsibilities. The Pastor wants those who are going to be confirmed this year to help with the Bazaar.

CAMILLA: You mean my presence is a danger to the confirmands?

MARTHA: What do you mean?

CAMILLA: Only that they'd stare at me—inquisitive and probably a little jealous.

MARCUS (*Very, very upset*) : God forbids that sort of behavior.

CAMILLA: Having tasted the forbidden fruit of sin I must bear the pain of shame for all to see. . . .

MARTHA: I'm so glad to hear you joking again, Camilla. I remember how you two used to scrap as children.

MARCUS: I don't know how you can joke about all this. How you have the courage—the moral strength.

CAMILLA: That I'm not ashamed to be precise. (*She gets up from her place, goes over to him and whispers*) Have you no pity for me, then?

MARCUS (*Unnerved by her proximity, tries to move away*) : Don't say things like that—and don't look at me like that either. I'll have to—I'm afraid I'll have to leave you now. My hat. I must thank you so very much. Aunt Martha, you won't forget the committee meeting tomorrow evening, will you?

CAMILLA: And I must thank you for the flowers. It is most generous of you to come and visit me in my great misfortune. . . .

(*He throws a desperate look at her and rushes away.*)

CAMILLA: The vultures join in the mourning and then make a meal of the corpse— (*Pause*) Mother, how much are you afraid of wagging tongues?

MARTHA: Wagging tongues?

CAMILLA: Aunt Viveka is inquisitive—Aunt Dolly talks too much, and Marcus thrives on gossip.

MARTHA: Dear child. What are you saying? They are all good old family friends. Viveka and Dolly were so helpful when Father died. Don't you remember?

CAMILLA: I only remember that each time we cried someone appeared with a hankie. I remember——Well—there was always someone with you pulling a long, sad face. As if they despised you. And you put up with it.

MARTHA: That's not true. I have never given them any cause to scorn us.

CAMILLA: But if I were to do something that would bring a rift between you and your friends—whom would you believe— whom would you stand up for? Mother. I've told Aunt Dolly I tried to commit suicide because I am pregnant.

MARTHA: Good God, Camilla!

CAMILLA: Of course it's not true. But I told her that story all the same. Now they all believe it. They will come here to get proof. They are going to stare and whisper at every meeting—at every tea party. You'll have to draw on all your courage to cope with them. You'll have to tell them that I'm a fraud.

MARTHA (*In great panic*): Why must you do these things? You only harm yourself—and me. You never show me any consideration at all.

CAMILLA: I told her that Maxi is the father.

MARTHA: Camilla. You've said enough. Now keep quiet. You can't do me any more harm. I don't want to hear any more.

I can't help what you've done. I'm scared for you. Why do you do these things? We don't even talk the same language. You aren't a woman like me—or Jen. I don't know what you are—but I loathe it—No, don't come near me. Don't say any more. Don't say anything.

CAMILLA (*As if she had been listening to her mother*) : I love Maxi, Mother. I'm not fooling now.

MARTHA: Why do you always have to take everything away from me? (*She bursts into tears and leaves the room.*)

CAMILLA (*In anguish*) : Mother, don't leave me now. Mother, Jen, Maxi. I don't want to be left alone. Can't any of you hear me. I can't bear it if you all leave me.

(*Only her bitter crying can be heard in the dark room. She puts out the only lamp still burning, and the room is plunged into almost total darkness. Jen enters from her room in the house—she stops in pity in front of Camilla and then deliberately goes and lights every lamp in the room—which by contrast is then brightly lit.*)

JENNIFER: I want to talk to you, Camilla.

(*Camilla sits up slowly, pulls herself together and then both sisters are sitting down facing one another, stiff and conventional.*)

CAMILLA: You haven't welcomed me home yet. You haven't said that you're glad that I'm alive.

JENNIFER: I'm glad that you feel so much better. Are you ready for further conquests?

CAMILLA: Thank you.

JENNIFER: You're not waiting for me to kiss you, are you?

CAMILLA: Oh no.

JENNIFER: You're smoking my cigarettes.

CAMILLA: I've finished mine. I'm sure you'll understand I didn't have any time to do any shopping yesterday. Do you want one?

(*Jennifer takes one, lights it, and starts to inhale deeply. Both sisters look at one another through the smoke, the tension eases very slightly. Jennifer tries to use a softer tone.*)

JENNIFER: Cam—

CAMILLA: Yes, Jen.

JENNIFER: You arrived at the boarding house at 6 o'clock, but the late bus gets in at 2:15. How did you spend the hours in between?

CAMILLA: I stayed at the station for a while. I walked around. Did some window-shopping. Remember that all-night café we once found by chance that time we went to the theater?

JENNIFER: You went there—all alone?

CAMILLA: You weren't with me, Jen. It was a terrible disappointment, dark and dirty, and no interesting types there at all. Not even one single tart—only sleepy policemen and drivers.

JENNIFER: And then you wandered around till 6 o'clock.

CAMILLA: I loved it. Everything seems so different at night. I walked through all the sleeping districts, looking at the dark windows. It all seemed so easy—and so much clearer.

JENNIFER: Weren't you frightened—of anything?

CAMILLA: It is only here that I am frightened. Of Mother—the vultures and you.

JENNIFER: And Maxi?

CAMILLA: And him, too. He doesn't understand anything.

JENNIFER: What have you told the neighbors, Cam? I met Aunt Viveka this evening. She said, "How simply terrible about Camilla. And what a blow for you. A dreadful catastrophe for the three of you." I said "This doesn't concern Maxi and me at all." Then she stared hard at me and said "Then you don't know yet." What don't I know, Cam?

CAMILLA: I told Aunt Dolly in the strictest confidence that I was expecting a baby—by Maxi.

JENNIFER (*Laughing relieved*): Cam—you're so ingenious. And they'll believe it. They'll swallow anything that smells of sensation.

CAMILLA: But I've never hurt Mother so deeply before.

JENNIFER: Poor Mother.

CAMILLA: Poor Mother. (*Mimicking her.*)

(*Pause. Jennifer gets up from her place, wanders round the room and finally comes to rest looking out over the garden. Camilla follows.*)

JENNIFER: Camilla, I'm in love with Maxi. No—don't interrupt me. This is not a story now. This is not one of the fantasies we used to weave lying awake at night, whispering in my bed when Mother thought we were both in our own separate rooms, mortal enemies. This is the first time I've wanted any man near me—when he comes near me I feel paralyzed.

CAMILLA: Jen—do you want him to be your lover?

JENNIFER: Yes, Cam, I do—but he's so stupid.

CAMILLA: Do you remember how we once said after having been to the cinema? He mustn't want to put out the light.

JENNIFER: That's how it is, Cam. I no longer feel that particular shame, any shame. Nothing matters any longer—only Maxi.

CAMILLA: Don't I?

JENNIFER: Not even you.

CAMILLA: You can betray me now. Any day.

JENNIFER: I have already betrayed you.

CAMILLA: Then you must put your signature to my secret document.

JENNIFER: And you must put yours on mine.

CAMILLA: I'll be left alone—to fight Mother—and all the ape-like vultures.

JENNIFER: I love Maxi.

CAMILLA: I'll be alone with Mother, the village, and the Pastor, and Mr. Trastheim.

JENNIFER: But that's life—you'll find a lover and then we'll be four.

CAMILLA: Not even Maxi can join our fellowship. He'll never understand us. Our secret determination, our secret oaths to Mother and the village. He didn't even understand my letter.

JENNIFER: He showed it to me. He didn't understand a word.

He was like a boy who'd got a very bad report from school.

CAMILLA: It took a lot of courage.

JENNIFER: I never believed you had such courage. I only remembered about it on the way to the hospital. You once said to me—remember—if you fall seriously in love, I shall pretend that I've fallen in love with the same man. I shall take my life for his sake, and write him a letter about it. (*Laughing*) It seemed very exciting then. We used to pretend to argue about him. He was going to feel that he was the most attractive man in the whole world. It wasn't a very funny game yesterday.

CAMILLA: We're grownups now.

JENNIFER: The time to be crazy has passed. An innocent man who sets a great deal of store on a stainless reputation is having to pay.

CAMILLA: Are you going to marry a vulture?

JENNIFER (*Bitterly*): They've all got something of the vulture in them—all but you. He wants to make a success of his career. The slightest whisper of a scandal would be fatal.

CAMILLA: I've hurt him by saying what I did—about our child.

JENNIFER: We must give the lie to that. "For the following reason I must make it known that my pregnancy by the aforesaid man is now terminated, the time was badly chosen."

CAMILLA: This will mean war to the death between the village and us.

JENNIFER: Between the village and you. I have already betrayed you—you can't count on my support any longer.

CAMILLA (*Slowly, with great bitterness*): I shall never have any support from anyone any more. (*She suddenly jumps up and hugs Jen passionately*) Oh, Jen—why must this happen. Don't you understand I can't be left alone. I'll be so lonely—so alone—you'll be with Maxi.

JENNIFER: Darling little Cam. I tell you I can't help it. There isn't room for you with us. It's always been you and I against the rest of the world—against Mother—and Mother's appalling

friends—against the whole village. Now it's Maxi and I. . . .
We've got to be able to rule our own lives. Surely you realize
that this had to happen some time. We can't play at being
terrorists all our lives.

CAMILLA: Then you're telling me that I'll have to die.

JENNIFER: And live again. This game is too serious to be
played twice.

CAMILLA: To play it twice.

JENNIFER: Yes, too serious to play. I shall tell Maxi about
our secret. He's lost faith in me. Because of all this. He thinks
I am hard and heartless—and jealous. I don't want him to suffer
because of us. From now I am going to protect him from you.

CAMILLA: This is a game to be played.

JENNIFER: Why do you have to go on repeating that all
the time.

CAMILLA: You are no longer my accomplice. Since you've
fallen in love you've become blind and deaf. (*Low and intense*)
Do you remember that time you stayed with Aunt Alice and I
didn't want to come with you? When you were bitten by a
snake—and I telephoned you during the night because I knew
that something had happened to you. I developed a temperature
at the same time you did——

JENNIFER: Yes, Cam—we knew everything about one another
then. Before . . .

CAMILLA: And now you don't know anything. You know
nothing, nothing at all.

JENNIFER: That's not true. You're not talking to Mother—or
one of the vultures.

CAMILLA: Oh, clear off. Go to Maxi. Tell him everything
about us. About our feelings about the village—Go on. . .

JENNIFER: Why don't you look at me? What are you doing?

CAMILLA (*Taking a piece of paper out of her dress and
tearing it up*): This is our document. You see—I'm tearing it to
shreds. We have been prised from one another. Now we hunt

alone. On different fronts. Against one another. Go away—you've become a vulture—one of them. You've developed into a really ape-like vulture. And I—I'll go my own way, too. *(Bursting into loud sobs.)* You didn't even know I was going to do it.

JENNIFER: Know what?

CAMILLA: Look at me. Listen to my thoughts, Jen—darling Jen, don't you know anything, anything at all. Can't you see. Can't you see.

(Pause.)

JENNIFER: It's not true. It's not true. You didn't want to die.

CAMILLA: I'm so clumsy. I fell and upset the water jug. It alarmed the housekeeper. Forgive me, Jen.

JENNIFER: No, Camilla. It was a game. A stupid silly game.

CAMILLA: You know the truth.

JENNIFER: I know it's time to stop playing. Cam. We are adults now.

CAMILLA: I am an adult.

JENNIFER: Don't you understand that the time for games is over.

CAMILLA *(Proud and simply)*: That was no game. I want your lover.

JENNIFER: And you tried to kill yourself because I'm alive, for my sake.

CAMILLA: I didn't die. I'm alive, and I want your lover, Jen.

JENNIFER: If you'd died I'd have thought it was a crazy game that ended badly. Why do you tell me now? Why must you hurt me—now?

CAMILLA: Because you're in my way. Mother is right. And all those vultures in the village are right too. We've always hated one another—we've got nothing in common at all. We laughed at everyone in secret—because there was nothing else to share. Now we've grown up—and we hate in the open, too.

JENNIFER: I can't begin to hate you—not like that—

CAMILLA: You won't find it hard. It only needs him to put

his arm round your shoulder, to kiss you. . .

JENNIFER: —for him to believe your sincerity. To believe in your letter. Now all hell's broken loose, Cam.

CAMILLA: Farewell sister—well met, my mortal enemy.

CURTAIN

ACT THREE

Scene One

Monday morning.

Mrs. Lien, Mrs. Haag-Seglidkin and Marcus Trastheim can be seen approaching the house through the garden. They would appear to be highly upset, continually stopping and arguing and gesticulating with one another. Eventually they reach the door—opening it very gingerly before they dare step into the room.

DOLLY: . . . but I am so distraught, Viveka. Supposing I begin crying.

VIVEKA: We have to carry out our duty.

MARCUS: This is an act of rescue to be precise.

VIVEKA: We are Martha's oldest friends.

MARCUS: We must not forget the children in the choir.

VIVEKA: I just can't forget Martha. Poor, poor Martha.

MARCUS: I think it would be best if I act as spokesman.

VIVEKA: You are too young, Marcus. I'll take care of any speaking to be done.

MARCUS: But, Aunt Viveka——

VIVEKA: Just you leave anything to be said to me.

DOLLY: I'm going to weep. It's all too sad.

VIVEKA: You are not going to shed a single tear. Sh— I can hear them coming now.

(All three heads swing round to the door leading to the main part of the house. Waiting. They look at one another, in silence. Maxi, deep in thought, enters the room: he lights his pipe before becoming aware of the deputation. Only when he moves towards the garden door does he notice them—then he moves back a pace. Pause.)

MAXI: Good—morning.

(They do not return his greetings. He looks at them puzzled,

then he turns away. They all stare at him with curiosity.)

Has anything happened? Marcus, what is the meaning of this?

DOLLY *(Beside herself with excitement):* I'm going to cry, I know I am.

MAXI: What is the matter? Why are you all staring at me?

MARCUS: If you're addressing yourself to me, I can only answer that I don't speak to scum—to be precise.

MAXI: What in heaven's name——

VIVEKA: We've come here to talk to Martha Behrens. We would like to help our poor dear friend in her misfortune.

DOLLY: How can you stand there so calmly—you've ruined the lives of three women. Viveka—I am not going to cry.

MARCUS: If I was a shot—it would be my duty to challenge you to a duel.

MAXI: I only hope you all know what you're talking about— I most certainly don't.

VIVEKA: A typically masculine attitude. Denial. Guilty, too.

(Maxi withdraws from the conversation and remains standing to one side, silent. The three turn to one another, gesticulating silently. They swallow hard, keeping quiet. Then Mrs. Behrens enters.)

MARTHA: I thought I heard voices in here. . .

(But her pleasure at seeing them disappears when she sees the expressions on their faces.)

VIVEKA: Poor Martha.

DOLLY: Dear dear Martha. I shall have to cry now.

MARCUS: Aunt Martha——

MAXI: Good morning, Aunt Martha—did you sleep well?

MARTHA: Thank you—I did.

VIVEKA: How can you speak to him?

MARCUS: I just don't understand how you can allow him to remain under your roof. Eat your bread—to be precise.

MARTHA: But my good friends. Let's sit down, shall we. How about something to drink—I'll just go and get a tray—

VIVEKA: Dear Martha—We—your oldest friends here—

Marcus: We consider it our duty to—(*Silenced by a look from Viveka*).

Viveka: Martha. You are a weak woman. Criminally weak. You were never able to rear your daughters properly. And because of this—because one of them has—Unhappiness has again cast its heavy shadow over your world. We want you to know that we shall stand by you.

Dolly (*A pathetic echo*): In this trying time.

Marcus: Precisely. Against a scoundrel like him.

Maxi: What do you want? Can't you tell me what it is you are holding against me? And stop giving us your pious sermons.

Viveka: There speaks a guilty conscience.

Martha: But my dears—I really don't understand.

Viveka: Martha—that man is a seducer.

Dolly: He has ravished your lamb, your little lamb.

Maxi: Are you all out of your minds?

Viveka (*Very loudly and worthily*): Camilla told Dolly the whole story of her tragic action. This man—engaged to your daughter Jennifer—is the father of the unhappy child that Camilla will give birth to in shame and misery.

Dolly: Bravo, Viveka. Well said.

Marcus: As a first step—we insist that you drive this adventurer from your door.

(*Maxi has moved right away from the village group—Mrs. Behrens, in an obvious quandary, looks out at the garden, silent. Pause.*)

Viveka: Dear Martha—I know what a terrible shock this must be to you. If our information is correct—you had simply no idea what was going on under your own roof.

Maxi: If you will allow me, Aunt Martha—I should dearly like to show these visitors out.

Marcus: The time for force has passed. We are staying here, my good fellow.

Viveka: Dear friend. We have come to help you decide on a course of action. Firstly—firstly—this profligate, this renegade

—must be thrown out, sent away from this village, out of our sight.

MARTHA: But none of this is true.

VIVEKA: I can understand how you shudder at the truth.

MARCUS: Aunt Martha, you must find it hard to believe your own ears.

DOLLY: We have come to you, dear Martha, knowing how weak you are.

MARTHA: I'm afraid you misunderstand me. Camilla has told me absolutely everything.

MAXI: Good Lord, Aunt Martha. Don't say any more. Let them get out with their overwhelming curiosity unsatisfied.

MARTHA: Maxi dear, I can't do that. I owe my very good friends some explanation.

VIVEKA: Martha—what are you trying to say?

DOLLY: Give me another handkerchief, Viveka.

MARTHA: Camilla is not expecting a baby—she has certainly never been pregnant. It was just a joke on her part—one of her sudden whims. I don't honestly think she knew what she was doing to me.

VIVEKA (*Breathing out like a pricked balloon*): Words fail me.

MARTHA: You must forgive Camilla. She is not very well.

VIVEKA: Not very well! I must say—of all the heartless, impertinent—

DOLLY: I'm so glad—so very glad.

MAXI: Well this is one expedition that got lost in the jungle. We would like to wish you a good morning. The path back lies through the garden.

MARTHA: No Maxi—we can't part like this. Viveka—you know I haven't much influence with my girls. They are so independent. But I know they don't mean any harm with their peculiar violent ways.

VIVEKA: Camilla drives me mad. She did this to make a laugh-ingstock of me.

DOLLY: She told me first.

VIVEKA: Don't be a goose, Dolly.

MARCUS: But why—why—why? Why did Camilla do this?

VIVEKA: To make laughingstocks of all of us. Come along, Dolly, Marcus. We no longer have anything to do in Martha's house.

(*They begin to make their departure in silence and bitterness.*)

MARTHA: Don't leave me like this. You've got to forgive Camilla. Forgive me. You all know how utterly miserable I am about Camilla.

(*Jennifer has come in during this speech and stands listening for a while before interrupting.*)

JENNIFER: Mother—must you always deprecate yourself—and us.

MARTHA: Jen darling—can't you tell them how miserable I am. No. You've never understood me either. You never wanted me to have any friends. And you wouldn't even comfort me in my grief.

JENNIFER: You found comfort alright. With your friends. What has there ever been that belonged to us—Camilla and I?

VIVEKA: There you see. This is a conspiracy. Jennifer was in on the whole story.

MARCUS: Jen. Please greet your sister from me and give her a message, will you? Tell her that after this, nothing, nothing will ever be the same again. From now on we go our own separate ways.

(*Maxi and Jennifer approach the three with determination, they are forced to move back, step by step.*)

MAXI: Do you think we're going to have to resort to force.

JENNIFER: Take Father's pistol. It's in the drawer of my writing desk.

DOLLY (*In panic*) : They're going to use a gun. Run Viveka—they'll shoot us.

MARTHA: Why must you hurt me so. You are driving my friends away.

JENNIFER: Oh—darling. How utterly miserable it all is. We waited for these few days together here. We made such plans to be carefree and happy, you and I and Camilla, too. We were going to have such fun—racing along the beach—we were going to see who could swim round the mouth of the river first. We were going to give you the taste of a home, a real home. Mother. . . .

MAXI: Oh Jen. All this business is so far outside my own experience. But surely—surely—Camilla—Camilla must be a very sick girl in some way.

MARTHA: They are both sick. They have no natural feelings for their mother at all. They isolate her from all human contact.

JENNIFER: Mother—please don't say more. Go and lie down for a bit. I'll make everything right again. I promise you that. Oh God. I shall go see Aunt Viveka—I shall go see Aunt Dolly. I shall bake them a cake as a peace offering. I shall give your friends back to you—and you back to your friends.

MARTHA (*Surprised*): You—you will put everything right again—between them and me?

JENNIFER: Between you and the village. Yes, yes. I shall polish our shield and give our house a face lifting.

MARTHA: Are you really going to do that? I can't believe that you're going to give me the happiness that a truly good daughter would. Are you?

JENNIFER: Me or Camilla. Now don't say any more, Mother—go and have a little rest.

MAXI: Jen—that is hardly the way to speak to your Mother.

JENNIFER: Forgive me, dearest. You don't really know me very well yet. Mother—give me just one day—one day—and you'll see everything will be alright.

MARTHA (*Vaguely murmuring as she goes off*): Just one day.

JENNIFER: You can't possibly be happy here with all this lunacy.

MAXI: I find you all rather strange—I don't understand so much that goes on here. Camilla—both of your relationship to your Mother. I'm frightened for you.

JENNIFER: Aren't you frightened for our love.

MAXI: Tell me something, Jen—is Camilla sick—mentally sick?

JENNIFER: Camilla loves you, Maxi.

MAXI: That's idiotic nonsense.

JENNIFER: She wrote the truth in that letter, Maxi. She wanted to die so that she could give me—you.

MAXI: She's mad.

JENNIFER: I thought she was playing a part—as usual. There's so much acting in this house—it's been our favorite game since Father died.

MAXI: You can't play around with life and death. These things are too serious.

JENNIFER: You've no idea of the games Camilla and I have been up to. Good God Maxi—if only you'd been here during those terrible weeks when Father was under suspicion. The whispers—Mother's tragic expression—and all the time those hyenas crept in and out. Camilla and I called them ape-like vultures—the worst possible name we could think up for them. We made a pact—Camilla and I. It was all very dramatic. We woke one another up at midnight and crept out to the cemetery—I can remember every detail very clearly—we pricked our fingers and collected the blood in a thimble—then we made a mixture with mould from one of the graves—and ate it. We swore an oath—to kill anyone who threatened Father.

MAXI: But I thought you and Camilla were never very friendly. I'm under the impression that you two had nothing in common.

JENNIFER: Mother never knew anything about this at all. We had our own secret language. Whoever came home first and saw that the ape-like vultures were here, would go upstairs and leave a sign in the window—then the other one wouldn't have to go in and be polite—we even tried to kill them.

MAXI: You tried to do what?

JENNIFER: Oh, we took some bleach and mixed it with the coffee. They all got ill. Aunt Viveka made Mother take a test of all the wallpapers and the kitchen utensils—but they recovered.

MAXI: I can just see you both. Two half-grown girls going around with sad eyes and tight-lipped mouths.

JENNIFER: We had a secret sign in our school books—in our napkin rings—we even had bracelets we'd made with AYS all over the place. The AYS stood for Are You Smiling—you see we had sworn never to laugh at them—or Mother.

MAXI: But surely your mother must have seen through you.

JENNIFER: We did think she'd found out something—she would question Camilla about me—and me about Camilla. But we used to lie—we were most accomplished liars. Oh, Maxi—it's childish to tell you all this about us—about myself.

MAXI: But you're a grownup now. You must see the hyenas in proper perspective. Meaningless, small-minded petty people in an obscure corner of the world. Grateful for any little sensation. You mustn't go on hating them—they're not worth it.

JENNIFER: Who said I didn't see through them a long time ago. I laugh at them now. No, it's not them I hate.

MAXI: Don't stand there like that—it scares me.

JENNIFER (*Laughing*): I don't want you to touch me under this roof—I don't even want you to kiss me.

MAXI: You're right. It's—stifling—don't you long for a storm, a breath of fresh air—something to break the tension? I feel I'm choking here.

JENNIFER: You're saying that we'll never come back here again—

MAXI: I don't follow you. . . .

JENNIFER: You must go back to town now. No—let me finish what I've got to say. You can't remain here—for Camilla's sake. You never know what we two girls from the backwood might get up to. We may both come to your room in the night—undressed. We might even pour a sleeping draught in your nightcap—and that would make you an easily hooked prey. You must leave today.

Maxi: But what about you?

Jennifer: Give me one day to sort out this problem. Then I shall come to you—and we'll hide ourselves. We will live together—only for one another.

Maxi: That sounds like an escape to me.

Jennifer: You would have been able to react like any other man who loves a woman with a charming little sister—if it wasn't Camilla and me it concerned. We would have spared her feelings—you would have been a big brother. (*Laughing*) I daren't let Camilla play her games with you—I know her power too well.

Maxi: But what of your mother and Camilla—when you leave them?

Jennifer: I have the whip-hand now. After that terrible deed of hers last night I shall offer her an ultimatum. She is going to have to choose between two painful alternatives—and she'll stay here.

Maxi: But you said that for a time you were very close. . . .

Jennifer: For ten years. When Father died I was nine, Camilla eight.

Maxi: But you can't just begin to hate her now. . . .

Jennifer: Oh, can't you see it. She loves you. I am frightened of her. I am scared of seeing you change. And one day. . . .

Maxi: Darling—you don't know what you're saying.

Jennifer: I know what I want. You must leave today. I'll come up to your room now and do your packing for you—I want to be alone with you in your room during these last few hours we have together. I've even written about it. In my very private diary. About the day when I am alone with the man I love.

(*Maxi follows her uncertainly out of the room. Camilla comes in as they leave, she has altered her hair style and wears a pretty, feminine summer dress. Seeing that she is alone she goes up to the mirror and starts to preen and pose in it. Jennifer finds her still in front of the mirror when she comes back.*)

JENNIFER (*Standing looking at her for a moment*): A darling sight, Cam. Our little sunbeam sees herself mirrored in a golden frame. You look charming, Cam, very charming.

CAMILLA: Good morning, Jen. You look pretty wonderful yourself.

JENNIFER: I have a high color and very red lips, Cam. Your lips take on this color when a man kisses you—hard and long.

CAMILLA: Officially you have a great advantage—but we haven't seen you as the bride yet.

JENNIFER: Oh, you will one day. My wedding will take place in town. You will wear white with a garland of modest flowers in your golden hair. What a pretty and touching part for you to play it will be!

CAMILLA: Do you mind if I open the window, Jennifer—there's an unpleasant smell in here.

JENNIFER: The hyenas paid a call—but we drove them out. Mother is most upset—she thinks they'll never come here again, on account of you. Because your baby—turned out to be just wishful thinking.

CAMILLA: You really ought to change your underwear more often. You stink like a farm hand.

JENNIFER: I shall indulge in the most fastidious personal hygiene—for my husband's sake. (*Pause*) Have you seen Maxi's tennis racket? That's what I came in for—but the sight of you rather took my breath away.

CAMILLA: It's on the table over there. Can I come and play with you in this dress?

JENNIFER: We are not going to play tennis. We're getting all Maxi's things together. He's going into town on the next bus.

CAMILLA: That's not true.

JENNIFER: He doesn't want to stay on—because of you. Give me the racket.

CAMILLA: So he's frightened of me, is he? And so are you,

dear Jen. You're frightened of me. (*Laughing*) You don't trust your fiancé—your baby sister has changed her hair style and donned a décolleté dress. Of course you shall have his little racket—you must rush to help him, sort out his lousy under-wear—He's not really taking that bus is he?

JENNIFER (*Looking at Camilla searchingly*): And don't go and change now. You can't travel in with him—you'll never find the money in time.

CAMILLA: I hadn't thought of that, Jen. I know you took all my money when you were in my room last night. . . .

JENNIFER: I have also taken the precaution of taking Mother's money too.

CAMILLA: Don't get so worked up—and so serious. You've got to concentrate on making yourself beautiful to say good-by to your young man. I am not going away today. It may even be three days before I go into town. I've got to put things right here with our dear neighbors, for Mother's sake. There are still one or two bones to be picked you know. Go on—take the racket. Run, run, he's waiting. . . .

CURTAIN

Scene Two

Two hours later.

Camilla comes into the room in front of Maxi—and moves slowly over to the window—she stands there looking out.

CAMILLA: No—don't go. Don't wait for Jen. She's letting me have these few minutes alone with you—to say good-by. It's really rather funny that you've got to go, isn't it? All because two people are in love with you you leave this lovely peaceful country house.

MAXI: Must we talk about it?

CAMILLA: No, we mustn't. What shall we talk about then— I like the color of your pajamas—I love the untidy way you keep your hair—your pipe smells better than any other pipe.

I love your long, powerful strides. . . . But we can talk about all this later on—in town.

Maxi: I love Jennifer.

Camilla: I believe you. I know that's what you believe for the moment. In fact you'll still go on loving her for a while. I don't know what plans you two have made for the future— If you're going to be together in town or will you get together in your room—surely you're not going to keep your passions in check any longer.

Maxi: Camilla—stop talking like that at once.

Camilla: Jen will be very happy for a short time—she must have that memory. You are the first man in her life—but mind you tire of her quickly—I don't want her around when I come to you.

Maxi: When you come where?

Camilla: I shall leave this damned hole. Soon. In a week, a month, I don't know. I shall have to pacify Mother's baboons first—then I'm coming to town.

Maxi: But good God, Camilla. . . .

Camilla: Call me Cam—it sounds so idiotic when you pro· nounce the whole name. Say Cam, Maxi.

Maxi: Cam. I'm not at all certain that you realize what you've done. You've ruined my holiday—and you're behaving like a stupid spoilt child.

Camilla: And I've been very disobedient, too. I tried to commit suicide without asking permission first. Maxi, forgive me. I adore you.

Maxi: You are not in love with me—this is just a hellish game on your part in order not to let go of Jennifer.

Camilla: I'm very fond of my sister Jen. But what I feel for you is a yearning stronger than death itself—I read that somewhere.

Maxi (*Very strongly—goes over and shakes her by the shoulders*) : Why can't you ever tell the truth. Stop feeding yourself on those senseless lies.

CAMILLA: You malign me—I am telling you the truth. I love Jen. I love you much more. I've had to make a choice. I've chosen you. Not Jen. Sometime or other we had to have enough of one another—and this house.

MAXI: I still don't believe you. But *if* you are telling the truth—then I must ask you to kill your feelings for me. Are you listening to what I'm saying? I love Jen, Jen, Jen.

CAMILLA: When you put your stern face on there are two small ugly lines on one side of your mouth. They're so touching.

MAXI: When Jen and I are married you'll come and visit us. We three will all be such good friends and we'll look back on all this. . . .

CAMILLA: You will never marry Jen. You're blind where she's concerned. Because you were the first man to kiss her you think it's your duty to marry her. It doesn't mean anything, Maxi. Alright—if I'm unlucky then you'll have to marry her—in a month or so. Even then it won't mean anything—Maxi, you've got to leave soon.

MAXI: Camilla, Cam. Don't you realize that this parting is final. We cannot meet again if you persist in playing your unholy game.

CAMILLA: We all realize that. Jen, you and I—we three can never all meet again. It's either got to be Jen—or me, and you. Today it's you and Jen, but tomorrow it's going to be Cam and Maxi.

MAXI: Oh, you're impossible. It's hard to be strict with you. You're just like some obstinate stiff-necked child. You refuse to accept and face reality, the truth.

CAMILLA: I'm a woman, Maxi. My mouth is soft and red— let my fingers caress your cheeks, run through your hair.

MAXI: Good-by Camilla. I would have dearly loved to be your friend. I want to be your friend—and stay your friend.

CAMILLA: I can hear the bus now. It's at the top of the hill. You can't pass me unless you push me aside—or kiss me.

MAXI: Please will you step to one side and let me go.

CAMILLA: You'll have to rush, Maxi—and you're going to kiss me or that bus leaves without you.

(*Maxi in a sudden temper approaches her and takes her in his arms. He kisses her once briefly—and then again at greater length. He rushes away.*)

CAMILLA (*Shouting triumphantly*): Maxi.

(*Mrs. Behrens comes into the room—dressed as though she were going out to the village. She moves quickly—avoiding looking at Camilla who follows her mother with her eyes.*)

CAMILLA: Are you looking for something?

MARTHA: My gray gloves. There they are.

CAMILLA: Where are you off to, Mother? Your committee meeting isn't till seven this evening.

MARTHA: I have something to do in the village. I'm surely allowed to go out when I wish to—or do I need to ask your permission first.

CAMILLA: Oh, Mother. Don't take all that nonsense about my baby too seriously. I'll talk to them. I'll go to Aunt Dolly, Aunt Viveka, and Aunt Marcus. They'll forgive me.

MARTHA: It's too late . . . they don't want to see us any more. I forbid you to visit them—you'll only make everything worse.

CAMILLA: Well, if you don't want me to. . . .

MARTHA: I don't know what I've done to deserve such punishment. I lost my husband, my son never grew up—and you two. What on earth is going to become of me. You'll both leave me—you'll go your own ways, not that you aren't doing so already—you'll leave me here in loneliness and shame.

CAMILLA: One of us will always live with you. Gentle and considerate. We'll go to church with you, accompany you to your committee meetings.

MARTHA: One of you—you?

CAMILLA: Me? Perhaps, perhaps not. We don't know yet. But you love Jen so much more than you do me.

MARTHA: I don't care what you do. Where you live . . . I have had enough. I have had more than enough.

Camilla: Isn't Maxi a nice young man?

Martha: Yes—and you had to drive him away—you and your disgusting ideas. What did he ever do to you?

Camilla: You will be so proud of him. And his wife. His darling small children. What highlights your trips to town are going to be. And when you come back home you'll have so much to tell all your friends "they've bought a new phonograph —with television and a four-speed turntable—and little Maxi is so gifted. He's in the top of his class."

Martha: You might at least stop trying to drive me away, too.

Camilla: Forgive me, Mother—I'm not really being spiteful now.

Martha: I just can't believe you any longer—I won't believe in either of you again. It's as if you both hated me for having given birth to you.

Camilla: We'll improve, Mother.

Martha: Jen says she'll go to my friends and ask for their forgiveness. It's too late. They don't want to know us any longer.

Camilla: Mother—do only your so-called friends mean anything to you? And what they think? Don't you care about Jen and me? Can't you see how we're both suffering—we've reached the critical moment of our lives.

Martha: You two bring me nothing but sorrow and shame. You laugh at me, you laugh at my friends. You laugh at the whole village—and I was born here.

Camilla: Perhaps one day you'll understand us.

Martha: Understand you. I do that already. You are heartless, cruel.

Camilla: Mother—that's just the right description.

Martha: Your only pleasure is found in—hurting others.

Camilla: Our only pleasure—bravo Mother! You find such appropriate words.

Martha: Hangmen—that's what you both are.

Camilla: Well said, Mother. Hangmen. Do you think a lady

hangman wears a red dress and black stockings? Or perhaps she wears a black dress and red stockings. No—she must wear a red dress—because of the blood. Aren't you going to say good-by to me—where are you off to anyway?

MARTHA: I am going to visit my friends. And they will refuse to open their doors to me. They put down the receiver when they hear my voice over the telephone.

CAMILLA: Mother—don't go.

MARTHA: I shall demean myself because of my daughters. I shall beg their forgiveness because I am the mother of two fully grown girls who are poisoning the whole of my life.

CAMILLA: You are a strange woman, Mother. Can you really go from door to door, abasing yourself. I don't recognize my mother. Don't you think that perhaps, perhaps you, Jen, and I should sit here together—and light the big open fire, and sit here together roasting chestnuts and laughing at the village.

MARTHA: You are a—blasphemer.

CAMILLA: Mother—don't go. Wait a few days. Then they'll come running to you.

MARTHA: I am going now—perhaps that will teach you both a lesson.

CAMILLA: I wouldn't put too much faith in that if I were you. After all, Jen and I are your unfortunate small daughters.

(*Mrs. Behrens leaves the room, bent and small, dressed in black. She meets Jennifer who shouts after her—but she does not respond.*)

JENNIFER: Where are you going, Mother?

CAMILLA: Our beloved mother is going on a journey of penance—to Aunt Dolly, Aunt Viveka, and Marcus—on account of me.

JENNIFER: How can she toady like that. So damnably undignified and stupid.

CAMILLA: Can you understand her?

JENNIFER: You know I've never been able to do that. Look at her. Look how shriveled she is. And she doesn't dare walk in the middle of the path any longer—she's got to make way for everyone she meets. She can't bear to be hurt by anyone—she so wants to be loved by all the world. It's heartbreaking to watch her.

CAMILLA: I pity her—but God how I despise her. Jen—I feel as though I could weep for her, just this once.

JENNIFER: We shall—we shall put everything right. That is to say, one of us will.

CAMILLA: One of us will stay here in the village. One of us—will go to Maxi in town.

(*Pause.*)

JENNIFER: And now, Cam—shall we have our final sisterly meeting in front of the fire?

CAMILLA: The last one, Jen.

(*They look at one another for a moment—then they each take a cushion and move to the fireplace. Jen lights the open fire—takes a dish with apples beside her and begins to throw them up in the air. They each place an ashtray beside themselves and sit facing one another. They have obviously sat like this thousands of times in the past years, exchanging confidences.*)

CAMILLA (*Sitting on her knees and making obviously ritual gestures with her hands and head*) : We shall drown the vultures in the whirlpool of the river.

JENNIFER (*Echoing*): We shall drown the vultures in the whirlpool of the river.

CAMILLA: With their foul mouths that reek of cabbage.

JENNIFER: With their hands that are washed for Christmas.

CAMILLA: And their dribbling lips.

JENNIFER: And their big white listening ears.

CAMILLA: Shall all go to the bottom.

JENNIFER (*Striking the floor with her fist*) : There drowns one vulture.

CAMILLA: Two have been drowned.

JENNIFER: Three have been drowned in the murky whirlpool

of the river.

(*They both laugh heartily—then light their cigarettes.*)

JENNIFER: You do understand, don't you, that I must arrange things for Mother before I go?

CAMILLA: You are such a loving daughter, Jen.

JENNIFER: When I leave—I shall not be coming back.

CAMILLA: It will be empty without you, dear sister.

JENNIFER: Maxi and I have discussed it pretty thoroughly. We shall be married as soon as I get to town. And we'll go abroad as soon as his grant comes through. Berlin, Paris, Rome. I shall be at Maxi's side, looking out over a strange and unknown world. I'm free, Cam, free.

CAMILLA: You will send me a picture postcard occasionally—won't you? And you'll mark your bedroom window with a cross—that room where you'll be both sleeping off your weariness side by side.

JENNIFER: We'll miss you, Cam—but we will write long letters. Only we won't be coming home for a good many years. Perhaps you'll be married too when we do get back.

CAMILLA: I shall have Marcus Trastheim. We shall take choir rehearsals, and form a new one, with the confirmands. I shall push the doctor's daughter out of the way and play the Madonna myself in the Christmas play—who knows perhaps I'll appear with my own child in my lap.

JENNIFER: You must have my room. You've always wanted it. And my stamp collection—and Father's fitted dressing case, and his revolver. In fact you're to have everything I possess.

CAMILLA: How good you are. While you're traveling around with Maxi I shall act out my penance—for Mother's sake. I have so many sins to answer for. Jen—I shall sacrifice myself.

JENNIFER: I don't like the tone of your voice. Why don't you look at me when you speak?

CAMILLA: What do you want me to do? Sing a hymn of gratitude? Shall I clasp my hands in joy at the prospect of a bright future.

JENNIFER: I don't like that voice of yours—or your gestures—or your face. Do you want to pick a quarrel, Cam?

CAMILLA: There is nothing to quarrel about. I'm leaving on Friday, Jen. And if you ask me what I'll do for money the answer is I've found the bank books—all of them.

JENNIFER: I'm afraid that you've misunderstood me. I'm serious, Cam, deadly serious. I order you to stay.

CAMILLA: I'm not joking either, Jen. I'm going my own way.

JENNIFER: For God's sake, Cam—don't start fighting. That will be the end for both of us.

CAMILLA: Don't you see—I'll go crazy, you and Maxi. You with Maxi—I can't let it happen. I couldn't go on living.

JENNIFER: You've got to, Cam. *You've got to!*

CAMILLA: No, Jen. No. There's nothing else for me.

JENNIFER (*In anguish*) : Good God, Cam. Don't you see what you're doing to me. Don't you know what beast you're bringing to life in both of us.

CAMILLA: I am not afraid, Jen. I have implicit faith in my victory. I know what power I have over my beloved. . . .

JENNIFER: Don't say any more. Shut up.

(*They remain sitting by the fire, but the atmosphere has changed—the former cosiness has given way to hate and violence.*)

JENNIFER (*In a different tone of voice*) : Don't forget that you gave me the trump card by what you did the other night.

CAMILLA: And don't you forget that it's a weapon I can use against you, for Maxi's sake.

JENNIFER: Don't forget the lie you spread about your baby, Cam.

CAMILLA: One day we'll all three laugh about that.

JENNIFER: Don't forget that I only need pay a few visits in the village—I shall whisper a few words here and there, to the Pastor, the squire, to the doctor—don't forget the doctor.

CAMILLA: How well you've taken a leaf from the vultures' book. (*Laughing*) You'll start to join them in their whispers about me.

JENNIFER: Oh, yes—and I shall whisper so carefully, so very regretfully, so insiduously, Cam.

CAMILLA: But there's nothing they don't know about me in the village—you won't find anything new to tell them about mad Cam.

JENNIFER: How about telling them that you're mentally ill?

CAMILLA: They'd pretend to be astonished and gape "But we've always known it."

JENNIFER: I'll tell them you've started wandering around the village at night with Father's revolver—that you may harm them. There are a thousand and one things I can find to say if you'll just stop to think.

CAMILLA: You're catching me up with all those expert lies.

JENNIFER: And after two weeks—I shall drop the bombshell. I shall ask for help, from the doctor and the farmers around. For Mother's sake and mine I shall demand that you are sent to a hospital—I shall let you become a certified lunatic.

CAMILLA (*Silent at first, then she laughs, a trifle strained*): Bravo, Jen. First round to you.

JENNIFER: The village hates us, for everything we've done to them.

CAMILLA: And how they hate us, Jen.

JENNIFER: But they'll believe in me now I'm an adult and regret the error of my childish ways. They'll have confidence in my word, Cam, now that I'm engaged and going to be married.

CAMILLA: That's what's so awful. I believe you. They will believe in you, too.

JENNIFER: If you drive me to it—I shall go to these lengths.

CAMILLA: You wouldn't do this to your own sister surely?

JENNIFER: Against a mortal enemy?

CAMILLA: They'll believe you—they really will believe you.

JENNIFER: They'll send an ambulance with a wailing siren for you, remember how scared of sirens we always were—and you will be taken off, to an asylum.

CAMILLA: Then I really will be ill—seriously ill.

JENNIFER: But *if* you stay with Mother—then I won't do it.

CAMILLA: So that's your little plan—clever strategy on your part, Jen. Either I remain and play the part of a sacrificing younger sister and loving daughter, or, I'm to be a lunatic and shut up in an asylum.

JENNIFER: Without him, nothing has any meaning.

CAMILLA (*Suddenly laughing wildly*): You are stupid, Jen—completely and utterly idiotic. If you get your own way—I mean if you start your whispering campaign and it succeeds—if I am sent away from my oppressed and unhappy . . . then you'll have to stay here. You won't be able to go away. Farewell to your happy future, with Maxi in Paris and Rome. Hahahaha, you'll tie yourself to this bloody village with such a firm knot— You didn't think of that, did you. . . .

JENNIFER (*Calmly and coldly*) : I have thought of everything, Cam. Even the possibility of my having to stay here.

CAMILLA (*Scared for the first time*) : Jen—you'd stay if. . .

JENNIFER: I cannot build my own happiness on my sister's downfall. I'd never know a moment's peace if I did that. Thinking of you alone . . . in a cell. And Mother, alone, here. And the village whispering, gossiping around here. Then I would stay, Cam.

CAMILLA: And Maxi?

JENNIFER: I should forbid Maxi to come here. I won't see him. I won't answer his letters. He'll forget me. I'd kill my love, Cam—because of you.

CAMILLA: I really must admire you, Jen. I can see it all so very clearly now. Your plans are incredible, foolproof. You really do hate me, don't you, Jen?

JENNIFER: We are very involved with one another. I am bound to you. You are the only person I have had to talk to all my life. We have opened our hearts to one another, exchanged confidences, Cam. Do you understand now, I am asking you to give me Maxi. Give me my travels—or else. . .

CAMILLA: Or else life is finished for us both.

JENNIFER: You've said it, Cam, finished for us two sisters.

CAMILLA: And you believe, you really think you could make me ill. Oh yes—I would be. What's happened, Jen? I'm frightened.

JENNIFER: I've never been scared of anybody—but I am now, of you. We've shown each other the way to hell.

CAMILLA: And I'm scared of you for the first time in my life. Isn't there anyone we can ask for advice?

JENNIFER: No one. We are alone in this Cam. We are completely alone in body, soul, and heart.

CAMILLA: Hug me, Jen—the way you used to. Hug me tightly.

JENNIFER: I would love you to stroke the back of my head, Cam. But I daren't cross the carpet to you.

CAMILLA: Jen—

JENNIFER: I daren't come near you—you could hurt me.

CAMILLA: Jen.

JENNIFER: Cam. Camilla. We have come to hate one another.

CAMILLA: I've been hurt, Jen. And I'm bleeding. Bleeding to death. I would have liked to stay here—for your sake. I can't, Jen—I can't—I haven't the strength.

JENNIFER: You must. Just for this once you've got to find the strength. For my sake. For Maxi's sake. For Maxi's sake, Cam—you love him as much as I do. . .

CAMILLA: Jen—I should never have kissed him. I shouldn't have kissed him.

JENNIFER: We never learnt to give up anything for one another.

CAMILLA: We were so strong—unbeatable together. We'll go under when we're parted.

JENNIFER: But I'm offering both of us a way out. . .

CAMILLA: Your life with Maxi—where strange birds sing. And mine here with Mother, in this village.

JENNIFER: Forgive me, Cam—forgive me. There's nothing I can do about it.

CAMILLA: Do you know you're killing me? (*Jennifer, unable to reply, starts to sniff.*) You give me two alternatives—to stay or to die. And if I stay, I die too.

JENNIFER: You love him.

CAMILLA: How strange it all is—and how simple. So easy to take the crazy way—no one will notice how it's done. We didn't know, we didn't know, neither of us, neither you nor I. We've locked each other in—there's only one way out—and I shall have to take it myself. For my sister has deserted me. She is on her honeymoon abroad. Shall I show you the pretty postcard she sent me. Shall I show you all the beautiful gifts she has showered on us— (*She crosses over to Jen*) My sister is wonderful—there's never been an older sister like her. We've always shared everything—our dreams—our plans—we had our own secret language and we stood alone against the whole world. But then a young man stepped into our lives—no one could guess, but they both fell in love with him. It was an odd coincidence, wasn't it? A little tragic, unworthy of the two sisters. Don't cry, Jen—not yet. There'll be such a long, long time for your tears. Forgive me Jen. Forgive me.

(*Camilla leaves the room on this last sentence—Jen looks silently after her, unhappy and troubled. Suddenly she shouts:*)

JENNIFER: Cam, Camilla, Camilla.

(*In terror she gets up, holding her throat, waiting for the sound of the revolver shot that echoes through the house, then she sinks to the ground where Mrs. Behrens finds her when she comes back from the village—from her entry one can gather that her mission was totally unsuccessful. She comes in—shuts the door, begins to draw the curtains, for it is getting very dark.*)

MARTHA: Why are you sitting in the dark, Jen? I had to turn round and come back, Jen. I was frightened they'd slam their doors in my face. Where is Camilla? I must have a word with her. Where is Camilla?

CURTAIN

CHAP. VIII

THE GOLDEN GATE
A PLAY IN FOUR ACTS BY
DAVIÐ STEFÁNSSON

TRANSLATED FRM THE ICELANDIC BY

G. M. GATHORNE-HARDY

INTRODUCTION BY

EINAR HAUGEN

INTRODUCTION

The Golden Gate (*Gullna hliðið,* 1941) is built upon an Icelandic folk tale. Davið Stefánsson, who was fond of adding the designation "frá Fagraskógi" (from Fairwoods) to his name, was one of the foremost representatives of the national romanticism that dominated Icelandic literature in the interwar years. In Iceland these were the years of home rule, granted by Denmark in 1918, crowned in 1944 by a complete independence which was only briefly marred by the wartime presence of English and American troops after 1940. Icelandic authors no longer looked to Denmark for their audience, and writers like Davið Stefánsson won themselves a great reputation as exponents of this first blossoming of a free nation. Even would-be realists and radicals like Thórbergur Thórðarson and Halldór Laxness, who scourged their countrymen, did so in the name of a passionate love for their country. Both of them delved deeply into the folk life of Iceland, and Laxness in his *Íslandsklukkan (Bell of Iceland,* 1943) produced a truly national saga.

Davið Stefánsson's patriotism was of an entirely different but no less real sort. In words and forms of the utmost simplicity he succeeded in giving voice to a lyricism which struck a new note in the often harsh atmosphere of Icelandic literature. His first collection of poems, *Svartar fjaðrir (Black Feathers,* 1919), expressed a tenderness, a warmth, and a humor which immediately won him tremendous popularity. His love poems are memorable, with a lilting quality reminiscent of the ballad, and at the same time a jesting tone that keeps them from becoming sentimental. He is particularly successful in his lulla-

---

This Introduction has been reprinted from *Fire and Ice,* published by the University of Wisconsin Press in 1967.

bies, melodious poems written for children and adults alike. His poetry deals with people and is close to people, appealing to their emotions through a combination of sound and mood. In many of his poems there is a deep symbolic concern with the great problems of human life, love and hate, life and death.

In a series of collections he established himself as the "national poet" of his generation. His lyric descriptions of Icelandic scenery, his espousal of the simple virtues of life, and his whimsical drolleries endeared him to a public which was rapidly moving off the farms and into the cities. He expressed perfectly their nostalgia for the old and simple virtues, the faith and the hope of the past, while also suggesting a new and romantic view of life that gave hope for the future. His political views were mildly socialistic, but he always preserved a deep sense of solidarity with the soil from which his ancestors had sprung. His father was a farmer in the northern region of Eyjafjörður, able and prominent enough to be elected to the Althing; his uncle, Ólafur Daviðsson, was a folklorist from whom he learned a great deal, and to whose memory he was later to pen a vigorous tribute.[1] Born at Fagraskógur in 1895, a graduate of the gymnasium in Reykjavík in 1919, a great traveler and lover of books, Davi ð was librarian at Akureyri 1925–52. He remained unmarried to his death in 1964.

The Golden Gate was not his only venture into the dramatic field. In *Munkarnir á Möðruvöllum* (*The Monks at Möðruvellir*, 1926) he tried his hand quite unsuccessfully at recreating the Middle Ages. After his success with *The Golden Gate* in 1941 he tried again in *Vopn guðanna* (*The Weapons of the Gods*, 1944), based on the oriental tale of Josaphat and Barlaam, and in *Landið gleymda* (*The Forgotten Land,* 1953), on the rediscovery of Greenland by the Norwegian missionary Hans

---

[1] His uncle published a collection of folklore entitled *Íslenzkar gátur, skemmtanir, vikivakur og thular* (Reykjavík 1887-1903); the article by Davi ð Stefánsson appeared in his book *Mælt mál* (Reykjavík: Helgafell, 1963), 108-18.

Egede. Somehow neither of these had the dramatic qualities that would ensure them life on the stage. His one novel was more successful, *Sólon Islandus* (1940), the symbolic narrative of a nineteenth-century Icelandic vagabond. In the words of Stefán Einarsson, "it is a truly Icelandic tragedy, the life of an ambitious, artistic dreamer with no means to realize his ambition, or to develop his talents which might have borne fruit in a bigger nation."[2] It is understandable that Daviŏ, with all his own success, nevertheless could feel a deep kinship with this Icelandic Peer Gynt. He was basically a dreamer, and most of his writing builds on dreams.

The folk tale on which *The Golden Gate* is based was written down by the nineteenth-century national poet of Iceland, Matthías Jochumsson, in his student days, and printed in the collection by Jón Arnason.[3] The title of it is "Sálin hans Jóns mins," a phrase weakly translated as "The Soul of My Own John." It is a short and salty tale about a woman who is married to a good-for-nothing husband, but who nevertheless loves him enough to make a quite extraordinary effort to save his soul. Just as he dies, she holds a leather bag to his mouth and ties the soul up in the bag before it can escape. She hides the bag under her apron and starts off for heaven. On her knock, Saint Peter comes out and she begs him to admit her husband; when he rather curtly dismisses her, she reminds him of the time he denied his master, and he bangs the door in her face. She knocks again, and has a similar encounter with Saint Paul; she reminds him that he had persecuted Christians. The third person to come is the Virgin Mary, and she has the nerve to remind her that she had had an illegitimate child. When finally Christ himself comes out, she sees her chance and throws the bag into

---

[2] Einarsson, *History of Icelandic Literature*, p. 307.

[3] Arnason, *Íslenzkar Thjódsögur*, vol. 2, 39-40 (1954 edition, vol. 2, 42-43); English translation in *Icelandic Legends* (Collected by Jón Arnason), tr. by George E. J. Powell and Eiríkr Magnússon, Second Series (London, 1866), pp. 45-48.

heaven before he can close the door. Similar stories are known from other countries, but the Icelandic one has its special twist in the woman's outspokenness.[4]

The story amused Davið sufficiently for him to make a narrative poem out of it, with the same title as the folk tale, which appeared in his collection *Í Byggðum* (*In the Valleys*, 1933).[5] The spirit of his poem is far removed from that of the folk tale, in spite of the common plot. The angry dialogue with celestial persons is dropped: the only one she meets is St. Peter, and their conversation is quite harmonious. The body of the poem consists of the long journey from her home to the door of heaven, described in great detail as a laborious mountain climbing operation. Once she has reached the top, however, the descriptions of heaven are a whimsical reflection of the peasant's conception of bliss: tall grass, fat cows, sleek horses, woolly sheep. This is just the place for her John, though she is not quite sure he is the man to manage such glorious possessions.

In a conversation reported by his journalistic brother, Valtýr Stefánsson, Davið said that he was not satisfied with his treatment of the theme in the poem.[6] So he delved into the religious world of his own past, studying the hymn books, devotional writings, and sermons of preceding centuries, steeping himself in the conceptions of the hereafter which had been entertained by the common people of his country. He found that these conceptions were of a singularly robust and tangible quality, sometimes so precisely expressed that an architect could have built the hall of heaven and a housewife prepared the meals

---

[4] For parallels see Stith Thompson, *Motif-Index of Folk-literature.* (Bloomington: Indiana Univ. Press, 1955-58), under motif K 2371.1.3 Heaven entered by trick: "wishing sack" thrown in.

[5] Reprinted in his collected poems, *Að norðan* (Reykjavík: Helgafell, 1952), vol. 2, 340-45.

[6] *Morgunblaðið*, December 24, 1941. Here cited from Matthías Johannessen's Introduction (p. 7) to the 1966 edition of *Gullna hliðið* (Reykjavík: Helgafell, 1966), to which the following discussion owes a great deal.

described! In an essay *Á leið til Gullna hliðsins* (*On the Way to the Golden Gate*), Davið wrote, "In heaven there was never frost, never storm nor hail, now and then a gentle rain for pleasure's sake, otherwise fair weather, eternal Icelandic summer. . . . There were neither taxes nor Danish merchants; all were masters of their own labor and their lives, and yet united in the spirit of God's love and wisdom. No one doubted the omnipotence of the Lord, but His mercy was so great and His views so noble that He reminded one rather of a graybearded, respected parish official and father than of the King's representatives."[7]

This play is a kind of Icelandic *Divine Comedy*. *Mutatis mutandis*, Dante's conception of the hereafter was not greatly different from that which the Old Woman of Davið's play harbors. In both works we find the conception of the other world as a high mountain up which a man must struggle, at the risk of losing his footing and falling into a bottomless pit. While these views have ample scriptural basis, they come with special appropriateness in mountainous and volcanic Italy and Iceland. In the play Davið spun this theme even further than in his poem, and got a chance to introduce the Devil and his followers, among whom were some of his favorite antipathies (as in Dante's poem). The authorities of this world, the rich and the rulers, even the ministers, do not come off well. Only the simple of heart are destined for heaven, and all of Jón's sins are not sufficient to outweigh the love of his wife. He goes to heaven in spite of himself.

The most important innovation in the play is the author's introduction of Jón as a major character. In the tale and the poem his chief function had been to die and be transported to heaven. In the play he furnishes dramatic contrast to his patient, long-suffering wife, and his blustering, colorful speech offers a welcome relief from her pious, loving manner. As the wife

---

[7] Davið Stefánsson, *Mælt mál* (Reyjavík: Helgafell, 1963), p. 221.

grows more saintly, Jón gets testier and more unwilling to be raised to glory. He retains his earthiness, even his hellishness, almost to the end. Matthías Johannessen, in a study of the play, points out that while her world has virtually vanished from Icelandic folk life, her husband's is still alive: "I feel as if I have often spoken with this fellow, chatted with him on the kelp-covered beach, while he takes his snuff sitting on the moss-grown rocks, or under a tumble-down farm well."[8] Jón has taken over from the folk tale some of the woman's saucy answers to the celestial authorities, here seen as the underdog's privilege of barking at the Almighty and carrying on the peasant's grumble at his circumstances in this life.

The play was first performed by the Reykjavík Dramatic Society on December 26, 1941, under the direction of Lárus Pálsson assisted by the author. The main roles were played by the well-known actors Brynjolf Jóhannesson and Arndís Björnsdóttir, while the author read the prologue. The performance was a tremendous hit; it attracted full houses throughout the season and received ecstatic reviews. Music for the four songs composed by Páll Ísólfsson added notably to the performance, wrought as they were in the spirit of old hymns and folk tunes.[9] Immediately after the war the play was produced in Norwegian at Det Norske Teatret in Oslo (March 5, 1946) and in Finnish in Finland, with great success. The present translation by G. M. Gathorne-Hardy was performed in the Christmas season, 1948, in Edinburgh, and again at the Edinburgh Festival, August 20–25, 1949. Students mounted a performance at Oxford University in 1949. The Icelandic troupe has presented guest performances in Denmark, Finland, and Norway.[10]

---

[8] *Gullna hliðið* (1966 ed.), p. 10.

[9] *Gullna hliðið*. Fjögur sönglög eftir Pál Ísólfsson. Reykjavík: Vikingsprent, 1942.

[10] All of this information comes from M. Jóhannessen's Introduction to the 1966 edition of *Gullna hliðið*.

Everywhere audiences were impressed by the spirit of religious humanism which breathes through the play. Daviỗ Stefánsson has here preached a powerful sermon against all forms of hypocrisy, while exalting the power of love to overcome evil. His folk parable is a charming and ingenious picture of an Iceland that will soon be gone.

EINAR HAUGEN

Harvard University

THE GOLDEN GATE

CHARACTERS

JÓN, A COTTER*
AN OLD WOMAN, HIS WIFE
VILBORG, A WISE-WOMAN
A SHERIFF'S OFFICER
A MAN AND WOMAN, JÓN'S FORMER EMPLOYERS
A THIEF
A JAILER
A DRUNKARD
A WOMAN, JÓN'S MISTRESS
A RICH MAN
A SHERIFF
PARENTS OF THE OLD WOMAN
HELGA, HER FRIEND
A PRIEST
A FARMER
A FIDDLER
SAINT PETER
SAINT PAUL
THE VIRGIN MARY
MICHAEL THE ARCHANGEL
THE ENEMY
FOUR IMPS
ANGELS AND THE ELECT

Sources: Popular folk tale and old hymns.

---

* Occupant of a cottage on a farm, paying with labor in lieu of rent.

PROLOGUE

Much by the veil of time is hidden yet
To which our creeds and customs are in debt.
Deserted crofts in glens remote and bleak
Tell much to those to whom their stones can speak.
Gold may be found in many a ruined hall,
And hearths long cold their former fires recall.
Here, long ago, a folk in rags and tatters
Groaned 'neath the weight of sacerdotal fetters:
Men prayed—but used in age their childhood's prayer;
Witchcraft and spells spread darkness everywhere;
Specters and goblins danced around the hall,
Brought death to men—and horses in the stall.
In crags was found the troll, in mounds the elf,
While down in hell lived the arch-fiend himself:
Each hamlet he with sin and evil filled,
Appearing there in any shape he willed.

Dark was the age. What sanctuary more
From ghosts and devils knocking at the door?
With ice and seas were barred, the springs were sealed;
Mountains spewed flame, the land with earthquake reeled;
The neighborhood with shameful lust was cursed;
Some men were tortured with a quenchless thirst,
Some lived a beggar's life on moss and leaves,
Others were turned by famine into thieves.
Men slew their brethren, maddened by disaster,
And recognized the Devil as their master,
His realm from hell extending to the sky.
In such a wolf-age, whither could they fly?

Yet some there were who sought to save themselves,
Pored over ancient volumes on their shelves,
Turned o'er the pages, blew the dust away.

And much would read, and fervently would pray.
In books, as many fancied, they could find
God's purpose, and his promise to mankind,
Seeking to point the road their souls to save,
In hope of better things—beyond the grave.

The pilgrim soul from each man's corpse was driven
To climb a mighty mountain—up to heaven.
Rocky and steep the slope, and hard to climb,
Bowed with the load of sins, through snow and rime;
While, as the rustic sages would declare,
Old Nick lurks in ambush everywhere.
Many a crippled soul climbs upward late,
But reaches in the end the Golden Gate.
After confession and beseeching prayer,
Some find eternal bliss awaits them there;
While others learn at last themselves to blame,
Hurled down to burn in everlasting flame.
Such was their faith of old—this race of ours,
A strengthless striving—'twixt two mighty powers!

Here we would sweep the stony path once more,
And resurrect our ancestors of yore
That thus the young may gain the power to feel
That inner strife which bygone times conceal;
Since buried in those secret depths, indeed,
Lie the main roots of custom and of creed.
The generations change. Age yields to age.
And what is now our children's heritage?

Take not offense, though our design be crude,
And dead men talk, with earthly speech endued.
Far be it from us to wound the trustful soul;
To bridge the gulf that sunders is our goal.
We breathe new life in hymns and peasant tale,
And show you thus the world behind the veil!

ACT I

A small cottage in a remote valley. Turf walls, earth floor. A pallet bed under a weatherboard roof, and above it a small window closed with a membrane. Opposite is a door, and a hearth with a pot on it. Firewood and cooking utensils. Against the gable wall is an old chest, and on it a carved wooden bowl and a couple of devotional books. Above the chest is a lighted train-oil lamp, fastened to the wall. There is a glimmer of firelight from the hearth. An evening in early winter.

Jón lies dying on the bed. He is in a red homespun shirt, and is old and bearded. His breathing is labored. The old woman (his wife) is sitting by him, knitting. Vilborg is busy at the hearth.

OLD WOMAN: Jón dear, Jón. (*Looks up.*) It's a fair caution how he can sleep.

VILBORG: Aye, 'twas real strong, the last dose he had. It's no use giving that Jón of yours extract of yarrow or thyme tea. I know the stuff for him. He's not the first I've ever treated when they're mortal bad with sickness.

OLD WOMAN: That's something to thank God for—being able to ease the sufferings of others.

VILBORG: There's all sorts of herbs. I've learnt by experience to tell them apart and know what's best in each case.

OLD WOMAN: No one doubts your knowledge, Vilborg, or people wouldn't come to you when it matters most.

VILBORG: There's some herbs as does away with unwholesome fluids and poisons in the body; others strengthens the blood and does good to the nerves as well. And then there's herbs just helps to get rid of wind from the belly. Some you have to boil on a slow fire, others over a roaring flame. And often a lot depends on your using the proper sort of fuel. One herb you must allus cook just with scrub or heather, others with bits of mahogany that drives ashore at spring tide, and a third sort with droppings of well-fatted ewe lambs. And then there's mixing the brew, with a drop of all sorts in one and the same dose.

OLD WOMAN: You want godfearing honest folk to handle these blessed herbs.

VILBORG: Ah, but 'tain't allus enough to say prayers right, seemingly. You have to suit your thoughts according to the nature and badness of the illness. Those herbs I gave your Jón a brew of just now is rare and hard to find, and they only grows where there's fire in the soil, close to hot springs and brimstone pools.

OLD WOMAN: Lord 'a mercy on us!

VILBORG: What's bad takes bad to drive it out. Supposing anything's to save him, it'll be that last dose, or another a trifle stronger.

OLD WOMAN: Seems to me he's terrible low.

VILBORG: Seemed to me he could use his tongue all right just now.

OLD WOMAN: Ah, that's only old habits from when he was a boy, God bless him! I'm ashamed to say I scarcely notices his bad language; you get used to that sort of thing quicker than in forty years of wedlock. At first I did all I could to wean him from this continual nastiness, but there as in other things I didn't get very far.

VILBORG: You're not the only one that tries and fails.

OLD WOMAN: Many's the time it's been difficult, living with him, and yet it allus seems to me there's something fine about my Jón. But he might at times have been harder working at home, bless his heart!

VILBORG: Those as is lazy and idle has got seven devils in their lap, and is scratching the back of the eighth.

OLD WOMAN: That's why it went as it did. It wasn't the way he was brought up as a lad, either. You might put it that he came into this sinful world without father or mother, so you needn't ask about his upbringing. Thrashed he was, plenty of that, and starved into the bargain. So was it to be wondered at if the lad couldn't keep his hands still?

VILBORG: It's a wicked world.

OLD WOMAN: I think there's other folk to be blamed for the way things went with him. But God in heaven above us knows I tried everything I could to keep him out of mischief.

VILBORG: No one as knows about it can doubt that!

OLD WOMAN: It may well be that I've grown as bad as him, but I had to try to share his burdens as long as I could. But God knows all the same that I refused for a long time to cook what he brought into the house, when I knew it was come by wrong and dishonestly.

VILBORG: Such ways didn't come to him by nature.

OLD WOMAN: Many's the one as has said that.

VILBORG: Many's the wiles of the Devil.

OLD WOMAN: And my Jón gives way, like lots of others. What was I to do? Of course I shielded him. Wasn't I his wife, as had sworn before God's holy altar to be true to him for ever?

VILBORG: Some people has a heavy cross to bear.

OLD WOMAN: And then we lost the children. God called three of them to him the same week, the others have flown off to the ends of the earth. It's often I've missed them, specially when I was left alone in the cottage.

VILBORG: It's a marvel what's left of you. You can't have been badly put together at the start.

OLD WOMAN: What do you think ought to be said of my Jón, then? Life's treated him harder still. Up to now his heart's never been known to fail, though I know he's never had his full health since they pinched him. It wasn't human, the way they treated him.

VILBORG: What else could you expect?

OLD WOMAN: He was mocked and scourged like our blessed Saviour. And it was as if each trouble seemed to harden him more. When I wanted to scold him, or opened the scriptures, he told me to shut my mouth, and at times he'd snatch the book from me and throw it into the corner.

VILBORG: It's as sure as anything that some folks are possessed by evil spirits. Didn't you ever look up someone who knew a thing or two?

OLD WOMAN: Oh no, Vilborg, dear. I've set my trust in the Lord and his word, and so I do still.

VILBORG: I don't know as it would have done any harm to read one of those exorcisms over him, if those had done it as understood about it.

OLD WOMAN: Oh, do you think so? (*Jón groans and tosses.*)

OLD WOMAN (*Attending to him*) : God help you, Jón dear.— He's dropped off again, same as before.

VILBORG: I'm inclined to think something foul is after him.

OLD WOMAN: I should think it might be the old lot, the sheriff or his underlings. They've been here before, and always on the same errand. God knows if they haven't got something fresh on my Jón. It's as if he couldn't leave that sort of thing alone. But they'd never take him away from me, sick to death as he is.

VILBORG: It's to be hoped not.

OLD WOMAN: Perhaps God'll release him from human punishment. And if he'd got rest coming to him, I'd be easy. But God is just as stern a judge.

(*Vilborg rakes the fire.*)

OLD WOMAN: My last hope is that Jón will repent his sins before he goes, whenever that may be.

VILBORG: I'm inclined to think that sickness and pain of body may sometimes purge a hard heart, same as fire clears the dross from gold.

(*Jón stirs, with a deep groan.*)

OLD WOMAN (*Attending to him*) : Are you feeling terrible bad, Jón dear? (*Jón is silent.*) Do you want to go on sleeping? Better try to wake up and pray, though there mayn't be much time.—There, he's dropped off again as usual.

VILBORG (*Goes to the bed and lays her hands on the sick man's forehead*): It's easy to see he's had the proper dose. It's a good thing he's sweating, 'cause sweat's nothing but poisonous fluids in the blood, as have got to find their way out, if things are to be better.

OLD WOMAN: It looks as if he was a scrap easier just now. Don't you think so, dear?

VILBORG: I don't like his breathing. Even if the dose was strong and good, it's a question how it'll turn out. He's an old man, and worn out.

OLD WOMAN: I'm ready for anything, Vilborg dear.

VILBORG: Well, there's nothing else to do but to bide and see how things go. (*Sits by the hearth, takes a tobacco pouch out of her pocket, rubs it a good while, and takes a pinch of snuff.*)

OLD WOMAN: I asked him this morning if he wouldn't like the priest to come and give him the holy sacrament, but that didn't suit him. He's never been wishful to go to God's table. (*Sits on the chest, knitting. A pause.*)

VILBORG: Last communion Sunday, two ravens were seen flying in a cross over the church.

OLD WOMAN: That's always been held a bad sign.

VILBORG: At the north end of the churchyard was an open grave. While the service was going on, there was rain fell on the soil.

OLD WOMAN: After that, I can expect anything!

VILBORG: Well, it's the way of life! You're too reasonable and steady a woman not to take things quietly as they come.

OLD WOMAN: We've all got to die. But, as you know, there's lots of places in God's holy word where it says that them as dies in their sins, without repenting, are in for a bad time.

VILBORG: I understand.

OLD WOMAN: My Jón, worse luck, has always been careless and hasn't got ready for death as a Christian should. That's why he mustn't just slip away in his sleep. He must repent, 'cause all his salvation depends on it. (*Jón stirs. She gets up and goes to the bed.*) Jón, Jón darling! (*Jón is silent.*)

OLD WOMAN (*Takes up one of the devotional books and turns over the pages. Goes up to Vilborg*): Sing this hymn with me, Vilborg dear. He must wake up, if it's possible.

VILBORG (*Looking at the print*): Don't you need to see the words too?

OLD WOMAN: I should think I knew this hymn by heart— "Lord be thou mine only peace." And the tune as well.

BOTH (*sing*): Lord, be thou mine only peace,
And take me in when life shall cease;
In through Heaven's glorious door,
Where none are hungry, none are poor;
And all thy flock sing words of cheer,
Most wonderfully pure and clear.

But then their chastisement begins
Who unrepentant die in sins:
Who lied and stole and falsely swore,
And likewise those that played the whore.
All those who covet earthly show
Into the flames of Hell must go.
JÓN: What's all this howling?
(*The Old Woman nudges Vilborg; they go on singing.*)
BOTH: Repent, my soul, from mockery flee,
And call on Him who died on tree.
Call thou on God and all his state,
And then shall ope the Golden Gate,
Where all enjoy eternal bliss
With angel hosts in Paradise.

JÓN (*Who has turned round during the singing*): What a devilish row!

OLD WOMAN: God forgive you. We were singing a hymn.

JÓN: No peace to sleep as usual. Suppose you want me to

suffer as much as possible?

VILBORG (*Gets up and goes to the bed*) : I think you're an abominable brute to your wife. I suppose she ought to have slaved for you a bit more! You should be ashamed of the way you've behaved to her before, sooner than chuck abuse at her!

OLD WOMAN: There, there, Vilborg dear. He can't help it.

VILBORG: I know what I'm doing. This isn't the first time I've stood by a sickbed.

JÓN: Each of you's as crazy as the other.

VILBORG: He's not fast asleep this time. (*Goes to the hearth and stirs the pot.*)

OLD WOMAN: Confess your sins to God, Jón darling, and pray the blessed Saviour of souls to have mercy on you. That's the only true remedy.

(*Jón groans heavily.*)

VILBORG (*Taking up the bowl*): He needs a fresh dose.

JÓN: Brandy!

OLD WOMAN: You know there ain't any. Try now to forget all earthly pleasures, and turn your thoughts on high. We're all sinful creatures. If you confess and make amends, you'll share the glory of the angels.

(*Jón gives a cry.*)

OLD WOMAN (*To Vilborg*): He's in dreadful pain.

VILBORG: I know what's wrong with him. It's not always the one that cries loudest that's the most hurt. (*Pours into the pot and stirs it.*) He'll soon get his dose. It's no good hurrying in a matter of life or death. (*Mumbles to herself.*)

OLD WOMAN: Eh, what are you muttering, Vilborg dear?

VILBORG: Leave that to me.

OLD WOMAN (*To Jón*) : Wouldn't you rather I sent for the priest, so that you could receive the last unction and the bread and wine, like a repentant Christian child of God? It'll give you peace.

JÓN: Baccy—brandy!

(*Wife looks at Vilborg in despair.*)

VILBORG: What's up? (*Goes to the bed with the bowl.*) Here now, Jón, it's best for you to swallow this down. (*To the Old Woman.*) He's done for, anyhow. (*Helps Jón to drink. The dose goes down the wrong way.*) Get it all down. That's real stuff. It's got a kick in it.

JÓN: Damned muck!

OLD WOMAN: I'm beginning to think there's something unnatural about his illness.

VILBORG: I saw at once, from the way the first dose acted on him, that the sickness was more than a bit queer. Don't you notice an odd smell in here?

OLD WOMAN: Like rancid butter?

VILBORG: I'm not so sure it ain't the smell of coming death. It's the stink of brimstone, no less!

OLD WOMAN: God help my Jón!

VILBORG: The air's stiff with foul spirits.

(*The light grows dim.*)

JÓN: Hey! Devils!

VILBORG: He's calling them.

OLD WOMAN: He's out of his senses.

VILBORG: Why? Why is he out of his senses? . . . They've drunk the oil out of the lamp.

(*The light goes out. The Old Woman screams, grabs the lamp in panic and goes with it into the corner to attend to it. In the glow from the hearth four imps are seen dancing round the bed.*)

FIRST IMP (*Fat and fiery red, holding out a keg of brandy to Jón, hisses*): Drunkard!

(*Jón laughs, rises half up and reaches for the keg, but falls back screaming on the pillow. His wife strides to the bed, takes one of the religious books from the chest, lays it on Jón's breast and bends over him.*)

SECOND IMP (*Gray and wooly, with a sheep's head, bleats*): Sheep-stealer!

THIRD IMP (*With fat white woman's breasts and red lips,*

waving a red rag) : Adulterer!

FOURTH IMP (*Coal black with red horns on his head, waves a rune-stick*) : Heathen! (*Jón screams.*)

OLD WOMAN: God have mercy on you!

VILBORG: Lie quiet as the grave and still as a stone. The croft's full of devils. Let me talk to them. (*Strides to the door and opens it, seizes a blazing brand from the hearth and makes the sign of the cross with it in the air. The imps howl.*) With the burning torch of light I make the blessed sign of the cross over this sick man. In the name of Holy Trinity, in the name of the archangels of heaven, the blessed Michael, Gabriel, and Raphael, I conjure from him venomous vermin and evil spirits, who have been sent out by the Devil to possess his soul and drag him to the abode of the damned.

THE IMPS (*Beckon to Jón, leaping about the floor and hissing*) : Come, come, come, come! (*Jón moans.*)

VILBORG: In the name of the Crucified, who gave sight to the blind and healed those possessed of devils, in the name of all healing herbs that grow on the earth, I conjure away venomous snakes and the generation of vipers which gnaw the life and lungs of this sick man, fill his blood with poisonous fluids and thus would destroy his heart and bowels, his gall, spleen, and all his entrails. (*Advances towards the imps, who retreat across the floor.*) Yield to the holy and almighty sign of the cross; depart to the confines of the realm of your black master, who awaits you in the lowest depths of fiery rain, with his glowing trident, ready to strike it into your coal-black bellies and plunge you in the seething brimstone cauldron of hell. (*The imps vanish through the door.*)

VILBORG: To the sick man let help come from the earth, victory from the sun, sustenance from the stars, and strength from the angels of God! (*Goes out after the imps. Wife looks up.*)

VILBORG (*Off*) : *In nomine Patris et Filii et Spiritus Sancti. Amen.*

OLD WOMAN: In His blessed name, Amen. Aren't you feeling

better now, Jón? (*Jón is silent. His wife takes the lamp and lights it from the hearth. Vilborg enters, shuts the door and crosses it.*) You've crossed the outer doors too, Vilborg dear?

VILBORG: I should think so! I know what suits them. We'll say no more about that.

OLD WOMAN: Blessing be with you, wherever you go! (*They go to the bed.*)

VILBORG: Ain't you a bit easier now? Everything's quite pure around you now.

OLD WOMAN: Don't you notice it, Jón dear? (*Throws the light on his face.*)

(*Jón is silent, his eyes staring. His wife looks questioningly at Vilborg.*)

VILBORG: It's easy to see the way things are going. (*Jón unconsciously strikes his hand on the book lying on him, so that it falls to the ground.*) That's likely to be his last act this side of the grave.

OLD WOMAN (*Picking up the book*): Perhaps he wants me to read him something. (*Sticks the lamp up on the wall, sits down and reads*):

Judge me, O God, and plead my cause against an ungodly
    nation;
O deliver me from the deceitful and unjust man.
For thou art the God of my strength; why dost thou cast
    me off?
Why go I mourning because of the oppression of the enemy?
O send out thy light and thy truth; let them lead me; let
    them
Bring me unto thy holy hill, and to thy tabernacles.
Then will I go unto the altar of God, unto God my exceeding
    joy;
Yea, upon the harp will I praise thee, O God my God.*

VILBORG: Are you going to go on reading? He's unconscious,

---

* Forty-third Psalm.

and his time's coming very quick. Oughtn't I to open the window?

OLD WOMAN (*Standing up*); No, for God's sake don't do that! (*She pulls out a leather bag from the foot of the bed.*) I'll not leave go of Jón's soul before it's in heaven!

VILBORG: Are you gone clean crazy, woman?

OLD WOMAN (*In a whisper*): I durstn't be sure St. Peter'll open the door for him, if he comes by himself. (*Aloud*) And Jón's got nobody but me.

VILBORG: So—your faithfulness won't stop at nothing! You've got a bit of string to tie up the bag, when it's wanted?

OLD WOMAN (*Takes off one of her garters and holds it up*): That ain't none too good for him, though it's woven in checks and with my initials. (*Short pause.*)

VILBORG: There doesn't happen to be any ptarmigan feathers in his bedding?

OLD WOMAN: No, none, Vilborg.

VILBORG: Then he should be all right this way. Didn't he often put his socks under the pillow at night?

OLD WOMAN: Yes, often.

VILBORG: As I thought. Put his socks at the head of the bed. That'll do no harm.

(*Wife takes a pair of blue woolen socks from the chest and puts them under the pillow.*)

OLD WOMAN: These are his best pair.

VILBORG: Seems to me he's taking a rare long time to breathe his last. Stick the psalter right under the pillow—since we haven't a priest's vestment handy, or the names of the Seven Sleepers on a bit of writing.

OLD WOMAN: With God's help, that ought to do. There's power in the psalter.

VILBORG: We'll see. (*Takes Jón's hand.*) I think that ought to do the trick. The ends of his limbs has got cold.

OLD WOMAN (*Stroking his hands*): God forgive your hands, Jón dear.

VILBORG: Now his soul's being released from the bonds of ungodly clay. Come here with the bag. (*The wife puts the bag over Jón's nostrils.*) That was the first!

OLD WOMAN: In the name of God the Father—

VILBORG: That was the second!

OLD WOMAN: And the Son—. Ready with the garter.

VILBORG (*Taking hold of the garter*) : Third! and the last.

OLD WOMAN: And God's Holy Ghost. (*Pulls together the mouth of the bag. They tie it up and cross it.*)

VILBORG: His earthly strife is over.

OLD WOMAN (*Lays the bag at the head of the bed, falls on her knees at the foot, and prays silently*) : God give your soul peace. Amen. (*Performs the last offices for Jón, kisses him, and signs him with the cross. Weeps.*)

VILBORG: "Dew falls at last, when day is past."

OLD WOMAN: I'd sacrifice my own salvation, if that'd give him a share in the bliss of God's children. (*Dries her eyes on the corner of her apron. Three knocks on the door.*) That'll be them, no doubt.

SHERIFF'S OFFICER (*Entering*): I make so bold as to step in. Good evening all.

VILBORG: Good day, officer.

OFFICER: Isn't Jón at home? Ah yes, he's on the bed. I have come here by the sheriff's orders. You have been charged, Jón, with a fresh theft, and the sheriff has instructed me to take you in custody and remove you to the place of trial. I have to obey his orders.

OLD WOMAN: Who doubts it? Everyone knows the way you do your duty.

VILBORG: Won't you sit down, officer?

OFFICER: I mustn't sit. Jón, you heard what I said. Show a leg, I've no time to wait. Are you deaf and dumb, or pretending to be asleep? Do you think that'll do your case any good?

OLD WOMAN: You might try shaking him.

OFFICER (*Does so*) : There then, dress yourself at once, Jón, and come along.

OLD WOMAN: He's not got much to say for himself. But this time he's go a lawful excuse.

OFFICER: Lawful excuse?

VILBORG: He's dead.

OFFICER: Dead?

OLD WOMAN: Aye, he's taken the liberty, though it might interfere with the sheriff's arrangements.

OFFICER: And you let me address a dead man, and summon him to court!

OLD WOMAN: It never struck me that the servants of the law wouldn't be sharp-sighted enough to tell a live man from a corpse.

OFFICER (*Makes sign of cross over Jón*) : Peace be with you.

OLD WOMAN: You can punish his body, but his soul you'll never get!

OFFICER (*Makes a move to go*): I'll report Jón's death to the sheriff.

OLD WOMAN: I've no doubt you'll both pray for him. But if you think he's for the bad place, that hope of yours'll never come off. In at the Golden Gate he shall go!

OFFICER: Good-by.

VILBORG: Good-by. (*Exit Officer.*)

OLD WOMAN: Waking or sleeping, my prayers and thoughts shall carry him there—since I trust in Thy mercy, O Lord, to lead me and remove me to Thy holy mountain and to Thy dwelling.

CURTAIN

ACT II

*A rocky, precipitous slope, veiled in mist. A yellow gleam
on the rim of the mountain.*

OLD WOMAN (*Enters, in her Sunday clothes, holding the
bag*) : Now I must sit down at once and take a breather. I'm
fagged out. (*Sits down.*)

JÓN (*Or rather his soul in the bag*) : You're not getting on,
woman. Do you think I want to lie for all eternity in this
damned bag?

OLD WOMAN: Now, you must have a scrap of patience, Jón
dear. As if I wasn't doing all I could to struggle on, and it's
no good my breaking down half way. This ain't no highway,
far from it. It's even steeper than the slope at home, and you
probably remember what that's like. And you know too that
I'm only an old worn-out creature that's been mother to ten
kids; you ought to know something about that, Jón dear.

JÓN: I've a dim recollection of it.

OLD WOMAN: And then you ask me to run up hill. Do you
think I can keep it up for ever, same as a fox? And it's not as
if I could be quite free and limber with your soul to drag along.
It doesn't take much to burden the traveler.

JÓN: Well, you shouldn't have been in such a hurry to start
on this trip—I'm stifled.

OLD WOMAN: It says in God's holy scripture—the body's
mortal, but the soul lives for ever. You must have known before
we set off that the road to heaven is long and hard.

JÓN: Anyhow, I'm sure most of what's in the scriptures is
nothing but a pack of lies.

OLD WOMAN: I might have known it! It's a sin to listen to
you. Surely you forget you're dead and on the way to the great
judge. Try now to mend your ways a bit, or all this trouble

will have been taken for nothing.

Jón: If you grudge taking this bit of a stroll with me, I bloody well won't accept your help. Do you hear?

Old Woman: Just like you! You're always the same.

Jón: You'd much better open the bag, so I can go my own way.

Old Woman: Let me settle that. If you want to shorten the trip, then say what few prayers you know and call your misdeeds to mind. The bag'll get lighter for every sin you repent. (*Jón laughs sarcastically.*) God help you, Jón.

Jón: No fear! When has he ever helped me?

Old Woman: You're never tired of blaspheming. Where do you think you'd be without the Lord's help and assistance? And then you mean to cap your shame by blaming him for the trouble you've brought on yourself. You took up with dishonest folks and let yourself be caught by the wiles of the Devil. I know there's forgiveness for them as is born weak. But you've gone on and despised the strength that's given by trust in God and by praying.

Jón: Oh, dry up!

Old Woman: All the same you might bear in mind the difference between living with angels and the chosen in heaven and wading breast high in fire and smoke with hardened sinners.

Jón: I'm stone-dead of thirst.

Old Woman: What do you think you'll be later on, if you've got to lie up to the waist in flame?

Jón: Don't you see a brook or a spring?

Old Woman: No. There's nothing here but mist and stone, stone everywhere, hoarfrost on the rocks and slippery at every step.

Jón: Open the bag at once, so I can lick the frost. It'll cool me.

Old Woman: I can't do that. You must put off cooling yourself while we're on the road. Say your prayers. They're the cooling water of life. Try that, Jón dear.

Jón: I'll get nothing by that. That's no good.

OLD WOMAN: God Almighty hears in heaven, as soon as you pray hard enough.

JÓN: Maybe. But wouldn't it be a good idea to get a trifle higher first? In fact, are you sure you're on the right track? It's likely you're quite astray.

OLD WOMAN: Leave that to me.

JÓN: You was always a damn fool in mist. You'd better have let me get out of the window.

OLD WOMAN: Oh, I'm sick of your grumbling! Nice reception you'd have out there in the dark, to be sure.

JÓN: I wish my soul was back in my body.

OLD WOMAN: Yes, so you say now, Jón my boy. But that can't be done now, till the last day, when the dead rise.

JÓN: Don't you think my carcass will get pretty high by then? Don't you see any tracks in the frost?

OLD WOMAN: You needn't worry. I'm on the right track. It says in the hymn—
"The way for all must upwards climb,
O'er crag and stone, through frost and rime."
No one goes astray, who follows God's holy word.

JÓN: The worst of it is—you can't be sure. Well then, try to get a move on.

OLD WOMAN: Yes, yes. Don't behave as if you was out of your senses. Just let me tuck up my skirts. It won't mend matters, to get to heaven with my petticoat all ragged and torn.

JÓN: Don't you see any signs of people?

OLD WOMAN: The hymn says—
"Through mist and cloud the way goes by,
Till verdant meadows greet the eye."
But I shouldn't be surprised if we happened to meet some old acquaintances from our country. (*Noise from the rocks.*) God be with us!

JÓN: What was that?

OLD WOMAN: Somebody's falling.
"The damned who up the mountain go

Must fall lamenting down below."

Jón: Hold the bag tight, so they don't take me with them in their fall.

Old Woman: Oh, so that's it! You can trust me, Jón, dear. But don't let on to anybody.

Jón: Do I generally talk out of fun? . . . But we might just ask them the way, even if they are damned.

(*A Man and Woman fall onto the stage, and lie moaning.*)

Old Woman (*Attending to them*): You must have hurt yourselves, poor things!

Man: We're all black and blue.

Old Woman: Why, you're the couple that starved and thrashed my Jón when he was a boy.

Woman (*Half rising*): It may be my man gave him a belting now and then, but he always got enough to eat, the young rascal.

Jón: That's a lie.

Woman: What was that?

Old Woman (*Trying to keep Jón quiet by beating the bag*) : The voice of truth, I fancy. You're the last people I expected to meet here. If I rightly recollect, it's a good thirty years since you passed away.

Man: Thirty thousand years, more like, I should think.

Old Woman: What, wouldn't they open the Golden Gate? But I suppose you counted up all your good deeds?

Woman: We wouldn't have been here otherwise.

Old Woman: So I should have thought.

Man: We were driven away like curs. (*Jón laughs.*)

Woman: What devil's laughter is that?

Old Woman: Oh, it came from somewhere down below.

Man: That laugh sounded to me like your Jón's. He can't be far off.

Old Woman: Why, whenever did you hear him laugh? It's likely he'd think of laughing, when he came home with the milking ewes, with his face all blue with the cold, and then got hard words and beating for his pains.

WOMAN: There was a mean streak in that good-for-nothing puppy.

MAN: We meant him nothing but good.

OLD WOMAN: So you think thrashings and starvation gave the child a better disposition? They generally does! The blessed heavenly Father don't treat nobody more severe than them as mishandles defenseless kids. And nobody does it but rogues, my good woman. But now the bruises on the child's body have got onto your own carcasses. (*Jón laughs.*) As you sow, so must you reap. But it ain't no pleasure to me to see you treated like this. I'd willingly help you if I could.

WOMAN: We must be getting on.

MAN: Down the hill. There's no other lodging to turn to.

OLD WOMAN: "Great is the misery of man."

(*The Enemy peeps out from behind a rock, sneering. He is black and scorched, with two horns projecting from a shining skull. He waves his hand, pointing downward. He appears, without the Old Woman being aware of him, each time when new arrivals leave her and continue their journey. The Man, the Woman, and the Enemy disappear.*)

JÓN: They've got the punishment they deserve.

OLD WOMAN: Can you laugh at those poor creatures of another world, who've got nothing before them but suffering? You should be ashamed of yourself, Jón. You'll sing a different tune if the gate ain't opened for you.

JÓN: We'll take things as they come. Now then, are you going to make a move?

OLD WOMAN: I'm sure it's all the same, even if the journey takes a long time. You're none too quick at mending your ways.

(*The Thief falls onto the stage, screaming.*)

OLD WOMAN: "They try to cling, but down they go,
        Like as the walls of Jericho."

So it's you, you swine, the chap who got Jón to pinch his first leg of mutton?

THIEF: I never heard but that you liked the taste of it all right.

OLD WOMAN: There wasn't a morsel of it passed my lips, nor the children's either, I can tell you, though it was a tight fit at home. I knew how it was come by. You'd have done better to have warned him of the risk, sooner than shove him over the brink.

THIEF: 'Twasn't me taught him to steal. It came more by nature than by schooling.

OLD WOMAN: After the mishap, it was as if all my Jón's finer feelings had given way.

THIEF: Finer feelings, ha, ha! I reckon folks don't care much about that sort of thing on earth, they mostly tries to look after themselves and their belongings as best they can. Is it better to die of hunger and poverty? All proper chaps is thieves. They pinches each other's time and job, their food, their characters, their money, their sheep, horses and women.

JÓN: *And* women! (*Laughs.*) Dead right, dead right, old man!

THIEF: Hullo! Is Jón here?

OLD WOMAN: I can't see him.

THIEF: There's plenty worse than me gets off all punishment in their lifetime, and yet slips into heaven after death. I think the same damned injustice applies there as on earth. The weaker gets turned away. Others is received with open arms.

OLD WOMAN: It's most likely you've read your lesson upside down and backwards—same as the Devil reads the Bible.

THIEF: But it never was so bloody bad where I came from that folks had to hunt over hill and dale to find a lodging.

OLD WOMAN: Ah, but there's a bit of difference between putting a chap up for one night and taking him in for ever and ever, amen. No, you scallywag. You've deserved to be shown out. Worse luck!

THIEF (*Angrily*): That's a lie!

OLD WOMAN: You've no call to quarrel with me about it. I've got no say in what happens to you. You settled it yourself, while you was alive, by your own faults. You paid no heed to God's word and the advice of good men.

THIEF: Blast the whole lot!

OLD WOMAN: You was always out of luck. It's awful to see you. Brand of a thief on your cheeks and both your ears bleeding.

THIEF (*Feeling his ears*): They've been cut to bits on the sharp rocks.

OLD WOMAN: It's the right marking. "Cropped and punched through." That was the mark on the first sheep my Jón pinched. (*Jón laughs.*) There's a queer echo among these rocks. What do you think me and the kids had to put up with, on account of what you whispered in Jón's ear, when you was showing him the way to thieve and rob? But all the same, I'd pray God to help you, if I thought it'd do a bit of good.

(*The Jailer falls onto the stage; stops by the Thief, groans.*)

THIEF: You had no pity on me nor Jón neither, when you was giving us the cat, you damned hangman! (*Jón laughs.*)

OLD WOMAN: "One mourns his suffering with tears,

        One curses, and another jeers."

That's straight out of the hymn book.

JAILER: Who was that speaking?

OLD WOMAN: Oh, it was only Jón's wife.

JAILER: I'm in agony. I'm smarting all over.

OLD WOMAN: You're being paid for what you did on earth.

JAILER: Just look at my hands!

OLD WOMAN: That's how it is with everyone that uses the cat.

JAILER: I caught them in a crack in the rocks, and couldn't get them free except by tearing off three fingers from each hand. (*Jón laughs.*) Was that Jón? Lucky for him I can't get at him!

OLD WOMAN: Don't you think that may have been an echo of your own brutal laugh. You didn't think it enough—thirty or forty stripes on the bare flesh, for quite a small offense.

JAILER: It was the sheriff's orders.

OLD WOMAN: Who asked you to take on the job, but your own hard heart? Why, no one could stop you from laying it on. This was no way to treat my Jón.

JAILER: He bloody well deserved it!

Jón: You're a liar!

Jailer (*Clutching the Thief*): What was that?

Old Woman: A spirit, giving evidence against you.

Thief: Let me go, blast you. (*They struggle with one another, shouting.*)

Old Woman: Ah, you're poor wretched creatures. But there's no saving you.

(*Jailer and Thief disappear.*)

Jón: Pleasant journey. Happy homecoming!

Old Woman: I'm ashamed to listen to you. As if it was any good to you, those curs getting a bad time.—We may meet more before it's over. If you want to get to heaven, you'll have to forgive them all, and pray for them with all your heart.

Jón: Those blackguards? Not much!

Old Woman: No one can tell whether they're a bit worse than you.

Jón: It's just as it always was. You excuse me in one sentence, and abuse me in the next.

Old Woman: That's quite true. But it's a bit of an uphill job trying to find excuses for you. That'll be proved when the time comes, Jón.

Jón: Well, start toddling on now.

(*A noise from the rocks.*)

Old Woman: "Great is the misery of man."

(*The Drunkard falls onto the stage, moaning.*)

Old Woman: "So must they too as outlaws pine
        Who are destroyed by ale and wine."

Drunkard: My head's done for. My head's done for!

Old Woman: Well, no wonder. The brandy you've took down is more than a drop.

Drunkard: I'm blind and muzzy, but I do know that voice.

Old Woman: That didn't hinder you, when you was giving my Jón the taste for it. You both drank yourselves to damnation.

Drunkard: 'Twasn't me as beat you and pulled your hair.

Jón (*In a low voice*): Oh, shut up!

OLD WOMAN: We won't quarrel about that. You've got a pretty heavy load anyhow.

DRUNKARD: It's the devil to have no brandy.

JÓN: Same here.

DRUNKARD: Have I started to hear things?

OLD WOMAN: You may have a little glimmer of conscience left.

DRUNKARD: I'm just dying of thirst.

JÓN: Me too.

OLD WOMAN: Poor chap. Wouldn't they open the Golden Gate to you?

DRUNKARD: The truth is I didn't exactly grovel to them. I was never given to licking the boots of the gentry.

OLD WOMAN: No one's without some saving grace.

DRUNKARD: It's all the same to me where I am, if only I've got enough liquor.

(*Jón laughs.*)

OLD WOMAN: How did the blessed St. Peter take it?

DRUNKARD: Oh, he started some drivel about reason and intelligence and the behavior of God's Christian children. Maybe the old billygoat was afraid I would tweak the apostles' beards or seduce one of those angel hermaphrodites. (*He and Jón laugh.*)

OLD WOMAN: What an expression! There ain't much risk of the blessed little angel bodies being like that.

A WOMAN (*On the rocks above*): Wait for me. I'm coming.

OLD WOMAN: You know the voice. And unless I'm much mistaken, so does Jón.

DRUNKARD: That's the wife of that—that—. How should I remember, with my head splitting?

WOMAN (*Falling on the stage*): Where's Jón?

OLD WOMAN: "All are reputed beasts untamed
Who are by fleshly lusts inflamed."

WOMAN: Where's Jón? I heard him laughing.

OLD WOMAN: It's an echo of him still in your ears. Time

was when it wasn't only your ears he tickled. (*Jón and the Woman laugh.*)

OLD WOMAN: It's hardly a laughing matter. Suppose you're laughing at your own sin?

WOMAN: I'm sure that was my Jón's laugh.

OLD WOMAN: Not a scrap of him was ever yours, you creature. But everyone knows you didn't mind being false to your own husband on the sly, and setting your traps for Jón, even though he was mine in the sight of God and man, and the father of my children.

JÓN: Oh?

WOMAN: What was that?

DRUNKARD: You're hearing things. Echo. Nothing else.

OLD WOMAN: And you dare say that to my face! Do you glory in your kids being bastards? Then why didn't you get Jón to acknowledge them?

WOMAN: Because of you and the law. But up at the Golden Gate they knew it all.

OLD WOMAN: Was that why they wouldn't let you in?

WOMAN: I was called a kept woman, a whore, a barefaced sinner—and so they slammed the gate.

OLD WOMAN: You had only yourself to blame. That was no way to live.

WOMAN: I liked forbidden fruit best. The greater the sin, the greater the pleasure.

OLD WOMAN: And the greater the suffering. I think there was some poison in your body, poor thing. We're all weak, but some of us controls ourselves better than others. You was loose in everything.

WOMAN: Yes, I was a sinner.

OLD WOMAN: And couldn't repent before you died?

WOMAN: No. I couldn't repent. (*Pause.*)

OLD WOMAN: My Jón would never have been led astray, if his will hadn't been crippled by drink and trouble of all sorts. Drink makes beasts of everyone.

(*The Drunkard laughs.*)

WOMAN: Jón was a lovely man—a lovely beast.

OLD WOMAN: Yes, he certainly could be that—the darling. But all the same you did wrong to tempt him.

WOMAN: I couldn't help it.

OLD WOMAN: No, you couldn't. I quite believe that. My Jón could be quite irresistible.

WOMAN: I love—love—

OLD WOMAN: But they wouldn't open the gate to you?

WOMAN: I love my sin.

DRUNKARD: Come along.

OLD WOMAN (*As they disappear*): Even if sinless Almighty God can't forgive you, I can all the same.

JÓN: So do I.

OLD WOMAN (*Sighing*): They knows everything in heaven. They can even tell from the looks of the children who was their father.

JÓN: I'd nothing to do with them, not a drop of blood.

OLD WOMAN: Do you mean now to tell lies to the Father of Heaven himself. You're a dreadful creature. It's surely not worth our carrying on any further.

JÓN: Are you losing your courage?

OLD WOMAN: Small wonder if I did. Hush, hush! (*Listens.*) Wait now, and keep quiet as a stone.

(*The Rich Man falls on the stage.*)

OLD WOMAN: "A spirit greedy and depraved
        By great possessions is not saved."
It says so in the blessed hymn.

RICH MAN: What are you mumbling, woman? Who are you?

OLD WOMAN: We've only lived a generation in the same parish, so it's hardly to be hoped as you'd know me. But perhaps you remember my Jón?

RICH MAN: Yes, yes. Now I remember you. Where are you going?

OLD WOMAN: I'm on my way up to the Golden Gate.

RICH MAN: You can save yourself that trouble.

OLD WOMAN: I trust in the mercy of the Heavenly Father. It says in the Bible that in his house them as was poorest on earth will find refuge and shelter.

RICH MAN: Nice people there must be then inside the gate! Tramps, paupers, thieves, and other criminal riffraff. Now I begin to see why I wasn't welcomed.

OLD WOMAN: They can hardly have turned you away without reason. And of course you had your pockets stuffed full of gold and silver. Didn't they ask how you came by the money?

RICH MAN: How I came by it? What do you mean? All doors were open to me before, even the house of the sheriff himself, and he wasn't generally free with invitations.

OLD WOMAN: Of course the sheriff and the Heavenly Father would be likely to have the same standards on human beings. Couldn't you soften the people that looked after the gate?

RICH MAN: I offered them handfuls of silver.

OLD WOMAN: And what did they do then?

RICH MAN: Do? Why, they spat on my hand.

(*Jón gives a low laugh.*)

OLD WOMAN: I thought you might have tried to bribe the servants of the Heavenly Father. But they're not that sort, I'm told. I wonder though if they didn't find one or two of Judas's pieces of silver in your fist.

RICH MAN (*Angrily*): Why do you think so?

OLD WOMAN: They're said to be still in steady circulation on earth, so it struck me in my simplicity that they might have got into your pocket some time or other. Wealth goes where wealth is.

RICH MAN: How dare you make such insinuations against a gentleman, you old hag?

OLD WOMAN: "Inasmuch as ye did it to one of the least of these my brethren, ye did it unto me." You remember who said that? And perhaps you remember too how the richest gentleman in the country charged the poorest of the cotters with stealing three of his sheep?

RICH MAN: That was my duty. Sheep thieves are outlaws.

JÓN: What was you yourself? A skinflint, a criminal, a rascal.

RICH MAN: Wha—what was that?

OLD WOMAN: This is where the stones cry out. It's not for me to judge if you or Jón was the bigger thief. But I know this—that he never took anything from the poor. He never grabbed the holdings of cotters and turned them into penniless slaves. And he never had your riches, nor your blood money. But what good is all your wealth to you now?

RICH MAN: What business is that of yours?

OLD WOMAN: Bitter is the tears of a woman, whose husband's in jail, with ten kids to feed and clothe at home. But now things have changed, so that you, my fine gentleman, are more to be pitied than she is. I'd help you if I could, though you'd probably be ashamed to receive my help.

RICH MAN: Your help!

(*Laughs. A noise from the cliff. The Sheriff falls on the stage.*) Why, it's the Sheriff. (*Goes to attend to him.*)

OLD WOMAN: "The land of light as lowly rates

    The quirks and pomp of magistrates."

RICH MAN: How are you, Mr. Sheriff?

SHERIFF: How d'ye do? Did you wish to speak to me? If I remember rightly, there was a small matter of an unsettled tax assessment. We can discuss that later.

RICH MAN: I'm afraid your memory has managed to play you false, Mr. Sheriff.

SHERIFF: We can go into that later, I said. Was there anything else—a complaint, a boundary dispute, or a case of larceny?

RICH MAN: Excuse me, Mr. Sheriff—

SHERIFF (*Interrupting*) : Yes, yes, yes, yes—. Good day. (*Tries to hurry away, but collides with the Old Woman.*) What are you doing, wandering here?

OLD WOMAN: Is this place in thy jurisdiction?

RICH MAN: A cotter's wife doesn't say "thou" to the Sheriff.

OLD WOMAN: Oh well, I've never learned fine manner, and if I can say "thou" to God Almighty, the Sheriff oughtn't to be more particular.*

SHERIFF: Who is this woman?

RICH MAN: She's the wife of that Jón Jónsson.

SHERIFF: I never served her with any summons to report here. What do you want? You should have applied to the Sheriff's Officer.

OLD WOMAN: You seem to think your authority extends beyond death and the grave.

SHERIFF: What do you mean?

RICH MAN: Excuse me, Mr. Sheriff, but—

SHERIFF: But what?

OLD WOMAN: You're both dead as mutton.

SHERIFF: Yes but—yes but—

RICH MAN: That's quite correct, Mr. Sheriff.

SHERIFF: But am I not bound to maintain law and order everywhere?

OLD WOMAN: You might think a man of your sort would be wanted in heaven. But I think the laws there is different.

SHERIFF: Those laws which are not signed and ratified by His Majesty the King are neither law nor justice. Do you realize that? Do you know who I am?

OLD WOMAN: It'd take less to make me see that.

SHERIFF: Do you think it is seemly to insult a royal officer and a judge, who has spent a full thirty years in the public service? What sort of justice is this?

OLD WOMAN: It's the judgment of God.

SHERIFF: This is a penal offense, under the law of Christian V.

RICH MAN: I entirely agree with you, Mr. Sheriff.

SHERIFF: Much obliged! *Vox regis, vox legis.*

---

* Translator's Note: The use of "thou" is a disrespectful familiarity. As this is not so in English, and it would be unnatural to use the second person singular where it occurs in the original, this passage might have to be changed or omitted in acting.

OLD WOMAN: And all the same they must have been able to see you was in gold braid and gold buttons.

SHERIFF: Do you suppose that they were all stone-blind? They might as well have been.

OLD WOMAN: No doubt they'd have opened the gate to you if they had been. But they'll have seen something through the uniform, as wasn't to their liking. What about that sentence you passed on Jón?

SHERIFF: Wasn't that sentence pronounced in accordance with the appropriate section of the relevant law? **Do you mean to teach me law and jurisprudence? Do you know to what you are liable for insulting a judge by royal warrant, a person in authority?**

OLD WOMAN: If my Jón had been rich, you'd have stopped the case. But that wasn't the way of it, so you sentenced him without mercy.

RICH MAN: Do you dare to bandy words with the Sheriff?

SHERIFF: Do you consider that I do not know how to deal with a delinquent of that kind? Are you taking the liberty of impugning my judgments?

OLD WOMAN: I'm not afraid of either of you any more, now. (*Jón laughs.*)

SHERIFF: I summon you for contempt of court. (*To the Rich Man*) You are a witness. Such persons should be arrested.

OLD WOMAN: But you're not a royal official any more, only a lost soul what falls down the great mountain, lonely and despised. Even them as suffered worst from the rod of your authority pities you, and is sorry for you.

SHERIFF: Do you know whom you are addressing? (*He stumbles.*)

RICH MAN (*Approaches the Sheriff and gives him a hand*): May I accompany you, Mr. Sheriff?

SHERIFF: As you please. But come at once then. I am very busy.

RICH MAN: It is certain, Mr. Sheriff, that I was absolutely

free from liability at my death.

OLD WOMAN (*As they move off*): I know that the King's law is not God's law, nor the judgments of men the judgments of God.

(*The Devil has peeped out from the rock.*)

JÓN: There's a rush of them down at the Old Boy's place today. But what's become of the blood of the Lamb, and all this salvation they preach about?

OLD WOMAN: There's some folks is past saving, and it's likely you're one of them. The soul can be so black that it mayn't be easy to wash it clean, not even in the blood of the Lamb. It'd be a sight better for you to cry over your wretchedness and the misery of mankind, than to laugh and please the Devil. (*Sees the Enemy, recoils and gives a cry of terror.*)

JÓN: What's up now?

OLD WOMAN (*crossing the bag and herself*):
Lord, support me in strife and woe,
Staunch the misery here below.
My soul, my heart and what else may be
Bow before thee and call to thee—
Drive the devils away from me

ENEMY: I hear your squalling, but feel no qualms
At the caterwauling of ancient psalms;
In me is a power too strong to be vexed
By the use fools make of a musty text.
I still need service about my throne,
For this I have made a man of Jón.
I saw from each inward and outward sign
The proper stuff for a rogue's design.
I moulded from childhood his condition,
In poverty, rancor, and superstition.
From pilfering crumbs and scraps he passed
To earn the name of a thief at last;
His conscience started to rot and perish,
And his rascal nature to grow and flourish;

His character turned to blackened ashes;
Then I gave him a taste of the jailer's lashes:
With fleshly passions I seared him first,
Then breathed in his spirit a drunkard's thirst,
Till his dross was purged of its precious metal,
And heaven and he could accord but little.
OLD WOMAN: That's God's to settle. (*She crosses the bag.*)
ENEMY: Who crosses thee, Jón? 'Twas a woman's hand:
The cross will fail, but the sin shall stand.
Thy soul, though small, is a useful chattel,
And 'tis mine to fight and to win the battle.
Thou hast served me in life and in death as well,
And shalt have thy pay—in the flames of Hell.
Nor prayer nor law can avoid the evil
That waits thy soul.
JÓN: That's the very devil!
OLD WOMAN: Be quiet, Jón.
ENEMY: Nay, for both 'tis best
No wise to vary from my behest.
Come then to me, nor clamber and crawl
On crags where all who attempt them fall.
Thou knowest, Jón, that thy dirty poke
Is a short-lived shelter for foolish folk.
Thy soul I have roasted far too well
To let it escape to heaven from hell.
And how can the Lord my power defy?
I am stronger than He.
OLD WOMAN: That is hell's own lie!
ENEMY (*While he speaks, the sky darkens*):
Full half of the world for mine I claim,
Its depths, its darkness and all its flame:
So shuffling subterfuge profits nought;
Gainst rebels my craft and my might are brought.
For the recreant soul that declines my hell
I will fashion a new and a potent spell.

I darken the sky with my mighty power:
I charm the clouds, and the lightnings shower.
(*Thunder and lightning.*)
The road of the thunder is my call;
I pound the mountains to atoms small,
And then my potency bursts its chain,
Which the Lord of Light would dare restrain.
His host shall break, as resistance ceases,
His heaven be cloven and dashed to pieces,
And down to the bottomless pit be driven—
(*Laughs.*)
OLD WOMAN: Save and defend us, God in Heaven!
ENEMY: Think you to 'scape my hand's control,
         You damned, bag-skulking, shrimp of a soul?
OLD WOMAN: Pray hard, Jón dear.
JÓN: Then open the bag, so as I can get a look at him.
OLD WOMAN: You're a damned good-for-nothing rascal, but
I'll never let you fall into his clutches. God be with us!
   (*Michael, the Archangel, appears on a high crag. Beams of
light from him shine on the Old Woman, who falls on her knees.*)
JÓN: What's up now?
OLD WOMAN (*In a whisper*): The Archangel Michael.
MICHAEL: Praise to the Lord Hosts,
Maker of heaven and earth,
The Lord of life and death.
Though heavy be your loads,
Yet climb the steep ascent
Up to the Golden Gate.
Wayfarers, undismayed,
Pass on, with me your guard,
Against the Fiend's assaults,
Till sentence is pronounced.
Heaven's messenger am I,
Sent from the source of light,
Where only justice rules,

And peace for ever reigns.

OLD WOMAN: Amen. (*Michael the Archangel disappears.*)

JÓN: Well, I thought that stuff of his was pretty feeble.

OLD WOMAN: How can you say such things, Jón, about our escort and guardian, the blessed messenger of light! (*Flash of lightning. The Old Woman leaps to her feet.*)

ENEMY (*Who has been standing on the watch*):
O slaves of light, I have known you too long
To lend my ears to your tuneless song;
The burden of all your bellowing seems
A feeble echo of ancient hymns;
I prefer the blast of a belly windy,
Or the literal version of hell's own shindy;
And sooner to stocks and stones I'd kneel
Than the drone of your star-crazed spinning wheel.
I know no angel ninny to equal
For empty-headedness that same Michael,
That sexless envoy of Heaven. No wonder
My sneer is lightning, my laughter—thunder.
(*Thunder and lightning. Howling from the depths below.*)

JÓN: Now I'm really enjoying myself.

OLD WOMAN: Are you losing the glimmer of sense that God gave you? It's a fearful disgrace to listen to you. If the lightning was to strike me, where'd you be then? Don't you hear the howling from down below?

JÓN: It shall never be said that Jón Jónsson went to heaven with his mouth shut and without a word to say for himself.

ENEMY: Well, go your ways, you will learn ere long
What doom awaits you, whose laws are strong.
Then you may pack in a smaller poke.

OLD WOMAN: That was a meaner devil who spoke!

JÓN: Do you mean to stick here forever, or what?

OLD WOMAN: Do you think it's weather for climbing slippery cliffs?

JÓN: Well, didn't he say he was going to look after you in

front and behind, that there ambassador of heaven?

OLD WOMAN: Well, all right then, in God's name! (*Climbs on a ledge of rock, and throws herself against the mountain side to shelter from the lightning.*)

ENEMY: E'en though the rocky ascent be passed,
My power is the same to the very last.
The prettiest souls have been oft my prey,
When once in the scales of truth they lay.
So let them the question of guilt dissect,
You'll see what wages Jón can expect.
On then, old woman, before much longer
We'll see and prove which is the stronger,
He who reigns in the fiends' abyss,
Or the Lord of Light in Paradise.
(*Laughs.*)

JÓN: The gall of the man!

OLD WOMAN: It wouldn't hurt if I was to say the old traveler's prayer that my poor old granny taught me, blessed be her memory! That prayer's always brought a lucky trip.

JÓN: Then be quick and cough it up.

OLD WOMAN (*kneeling*):
Show me the light of your guiding star,
Melchior, Kaspar, and Balthasar:
Abraham, Isaac, and Jacob too
Follow me all my journey through.
Holy Spirit, thy comfort lend,
Angel Michael, my head defend.
Gentle Saviour, with me abide,
Blessed Mary, be by my side.
Guard the heart of me, Peter and Paul,
Then am I safe, whate'er befall.
Blissful then shall my journey be
And home and flock I again shall see. Amen.

JÓN: Amen and hallelujah. And let's be getting on.
(*The Old Woman gets up and starts climbing.*)

ENEMY (*Looks out from the rocks in the flashes of lightning,
and stares menacingly up the hill*):
I follow the laggards who go astray,
And show them their path—
JÓN: Till then, good day!

CURTAIN

ACT III

Woodland trees with green foliage on both sides. In the center is a view across green meadows. In the distance are rays of light from heaven and the Golden Gate. Sunshine and clear blue sky.

OLD WOMAN (*Entering with the bag*): Lord God and Heavenly Father! How glorious! I must say, Jón, this is a land of plenty.

JÓN: So?

OLD WOMAN: Yes, don't you know we've crossed the border of the Heavenly Father's estate in heaven?

JÓN: Oh, have we?

OLD WOMAN: This is what I can see—and more: trees in full leaf on both sides, green fields stretching on and away, pasture for I dunno how many hundreds of horses, and far away the light from the Heavenly Jerusalem and the Golden Gate.

JÓN: Oh, really?

OLD WOMAN: It's as if you didn't care about it. You're so dull and sluggish.

JÓN: It's not as if I could see anything.

OLD WOMAN: No, poor boy, I know. But you must feel that there's perfect calm and sunshine here, none of them storms and lightning we had going up the mountain.

JÓN: Blowed if I notice a bit of change.

OLD WOMAN: You just doze away in your bag, and if you open your mouth it's only to curse and swear—just as if you really wanted to get into trouble.

JÓN: Ain't you pitching it pretty strong?

OLD WOMAN: Well, is it strange if I'm hurt? Why do you think I took on this trip?

JÓN: You wanted it. I never asked you.

OLD WOMAN: I might have known it. You get more and

more ungrateful as time goes on. How do you think you'd be now, if I'd let you go into the monster's open jaws, as you wanted yourself?

JÓN: Do you think I'd have been any worse off?

OLD WOMAN: Ain't you afeared for your soul's salvation, Jón?

JÓN: I've never been afeared of anything.

OLD WOMAN: Maybe. You get cheekier and cheekier as we get near the gate. Do you think that's the best way to save your soul? No, Jón, now you must look to yourself. Now or never. And in this heavenly spot. How lovely all round!

JÓN: Open the bag.

OLD WOMAN: No, I daren't. The Enemy may very well be close by—you're never tired of harping on his name. He can change himself into the shape of every living thing, the wretch, beasts or men or even angels. Are you feeling bad?

JÓN: Need you ask?

OLD WOMAN: You'd better call to mind your schooling a bit, before we get to the gate. You'll have to confess there, and there's no hope if St. Peter doesn't feel that everything you say is steeped in burning remorse and penitence.

JÓN: I think I can do quite well without confessing to him, the old billy goat.

OLD WOMAN: You can't get out of it. Anyhow he knows all about every mortal thing folks have done on earth.

JÓN: You don't say! I'll bet he knows!

OLD WOMAN: You'll find out before the end. I mean to tidy myself up a bit, before we come to meet anyone.

JÓN: Are you expecting all the hosts of heaven to come and meet you?

OLD WOMAN: Who knows but that the blessed Archangel Michael may have told them I'm on the way. I may be of little account on earth and still less up here in heaven, but it don't follow that everyone will have forgotten me. (*Goes a few steps from the bag.*) I'm going to wash off most of the sweat in this here spring.

Jón: Hi! Shove the bag down into the spring in the mean-time, to cool me a bit.

Old Woman: Are you dreadfully hot?

Jón: Hot? What do you think?

Old Woman: All right, then. (*Puts the bag into the spring.*) Are you more comfy now?

Jón: Ah-h, that was good!

Old Woman: There you have a foretaste of heaven. Say your prayers now, Jón dear.

Jón: I'll say them quietly to myself. That will do just as well.

Old Woman: Do so, dear, (*Unfastens her dress, and washes and dries herself.*) I see myself in the spring as if it was the finest looking glass.

Jón: Must be a sight to see your ugly mug.

Old Woman: Is that how you says your prayers?

Jón: Don't interrupt me. (*Pause.*)

Old Woman: I feel I've grown many years younger by wash-ing myself in this holy well of heaven.

Jón: That's quite likely. You haven't got your virginity back?

Old Woman: There's something moving in the woods. If they was to come here, then mind and don't say a single word unless you're spoke to.

Jón: Anything that comes from you will be clever enough.

Old Woman: You're not funny.

(*Enter the Priest and the Old Woman's Parents. They are dressed in white and hold palm branches, with their hands crossed on their breasts—very solemn.*)

Priest: We greet thee in the name of the Eternal Trinity.

Old Woman: God be with you.

Mother (*Aside*) : She doesn't recognize us.

Priest (*Speaks all the time in his pulpit manner*): It is not to be hoped that thou shouldst perceive from our countenances who we are, seeing that it is long since we, by the Lord's mercy, were called forth from the great vale of sorrow, where men walk clad in curses as with a garment, and the teeth of sin are

as teeth of lions whose bite is mortal. I am a servant of God
and thine ancient spiritual counselor, and these are thine
earthly parents.

(*The Mother takes a step nearer to the Old Woman and
spreads out her arms. The Old Woman kisses her.*)

MOTHER: A hearty welcome to you, my child.

FATHER (*As the Old Woman kisses him*): The Lord bless
your coming.

OLD WOMAN (*Drying her eyes on a corner of her apron*): I
knowed you at once—but you've grown so white and fine. But
how nice of you to come and meet me.

PRIEST: Submit thyself in all things to God's will, and thank,
above all, thine intercessors, thy Redeemer and Comforter,
who offered himself to death and paid with his precious blood
for the sins of mankind.

OLD WOMAN: Oh, you're still the same blessed light.

PRIEST: I rejoice unspeakably to see once more the children
of my former congregation, within the bounds of eternal life.

OLD WOMAN: Well, what can you tell me about my boys?

MOTHER: They were given wings at once, like everyone who
dies in childhood, and now they flutter round the sky, singing
with the angel children.

FATHER: You needn't be the least uneasy about them, my
daughter.

OLD WOMAN: Bless their little hearts. I'm terribly anxious
to see them. (*Sobs.*) But no doubt I don't deserve that mercy.

PRIEST: As it is necessary for thee to comprehend, and as I
have ofttimes declared unto thee aforetime in the house of God,
it is here, in the land of the living, that the scriptures are ful-
filled, which declare that the mortal children of earth shall meet
again and be welcomed by their beloved ones, so soon as they
are called away from the realm of the world, provided that they
have been pure and devout and submissive to the power of the
Lord in their daily lives, and behaved themselves prudently and
in accordance with his word, as is purely and clearly set down

in his holy book. If thou hast so done, here is neither room nor occasion for sorrow, seeing that thou shalt then shortly be allotted a lasting dwelling place within the Golden Portal and partake of the habitation of the angels and the elect.

Jón: He talks just like a prayer-book. (*Laughs.*)

Father: What was that?

Old Woman: The rejoicing of the redeemed can be heard all the way here. They must be wonderful happy.

Father: You should know that quite well, my daughter. We, who live in the heavenly Jerusalem, have received the highest prize of victory.

Priest: Even as thou seest, we have put off the earthly rags of our sin, washed in the regenerating fountains of the Holy Spirit, put on the white robes of innocence, and thus, bearing branches of palm, we sing and dance around the throne of the Lamb in an ever shining choir of glory. There is no poverty there, nor wrath nor adversity, but absolute plenty and health, thoughts of peace and a most blessed welcome. There we are satisfied with the love and mercy of the Lord.

Old Woman: That's just what it said in the revival hymns you gave me.

Father: We believed God's word and acted accordingly. It's always been our one wish and prayer that you'd do the same.

Mother: As if our daughter hadn't done that! Hasn't she shown the fullest faith, and Christian patience in word and deed?

Father: Obedience to parents is one of the highest duties of God's children. You broke that obligation, my daughter, when you went and married Jón, who by his ungodly life disgraced the word of the Lord, you yourself, your parents, and all the family.

Jón: You'd have been more at home in the place down below, old man.

(*The Mother catches hold of her husband.*)

Father: We are saved. No harm can come to us.

OLD WOMAN: I won't argue with you, father. But I thought that you and everyone else that lives in heaven ought to be able to forgive my Jón his trespasses. Isn't it written somewhere —love your enemies, bless them that curse you?

FATHER: Justice will judge him, when the time comes.

PRIEST: Though Jón has too long hearkened to the ungodly, whose fellowship is as fuel of fire, and thus by his behavior and course of life and pride run the way of destruction, even as bloodthirsty and false traitors, who betray their Lord and Master, as did the traitor Judas, yet may he be enabled mercifully to escape from the claws of the Enemy, but only if tears run down his cheeks, and his prayers are even as those of the penitent robber on the cross.

FATHER: Whatever's in store for him, we wish with all our hearts that you may not have to pay for your fault, since you must have repented it bitterly.

OLD WOMAN: No, father, I haven't.

MOTHER: God help you, my dear child.

OLD WOMAN: I loved my Jón. And it says in God's word that those who love a lot shall be forgiven a lot.

PRIEST: In the last moments before a human creature comes to the great portal, it serves him best to tarry alone and confer with his God and his conscience. Wherefore we will walk a little longer in the wood, but soon after return. God be merciful to us all. Amen.

MOTHER: I will pray the holy mother of God to pity you.

OLD WOMAN (*As they move away*): Nay, I'd rather you prayed for my Jón.

JÓN: Damned if I care for their prayers. It's like you to demean yourself to these spirits out of the hymn book, this precious trio!

OLD WOMAN: It's a shame to listen to you.

JÓN: Have you no self-respect—or what is it?

(*The Enemy, disguised as an angel, peeps out from among the trees close to the spring, and reaches for the bag. He has a fiery red shock of hair, which hides his horns.*)

JÓN: Pick me out at once from this poisonous hole. Do you want me to catch my death of cold?

(*The Old Woman sees the Enemy, and snatches the bag in a panic.*)

ENEMY (*Mimicking the Archangel Michael*) :
Praise to the Mighty, him alone,
From him have I been sent
To guard you, wayfarers, upon your road.
Put not your trust in any word of those
Who swell with overweening arrogance,
Born of their own success.
Entrust to me your load,
And I will bear it on,
Home to the Golden Gate.
Since Might has sent me as his messenger.

OLD WOMAN: Get thee behind me, Satan!

JÓN: That's a nice way to address him.

(*The Enemy disappears.*)

OLD WOMAN: Oh, his looks suits his talk, even if he is got up as an angel. Trust me to spot him!

JÓN (*Laughing*) : But what are you dawdling here for? Ain't you done titivating yourself enough.

(*Enter the Farmer and Helga, dressed in white. He is elderly, she is young and sprightly.*)

OLD WOMAN (*Welcoming*): Can I believe my eyes? Is it you, darling?

(*They kiss one another repeatedly, pat one another on the shoulders, and both talk at the same time, while greeting one another.*)

HELGA: How are you, darling. Welcome, welcome!

OLD WOMAN: Bless you, bless you, and thanks from my heart for all the good old times.

HELGA: And thank you ever so much more (*They finish kissing.*) But what fun to see you again!

OLD WOMAN: What ought I to say, then? (*Shakes hands with the Farmer.*) How do you do, old friend.

FARMER: Good day and welcome. So you know me, even though I'm not in my old duds?

OLD WOMAN: Do you think I don't know your face?

HELGA: I wanted to be the very first to meet you on this side. But I came after your parents and the priest, after all.

OLD WOMAN: Yes, they were with me for a little while and have just gone off into the wood. But I couldn't help it: I felt somehow so unworthy compared with them.

HELGA: I think they've been much too godfearing while they were on earth. But aren't you tired after your journey? I should almost think so. But now it's pretty well over.

OLD WOMAN: Just like you. You're just as young and pretty as ever, and your nature's not altered. But what a pretty dress you've got, and how it suits you!

HELGA: That's the sort they weave now in heaven.

OLD WOMAN: I'm sure that not even the storekeeper's wife ever had such a fine frock, nor of course the priest's wife when she was alive, neither. (*Feels the dress.*) I should think this was good wearing stuff—even though it may be thin—and stands washing? But does it give you any cover, dear?

HELGA (*Laughing*): Here you could easily go stark naked all the year round.

OLD WOMAN: Now you're at your old jokes. But ain't they terrible strict here—about morals and such?

HELGA (*Laughing*): Bless you, don't ask me that! Here they're all saints—much too saintly. At least the lads at home in our parish had some life in them.

OLD WOMAN: Yes. Reckon they was not too good to kick over the traces a bit.

HELGA: Some folks are shocked at everything. But a lot of what men call sin is no more than fun, innocent fun.

OLD WOMAN: That's what I've always said too.

FARMER: Was the cattle in middling good condition down

there, when you left home?

HELGA: He was bound to get onto that. He'll never talk about anything but cattle.

OLD WOMAN: Thanks. I should say they'd done pretty moderate. It turned wintry early in the autumn, and though really there wasn't much snow, the frost as you might say killed all the grazing for the sheep.

FARMER: Any losses from disease?

OLD WOMAN: Well, it hit them here and there.

FARMER: That's bad. Folks must have started folding them at the first gathering. But the horses are still at grass?

OLD WOMAN: Oh yes, they're left to God and the frost.

HELGA: I remember when the village lads used to saddle the ponies and gallop about the farm, like princes in a fairytale. Many's the horse whose flanks I've patted. I gave some of them milk to drink, when I left them.

FARMER: Blessed creatures. It was always a poor soil at home, the hay crop was scrappy and the grazing mostly bad.

HELGA: But I feel at times I'd almost like to swap heaven for my old parish.

OLD WOMAN: Lord, fancy that now! Why, the soil there is nothing like what it is here.

FARMER: It was wonderful what the lambs was like this autumn. But how did the farmers do on the whole?

OLD WOMAN: Oh, it seems as if some can't never make ends meet, even though they scrapes every penny and breaks their backs.

FARMER: That's true as day, but still farming's the best way to live. How was your Jón, when you passed on?

JÓN: Damn bad! (*They look at one another.*)

OLD WOMAN: Did you hear anything?

FARMER: I wouldn't say no.

OLD WOMAN: You was the best and truest friends to Jón and me, while you was on earth. Private-like to you, I've got a little something with me on the trip.

HELGA: Now I'm getting curious.

OLD WOMAN: You see that bag there. What do you think's in it?

JÓN: Me.

HELGA: How in the world—?

OLD WOMAN: Say howdyedo to the folks, Jón dear. You know that namesake of yours, that was always so helpful and kind to us?

JÓN: Good day, namesake.

FARMER: That's his voice.

OLD WOMAN: Now the lady too. You know who she is.

JÓN: Good day to you.

HELGA: Am I to believe it's you, Jón?

JÓN: Oh yes, it's me all right, worse luck.

OLD WOMAN: It's his soul, bless it.

FARMER: Well, I'm clean flummoxed. How are you, name-sake?

JÓN: I suppose you've grown so proud from living in heaven that you didn't mean to speak to me, you damned old scoundrel.

OLD WOMAN: Don't he sound still like his old self?

HELGA: It's refreshing to hear old Jón talking our blessed mother tongue. How did you manage to pack your husband into this bag?

JÓN: She shoved it in front of my lips just as I popped off, and so I spat my rotten soul into the bag.

HELGA (*To Old Woman*): However did you think of it?

OLD WOMAN: Oh, don't ask me that.

JÓN: She thought I'd have to go to hell, like all the great sinners.

HELGA: But you're not a great sinner, Jón.

JÓN: Listen to that now, old gal.

OLD WOMAN: Of course you're a sin-afflicted soul.

JÓN: That's a whopping lie. Open the bag directly, and let me out of this hell. I'm not a great sinner.

OLD WOMAN: Have a little patience, dearie. It won't be long

now.

Jón (*In a rage*): I'm not a great sinner!

OLD WOMAN: Well, it don't matter. I'll not let you out of my hands till we're at the gate.

FARMER: I can't make head nor tail of all this.

OLD WOMAN: That's what I'd expect you to say. I hardly know myself whether I'm dead or alive, but I do know that's my Jón's soul, in that there bag. However things go, I intends to bring it safe to the gate.

FARMER: I always knew, namesake, that you had a good wife.

Jón: Rot!

FARMER: You mustn't talk like that, namesake.

OLD WOMAN (*In tears*): I had ought to be used to them kind words of his.

FARMER: In heaven we have to mind our speech, like steady respectable farmers, and keep up the reputation of our old parishes.

Jón: This is a damned dog kennel!

HELGA: Well, in spite of everything, it was often good to be on the earth. When do you think you've enjoyed yourself most, Jón dear?

Jón: When I had enough booze and baccy.

FARMER: And I, when I carried the fresh hay to my sheep.

OLD WOMAN: Though I'm ashamed to say so, I never enjoyed myself better than in the arms of my Jón.

Jón: Ah, it's something that you should think that!

HELGA (*Sighing dreamily*): Happiness came to me like a lovely song that you can't ever forget. (*Pause.*)

Jón: Well, it wasn't altogether such a damn bad place—our dirty old world! And to tell you the truth, I've never had a slavish belief in this everlasting bliss of the hymn book.

FARMER: You'd talk different if you saw what we see.

Jón: Oh, do you think so?

FARMER: Here there's unlimited land and masses of grass.

Jón: You get a tidy crop of hay, then?

FARMER: No, we never puts a scythe to the ground here.

OLD WOMAN: What's that you say? Don't you never make no hay?

JÓN: What, are you all so bone-lazy, or haven't you any live-stock?

OLD WOMAN: Need you ask that? Don't you remember how I told you on the way, when I was passing the blessed cattle: first the flocks of sheep with silver fleeces, and then the stud of horse—but you must have managed to hear them whinnying, they neighed quite a lot—and then the herds of cows, and they was something like cows, Jón. And the bulls, sleek as a mass-cope.

JÓN: All this stock must take a tidy bit of feeding.

FARMER: All the stock finds its own grazing here, all the year round.

JÓN: Now you're pulling my leg, namesake.

HELGA: No, he's telling nothing but the truth, Jón dear. All the same, at first folks can get bored with all these joys of heaven. Never a storm, always flat calm—as you might say.

OLD WOMAN: Aye, it was always refreshing to come from the fire out into the cold.

HELGA: That's why I sometimes feel too well off, and long to be back on earth, with all its toiling and moiling.

OLD WOMAN (*Patting her shoulder*): Oh, my dear!

HELGA: I miss most of all never seeing snow. I never forget how lovely the mountains were, with their white peaks gleaming in the sunshine. At times I've even wished to be out in an Iceland blizzard.

OLD WOMAN: I can easy believe it may be dreadful wearisome, this eternal mild calm, this never-ending heavenly weather.

HELGA: To say nothing of the dark. What fun it was, and often how handy! (*Jón laughs.*) But here we have sunshine all the year round—glaring bright, everlasting day.

JÓN: Damned if I believe what you say. But, tell me, namesake, are there any cattle that live out all the time?

FARMER: I'd never have believed there were any such sheep. They never falls off. It's a sheer pleasure to take a look at them.

JÓN: Them fat-bellied ones can't be bad eating?

OLD WOMAN: But the cows—I suppose they don't stay dry long? Ain't they all wonderful milkers?

FARMER: They're first rate.

JÓN: But the horses? Do they ride them?

FARMER: It's just like sitting on your bed—it feels just like a bird in flight. And as to the build of them—there's simply no describing it in words.

JÓN: I can hardly believe that you can't describe them in Icelandic.

OLD WOMAN: These are heavenly animals. You have to mind that, Jón dear.

JÓN: Even if they are heavenly, as far as I remember, folks used sometimes to describe the Lord himself. So I should think it ought to be easy to describe his cattle. But tell me, namesake, do you own many sheep?

FARMER: I can't exactly answer that.

JÓN: Eh?

HELGA: He owns all the livestock in heaven—and so do I. And soon you'll own them all—every single one.

JÓN: Now I can't understand anymore.

HELGA: In heaven no one is poor and no one is rich. Everyone owns everything there.

JÓN: Now you're at your jokes again. (*Laughs.*)

OLD WOMAN: Are you laughing at it, Jón dear?

JÓN: You must think that I'll believe everything you stuff me with. Hasn't each farmer got his own house?

FARMER: Nobody cares about that.

JÓN: Indeed. Then don't people marry up here, in this heavenly village?

HELGA: No. No one marries here.

JÓN (*Laughing*): I like that! What do the women say to those regulations? Can the men take them altogether without ceremony, so to speak?

HELGA: It's you that's joking now, Jón dear.

JÓN: Perhaps it's not quite as mad an arrangement here in some ways as I thought.

OLD WOMAN: Mayn't Jón and I be together, if both of us is allowed to get in?

HELGA: Yes, yes, bless your innocence, if you want to yourself.

JÓN: Oh, but mightn't a man now get himself someone younger and slimmer than you, old gal?

OLD WOMAN: You'll be glad to have your old grievance, if I knows you right.

JÓN: Then do people lie out of doors at night on all the crofts?

HELGA: It's nice to sleep in the grass.

JÓN: In the grass? No thanks! But since all the stock fends for itself—what do you really do? Nothing?

FARMER: I can hardly tell about that.

JÓN: Now you're telling me a lie, namesake.

FARMER: There's some goes round the stock for pleasure.

HELGA: Some pick fruit from the trees, others make garlands of flowers.

JÓN (*Contemptuously*): Make garlands of flowers? Is that a job, now? No one can live on that damned nonsense.

HELGA: Some play with little birds.

(*Jón shrieks with laughter.*)

OLD WOMAN: Pretty thoughts you've got now!

HELGA: Some listen to the singing of the heavenly choir.

JÓN: I shouldn't think that howling would be edifying. Do you eat at all, namesake? You surely don't live on garlands and the songs of angels.

FARMER: We're fed on heavenly food.

OLD WOMAN: The Lord's everlasting love and mercy, as the priest used to say.

JÓN: He can eat his eternal love himself, the poisonous old

glutton. I want something more solid.

OLD WOMAN: You remember what it says in the hymn—"clear wine, with marrow and fatness too shall there be freely given."

JÓN: Is that true, namesake?

FARMER: Here there is all that the heart can desire.

OLD WOMAN: Do you hear that, Jón dear?

JÓN: I believe you're all lying about this, but I believe my namesake more than the priest.

OLD WOMAN: Wouldn't you like to ask now how you ought to behave to get into all this happiness?

JÓN: Do you think you won't be able to save me?

OLD WOMAN (*To Helga*): Please tell me, dear, how I ought to behave at the gate.

HELGA: That's quite simple. You knock three times. St. Peter comes out, and you tell him all the truth.

OLD WOMAN: I know he must be quite straightforward and simple. But—I suppose no one needs to try hiding anything?

FARMER: It's best to make a clean breast of everything.

JÓN: Oh, is it?

OLD WOMAN: And oughtn't the soul to be full of remorse and penitence?

FARMER: Yes, there's no denying that.

OLD WOMAN: You hear, Jón. And if now he should get in, which is quite uncertain, what happens then?

HELGA: Then he's washed in the water of regeneration, and dressed in white robes. It's all done in a flash.

JÓN: Really? They must be damned spry.

OLD WOMAN (*Whispering*): Do I have to tell my parents about Jón?

FARMER: That makes no difference.

(*Enter Priest and Parents.*)

PRIEST: Now the great hour is swiftly approaching when thou shalt stand trembling before thy Lord and Judge, and beseech him with prayers and humble supplications; since it is my hope that thou hast gained that blessed humility, likewise that gracious state of penitence, as also the one true faith: for thou hast been taught as a child of God and frequented constantly his Holy Church.

OLD WOMAN: Certainly I couldn't count the times I've been to church. But it did me good—no stones for bread. Oh them sermons of yours, what a help and consolation!

PRIEST: Ofttimes didst thou make thy way thither by hard roads and in foul weather, whilst others rested at home in their sins, who had a shorter road and were in every wise stronger in body and constitution.

FARMER: Some of us couldn't leave home. If I knew the beasts was short of food, I paid no attention to nothing, not even to God's word.

HELGA: You certainly had your sheep as much to thank for your salvation as our blessed priest.

PRIEST: It is good for us to be here. And I can still pray my old prayer for the children of my congregation, both those who are here and those who are dwelling yet in the world below, in the weakness of the flesh and the hurts and perils of the temptations of the Devil. (*Sacred singing in the distance. The Priest clasps his hands on his breast.*)

O thou most mighty Lord of glory, thou who alone art crowned, spotless and innocent, bless thou all our counsel and condition, our aspirations and intentions, our going out and our coming in, and make all thy handiwork to prosper. Grant good fortune to our fishermen, and fruitfulness to our cattle, protect us from pestilence and famine, flood and tempest, lightning and thunderstorms, and impending perils of the elements. Defend us from spirits of the air, wild beasts, venomous serpents, and all the assaults of the Devil, from mortal peril and from extinction. Grant us that we may make ready in time and fill our lamps with olive oil and, endued with the breastplate of faith and the helm of hope and the sword of charity, may meet our beloved bridegroom and go in unto thy wedding feast, before the door of mercy has been shut. And when thou dividest the sheep from the goats, let thy blessed right hand lead us, thy spirit control us, thy seraphim guard us—and sweeten all our adversity with a foretaste of the heavenly joy. (*Jón makes a sound to show that he has grown bored.*) Amen.

THE OLD WOMAN'S PARENTS: Amen.

JÓN: Amen.

OLD WOMAN: If the precious gift of mercy is vouchsafed me, it'll be thanks not least to my old minister.

HELGA: While I was on earth, I never thought about death, I very often forgot to say my prayers, and very seldom went to church—and yet they let me in. If I've managed to deserve that, in spite of everything, I think everyone ought to deserve it straight away.

FARMER: I think so too.

OLD WOMAN: If you had your way, my Jón wouldn't need to worry.

HELGA: Your Jón? (*The Parents look at one another.*) God knows, he's deserved many times over to live in heaven for all eternity. If I had my way, I'd forgive everybody everything.

OLD WOMAN: It's always been a sort of heavenly joy to be in your company.

PRIEST: As one having the cure of souls, I take leave to ask: Has your Jón done anything wrong since last time?

OLD WOMAN: That's not for me to judge.

FATHER: Is he still in the cottage?

OLD WOMAN: If he ain't on his way up to the Golden Gate.

FATHER: On the way here?

JÓN: Oh yes. Did you think I was immortal? Put that in your pipe and smoke it!

(*The Parents look at one another.*)

PRIEST: We will all accompany you home, but at the Golden Gate you, like others, are obliged to stand alone. We will also pray for you fervently in the meantime, and when you enter into glory we will sing Hosanna in our hearts.

OLD WOMAN: Oh, I'd rather you prayed for my Jón.

PRIEST: We will do that also.

JÓN: I suppose the Lamb's food has made you keen on praying.
(*Violin music and singing of angels.*)

PRIEST: What was that?

OLD WOMAN: The angels—oh, how prettily they sing!

PRIEST: You cannot really have heard them.

FATHER: I heard too.

JÓN: You're just the same damned bootlicker. (*The Old Woman hides the bag under her apron. Enter the Fiddler and Three Child-Angels. They are all dressed in shining garments. The fiddler is playing his fiddle, and the angels on small violins. They dance round the Old Woman, singing "Eia, eia!"*)

OLD WOMAN: My darling boys!

ANGELS: Yes, that's who we are, mummy. (*They kiss her on the cheeks.*)

OLD WOMAN (*In tears*): I can't hardly believe them's the sons of Jón and me—such divine creatures! And yet I recognize them, my blessed little goldilocks.

FIDDLER (*Plays and sings. The Angels join in*):
Horsehair on catgut,
And hollow wooden frame;
That was all the fortune
To the fiddler's name.

He sang in the cottage,
And the goodwife soon
Gave him his supper
And some nice new shoon.

The fiddler was a lover
Of beauty and of song;
So now he lives for ever
In the ages long.

Horsehair on catgut,

And hollow wooden frame;
That was all the fortune
To the fiddler's name.

OLD WOMAN: I reckon he hadn't much to be grateful to me for, poor lad.

HELGA: You remember him, then?

OLD WOMAN: I've never forgotten. I told you you two would meet again, and yet he was only a bird of passage, same as a wild swan from the hills.

(*The Fiddler and Helga look into each other's faces with sparkling eyes.*)

HELGA: Sing some more, my dear. Sing that old song of yours about love.

FIDDLER (*Addresses his song to her. The Angels accompany and dance. Before the end of the song, all except the Old Woman start dancing*):
Long was the time I tarried,
My lily fair, for thee:
My tuneful strings I carried
When wintry storms blew free;
I trysted neath the birches
That grew by Greenwood Lea.

Through shady groves I wandered,
My lily fair, with thee;
While livelong summer squandered
Its sunlight on the sea,
And zephyrs stirred the birches
That grow by Greenwood Lea.

Now, heart with heart combining,
My lily fair, we see
A flaming radiance shining
Across the welkin free;

And blithe 'tis neath the birches
That grow by Greenwood Lea.

(*Helga throws herself upon the Fiddler's neck and kisses him. Dance with music.*)

OLD WOMAN (*Fascinated*): Oh the blessed angels! (*Aside to Jón.*) Do you hear, darling?

JÓN: Do you think I've gone deaf? Have the kids got wings?

OLD WOMAN (*Trying to keep Jón quiet, whispers*): Angels' wings.

FIDDLER AND ANGELS (*Show themselves about to go away, sing*): Eia, eia!

ALL (*Draw up in file and sing as they move off*):
To the Golden Gate we go,
—Eia, eia!
Bright the heavenly legions show;
—Eia, eia!
Mary maid, and Saviour high
Pity those who live and die.
—Eia, eia!

CURTAIN

ACT IV

At the Golden Gate. Music and wordless songs are heard in the distance. The three angels enter, take their places, and point to the gate. The Old Woman comes after them, crosses herself, falls on her knees and prays in silence.

ANGELS: We await you inside the gate. (*Exeunt.*)

OLD WOMAN: Amen. In his blessed name, amen. (*The song stops. Old Woman looks up.*) Then the time has come. (*Sees that the angels have gone and rises to her feet.*) So we two are alone outside the Golden Gate.

JÓN: At last!

OLD WOMAN: Have you repented your sins now, as humble sinners should?

JÓN: I'll hardly change for the better from this.

OLD WOMAN: Remember then to mind your speech like a Christian.

JÓN: Haven't I always?

OLD WOMAN: If you're asked to speak, then tell the truth honestly. St. Peter knows everything.

JÓN: You think so?

OLD WOMAN: And try now to talk a bit gentler like, Jón dear. That'll make a bettter impression on strangers than this continual off-handedness.

JÓN: Oh?

OLD WOMAN: If, by God's help, you should be let in, then you must give my best love to our boys. And so I wish you everlasting—

JÓN: Look here, just go and knock.

OLD WOMAN: Are you ready now to meet your judge.

JÓN: Oh yes, just as I've always been.

OLD WOMAN: Then I'll knock in the Lord's name. (*Knocks*

three times.)

JÓN: Looks as if they wasn't in any hurry to come to the door.

OLD WOMAN: In the realm of heavenly peace, there ain't no hurry about anything.

JÓN: Perhaps they thinks it's good manners to keep folks waiting. Knock again, woman.

OLD WOMAN: Take it easy, Jón dear, and mind you don't speak till you're spoke to. (*The gate opens, showing a vision of glory inside. Enter St. Peter. He is in a long blue gown, with a bunch of keys at his belt and a big ledger under his arm. In face and appearance he suggests an old church deacon.*) God bless you, Holy guardian of heaven, servant of the Lord and blessed apostle.

PETER: So you are from Iceland? Peace be with you, my good woman. (*Shuts the gate.*)

OLD WOMAN: I'd humbly beg your pardon for giving you this trouble, poor wretched creature that I am.

PETER: It's never been exactly restful, having charge of the keys here in heaven. But so far I've tried to do my duty, and as far as I know the Holy Trinity haven't yet wanted to find anyone else for the job.

OLD WOMAN: Well, and it's certainly most unlikely that they'd hit on anyone else who was better and more trustworthy. I knows that much about you from my reading of the Holy Scripture. But what a grace it is—to stand face to face with you.

PETER: No one who has read the scriptures wonders who I am. But isn't there a widespread neglect of that study? So I have gathered anyhow, from some of those who have come here.

OLD WOMAN: I've often seen pictures of you in religious books and on altar-pieces, and I must say that you looks and behaves even grander in reality. But in the pictures there was always a ring of light round your head—but of course you only wears that on special occasions, though. But it suits you uncommon well, blessed man of God.

PETER: That's enough now, my good woman.

OLD WOMAN: Oh naturally you've got other things to attend to but listening to me. But, as you see, I've come here, and it's a long way from Iceland to heaven. I must say it's a long and weary way. And in fact, I hardly knows myself whether I've got here awake or asleep, alive or dead. But I've trusted all the time that you'd have mercy on me when I came.

PETER: Everyone trusts Peter, old as he may be. And it may not seem much, at first glance, to turn a key in a lock, but when it's this one (*Lifting up the key*) it's not all the same who holds it. It looks as if some people thought it was no more than a trifling favor to open the door for them, but it's really no small matter to grant men everlasting happiness.

OLD WOMAN: Well, it wasn't really on my own account that I came to take this on. I just wanted to have a talk with you and find out if it'd be quite impossible for you to have pity on my Jón.

PETER: I like nothing better than to take in those who have deserved it, and it was never my habit to turn innocent folks away. On the other hand people must understand that heaven is an old and respectable establishment, which will not have a stain put on its reputation. It ought to be enough if we settle about your husband when he gets here.

OLD WOMAN: He died a little while back, and isn't far off. He's had his share of trouble—plenty of it—on earth, poor chap, and seeing as how I'm his wedded wife and have had ten children by him, it was my duty to come with him from our cottage, since he hadn't many to lend him a hand, barring me and the children. But you see it'd be a great relief to me to know Jón was comfortably housed, with kind and real quality people.

PETER: Well, we shouldn't think of lodging him just in a shack here in heaven.

OLD WOMAN: If I know anything of my Jón, he'd be ready to take on a job of work to pay for his board and some old rags to wear. He was always a bit demanding, but they surely won't skimp the daily bread here in heaven. I can safely say that he

                    DAVIÐ STEFÁNSSON

was clever with his hands and especially good with animals.

PETER: That won't hurt any. But it often seems as if people don't realize till too late what is agreeable to God. Men rush through life and trust to mercy, but things can sometimes turn out differently from what they expected. We make a practice of examining all their papers here at the gate.

OLD WOMAN: I know that heaven won't be mocked. But no one expects anything special for my Jón; he'd do better in some job like minding cattle, or looking after a dairy in the summer pastures, than making up wreaths of flowers, or fiddly little chores like that.

PETER: We've never had any trouble with our folks, once they were inside the gate.

OLD WOMAN: I've no doubt Jón would get on all right with sensible folk, even though he may have had his little faults, same as all us children of men. I've had no reason to complain of him, that much is sure. And our kids wasn't no weaklings. Three of them came to meet me just now—my little lads. They've been well treated with you, and we their parents can be very thankful to you and the Heavenly Father.

PETER: Yes, they're in the best of health, the young things.

OLD WOMAN: If Jón could be father to such nice children, it's hardly likely but he was good himself at bottom. Oh, he could be a real gentleman, if it comes to that, and that was exactly his real true nature.

PETER: If that's so, there oughtn't to be any difficulty about him. But sometimes things turn up when I look at this (*Lifting the ledger.*) It's not everyone who takes care to guard against it.

OLD WOMAN: Well, you couldn't really say that my Jón was a regular churchgoer, if I'm to be quite honest, but he often read his Bible, so it didn't make much difference. He wasn't the sort of man to show off before others.

PETER (*Opens the ledger*): I'll have to take a look at his record. Oh, dear, dear, I remember. It isn't good.

OLD WOMAN: But he was a godfearing man all the same, in

his own way.

PETER: You wish Jón well. That is nice of you and will be borne in mind. But I have to answer for all I do to the Holy Trinity.

OLD WOMAN: I once read that there would be more joy here over one sinner that repented than over ninety and nine just persons.

PETER: Quite correct. But always provided he repents.

OLD WOMAN: I hope too that my Jón has done that—with God's help.

JÓN: I've never been a great sinner.

OLD WOMAN (*Looks imploringly at Peter*): You mustn't imagine that I meant to keep it from you that I'd got Jón's soul with me. It's for his sake I've come here. (*Pulls out the bag.*)

PETER: Best that I talk to the lad himself.

JÓN: Of course. And no offense.

OLD WOMAN: It'd be awful nice of you if you'd be lenient with his faults. Isn't it best for him to stay in the bag meanwhile, or should I untie it?

JÓN: Untie it, untie it directly!

PETER: The soul must appear naked before its judge.

OLD WOMAN (*Sits down and bends to untie the bag. Looks up*): But the soul is perhaps just a mere vapor, drifting out in the wind?

PETER: In your eyes it will have the appearance of Jón, just as he was in his lifetime.

OLD WOMAN: Oh then you'll let him keep his shirt and underpants. They're snow-white homespun, white as ivory. I'm so afraid he'll catch cold, if he's stripped for long. Well, I don't think I shall ever get this untied. I don't like cutting my garter.

PETER (*Stretching out his hand*): Rise up, farmer Jón, and give an account of your deeds.

JÓN (*Rises gradually till he breaks out and shakes himself*): I'm glad of this. How d'ye do, Peter old boy.

PETER: Good day, my man.

JÓN: That's the worst that has ever happened to me—to be rolled up in that rotten bag. But it's all owing to my old woman.

OLD WOMAN: Talk like a Christian, Jón dear.

JÓN: I should think I can talk exactly as I please—just like every other Icelander. I've never heard they had occasion to be ashamed of their mother tongue, so far. The clergy thinks that prayerbook language is what you talk here in the heavenly village, but—

PETER: By their fruits ye shall know them.

JÓN (*Laughing*): You talk pretty good Icelandic yourself.

OLD WOMAN: What do you suppose, man? Him, what speaks with the tongues of men and angels. But he knows, bless him, that we're simple common folks what only knows their mother tongue.

JÓN: Hold your tongue, woman. Of course Icelandic is spoke in heaven—and nothing else. Do you think they talk some kind of Latin up here?

PETER: I speak the languages of all Christian peoples.

JÓN: Have you talked to Luther?

PETER: Why do you ask?

JÓN: Have you talked to the Pope? You'd hardly care to waste words on that old scoundrel. Are there any Danes here in Heaven?

PETER: Why shouldn't I take them in?

JÓN: Are they here too, then? Well, it's all the same.

PETER: You're plainspoken people, you Icelanders.

JÓN: Yes, Peter old boy, we're used to speaking plain, so it can be heard through the roar of surf and the rumble of volcanoes. You know that Iceland's way out at sea, and that it's powered by fire and glaciers. It hasn't its like in the wide world.

PETER: True, it's a beautiful country. But somebody who came here told me that the people very soon lost their freedom, because of the quarrels and tricks of the inhabitants.

JÓN: Don't speak of it, it's a sad story. Such a thing would never have happened, if I'd been alive in those days.

PETER: It might have been expected that the men would have changed for the better, when the church was encouraged and her ministers increased.

JÓN: Not at all. It was more the other way. That was when the Devil got into the game.

OLD WOMAN: But the blessed priests, they bring us the gospel of salvation.

JÓN: They have a go at it. Much help for the soul I'd say it was, to see them yawning before the altar and slobbering in their pulpits.

OLD WOMAN: Mind what you're saying, Jón dear.

PETER: We've often had trouble with this little people, and the Prince of Darkness expects much of it. But the fight's not over yet.

OLD WOMAN: Ah, but ain't a lot of these here transgressions more pranks than real crimes? But it's nothing but the truth— we makes a very bad use of God's gifts.

PETER: Perhaps you have met some of your acquaintances who were on the way down?

(*The Old Woman sighs.*)

JÓN: I hope you're not going to compare me to that damned riffraff. Do you happen to know who I am and what my stock is, Peter old chap?

PETER (*Taking up the ledger*) : I'm pretty well informed of it, Jón Jónsson.

JÓN: Certainly my name's Jón, son of Jónsson the rich, son of Svein the hymn-writer, son of Grím the lawman, son of Klæng, son of Kári, son of Bishop Brand. I come in the direct male line from the kings of Norway.

PETER: You Icelanders don't exactly lack family pride.

JÓN: Do you know anything about family history?

PETER: I know this much, that some of your ancestors went straight to hell.

JÓN: Who told you that lie? But on the other hand, the Norse vikings didn't ever spend their time torturing sticklebacks and minnows to death, like your countrymen in Galilee. When you put to sea and had a tiny bit of a tossing, you fell to praying, shaking in your shoes and in a blue funk!

OLD WOMAN: You should be ashamed of that kind of talk to this holy man. (*To Peter.*) But seeing as he was born with this taint in his blood, and bad instincts in his body, you should make more allowances for him.

PETER: He was granted full intelligence.

JÓN: And plenty of it.

PETER: He was given sense to choose or reject.

JÓN: And I've done it too, proper.

PETER (*Turning the pages of the ledger*): Now that I know your reason for coming, I will, in accordance with my official duty, and for the further revision of your record, as it is set down in the protocol of heaven, put a few questions of conscience to you, Jón Jónsson, which I ask you to answer directly and definitely.

OLD WOMAN: Remember you're standing before your judge.

PETER: Do you acknowledge that you have received in your youth the ten commandments of God, and have also had a Christian education?

JÓN: Yes. And for every commandment I learnt, I got ten whacks from my masters.

OLD WOMAN: That was all the Christianity he had.

PETER: Do you admit the validity of the ten commandments?

JÓN: What do you think? Need you ask?

PETER: Do you claim to have acted in accordance with these commandments and lived your life as befits a child of God?

JÓN: Yes, you can put that down.

PETER: Do you remember any sins which you have committed and need to confess?

JÓN: Oh no. I don't think I remember anything of the sort. Though I might perhaps admit that I've sometimes happened to make a little slip, like everyone else. But I'm sure you're not smallminded enough to take account of that sort of thing.

PETER: Do you call it a little slip to take God's name in vain?

JÓN: Have I done that? Besides, I've always thought the Creator was above eavesdropping.

PETER: Do you call it a little slip to covet the goods of another?

JÓN: Everyone in the world does that—every man jack of them. I've never had anything of my own—not a brass farthing.

OLD WOMAN: There you're telling the truth, Jón dear. We lived on starvation level.

PETER: What are the words of the eighth commandment?

JÓN: The eighth? Is there anything special about it?

PETER: Do you remember having broken that holy commandment?

JÓN: Oh no.

OLD WOMAN: What about that leg of mutton, Jón?

JÓN: Who cares about one leg of mutton? Do you think the Heavenly Father is some kind of miser?

PETER: But what about the sheep?

JÓN: What damned sheep? Do you mean when I mistook the earmarks of those two or three scraggy sheep? That's all done with now!

PETER: Are you ready of your own will to confess your principal sins to me?

JÓN: I'll get along without admitting sins I never committed.

OLD WOMAN: But perhaps you might remember a few trifles, Jón dear.

JÓN: Shut up, woman.

PETER: Do you remember no sins which you committed with a woman?

JÓN: With a woman? Now you're joking, Peter old boy. Do you mean with my old gal?

PETER: With the wife of another man.

JÓN: That's the way! You sniff out everything. Do you suppose I've got no natural instincts? I can tell you, Peter Jóhannesson old boy, that every single man on earth is intimate with more than one woman. Fellows that had no leanings that way would be damned feeble creatures—more like. It's not the will they lack. You can write that down.

OLD WOMAN: That's true what you say, Jón dear. There's not many that don't have plenty of trouble with their bodies.

JÓN: And I asks myself—ought you to count against us as sins those instincts we've had put in our blood on purpose to keep life going in heaven and earth? Why, no child comes of itself. Is it wrong for a man to give in to a law of nature?

(The Enemy appears on the watch, dressed as before.)

PETER: Do you consider that is serving God, Jón Jónsson?

JÓN: And you can talk like that, you who denied your Saviour three times while the bloody cock crowed twice!

OLD WOMAN *(Falling on her knees)*: O Lord, have mercy on him. Draw, in thy mercy, a bloodred stroke through the record of his sins, and bathe him in the gracious fountain of salvation!

PETER *(At the gate)*: In the name of the Holy Trinity, I close the Golden Gate. *(Goes in; the gate is heard to lock.)*

OLD WOMAN *(Gets up, in tears)*: Oh, Jón dear!

JÓN: I thought he wanted taking down a peg.

OLD WOMAN: You talked just like a raving lunatic. You might have known it don't pay to quarrel with the judge.

JÓN: There was nothing else for me to do, if I wasn't to let him get the best of me. I couldn't see any different but that he was a man, same as myself.

OLD WOMAN: Have you given up all hope, then?

JÓN: I dunno as I've ever had any hope.

ENEMY: Here you can see which is the better
And stronger man—myself or Peter.
Often enough he has fled the fray. *(Laughs.)*
Checkmate! The board may be put away.
The gate is locked in the heavenly city,
Mine's open.

JÓN: It's Master!

OLD WOMAN: Oh God, have pity! (*Seizes hold of Jón.*)
ENEMY: Away with these heavenly trappings vain!
  (*Tearing off the angel disguise.*)
For all that is heaven's I here disdain.
I left it young, and I hate and scorn
Its blind insistence on creeds outworn.
'Tis not my nature to cringe and crawl:
I was made to conquer—the Lord of all!
  (*The Old Woman crosses herself and Jón.*)
ENEMY: I need no Michael to be my guide,
Though the crags be steep, on the other side.
I stick to my slave with the scourge-scored back;
I have followed Jón, I have dogged his track;
For often the dross from the soul is cleared
At the final moment—
JÓN: (*Shaking his fist at the Enemy*):   I ain't afeard!
  (*Tries to tear himself from his Old Woman.*)
ENEMY: Your wife's endeavors are vain to save you;
You are weighed and damned—come Jón, I'll have you.
Though the cross be marked upon belly and breast,
Nor life nor record are changed the least.
For ever and ever you bear my brand,
My cringing bondman, in heart and hand.
'Tis I that have fooled you altogether,
And beaten the Lord—
JÓN: Oh, hold your blather!
  (*Old Woman draws Jón toward the gate.*)
ENEMY: For both of you, 'twould have been much better
To have followed my counsels to the letter:
Yet, true to a good time-honored custom,
Folks will start climbing, till down we thrust 'em.
And if anyone's hurt, and his wounds afflict him,
I've plenty of brimstone to treat the victim.
  (*Old Woman knocks three times on the gate.*)
I'll soon singe the cross-mark from your pate,

So come now, Jón, they have shut the gate.

OLD WOMAN: I trust you to talk like a Christian, if anyone should come out. (*Knocks again.*)

JÓN: It's no use knocking.

OLD WOMAN: Why, it looks just as if you was desperate to get down into the brimstone. There's someone coming.

(*The gate opens. Paul the Apostle comes out and shuts the gate. He is in a long red robe, and has a gray beard and a heroic appearance.*)

PAUL: Paul the apostle greets you in the Lord.

(*The Enemy hides.*)

OLD WOMAN: God be with you, great preacher to the heathens, rock of help to all that's in trouble. I knew you wouldn't disappoint me.

PAUL: On the earth I dwelt among heathens. I journeyed from land to land, to save them who dwell in the habitation of unrighteousness which is their heart, and preached faith to infidels. Many I drew up from wallowing in the mire and abomination of their sins and made them the finest of God's creatures. But what was my reward? On behalf of these sinful worms of earth, I had to endure scorn and torments, and finally I was beheaded by the Roman axe. Though many gave ear to my words, yet more have refused my message, and have hidden their infirmity in the darkness instead of being clothed in the armor of light.

JÓN: If the clergy spoke up like you do, the faith wouldn't be all smothered by the coughing in church. I'll stand by that. You're a fine speaker.

PAUL: My speech and my preaching were not with enticing words of man's wisdom, but in demonstration of the Spirit and of power, that your faith should not stand in the wisdom of men, but in the power of God.

OLD WOMAN: Where should we be without Him? We have Him to thank—and His apostles—that the world ain't like a whited sepulchre.

PAUL: Do men believe those who preach the truth better than false prophets? Far from it. Where is the wise? Where is the scribe? Where is the disputer of this world? Hath not God made foolish the wisdom of this world?

JÓN: Yes, that's for certain. Everyone on earth is a damned ass.

OLD WOMAN: We're ignorant folks. But didn't you say once: He that is weak in the faith should be cared for and not shaken in his conscience?

PAUL: That is so.

OLD WOMAN: And in your Epistle to the Romans it says: Be not wise in your conceits. Recompense to no man evil for evil. And—as much as lieth in you, live peaceably with all men.

PAUL: That is true likewise. Hath God cast away his people? God forbid.

JÓN: Well, but it takes two to make friends.

PAUL: I have heard your discourse with the apostle Peter, my fellow-worker and brother, and know your business in coming hither. Wherefore I ask you, Jón Jónsson: Do you not yet know that the all-seeing God is a searcher of the hearts and reins, while we are his servants? Have you not yet been convinced that you are unworthly to enter and consort with the elect?

JÓN: Not in the least. Certainly not.

OLD WOMAN: I implores you, sir. Show mercy to my husband, and open the Golden Gate to him.

PAUL: Wherefore should I transgress the laws of heaven? Wherefore should I despise the decision and act of my fellow-worker? Know you not that the unrighteous shall not inherit the kingdom of God? Be not deceived: neither fornicators, nor idolaters, nor adulterers, not the effeminate, nor abusers of themselves with mankind, nor thieves, nor the covetous, nor drunkards, nor revilers nor extortioners shall inherit the kingdom of God.

(*The Enemy, on the watch, chuckles with delight.*)

JÓN: You're a proof of that, or rather the opposite. It can't hardly be so. To the best of my knowledge you was yourself an idolater and a reviler. Wasn't you pleased, when the martyr Stephen was stoned to death? Didn't you persecute Christian folks and want to wipe out the gospel of Christ from the earth? Perhaps that's not reckoned as sin?

OLD WOMAN (*Who has stared at Jón in consternation*): You're behaving like a brute and not a man. (*Produces the bag and shows it to Paul.*) You knows my thoughts, sir. This is my last wish.

(*The Old Woman crouches down in front of Jón with the open bag. Paul raises his hand. Jón, covered by his wife, sinks down into the bag with a cry.*)

OLD WOMAN (*Stands up, gathers the mouth of the bag together and ties it up*) : This is the best place to keep you, you bundle of rubbish!

JÓN: Open, open at once!

PAUL: You hear my words, Jón Jónsson. By no means would I contend with you, but if you had altogether turned from your way of life instead of becoming hardened, had preferred truth to lies and purged your heart, then these merciful doors of salvation would stand open to you. Let no one deceive himself. Those who defile the temple of God, them shall God destroy. (*Goes to the gate.*) To this my conscience in the Holy Spirit bears me witness. (*Goes in and shuts the gate. The Enemy laughs.*)

JÓN (*Roars*): Open the bag, you devil of a woman!

OLD WOMAN: Be quiet, you brute.

THE ENEMY: Mine art thou, Jón, and I better merit
To claim thee kin than the Holy Spirit.
Though great St. Paul may have cause to feel
Thy manly courage and voice of steel,
Though priests their pages with ink may stain,
Beside my wisdom it all is vain.
Nor peace nor mercy thy soul shall know,

O'er screes and lava thy road must go,
Back to the north and down below. (*Laughs.*)
And down below!

OLD WOMAN: God must have forsaken you, Jón dear.

JÓN: Open the bag! It's all the same to me, damn it!

OLD WOMAN (*Taking a hasty look at the Enemy*): Now he's stretching out his claws. This is what I came here for, to save you from everlasting damnation.

JÓN: Nice sort of saving I call it! Now then, open the bag, I tell you.

OLD WOMAN: I don't believe as how Mary the mother of God won't take pity on you, if I can manage to get a word with her. (*Knocks three times on the gate.*)

JÓN: Surely you're not going to knock for the third time?

OLD WOMAN: Don't you say a single word, and hold your breath.

(*Soft music and ringing of bells*)

THE ENEMY (*Starts, stretches out his claws, hisses*): Jón, Jón. (*Withdraws into cover.*)

OLD WOMAN: Now, be humble, like a child. (*Goes a few steps from the gate.*)

CHOIR OF ANGELS:

> O Mary, mild and great,
> The mother of Our Lord,
> To thee we consecrate
> Our song of thanks outpoured
> Thou breathest faith and heat
> Upon earth's frozen sward,
> O Mary, mild and great,
> The mother of Our Lord.

(*The gate opens of its own accord. The Virgin Mary comes out before the end of the song. She is in a snow-white silk robe, with her hair hanging down and a wreath of flowers on her head. Accompanying her are angels and saints, who arrange themselves behind her in the gateway.*)

OLD WOMAN (*Falling on her knees*) : Holy Queen of Heaven!
Merciful mother!

MARY: I heard thy sighing.

OLD WOMAN (*In tears*) : You wept by the cross. Have pity
on me!

MARY: All shall be well with those who love most fervently.

OLD WOMAN: I would sacrifice my salvation for him—Will
you speak to your blessed Son, and ask his help?

MARY: I will speak to my Son. God bless thy love and care,
and give thee peace. (*Exit with her escort, who finish their
song. The music dies away gradually.*)

OLD WOMAN (*Crossing herself and standing up*) : I've never
seen a more godlike face.

JÓN (*Shyly*): It was like a sweet breath of spring playing
round me.

THE ENEMY (*On the watch*):
Come now, Jón, it's a woman's way
To kneel and grovel and whine and pray.
Your soul's my prize—though it wants inflating,
And the end of the story needs no stating.
So come this minute, I'm tired of waiting.

JÓN: Who asks you to wait?

PETER (*Comes out and shuts the gate*) : So you're still here,
my good woman.

OLD WOMAN (*Hopefully*) : Mary the mother of God was
going to plead my cause with her beloved Son.

PETER: You can trust my verdict. It will not be changed.

(*The Enemy gesticulates exultantly to the Old Woman.*)

OLD WOMAN: Ah well, them as lives by the land has plenty
of troubles, in heaven as well as on earth. But it's not your fault
that things went wrong. I mustn't think how grand it would
have been for my Jón, to come to live in bliss among the
angels. Isn't the glory inside the gate quite unspeakable? I
guess I needn't ask. And is every soul, what gets in, allowed
to live there for ever?

PETER: World without end.

OLD WOMAN: And it'll never be thrown into the fire, no matter what it does, and whatever happens?

PETER: No, never.

OLD WOMAN: I suppose it'd be sinfully forward of me, if I was to ask you just to let me peep in—through ever so little a chink?

PETER (*Considering*) : Why should I refuse you that?

OLD WOMAN: I'd like so dreadfully to have a look in.

(*Peter opens the door slightly. Music in the distance.*)

OLD WOMAN: Oh! Oh! Are the flowers of gold? I'm thinking what a joy it would have been to my Jón to be here. And then of course, as I see, it must be many times more lovely the nearer you get to the Lamb's throne and the shining choir of glory. (*Peter nods his head in assent.*) Do you think my eyes would be dazzled too much, if you was to open it just a tiny bit more?

PETER (*Complying with her wish*): The light of heaven heals all the ills of Christian people.

(*In the beams of light are seen many-colored flowers and shrubs. Angels and other beings in white move to and fro.*)

OLD WOMAN: My Lord and my God! There I see my blessed little lads! (*Moves a few steps backwards as she speaks.*) And there's my father and mother, and the priest, and the farmer, and my friend Helga, and the Wild Swan, and— (*As she makes a spring and throws the bag as far as she can into heaven*) and in you shall go too, my Jón—and may God have mercy upon you!

(*Cries of welcome. Peter is thunderstruck.*)

THE ENEMY (*In a furious rage*) :

Heaven's pages are torn, and can ne'er be mended,

Commandments are lies, all justice ended,

And the laws of heaven and hell suspended!

(*Disappears.*)

PETER: Do you know what you have done, woman?

OLD WOMAN (*As she runs away*): Good-by, Peter dear, and give my love to my Jón!

(*Exit. Music begins at this point, and lasts to the end of the play.*)

PAUL (*Entering*) : Great things have been happening here.

PETER (*Bowed*) :—which will probably cost me my post and my job?

PAUL: God forbid. Love suffereth long, believeth all things, hopeth all things, endureth all things. To Him be the power and the glory.

CHOIR OF ANGELS: Amen, Hallelujah!

(*The apostles stand one on each side of the gate.*)

JÓN (*Appears in the gateway. He is dressed in white, and holds a palm branch to his breast. Behind him are angels and saints. He makes as if he did not see the apostles, and looks round on both sides*) : What, has my old gal gone, dear old bird? (*Looks mockingly at the apostles.*) So here you are, you men of God?

(*The apostles say nothing. Jón flourishes his palm branch, and goes quickly into heaven. The Angels and Saints dance round Jón, singing "Eia! eia!"*)

JÓN (*Gazing in all directions, as if the glory was only now apparent to him, notices his attire, half bewildered*): Why have I now become as white as driven snow?

THE REST (*Sing*): Thou art a child at heart, and all of us are so.

Eia, eia!

JÓN: Why have I now been given this palm branch, fair and green?

THE REST: This is to testify thy conscience now is clean.

JÓN: Why do the flowers I see appear like burnished gold?

THE REST: Because the soil is rich with mercies manifold.

JÓN: Who in those homes reside, whose gables this way face?

THE REST: This is the city of heaven, the Godhead's dwelling-place.

JÓN: Come they from stars or sun—these ever dazzling beams?

THE REST: From the Lamb's glorious throne this holy radiance streams.

Jón (*Rejoicing*): What, like a snowcapped isle, is yonder lofty tower?

The Rest: That is our Mary's home, the blessed Virgin's bower.

(*The music grows louder. Ringing of bells. Jón is resplendent.*)

The Rest: With joy the vault of heaven is trembling, as you see.

Fiddler: " 'Tis blithe beneath the birches that grow by Greenwood Lea!"

All: Eia! Eia!

(*As the singing ends, the apostles close the gate slowly and quietly.*)

CURTAIN

OUR POWER AND OUR GLORY
A DRAMA BY
NORDAHL GRIEG

TRANSLATED FROM THE NORWEGIAN BY

G. M. GATHORNE-HARDY

INTRODUCTION BY

HARALD S. NAESS

INTRODUCTION

I

Literary sociology can reveal and explain some very irregular value patterns. While Nordahl Grieg's name is not mentioned in the *Columbia Encyclopedia,* Scandinavian encyclopedias place him among the first of his contemporaries, and the Russian *Bolshaya Sovietskaja Entciklopedya* makes him one of the most important Scandinavian writers of all time, greater than either Hans Christian Andersen or Knut Hamsun. Clearly Nordahl Grieg's socialist sympathies have impressed critics in the communist countries, while in the West, the quality or popularity of his works has not secured him a place among the more well-established Scandinavian moderns like Karen Blixen (Isak Dinesen) or Pär Lagerkvist. In Scandinavia his prominent position is due not least to his wonderfully active life, which also explains the still towering position of a Björnstjerne Björnson, of whom Ibsen said: "His life was his greatest poem; to express oneself in one's life is, I feel, something of the finest that a man can achieve—we all try to do this, but most of us make a mess of it." Along the same lines, the Norwegian novelist Sigurd Hoel, whose temperament was much like Ibsen's, said of his younger contemporary Nordahl Grieg: "He was the most richly endowed of all men I have met, when you consider the sum total of his talents as well as their relative harmony."

That harmony was one of violent contrasts, as startling as the rugged idylls of the Norwegian landscape, which Grieg loved. The poetry in which he declared this love of Norway was too passionate for his urbane colleagues, they suspected him of chauvinism, even fascism, though it is now clear that, of

all Norwegian writers in the twentieth century, he was not only
the most internationally oriented, but, as a communist, the
bitterest enemy of National Socialism. Similarly, while he was
by nature a rather lazy, gentle, and peaceful person, he always
seemed intensely active, and he admired men of action, athletes,
empire builders, and revolutionary soldiers. Though he came
to measure literature more and more by its pure propaganda
value, and practiced his utilitarian theories in plays and novels,
he could not use Ibsen's drawing-room sets, and so found it
necessary to revolutionize the shape of Norwegian drama. Nor
could he suppress his love of rhetoric, and actually reached his
widest audience through the medium of poetry, where his youthful exuberance, if not his poetic talent, recalled the name of
Henrik Wergeland, Norway's greatest poet, and like Grieg a
playwright, publicist, Norwegian nationalist, and international
political crusader.

As a young man Grieg went to sea, and while he never became
a good sailor, in temperament he remained one throughout his
life. Like his colleagues in this most Norwegian of professions,
he was driven by a restless and adventurous spirit and in the
course of time experienced much human misery and social
injustice of the kind that feeds the revolutionary mind. But on
his journeys he also carried with him a sailor's dream of his
home, which, because it is the one fixed value in his ever-
changing world, tends to produce conservative attitudes: sailors
have always believed in idealized womanhood, a well-ordered
family life, and in patriotism. With so many contrasting forces
at work in his personality, it was possible for Nordahl Grieg
to listen to and sympathize with people of all convictions. He
wrote with understanding of Ibsen, whose temperament differed
entirely from his own, or Hamsun, whose political views he
despised, or the German soldier, whom he fought in World
War II. On hearing of his death Graham Greene wrote: "He
was the only man I have ever met with whom it was possible
to disagree profoundly both on religion and politics and yet

feel all the time the sense of good-will. He had not only good-will himself, but he admitted it in his opponent—he more than admitted it, he assumed it. In fact he had charity. I wish we others had as much of it."

II

Nordahl Grieg was born and raised in Bergen. Whoever wishes to attach any real or symbolic importance to this fact might point to Bergen's traditions as a city of shipping, commerce, and international outlook, and to its inhabitants' reputed love of big words and light poetry. He grew up in a comfortable middle-class home with strong family ties, sharing with the composer Edvard Grieg (1843–1907) a common Scottish forbear, and with another famous relative, Bishop Brun of Bergen (1745–1816), his curious first name (Johan) Nordahl. This great-great-great-grandfather produced not only Norway's first national anthem (1772), but a series of warm and refreshing songs, and, in the hour of Norway's greatest need during the Napoleonic Wars, speeches full of eloquence and national etnhusiasm.

After passing his *examen artium* in 1920, Nordahl Grieg planned to study for a higher degree, but first he wished to see the world and so signed on as a deckhand on board the S/S *Henrik Ibsen*, bound for Australia. Apart from his experience of North Atlantic convoys during World War II, it was his only extended sea voyage, yet it remained a source of inspiration for him throughout his life, and, after his return to Norway (1921), resulted in a collection of poetry, *Around the Cape of Good Hope (Rundt Kap det gode haab*, 1922), and a novel, *The Ship Sails On (Skibet gaar videre*, 1924). His "verses from the sea dedicated to my comrades on board" include sentimental but well-made poems about the quiet joy over a letter newly arrived from home, or the pride at sighting Norwegian flags in foreign lands, and this harmless emotionalism and the healthy enthusiasm of the title poem ("Oh, this is life nonetheless") must have struck readers as more typical of the collection than its realistic accounts of daily drudgery, fights on board and "the harbor's hideous pleasures." On the other hand, these last elements are more consistently the subject of Grieg's first novel, which was based upon actual memories and was received, partly as a social document dedicated to the expo-sure of venereal diseases among Norwegian sailors, partly as a vicious caricature. Unfortunately, to the surprise and sorrow of Grieg, this last view was shared by many of his shipmates. Sophisticated readers now will find the book repetitive and overly charged with melodrama and pathetic fallacies, but it was eventually translated into nine languages and already in its first year received eight printings in Norway. One reason for its popularity there can be found in the fact that this little giant among shipping nations had produced next to no litera-ture describing life on board a steamer on the seven seas. Per-haps the greatest merit of Grieg's first novel was that in it the author changed the scene from Captain Marryat's distant terri-tories to Norway and our own times.

By the time *The Ship Sails On* appeared, Grieg had spent a summer walking from Hamburg to Rome, another summer writing in Finnmark, and one year studying at Wadham College, Oxford. He loved English university education with its equal emphasis on mind and body culture, and joined the rowers on the Cherwell as well as the debaters in the Oxford Union. Here, during its centenary dinner, he could see, from his seat beside Lord Asquith, the Archbishop of Canterbury, Lord Cecil, Lord Birkenhead, Lord Curzon, and other famous builders of the British Empire, which he was then studying. In "Rudyard Kipling and the British Empire," which he eventually devel-oped into a publishable thesis, Grieg does deplore his hero's attitude during the Boer War, but generally Kipling's verse, with its masculine drum and brass tone, appealed to him during his first Oxford days. Later in life Grieg's memories of his stay in this city of learning and good companionship became an effective counterweight to his eastern sympathies and contributed to a truly international outlook in him.

In 1925, one year after his return from Oxford, Nordahl Grieg received his M.A. degree. He also worked as a journalist—with the pen name Fortinbras—and published a second volume of poetry, *Stones in the Stream* (*Stene i strömmen,* 1925). It is a miscellany of love and nature poems, most of them low-keyed and less original than his first poems, though some contain interesting early versions of ideas which later became very central in Grieg's work: "The Chapel of Wadham College," describing not architecture but the poet's sentiments during a memorial service, points to his lifelong preoccupation with the "Young Dead." Another important Grieg theme, The War, is often referred to, more particularly in the poem "Woman, Death, and Jehovah," where a young expectant mother implores Jehovah to destroy the world, so that her child will not be used in the war of revenge which her husband so eagerly waits for.

The problem of war continued to occupy Grieg's mind during a stay in Greece the following year (1926). If war meant aggression, there was also a war to end aggression, and participation in this kind of war Nordahl Grieg came to view as the highest form of engagement, indeed—under the influence of Greek art and natural beauty—as a form of art. The first of Grieg's "Greek Letters," which he published in *Oslo Aftenavis* during the summer of 1926, has the heading "Marathon" and the following passage: "For Aeschylus was not the only artist who fought there, they were all artists, whether they were themselves creative, or only loved art, in the theaters, in the temple square. Marathon means Art fighting. Beauty under arms."

On his return to Norway, Grieg published a play, *A Young Man's Love (En ung mands kjærlighet,* 1926), which received its first performance in Bergen in 1927. The protagonist, Jan, is torn between his love of two women, Aimé, older and more experienced, whom he finally marries out of pity for her, and Berit, younger and more idealized, whom he forsakes with the result that she commits suicide. Outside the action, but actually its evil driving force, is Aimé's former lover, Bernhard, brutal and indestructible like the ship that sails on. As in the novel, where young Benjamin represented a humanity destroyed, Jan is another loser, continuing a line of Grieg characters who embody "the Christian love of defeat." In Grieg's wars between sexes, social groups, nations, Truth is bound to be beaten, though never in a way that destroys *all* hope. *A Young Man's Love,* though it has suspense and, in part, good dialogue, is a rather immature work. Grieg's love of melodrama and emotional language did not work in a technically conventional piece based upon as old a motif as a man's jealousy of his lover's past. But in his next play Grieg began the modernization which Norwegian drama had needed since the days of Ibsen.

The spring of 1927 Nordahl Grieg spent in China as a newspaper correspondent. He was moved by the distress and ignorance of the common people and by the political humiliation of a once powerful nation: "With our intellect we place ourselves on their side. China has been violated, China continues to be abused, China has been right all along." But in his *Chinese Days (Kinesiske dage,* 1927) he also described H.M.S. *Vindictive* plowing up the Yangtze to intimidate the Chinese: "The steel, the froth, the flags, the brass band become one call: 'This we understand, this freezes our blood, this is the song of youth which has called men under the colors and will always do so.' " Two people who helped Grieg get Kipling out of his system were Madame Sun Yat-sen, "a complete Chinese madonna," and Michael Borodin, a person whom the Russian communists might well refer to as "our man in China." "His tactics are quieter, not aiming at little concessions or an immediate victory. His game is one of centuries." During a conversation Grieg had with Borodin he got the idea of a new play, which he wrote in seven days and seven nights. The title and subject is *Barabbas (Barrabas,* 1927), symbol of war and violence, but Jesus is also in the play, representing the doctrine of love and conciliation. Although Grieg recognized the value and beauty of this doctrine, he was already moving toward an acceptance of violence, not the senseless brutality of Bernhard in *A Young Man's Love,* but the joy of battle which also goes with the revolutionary spirit. The play was written at a time when great changes took place on the Norwegian scene (the Socialist party was winning its first victory at the polls), and therefore, during its first production in 1928, proved to have considerable striking force. A poor performance in 1949, however, showed up the weakness of a play which was already dated, even though its chief technical merit had been the author's attempt to produce an atmosphere of timelessness: "The action can take place in China today. In India tomorrow. In Palestine 2,000 years ago."

In the fall of 1927 Nordahl Grieg was asked to write a cantata for a Bergen exhibition. The result was "Norway in Our Hearts," which two years later became the title of a whole collection of patriotic verse *(Norge i våre hjerter,* 1929). Grieg had spent most of this time in North Norway, but he also traveled in the western, southern and eastern parts of the country, since his aim was to write an epos honoring the land and its people. All provinces were to be represented and, if possible, all major professions. The emphasis on action as ultimate beauty, which Grieg had admired in Oxford and Greece, is unmistakable in this poem, written, as Grieg said, more in Björnson's than in Bull's or Wildenvey's style; that is to say, celebrating, not the colorful or sublime, but the homespun heroes of everyday life. Although there are poems about the pleasures of a northern summer, the tone is mostly dark, as it should be north of latitude 60, but with the theme of hopeful waiting generally applied to characters both animate and inanimate: a mother over the cradle, fish spawning in winter, and the night train racing toward its goal. In retrospect *Norway in Our Hearts* can be seen as an attempt to write for the com-

mon people, a *biblia pauperum,* which was frowned upon by
many critics, who found it too national or too sentimental. But
those for whom it was intended thought otherwise: 8,000 copies
of the book had to be printed within three months.

Perhaps the most striking poem in *Norway in Our Hearts* is
Grieg's description of the stallion Sikil let loose among five
dozen mares in a mountain valley. The poem, which is exu-
berant to the point of parody, touches Grieg's version of the
élan vital, here as potency or pure power, and entirely non-
political (except, perhaps, as "male chauvinism"). But Grieg
must have had second thoughts about his activity complex. In
his next play *The Atlantic (Atlanterhavet,* 1931), about the
promotion and tragic end of a transatlantic flight, he shows
how the press in its search for sensation helps disseminate a
pathological restlessness, indeed the "Americanism" which
Hamsun had exposed in his satire forty years earlier. Hamsun
was also one of the few readers who received the play with
enthusiasm; after *Norway in Our Hearts,* he and other conserva-
tives had reason to look upon Grieg as a modern back-to-nature
prophet. They were mistaken: like his young journalist here in
The Atlantic, the bourgeois poet Grieg vanished from the scene,
and they did not recognize him in the newly converted socialist
who returned from Moscow three years later. The intermediate
period is one of many crises concerning his failing economy,
productivity, ideology. Part of this time (1931–32) he spent in
Oxford, England, where he completed—after six years—*The
Young Dead (De unge döde,* 1932), perhaps the most personal
of all his books. In each of the six portraits—of Keats, Shelley,
Byron, Brooke, Sorley, Owen—Grieg has emphasized features
which he recognized in himself. In Keats the love of beauty, in
Byron the dream of battle, and in Shelley, whom he probably
found most congenial, the experience of poetry and action as
identical. These features he also saw reflected in the works of
three poets who died a hundred years later, during World
War I: Rupert Brooke, whose last word was hello, "the happy
greeting of friendship and youth"; Charles Hamilton Sorley

who possessed at one time the "Christian love of defeat and the furious activity of the Roman," and Wilfred Owen, a soldier like Aeschylus, who knew "of greater better wars, where men would fight—not for flags, but for the power of life; against death, not against men." A mixture of cool analysis and ecstasy characterizes Grieg's treatment of the six English poets, but his joking reference to *"The Young Dead,* by one of them" shows him to have been at the end of his tether. In a newspaper interview after his return from Russia two years later, he referred again to Brooke, Sorley and Owen:

It is hopelessness that characterizes their individual resistance to war. And when I, during my work with the book, lived in the country of these young dead, I felt a desire to see the country in which people had risen against imperialistic wars and put an end to them. That is why I traveled to Moscow. *The Young Dead* expresses a very private desperation regarding existing society, and I traveled to a country where this desperation had been overcome and where there is a life with a future.

The famous actress Gerd Egede Nissen, Grieg's friend and, after 1941, his wife, tells of how he loved to talk about his two years in Russia (1932-34). Most impressive he found its people: "they smile, they are so good, they are all children, all kindness. And their art, also fantastic. People and art go together. They use art in the service of culture." By art Grieg meant first and foremost stage art, which he studied with enthusiasm during this golden age of the Moscow Art Theater. He admired directors like Stanislavsky and Meyerhold, and perhaps even more Sandro Achmeteli, the director of the Georgian State Theater in Tiflis. It has been said of Grieg's two years in Russia that it was a period in which he studied, rested, and wrote nothing, which is not quite true. Both the play *Our Power and Our Glory* and the novel *Young the World as yet Must Be* were planned there, also the periodical *Veien Frem. Our Power and Our Glory,* which Grieg completed in Bergen in 1935, became his first stage success and helped him overcome his old fear—after three failures—of writing for the theater. His next play, however, in which he employed Ibsen's drawing-room technique, fell to the ground.

But Tomorrow (*Men imorgen,* 1936) is about a Norwegian industrialist, forced by foreign shareholders to adapt his fertilizer plant to war production of poison gas. With the general acceptance of mass murder as background, a cold premeditated private murder is carried off, showing that in the author's mind one form of killing is no more objectionable than the other. The play, which is somewhat in the style of *Little Eyolf,* shares with Ibsen's work a topical theme and many moving scenes, but also some serious flaws. Although its more immediate meaning was plain enough for the Norwegian Nazis to boo during the Bergen performance, some of the liberals also criticized it for confusing characterization and poorly motivated action. Grieg explained his intentions in an angry article ("a sad and meaningless waste of my time"), which is extremely useful for an understanding of the play. Readers are told, for instance, that the industrialist's wife should not be seen as sympathetic. Under a surface of philanthropy and quasi-religion, she continues to cultivate her sexual appetites, and so, on the day of reckoning, will not be found on the side of Truth. If Grieg and Ibsen can be said to have shared one single quality, it must be the fact that neither of them thought much of sex.

Grieg's monthly journal *Veien frem* (*The Road Ahead,* 1936-37), which stopped publication after only two years, was a unique periodical in Norway during the mid-thirties. Not only was it edited by one of that country's few brilliant journalists, but it contained within its pages contributions by many of Europe's famous men of letters, Maxim Gorky, Aldous Huxley, André Malraux, Thomas Mann, and others. Most of its articles dealt with culture, particularly theater, and politics. It brought reports from places where things happened in Europe —Russia and Spain—and launched repeated attacks upon people that were still unrecognized as dangerous enemies by many

Norwegians—Mussolini, Hitler, Franco, Quisling. Its style was simple, honest, intense; Huxley, the humanist, was treated with respect, but Hamsun, the old Grieg idol, was not spared, and for Gide, the communist renegade, there was nothing but disdain. *Veien Frem,* though it was considered a worthy enterprise by most of Norway's radicals, did not receive their support, with the result that the last issue appeared in December of 1937. By that time Grieg had spent a summer in Spain and published his experiences in a book, *Spanish Summer (Spansk sommer,* 1937), also his best play, *The Defeat,* had been published and performed.

Some of the inspiration and background material for *The Defeat (Nederlaget,* 1937) Grieg found in the family history of his friend Gerd Egede Nissen. Her grandfather Christian Nissen had fought for Garibaldi in the 1860s and her granduncle, Doctor Oscar Nissen, had been with the Paris Commune in 1871. In the play, which describes the Communists' last heroic stand against Thiers's government troops, Grieg gives a new version of the old Barabbas versus Christ theme. It uses all the theatrical devices he had learned in Russia and used effectively in *Our Power and Our Glory,* but it differs from it in having more fully developed characters, each of them representing, not only an idea, but a personal life. The philosophies of Barabbas and Christ seem to unite here in some strange dialectic. The young teacher Gabrielle, the peaceloving Varlin, and Delescluze, who has learned the bitter lesson that what is good can only survive through force—or even the boastful, cowardly Courbet, and Rigault, the cynical advocate of violence, all of these have the author's sympathy, but mostly Gabrielle, who, as the executioners approach, teaches her last lesson: "Come children, we shall tell the soldiers about the future, about our uncompromising faith. They shall see it in our smiles." What finally raises *The Defeat* above other Grieg plays is the beauty of its language. It was written in one of Grieg's more utilitarian periods, when what little verse he wrote was strictly revolutionary, conforming with his new esthetic theory: "A true work of art is precisely a product of its time. It will have the honor of being devoured completely by living beings who absorb it into their blood and tissue and use it in order to grow out of it. Happy and consummated, this work will be left behind like an empty crab shell." This is not true of *The Defeat,* whose characters and poetry are timeless, but it does apply—at least in some degree—to Grieg's next major work, a novel based upon his experiences in Russia and Spain.

Young the World as yet Must Be (Ung må verden ennu være, 1938) has sex, suspense, violence and all the other ingredients of modern international fiction, it is both excellent journalism and forceful propaganda, but, for a work of art in the traditional sense, too superficial, particularly in details of characterization. Though it cannot now have the impact it must have had in 1938, the book is still readable as an exciting exposé of prewar political debate. It shows the defeat of western humanism and extolls the fervor of the young communist believer; it also demonstrates a new attitude to women, which Grieg explained more fully in a letter to his brother:

To a ridiculous degree Norwegian radicals have concentrated their liberalism within the field of sex. It is a rather harmless topic. You would be surprised to see the almost ascetic austerity of Russian literature in this respect, it is also evident in the theater. Furthermore, the relationship between the sexes has been a fantastic triumph here, Marxism has clearly proven its point, both parties will have to be economically independent, both must have their work, their quite individual worth as human beings, not until this is so, will their emotional lives become truly free. All in all, they have created here a new standard of humanity, which no one can overlook.

Grieg's portrait of Kira Dimitrovna shows that he has left behind him the sailor's madonna concept of woman, but Kira is also idealized, and in a somewhat disturbing manner: because her attitude of no compromise is so devoid of human features, her personality often appears more Nazi that communist. *Young*

the World as yet Must Be deals more particularly with the
Moscow Trials, which were then attacked by all radicals in
Norway, but which Grieg defended, even though his description
of them are frightening enough. Grieg was never a member
of the Communist Party, but any attempt to deny or modify
his communist sympathies would be futile. Thus, of the socio-
anarchist philosophy, which he had earlier admired in Shelley,
he said it was nothing but bourgeois attitudes turned inside
out. On the other hand, it is not certain what would have happened to Grieg's communism after Czechoslovakia and Hungary.
His main concern was always war, the combination of business
and war was the ultimate evil, and he sympathized with communism first and foremost because he considered this ideology
to be the strongest power against war. It is true that Grieg did
not share his countrymen's concern when the Russians attacked
Finland in 1939, but his Norwegian nationalism included a
belief in the self-determination of other small nations, and this
nationalism grew in strength as World War II approached.

Nordahl Grieg spent the fall of 1939 as a soldier in Finnmark. His stay there ten years earlier had resulted in a book
of patriotic verse and this time also he concentrated his creative work on national themes; he had plans for a novel about
Finnmark, a film about the bird sanctuary Fuglöy, and a play
about Norway's national poet, Henrik Wergeland. All of this
material disappeared during the following years, which were to
be the most eventful in Grieg's life. A posthumous collection
of speeches and articles, *The Flag* (*Flagget,* 1945), contains an
interesting miscellany of war impressions, and, judging from
a note found after his death, he probably intended to work them
into a complete volume of memoirs. It would have opened with
Grieg's military service in Finnmark, and continued with the
German attack upon Norway in 1940 and his personal participation in the adventurous removal of Norway's gold reserves
across the North Sea to England. Other chapters would have
been devoted to his education at the officers' training camp at

Dumfries, Scotland, and his memoirs of transatlantic convoys and flying sorties over Norway as well as his visits to Iceland and Jan Mayen. Several of his gallant comrades from the war are mentioned in the note, among them the Norwegian lawyer Viggo Hansteen, a personal friend of Grieg's who was executed by the Germans in 1941. The last chapter, with the precarious number 13 changed to 14, was entitled "Over Berlin." This sketched list of contents has no mention of Grieg's achievements as a writer, even though he wrote his best poetry during these years, and, through his speeches and readings of this poetry, aided Norway's contribution to the Allied cause. Like a good soldier, he wanted to be where the fighting was, among the sailors at sea or the bomber pilots over Germany. On December 2, 1943, he set out for Berlin as a reporter in a Canadian bomber. It did not return. He was found and buried by members of the Red Cross, but his grave was destroyed in new allied bombing raids.

Ironically, the war, which Nordahl Grieg had foreseen more clearly and warned against more intensely than any other Norwegian, provided him with the perfect concluding years of a life dedicated to poetry and action. Not only was his verse technically more accomplished than before, but its dithyrambic qualities had the right setting. What had earlier seemed exaggerated or bombastic was now at one time deadly serious and uplifting. Among the poems in Grieg's posthumous collection, *Freedom* (*Friheten,* 1945), perhaps the most striking are those dedicated to people he loved and admired: King Haakon VII, his wife Gerd, his friend Viggo Hansteen, and other men such as the actor Captain Martin Linge, whose life was truly consummated in death:

> When the fatal bullet dropped him
> He, in blood, had rendered well
> All an artist's heart can give us.
> 'Twas the end. The curtain fell.

Grieg at his death was only 41, and there is reason to believe that, had he lived, he would still have had much to give. On the other hand, his artist's heart might also have received more than it could take: already he saw signs that soldiers' and sailors' sacrifices would not change the world, and the last poems often speak of his doubts about man's will to avoid future wars. In this respect, too, his death was not premature, since it allowed him to retain his hopes. If Defeat is the subject of Grieg's art, Hope is its basic inspiration, that is why his death is tragic only in the true classical sense of something great and beautiful, which, as it meets with physical disaster, rises spiritually to set a mighty precedent. This process, by which a life is transformed into poetry has also been illustrated by Grieg in the eight stanzas of "The Best," which were inspired by the death of Viggo Han-steen. Midway in the poem the theme "they are the best who die" is suddenly inverted, preparing the reader for the last lines, which may well serve as an epitaph for Grieg and the other young dead:

> Increasing the life they yielded
> Their ghosts in new men survive.
> Upon their graves shall be written—
> For ever the best shall live.

III

Our Power and Our Glory (Vår ære og vår makt) was written during the winter and early spring of 1935. Nordahl Grieg had recently returned to Bergen from Russia, where he had studied theater and made preliminary plans for a drama about the Norwegian shipping boom during World War I. He first intended to use the material in a film, but after much encouragement from the Bergen Theater director, Hans Jacob Nilsen, he was persuaded to prepare it for the stage. That Grieg had profited from his study tour can be seen in his articles on Russian theater, but particularly in his new plays, which, like those of Bertolt Brecht, belong to the "epic theater" tradition. They do not depend on a "suspense of disbelief" in the audience, rather they demonstrate what Brecht calls "alienation," whereby everyday events are used in a manner that makes them strange, striking, and, above all, instructive. An interviewer who expressed concern about Grieg's use of living models, was told: "Since real life, in all its grotesque brutality, is so much more powerful than anything a person can think up, one would have to be very stupid not to use archives and old newspapers." Which is exactly what Grieg did. He searched for his material in the daily press from World War I, and in the papers of various seamen's organizations; he also stayed in a hotel on the waterfront, where he could observe and converse with shipping people and sailors. Some of them he invited to his hotel room, where they taught him the songs he used in the text of the play. As he completed the scenes—rarely in chronological order— he read them and discussed them with Hans Jacob Nilsen, also with his friend Gerd Egede Nissen, who approved of Grieg's sailors but criticized his shipowners for being too exaggerated: as an actress schooled in the naturalistic theater, she found them artistically and psychologically unacceptable. "But why," Grieg asked in an interview, "should I concern myself with a person's psychology in the bourgeois sense. What's the use of giving a psychological close-up of a shipowner in this connection? It may lead the person to various crises, for instance in his relationship to his wife, but interesting he is only in his societal emplacement." Rather than operating with complicated individuals, as Ibsen did and his followers, Grieg arranges his people in social groups, each character representing certain facets of the group spirit. The shipowners are ruthless, but sometimes jovial and sentimental (Ditlef Mathiesen), sometimes cold and calculating (Freddy), sometimes coarse and socially insecure (Konrad, Birger), sometimes full of law and order (Skipper Meydell). Their interests include gardening, playing with their children, cultivating the family tree, occasional orgies, and honoring the flag. What the sailors have in common is a basic sensitivity, even the robust Swiller has it, where he guards Alf against disturbing news, or the embittered Malvin, defending the informer's son. Ditlef's attitude to modern art, to his snowdrops, and even to his children, is seen as something artificial. The sailors, on the other hand, all belong in some sort of genuine relationship, usually to a woman—mother, wife, sweetheart—or, as in the case of the Swiller, to good companions in general. Otherwise the purpose of the social idea theater calls for a radical reduction of "character," whereby realistic action sometimes develops into allegory. This has been the case in the last of the fourteen scenes, where Grieg's two character groups are pitched in battle array around the soldiers. The shipowners with the stock broker to the left, preparing the war, the sailors to the right, retaliating with general strike. Peace, however, is on the sailors' side, in the shape of a young woman. Probably her part should not be too stylized, but rather played with the force and warmth that colors most of the whole play: it is indeed remarkable that Nordahl Grieg, in spite of necessary simplifications, has been able to give so many characters life and individuality.

In its tone (character, language, use of dialect) *Our Power and Our Glory* is very much a Bergen play, in its ideas it is more generally Norwegian. Shipping has long been a major industry in Norway, contributing to the country's relatively high standard of living and providing a field—one of the few still left open—for large-scale free enterprise. Shipping has always been particularly profitable in times of war, especially for so-called neutral countries, which have everything to gain and nothing to lose, except the lives of their sailors. For a pugnacious playwright like Nordahl Grieg, the ruthless speculation in shipping during World War I was a remarkably fitting subject. Not only was he able to demonstrate a very palpable example of the War-Business complex, but, equally important, he could now prove his solidarity with Norway's seamen, whom he had partly estranged by writing *The Ship Sails On.* The title of the play is taken from Björnson's poem "The Norwegian Sailor" (". . . Our power and our glory/White sails have brought to us."), and used ironically: those who are really responsible for our power and our glory, the Norwegian sailors, are either killed in war, or left to die in poverty. Actually Björnson need not have been taken ironically; his poem, which honors the Norwegian sailor no less than *Our Power and Our Glory,* may even have inspired Grieg:

> And many a seaman's head
> A wreath of seaweed wore when dead,
> Whose name should shine in gold
> Among the heroes bold.

Ditlef Mathiesen's medal is also mentioned in Björnson's poem:

> Saint Olav's Cross's praise
> Would on that pilot fitly blaze
> Who saved a hundred men,
> And hundred once again.

All in all Björnson's song was rather democratic for the occasion (a Stavanger yachting event, 1868), but it was not revolutionary. Grieg's play is, and it is also more deeply felt: of all people, sailors were closest to his heart. His first poems were dedicated to them, also his last. The fragment "Sea Folk," left incomplete when Grieg set out for his flight over Berlin, ends with an explosion, exactly as in Scene 3, Act II, of the play. Only these are sailors sacrificed in World War II.

Perhaps the most interesting aspect of *Our Power and Our Glory* is its technique—Grieg's reliance on contemporary theater resources, more particularly his use of sound and lighting. The play departs from the naturalistic theater with its unified action and coherent character development, rather the effect is expressionistic, with a series of disconnected tableaux, making up a startling picture book of Norwegian shipping. The scenes shift from the shipowner's office to the agent's home, from the German submarine to the *Vargefjell* forecastle, from the Bergen restaurant to the lifeboat at sea, etc. The intention—to create contrast and thereby making Reality strange, striking, and instructive—is underlined by special light and sound effects. Much of this Grieg had learned in Moscow, not least the use of music for emphasis rather than ornamentation. In his articles about Russian theater he mentioned some of Nikolaj Okhlopkov's productions, where the conventional division of stage and audience was eliminated, making a kind of "total theater." In a somewhat modified form Grieg employs this method where, immediately following the curtain at the end of Act III, we have a Gentleman address the audience from a private box.

Grieg also wrote about Vsevolod Meyerhold with admiration (one scholar, overlooking Mischa Elman, suggests he is the model for Sascha Erdman!), in particular he commented on his ability to create sudden life and activity through his use of lights. This again points to Grieg's practice in the Epilogue, where, after the Gentleman's speech, we hear the gong, and then see 1935 projected on a curtain moving aside to reveal the Lodging for Homeless Men.

Grieg told Gerd Egede Nissen that he could not have written the play without having first watched Noel Coward's film *Cavalcade*. He did not want this to be known, however, since journalists would then say he had learned nothing in Russia, "And, by golly, that I have," he added. That he has also learned a lot from *Cavalcade* can be seen immediately by comparing the plays. Both consist of a chronological arrangement of scenes with a final 10-15 year jump. Both use light and sound,[1] popular songs and music hall refrains[2] as well as patriotic or religious

---

[1] "The lights fade as the noise of chimes and sirens grows louder" is an often repeated type of stage direction in *Cavalcade*.

[2] *Cavalcade:* "What is—what is the matter here?" *Our Power:* "Who goes there? Who goes there?"

hymns[3] in much the same manner. More strikingly reminiscent of *Our Power and Our Glory* is the following *Cavalcade* stage direction (II,7) : "Above the proscenium 1914 glows in lights"; also the scene with the women saying good-by to the soldiers (II,9) , and the scene from "The Epilogue," in which six "incurables" in blue hospital uniforms sit making baskets. In spite of such corresponding features, *Cavalcade* and *Our Power and Our Glory* are very different in mood. Noel Coward is sentimental and patriotic, Grieg aggressively ironic: the warmongers cultivate snowdrops and Moral Rearmament; the sailors' death cries are silenced by chorus girls; the shipowners revel to the tune of Wergeland's moving song about the sailor's last voyage, arranged for a jazz band.

Naturally Norway's shipowners did not like the play. The Bergen Theater board of directors, hearing of the try-outs, voted to stop production immediately: "We have come to the conclusion that some demarcation is needed between tendentious literature and propaganda. This piece by Nordahl Grieg is the prototype of Russian propaganda theater. It will serve no purpose in Norway, but cause enmity and violate the neutrality of the stage, since art is here used in the service of propaganda." However, after director Hans Jacob Nilsen threatened to leave the theater and actress Gerd Egede Nissen to stop playing Hedda Gabler, the board rescinded its resolution. By that time the conflict had become nationally known, resulting in a sale of 40,000 tickets. The Bergen première took place on May 4, and Norway's leading critic wrote: "At long last a young poet who has something to tell us from the stage, so clear that it strikes us, so daring that we get new courage, so simple that we feel we have always thought exactly that. *Our Power and Our Glory* is straight out of our own times."

HARALD S. NAESS

University of Wisconsin

---

[3] *Cavalcade:* "Land of Hope and Glory." "Nearer My God, to Thee." *Our Power:* "Sing Me Home." "Sailor's Last Voyage."

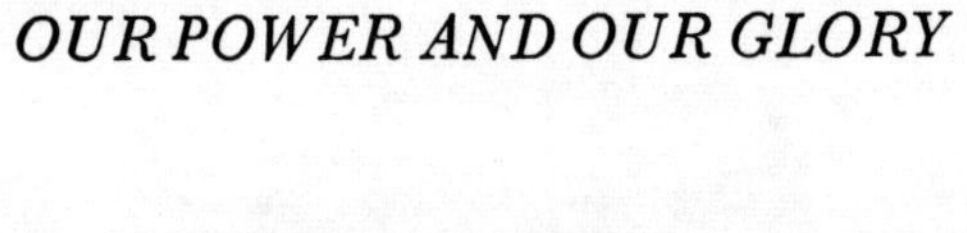

OUR POWER AND OUR GLORY

ACT I

*A coffin, covered by a Norwegian flag, with a wreath of sea-
weed and rushes: the dead Norwegian seaman. The orchestra
plays "Sing Me Home." The music suddenly breaks into a wild
discord, like an explosion. The date "1917" is projected in
flames. The curtain is drawn aside.*

Scene 1

*The shipping office. High above the harbor, with peaceful
sunlight streaming in through the window. Ditlef S. Mathiesen
is standing, on the spot where the coffin went down, a well-
developed man, vigorous and robust, about thirty-five years old.
He speaks with a strong provincial accent, expressing an easy-
going sense of authority. His Secretary, Miss Berents, sits and
follows him with her eyes, discreetly devoted.*

DITLEF: When does the charter for the "Vargefjell" expire,
Miss Berents? March 6th, eh?

MISS BERENTS: Yes.

DITLEF: Englands' requisitioned 'em both for the run between Newcastle and the French ports. 45 shillings—no objection
to that! Tonnage gets shorter every day over there. Yesterday,
"Ole Viig" struck a mine, and today I hear that old Birger's
new boat's been torpedoed; eight men went down with her,
worse luck! It wouldn't surprise me if freights are up to fifty
shillings soon—not a bit. I know there's some who don't like
the idea of putting their ships into that trade. But what I say
is—we've obligations as a seafaring nation. And—as you know—
I've never been afraid of taking a risk. (*Stops by the window*)
What a lovely day! This spring *before* the spring—you don't
get it anywhere but here. Nowhere else in the world. Don't
you think the gardener'll have sent in snowdrops from the

garden at Milde today? I love that place, I can tell you, Miss Berents. You can keep all my other properties, so far as I'm concerned. I have to see the sea. Old sailor blood, you know. And how fit the kiddies keep down there! You must come over one day, when the children are there, and play with 'em. If only you weren't so indispensable in the office, I'd say to you—get yourself children, Miss Berents. They're the best that earth has to give. (*He has sat down, and drums contentedly on the table*) Fifty shilling a ton! Not bad, eh? Can you remember—before the war we were pleased if we got four. It's fantastic, what we're in now—a reg'lar fairy story. Only thing is—not to lose your head. And I must say that's what those chaps in the Seamen's and Stokers' Union are doing. Demand, demand—do they ever think of anything else? What's it all coming to? You should have heard the yarns my grandfather used to tell when he was at sea. Things were different then. Don't misunderstand me. For instance, I've nothing against two kroner a day extra for crews that go into the danger zone. I'll willingly grant them that recognition, even if it does mount up. But a rise in sailor's pay from 70 to 120 kroner a month, *plus* 25 per cent for the cost of living! May be all right today, but what do we know about tomorrow? No security anywhere. This ain't the time for it. Write and tell 'em I regard it with great misgiving. You don't look well, Miss Berents. White about the gills. Spring air, eh? Now I'm going to say something to you, and you're to treat it as an order: when I go to Copenhagen, off you go to Geilo and take a rest. Here's 300 kroner. Don't stint yourself in any way; you're to have a real good time.

MISS BERENTS: Oh, that's far too much—

DITLEF: Nice to be able to give you a treat—to have the chance of it.

(*Enter Freddy, Ditlef's brother-in-law. He is the same age as Ditlef, handsome, distinguished looking, English tailoring.*)

DITLEF: Evening, Freddy. Well, you can go now, Miss Berents. (*Exit Miss Berents.*)

FREDDY: I've got hold of the "Vöringen" for us, Ditlef.

DITLEF: Good job, Freddy.

FREDDY: Two hundred thousand each.

DITLEF: I'm agreeable.

FREDDY: A good bargain, but not *so* good as they're saying in town. Two hundred for each of us is O.K. But the fact is that I've now secured an option on another hundred. What do you say to our letting Konrad have them?

DITLEF: All right by me.

FREDDY: He'll look on it as a really special favor. And he may be useful one day.

DITLEF (*Suddenly laughing*): Old Konrad! He's a queer card. Decent chap really. Have you heard the latest? It was last night. Only you were so damned tight—you must keep it to yourself. You know Konrad has less idea of music than anyone in the world, and now he's gone and bet Birger fifty thousand that in a month he'd learn to play "Old Man Noah" with the bass and treble. And what do you think? Today he's hired a music teacher and got down to it. Oh, Konrad's all right!

FREDDY: Hm—Konrad's never really belonged to our set, even though we were in the same class at school. But I know he was allowed to come to us once or twice when I had the boys over and I know that Konrad appreciated it in a touching way.

DITLEF (*Digging him in the ribs*): Yes, and so you've gone on being touching to the whole family. Specially his sister, eh?

FREDDY: Oh, you will have your joke.

DITLEF: How *is* Edith? Pretty little gal. Hot stuff—what?

FREDDY: Edith's to go to school in England. Anyhow, all that is very ancient history. Dead and done with.

DITLEF: And everything is going well up at the Minister's house? When are you going to be married?

FREDDY: When Margrethe comes home.

DITLEF: Plenty to tidy up before then, eh? Well, there's really a lot of pretty stuff to look at here. And the little girls know how to enjoy life. You can actually *have* most of 'em.

FREDDY: But they must be young.

DITLEF (*Admiringly*): Ah, Freddy, there's certainly been some goings on in that sail boat of yours.

FREDDY: Look out now. What about that apartment in Oscar Street? I do think that was disgraceful of you. Disgraceful—how's Augusta?

DITLEF: Oh, your sister was a bit sticky to begin with, when she got to know about it. But now it's settled that she is to go to Sweden, to her cousin's place in the country, so you see things are looking up. Worst of it is she's taking the kids with her. I don't know how I shall get through two months without my children. Not to be able to say good night to them, Freddy.

MISS BERENTS (*Comes in*): Mr. Cummingham would very much like a word with you.

DITLEF: I'm always in to Mr. Cummingham.

CUMMINGHAM (*Enters*): How are you, gentlemen?

DITLEF: Very fine indeed. Always glad to see you (*Pleasantly*) Surely England isn't going to requisition any more of my boats today?

CUMMINGHAM: No; you can be let off today. I have a request to make to you. And I can talk freely in the presence of Mr. Bang. I know England has a loyal friend in him. We have done business with him. To come to the point, Mr. Mathiesen. I wish to ask you to emphasize to your captains and crews that they are to preserve the strictest silence as to what they see in the North Sea. Mines, U-boats, warships. And perhaps you'll be kind enough to pass on this order—this request—to your colleagues this very day. That sort of information can easily get into the wrong hands. They—the other side—have begun to show rather a troublesome interest in these matters.

DITLEF: Rely on me. It shall be done.

CUMMINGHAM: Then, about the information to *me*. It's not enough for me to *get* reports on what has been observed at sea. I must have them quickly. Here, as you will understand, it's a matter of minutes. That's all.

FREDDY: Any other news, Mr. Cummingham?

CUMMINGHAM: Oh no. We began a big push on the Marne this afternoon, but that's hardly of much interest. I expect it's in the papers. Personally, at present I'm kept pretty busy by the Norwegian copper exports to Germany. An interesting chapter.

FREDDY: A sad chapter for a friend of your country.

DITLEF: It's not always easy to be a Norwegian, Mr. Cummingham.

CUMMINGHAM: Perhaps not.

DITLEF: To know that such things go on.

CUMMINGHAM (*Taking up his hat*): Well, I must be off, gentlemen.

DITLEF (*Accompanies him to the door*): Lovely evening. Peaceful, what?

CUMMINGHAM: Yes. Good evening. (*Exit.*)

DITLEF: We must see about getting rid of those copper shares.

FREDDY: Sooner or later. But we'll wait a bit. They're rising all the time. And they've been transferred so neatly—if I do say so—that the devil himself couldn't guess we've a finger in the pie.

DITLEF: I don't like it.

FREDDY: And I don't like accepting a quite unnecessary loss.

DITLEF: Well, that's that, Freddy, that's that. I'm just going in to Johnson to speak about the message Cummingham wants circulated. Will you wait? Then we can walk home together.

(*Exit Ditlef. Freddy is alone for a moment. Enter Konrad.*)

FREDDY (*Cordially*): How are you, Konrad?

KONRAD: Do you know what ought to be done with you? You ought to be shot. Swine that you are.

FREDDY: Do you think we should miss a lot if you expressed yourself a trifle more politely?

KONRAD (*Depressed and hopeless*): What have you done to Edith? What have you done to that poor innocent child?

FREDDY: As to innocence, I'm not so sure—

KONRAD: I'll kill you.

FREDDY: Splendid, Konrad. But what do you say to our trying to help her instead? Now that the accident has happened.

KONRAD: I've heard about that help, you slimy devil. Sending her to one of your smart doctor friends in London, eh? So that was the college for young ladies that Edith really must go to?

FREDDY: When the operation's over, she can still go to college. The one thing doesn't stop the other.

KONRAD: But the girl is to stay here—see. And you're to marry her. Do you understand?

FREDDY: I'm sorry, you're mistaken there, Konrad.

KONRAD: Perhaps we're not good enough for you!

FREDDY: Konrad! You know as well as I do that I'm to marry Margrethe Harmens.

KONRAD: My sister didn't know it.

FREDDY: Know it, know it! One doesn't talk about a thing like that. Bear that in mind.

KONRAD: So you won't. Then you'll have to put up with a scandal, old man.

FREDDY: We differ about that, too. Because you daren't. Who do you think would lose?

KONRAD: It's queer about you. You cheat all the time, and still you're respected.

FREDDY: Respected. That's the first sensible thing you've said. (*Sneering*) Respected, ah, but feared. (*Suddenly changing from coldness to charm*) Listen to me, Konrad. Let's get this thing out of the way. Does anyone else know about it?

KONRAD: No, but they shall.

FREDDY: Let's not part as enemies. That mustn't happen. Remember our schooldays together—all our memories. Let's cross out the whole painful episode, Konrad.

KONRAD: Never! Never! I tell you.

FREDDY: Ditlef and I were just talking about you. In connection with a deal that we thought might interest you. I shall be sorry if nothing comes of it now.

KONRAD: What sort of deal?

FREDDY: Since you ask me, it was the "Vöringen."

KONRAD: The "Vöringen"? Oh, no, old chap. There's not a broker in the town who can get me the "Vöringen." I've been trying all day.

FREDDY: Are you game for a hundred thousand?

KONRAD: Chuck it, Freddy.

(*Freddy bangs down the papers on the table in front of him.*) Good lord!

FREDDY: Remember, Edith's young, Konrad. Only sixteen.

KONRAD: Yes, that's just what's wrong about it.

FREDDY: Look at it from the other side, Konrad. You're generally an optimist. She has got all her life before her.

KONRAD: Keep Edith out of it, as much as you can.

FREDDY: You shall have them at 160.

KONRAD: What did *you* get 'em at? Well, never mind about that, this is business.

FREDDY: They'll stand at 200 tomorrow.

KONRAD: They will. No doubt about that. And you know of a good place for Edith, Freddy? Somewhere where she'll get kindly treatment—sympathetic attention?

FREDDY: A safe place, Konrad, take my word for it. A place in which you can have every confidence.

KONRAD: They say she'll make 50 per cent on the first trip alone.

FREDDY: That's hardly putting it too high.

KONRAD: I'm on, then, I should damn well think so.

DITLEF (*Entering with overcoat and hat*): Morning, Konrad. Nice to see you. How's "Old Man Noah" getting on?

FREDDY: Konrad's coming in with us, Ditlef.

DITLEF: I should jolly well think he was! Must stick together, what?

KONRAD: Me and you and old Freddy.

DITLEF: Just so.

KONRAD (*With emotion*) : Thanks for being such a friend, Ditlef. And you too, Freddy.

FREDDY: There are one or two points which perhaps we ought to settle, Ditlef.

DITLEF: I won't hear of it. Tomorrow. I must get home now. Seven o'clock's the kiddies' bath time. Think I'd miss that sight? You should see Hannemor riding all round the nursery on her pot! God bless 'em. Well, we're off, eh?

Scene 2

The home of a commission agent. A dark, chilly room: daz- zlingly bright daylight outside. The faces show white in here in the semidarkness.

Aslaug is sitting shivering, and pulls on a knitted jumper. Her husband, the agent Eilif Olsen, a shabbily dressed man in his forties, enters hurriedly.

OLSEN: Did you see them? Did you see those two cars?

ASLAUG (*Indifferently*) : What are you talking about?

OLSEN: They came in from Milde, Mathiesen and some people from outside the town. They were to meet at the "Norge" at three, to draft the prospectus for the new bank. But in Viken and at Nygaard and the whole way along, they came across people who wanted to be in on it. So they had to stop and go in wherever it might be, and arrange for the applications.

I was up at Grönsæter's when four or five of 'em came in. No sooner did Grönsæter hear what it was all about, than he puts down his name for twenty-five thousand. Of course he's well off; had a fine warehouse when the war broke out, and ran it sensibly. And right there, over the counter, there were applica- tions for 270 thousand. So then they drove on till they were stopped again. Do you know how much had been applied for,

when they arrived at the "Norge," where they were really meant
to start? Eight million!

ASLAUG: What's that to do with us?

OLSEN (*Gently*) : No, there may be something in that. (*Flares
up again*) If only I'd a few hundred kroner, you'd see; I don't
ask for more. That's enough for the first installment—ten per
cent. I met old Konrad this morning. He said he could hand
me over some shares in the "Vöringen" at a reasonable rate. Just
for old times' sake, he said. I'm certain I should make a success
of it. Sell at the right moment, buy some more, sell again, get
a lot more, and then one day I'd be *in*.

ASLAUG (*Sounding bitter*) : Where are you to get the money
from? (*Silence*) Have you sold anything today?

OLSEN: Oh, of course you think it's easy, when one's agent
for a firm on the blacklist. They say there was a German up
here today, asking for me. He was to come here again later.

ASLAUG: Yes, we've had our fair share of disappointments.—
You must go down and empty the garbage can. The kitchen's
a fair sight!

OLSEN: Would it be asking too much for you to do it before
I come home? I slave all day for you.

ASLAUG (*Suddenly bursting out*): Oh, I'm too good for this
sort of thing. I was meant for something better. This room
smells moldy, it's so dark and cold here—Haven't you enough
cash for me to go to the movies this afternoon? It's Psilander.

OLSEN: I believe I shall get some money tomorrow. There's
no help for it, this evening you must put up with me.

ASLAUG: Well, you're someone too, I suppose! You've got
no drive. Why can't you make money, just as well as the rest?
You seem to me just like what I see when I open my eyes every
morning: there you stand in the half-light, over by the wash
stand, with your suspenders hanging down—all limp and flabby.
That's you!

OLSEN: You might get up yourself. Then you'd be spared
that sight.

ASLAUG: What have I got to get up for? I know there's never anything to hope for. But why couldn't some of our friends have a little thought for others? Why for instance couldn't one of them send me 500 kroner? Anonymously.

OLSEN: You ought to get out more, Aslaug. While the weather's fine.

ASLAUG: You think I can go out and show myself to people in this coat! Why it's so old that it's green. I hate the sunlight. I won't go out.

OLSEN: Perhaps you could get Vaardal the tailor to turn it. They say he's pretty cheap.

(*Enter Leif, a boy eight years old.*)

ASLAUG: Have you been fighting again, Leif? Ought to be ashamed of yourself. What a sight! Here we are, slaving to keep you going, and your whole suit's in rags. You'll be the death of me!

OLSEN (*Shaking the boy*): Will you answer? Who've you been fighting?

LEIF: Eilert.

OLSEN: Why?

LEIF: We were photographed.

OLSEN: Yes, you look as if you'd been photographed! But that's no answer.

LEIF: It was Eilert's idea.

OLSEN: What was his idea?

LEIF: Well, we were photographed in the school, and were to give the picture to the teacher, 'cos it was his birthday, and then I had no money to join in, and so they wrote—"To our teacher Mr. Berg, from the class, minus Leif." Yes, and so I fought Eilert afterwards in the playground.

OLSEN: So that's the way it was! Why didn't you come to me?

LEIF: I knew you'd sold nothing.

OLSEN (*Gently*): Well, well. (*Abruptly*) Did you lick him?

LEIF: Darn right I did!

OLSEN: You'll be photographed all right one day, Leif my

boy. You can bank on that. (*He goes to his coat and takes out a parcel.*)

ASLAUG: "Minus Leif"! Seems to me it's minus you and me too. Such is life! (*Sees that her husband has a bottle*) Have you been buying brandy, when we've hardly a scrap of food in the house?

OLSEN: I had to, since there's a customer coming.

ASLAUG: Well, I must say, you're really something! I know what you're like when you've had a drop. Then you start playing the fool. And I won't have any more children! Leifie, go out and play.

OLSEN: Will you hurry up!

ASLAUG: No, I won't. You're so difficult always. You must behave yourself.

(*A knock at the door.*)

DR. RUDOLPH WEGENER (*A man in his thirties, with a limp, enters. Speaks Norwegian with an attractive accent*) : My name is Dr. Wegener. Would very much like to have a few words with you.

OLSEN: My name is Olsen. This is my wife. Delighted. Aslaug, please get out some glasses.

WEGENER: Not on my account. I do not drink. (*To Aslaug, as she goes out*) *Auf wiedersehen,* ma'am.

OLSEN (*Making conversation*) : You speak our language very well, Herr Wegener.

WEGENER: I studied in Kristiania at the university for two years. From 1901 to 1903.

OLSEN. Oh, so that's it.

WEGENER: I took my doctor's degree in Norwegian literature. Ibsen.

OLSEN (*Suspiciously*) : Interesting. (*A pause*) I see you've a game leg. I suppose you were in the war?

WEGENER: Till October last year. Now it is pleasant for me to return here, after all these years.

OLSEN: A lot of changes.

WEGENER: I have obtained a fuller and richer picture of your country this time. I was so young last time.

OLSEN: I see.

WEGENER: When I have thought of Norway, now in these years when mankind is going through so much that is frightful, it has been with such happiness. I felt—this land is alive, it has been spared by the war. We others are perhaps blind, our eyes are smothered in blood, but over there are some eyes which see. This land with its great spiritual insight will give to mankind a new clarity—a new knowledge. You will be able to do it, because you have suffered with the world: and the greatest wisdom is that which springs from a great sorrow.

OLSEN: I must say, I don't quite follow.

WEGENER: That was how I thought. And then I came back. (*Smiles*) I had a little experience today which was quite interesting to me. I passed a new house outside the town—a fine house, a palace—I was told that it belonged to a shipowner, Mathiesen. . .

OLSEN: I know it.

WEGENER: Over the entrance porch, a workman was employed in cutting on stone the date: 1917. He sat in the sunshine and swung his hammer against the chisel. It had such a cheerful ring. And it struck me that many fine houses had grown up all round, on the headlands and cliffs, and all had the same amusing inscription. That made me think of some words of my old friend Ibsen.

OLSEN: What does he say?

WEGENER: He says, in a letter, that he does not think his people "has that exaltation in the soul which is needed to enable them to mourn," and only so long as a people can mourn—he says—can it live.

OLSEN: And you think that's a good saying? I don't. Do you think Mathiesen and those chaps mourn? But they live all right, and well too.

WEGENER: You have a great admiration for that sort of

person?

OLSEN: Smart fellows.

WEGENER: You should join them. (*His words are gradually marked by a bitter pleasure in speaking directly and contemptuously.*)

OLSEN: It isn't everyone who can be in with them. (*Ironically*) Do you want to do business, by any chance? Buy canned goods? First-rate quality!

WEGENER: Not exactly.

OLSEN: So I can imagine. I thought that talk of yours was a trifle odd. What are you, actually?

WEGENER: Let us say I am a journalist who is to work for a better reciprocal news service between our two countries. It is here that I have a use for you.

OLSEN: Oh, you have, have you?

WEGENER: You have contacts. You frequent the cafés down by the harbor. I want you to provide me with reports on what the sailors see during their trips.

OLSEN: More or less what I thought. Oh no, this thing *stinks.*

WEGENER: What is your price?

OLSEN: Price! I tell you I won't; it ain't right.

WEGENER: Need we waste our time over that sort of thing? In a land where highly respected men triumphantly carve on their porches the date 1917, the year of agony and death, fine feeling is surely unnecessary. You will have 200 kroner a month.

OLSEN: But this is a criminal offence.

WEGENER: There is a provision in the law—that's true. But it is transgressed every day, without penalty. The English get all the intelligence they desire.

OLSEN: But it's you who sink our ships.

WEGENER: Because you support the enemy; because you are in league with the other side; though, when it suits you, you call yourselves neutral. You have one statesman in Norway, and only one. He has said bitter things about us who sink your ships. But he has also said another thing: English authorities—

he says—do as they please in this country, as if Norwegian authority and the sovereignty of the Norwegian state did not exist. And he adds: Personally I have often found it difficult to decide what has shocked me most.

OLSEN: It shocks me too.

WEGENER (*Scornfully*): Just so! It shocks you. Listen to me. People in this country think the English are winning; they act accordingly. As far as I understand you, you would like to take a hand in speculation. Gamble on our winning. Back us. Play boldly, play for high stakes. If we win, we shall not forget you.

OLSEN: Now that's something I should like to do. (*Bending suddenly forward*) Will you give me a thousand kroner?

WEGENER: No. We have no superfluous money to give away. We have many to pay. You shall have two months in advance. Four hundred.

OLSEN: I accept.

WEGENER: Here is the address for you to send the reports to. Here is the code. Burn the papers after you have learnt them by heart. Good-by. I am leaving this evening. But I shall keep in touch with you. Be sure of that. (*Exit.*)

ASLAUG (*At the door*): Well? Was it anything?

OLSEN (*Walking excitedly up and down*): I've had a stroke of luck, Aslaug, and I mean to use it. I can buy two shares. I'm not outside any longer. We shall get out of this—you and I and little Leif. I fancy I'm just as smart as the rest of 'em. Now I'm in the game! Money, money, money!

Scene 3

In front of the curtain. On the road to the harbor. Ditlef and Freddy arrive, walking.

FREDDY: Six o'clock is when the "Vargefjell" sails, isn't it?

DITLEF: That was the intention.

FREDDY: Perhaps the captain would be kind enough to take a letter from me with him. I'm in a very awkward situation. When the "Lyderhorn" was torpedoed, I lost four new suits that I'd had made up in London.

DITLEF: What about me? I had six cases of whiskey on board—so good that it's not on the market. What times we're living in!

FREDDY: As you'll recollect, it's not the first unpleasantness of the kind I've had.

DITLEF: What I always say is—there's no help for it. We must tighten our belts, and accept it cheerfully.

(*Captain Berg comes towards them*)

DITLEF: Evening, Berg. Don't look too bad, eh? Nothing but fine weather.

BERG (*Slowly*): There's nothing to say against the weather. But perhaps you remember what I told you. When we were stopped on the last trip, and I rowed off to the U-boat with the papers, their commander said to me, "Next time you go with pyrites to England, we'll sink you!" Next time is today.

DITLEF: The North Sea's a big place, old man. And I'm sure you'll find room enough to change course and dodge the Germans. (*Cheerfully*) Copy me, Berg; don't look so much on the black side.

(*All three move on and exit. Sailors and stokers with seamen's bags come down towards the harbor. Women and children are with them. We notice a young couple—Ingolf and Berly: also an elderly man, formerly a seaman, and his son, Alf, seventeen years old. More slowly than the rest come Henry and Lillian. Henry is a young stoker, with a sensitive, open face, full of gloomy thoughts. Lillian is normally lively, but is quiet this evening, as she walks arm in arm with him.*)

HENRY (*Stopping*): How lovely it is here! Our last evening!

LILLIAN: But you'll soon be coming back to me and the baby. You promise!

HENRY (*Smiling at her*) : I promise.

(*Two Boys enter R. They are playing "syl"—a local Bergen game, played by throwing a knife or pointed instrument in various intricate ways—with great skill.*)

FIRST BOY: This is a good place. I can do a "double 'ead" here.

SECOND BOY: You ain't bin "through the 'ole" yet.

FIRST BOY: Oh, ain't I just? (*Does the "double head"*) Not so bad, eh?

SECOND BOY: So you think that was something. (*They squat down and go on with the game.*)

LILLIAN: I used to be pretty good at playing "syl." (*Looks at Henry*) Now your thoughts are far away again.

HENRY: No, they're not. I was thinking about these boys here. How happy they are. Everything's a joy to a boy like that, from the time he turns out in the engine room in the morning. What liveliness, what pluck! (*Sadly*) Seems to me chaps are too good for what's in store for 'em.

LILLIAN: You've seen such a lot of dreadful things, Henry. Torpedoings—what you were telling me about the war.

HENRY: Oh, you soon get used to that.

LILLIAN: What is it you don't get used to then?

HENRY: To leave you, that I don't get used to.

LILLIAN (*Kissing him*): Oh, Henry!

FIRST BOY: They're kissin' each other. Did you see? They kissed each other. Ought to be ashamed of themselves.

LILLIAN (*With emotion*) : Yes. We kissed each other. And we're not ashamed. Are we, Henry? Not a bit.

(*They walk off. Olsen and Leif—with a hoop—enter.*)

SECOND BOY: Look at old Leif! Quite the little gentleman. New clothes, wot?

BOTH BOYS (*Sing with their hands cupped at their mouths*) :
> 'Is Sunday pants is split in two,
> Across 'is dirty bottom;
> Such things don't worry me and you,

Becos we 'aven't got 'em!

LEIF (*Stopping the hoop and turning round*): Will you shut up!

OLSEN (*Shaking his stick at the boys, who run off L.*): If I got hold of you, you'll catch it!

THE BOYS (*Off*): Think we're afraid of you?

OLSEN (*To Leif*): And you ought to be ashamed of yourself. Get off home directly. What are you following me about for? (*With a sudden melancholy, bitter expression*) No one asked you to come here with me.

(*Before they go out, Cummingham and a Man in a Raincoat have entered, on their way to the quay.*)

MAN IN RAINCOAT (*Nodding towards Olsen*): That's the man I told you about.

CUMMINGHAM: So that's our new friend.

MAN IN RAINCOAT: He sent off his first report today. Cover address. Stockholm.

CUMMINGHAM: Which code?

MAN IN RAINCOAT: The old one.

CUMMINGHAM (*Contemptuously*): Good god! They're like children. What was in it?

MAN IN RAINCOAT: Five destroyers observed outside the Marsten.

CUMMINGHAM: Ah! The usual thing. Pack of lies. Who does he get it from?

MAN IN RAINCOAT: One of the hands on the "Jötun."

CUMMINGHAM: We must see how far he goes. (*Sneering*) Then we'll squash those vermin. (*Exit Man in Raincoat, R.*)

(*Cummingham stands in the center of the stage. The curtain is drawn aside. The scene is the harbor, with a ship alongside the quay. Seamen with their friends are moving about in the background. Ditlef and Freddy are talking to Berg. Cummingham enters the picture.*)

DITLEF: Good evening, Mr. Cummingham. (*In a low voice*) Well, tonight there's a cargo leaving that I hope will do you good. Pyrites for Newcastle. Guns, eh?

CUMMINGHAM: Splendid. By the way, there's another cargo leaving here this evening.

DITLEF: What sort of cargo?

CUMMINGHAM: Copper for Germany.

DITLEF: You know my feeling about that. How it shocks me.

CUMMINGHAM (*Slowly*): The copper that is being exported from Norway will be used to make the shells that cripple and kill our soldiers day after day. (*Violently*) And what would this country be without us? (*Pause*) There's another side of the case too, which isn't really my concern, but which is of some interest. You know perhaps that Norwegian copper—extracted from Norwegian mines—is used in making the U-boats which are sinking Norwegian ships and killing Norwegian sailors all the time. (*Turns towards them*) The inflated price of Norwegian copper is the price of blood. Good evening, gentlemen. (*Exit.*)

DITLEF: I've never seen him like that before.

FREDDY: I must say I prefer him as he generally is. Not so off-balance, so un-English.

BERG: I heard, up at the consulate, that he got a telegram this afternoon which can't have been a nice one to get.

DITLEF: What? Can he have been gambling too?

FREDDY: I should never have thought so.

BERG: No, it was another kind of telegram. They say his son has been killed. (*The Chief Engineer comes up to him.*)

BERG (*To Ditlef*): One moment, sir. (*Starts talking with the Chief Engineer.*)

FREDDY (*To Ditlef*): Son or no son, when a chap like that takes on so, it means something. England's going to forbid the export of Norwegian copper. We must sell our shares, and at once. I'll go make a long distance call. (*Exit.*)

DITLEF: I'll come in a moment. (*Turns to the Captain and speaks with feeling*) Well, I wish you luck, captain. You realize that a lot of warm wishes go with you. And you must remember one thing—you're sailing with a cargo that's *important,* and you're taking it to a country that is fighting for civilization. Bear that in mind.

BERG: Ah well, you know, when one's the skipper one has a lot of other things to think of.

(*They shake hands. Exit Ditlef, Berg turns again to the Chief Engineer.*)

CHIEF ENGINEER: Yes, I'm stuck. The man had to go to hospital and I know of no one else.

BERG: You must do what you can. We sail in ten minutes. (*Goes on board.*)

(*The sailors and those with them have gathered in a small group. They are: Ingolf and Berly, Alf and his father, Henry and Lillian.*)

THE FATHER: It's queer being down here again, after living so long up country. This is where I once walked with *my* dad, when I was off on my first trip. That's 45 years ago.

ALF: Oughtn't I to be getting aboard soon?

FATHER: Oh, there's no hurry. (*Smiles at him*) Are you impatient? Well, there's nothing wrong with that.

(*A crowd of sailors, pale and exhausted, arrive, accompanied by a few relatives and curious people; among them the two boys and Olsen.*)

BERLY: Who are they?

INGOLF: They must be the fellows who were torpedoed on the "Lyderhorn." They've just come in on the boat from England.

ALF: What if we were torpedoed!

FATHER: How you talk, boy!

OLSEN (*Mixing with the "Lyderhorn" men*): Care to have a drink with me?

AALESUND (*A sailor*): Sure thing!

FIRST BOY: How long was you in the lifeboat?

SECOND BOY: You heard me. Forty-eight hours.

OLSEN: What was it like?

THE SWILLER: Oh, it was a fine fishing trip.

FATHER: Did you manage to save anything?

SWILLER: Nothing but the concertina. I went back for that, 'cos it was new. (*Fingers the keys.*)

BERLY: Play us a tune.

SWILLER: I don't know nothing but the Bedtime Waltz.

LILLIAN: How he talks!

(*The Sailor plays a catchy sailors' waltz.*)

CHIEF ENGINEER: Hi! Swiller!

SWILLER: I'll 'swill' you, you fat devil!

CHIEF ENGINEER: Listen to me. I'm absolutely in a jam. One of my stokers has fallen down the ladder—bilged, of course— and I'm a man short in the engine room. You and I have been shipmates before, and I couldn't wish for a better stoker. Can't you take it on?

SWILLER (*Annoyed, but secretly pleased at being the center of attraction*): D'you know what you are? You've the cheek of a bedbug! Here am I, not gone twenty yards over the gang- way, and you want me off again. Ain't I even to get into the town and have a look at the gals? I got eighteen pounds when they paid off, and ain't I going to spend that first!

CHIEF ENGINEER: Oh, there's fine girls in Newcastle, too.

SWILLER: Gals is all the same, wherever you pick 'em up. But do you want to do me out of a drink, you old devil?

CHIEF ENGINEER: Oh, we can fix up a drink all right, on the "Vargefjell," too.

SWILLER: Well, if you stand me a drink, I'm not too mean to take on the trip. (*Crosses the gangway, saying good-by to his mates*) Well, thanks for the trip, Aalesund; good-by Larvik; give my love to Lousy-Astrid, Doggy!

CHIEF ENGINEER (*Following him on board*): I shan't forget you for this.

(*The concertina is heard off, playing in the mess.*)

FATHER: Well, there's nothing mean about that chap.

BERLY: There's another of them.

LILLIAN: Oh! The poor fellow!

(*Malvin enters, supported by his wife, Alma. One of his arms is hanging down; he limps. His face is white and drawn.*)

ALMA: Does it hurt so much?

MALVIN: Oh, I can manage. (*They go on out.*)

AALESUND: He had torpedo splinters in the head and the leg and the arm. At first we thought he was done for. He lay bleeding on the deck, without a sign of life. His old lady can be thankful she's got him home—that it wasn't the parson that called this evening.

BERLY (*In a whisper*): The parson! (*She catches Lillian's eye.*)

OLSEN: Now we'll be off to the pub, eh? (*The "Lyderhorn" men and their friends leave. The quay grows quiet and deserted.*)

ALF (*Who begins to feel the parting for the first time—that chilly breath of loneliness*): Well, mum'll soon be home now.

FATHER: Yes, it was sad for her not to have been able to stay to the end, but she had to get back to cook supper, you know.

ALF: The train will have reached Stend station by now.

INGOLF: Give my best love to Anton and Ruth.

BERLY: Yes, I won't forget.

INGOLF: And you must write.

BERLY: Yes, and you too.

FATHER: And behave yourself.

ALF: Yes, dad.

FATHER: And write to us.

LILLIAN (*Like an echo*): And write——

HENRY (*As if afraid*): No, no. Don't say anything.

LILLIAN: Why not?

HENRY: No, you see, it makes me feel as if I had to begin to leave you already. Then it's as if all the trouble here, all that isn't ourselves, begins to part us, *even while I'm still here;* do you understand? I've enjoyed these three weeks so much; it has just been you and me—no one else in the world. Don't say anything; let these weeks go on to the very last second—just you and me. Let me stand and keep quiet and look at you. Do you see what I mean, Lillian?

LILLIAN: Yes. (*They stand with white faces, gazing at each other.*)

INGOLF: Well, Berly, thanks for our time together.

FATHER: Good-by then, my boy.

ALF: Good-by, dad. (*He goes on board.*)

BERLY (*In a sudden outburst*): I can't stand it!

INGOLF: Belay there, Berly. You've been so wonderful all the time.

BERLY: But I know it! I feel it! This time——

BERG (*From the deck*): Well, lads, we can't help it. We must get aboard.

BERLY (*Wildly*): Don't go! You mustn't go!

INGOLF: You heard what he said. There's no help for it. (*He wrenches himself loose and goes aboard.*)

VOICE OF THE MATE: All clear aft!

HENRY (*Almost in a whisper, while his eyes do not leave her face*): Good-by and good luck.

LILLIAN (*Motionless, gazing at him*): Thank you, you too. (*He hurries on board without turning around. The steam whistle blows.*)

CURTAIN

ACT II

Scene 1

(*In front of the curtain, Alma and Berly come hurrying on in the rain.*)

ALMA: What are you so nervous about? You know you'd be the first to hear of it. *You* don't need to look at the papers.

BERLY: But I've been away several hours, with father and mother in Viken. Anything can have happened in that time.

ALMA: Just keep calm, Berly.

BERLY: Yes, it's easy for you to talk, with your Malvin at home. But I've got my Ingolf on the worst run between England and France—

THE SECOND BOY (*In a shiny wet waterproof, sings out in a repeated rhythm*): Bergens Tidende, Aftenbladet, Annonsen, Arbeidet, Folkets Avis!

BERLY (*Who has snatched a newspaper*): Oh, thank God!

ALMA: Is there nothing this evening?

BERLY: Oh yes. A Tönsberg boat sunk without warning. Six men drowned.—Without warning, Alma! There are the Germans sitting safe and snug in their U-boat. No one sees them sneaking up. And then they kill *our* people, Alma.

(*The gong sounds. The curtain rises on the U-boat.*)

Scene 2

(*The U-boat's control room. The Commander and the Lieutenant are standing by the periscope. Two sailors stand at separate wheels, steering. All in working clothes. It is a narrow space, with an uncanny, oily yellow light. It conveys the spirit which marks them all:—quivering, exhausted nerves.*)

COMMANDER (*Giving the orders*) : Fifty degrees.

THE SAILOR (*Turning the wheel*) : Fifty degrees.

COMMANDER (*To the Lieutenant*) : Should be a Norwegian steamer just ahead. The operator took the report just now. That will be the twenty-fifth in the four months since we left Wilhelmshafen. A nice little jubilee. (*To the Sailor*) There'll be extra rations this evening. That'll go down well?

SAILOR: Yes, Herr Commandant.

COMMANDER: We're leading by seven. U 40 has only sunk seventeen. Won't Von Mühlen be annoyed?

LIEUTENANT: We haven't heard from U 40 for several days.

COMMANDER: Their radio must be out of order.

LIEUTENANT: Probably.

COMMANDER (*Sharply*) : Their radio must be out of order.

LIEUTENANT: Very good, sir. (*Pause.*)

COMMANDER: We must soon think of something to cheer us up. When we get to the Shetlands, we'll row ashore and steal sheep. Do you remember that night outside Homborsund in Norway?

LIEUTENANT: I remember what a good smell there was, of autumn and the earth. The sea was phosphorescent, the dark sky was full of stars. It was so high overhead that breathing was a delight. Oh, if only I could breathe like that once again, I ask nothing more—

COMMANDER: Nothing more! (*Looks through the periscope*) We ought to have that ship soon now.

LIEUTENANT: Are we to board and check their papers?

COMMANDER: No, we're sinking them without warning.

LIEUTENANT: Must we?

COMMANDER (*Sharply*): Remember the "Baralong." She was flying a neutral flag too, and when our men surfaced and demanded the papers for checking, they dropped the screens and there were the guns, and they sank the boat. My friend Herwart was among the forty who jumped into the sea and swam for their lives. But on board the "Baralong" the English stood and shot them down, picking them off like ducks in the sea. Some got safe aboard the enemy ship, but they went after them and killed them wherever they found them. There's more than one "Baralong" at sea. It's swarming with them. Am I to trust a ship because it looks neutral?

LIEUTENANT: I suppose not.—But we needn't revenge ourselves on the helpless, for all that.

COMMANDER: What do you mean?

LIEUTENANT: You fired on the sailors in the lifeboat yesterday, and there were children on board.

COMMANDER: *That's a lie!* I thought it was an enemy submarine surfacing: It looked like that in the sea. And I had no time to lose. (*With a bitter, melancholy smile*) Ah, Erwin, I'm the commander.

LIEUTENANT: My mistake, sir. (*Pause.*)

COMMANDER (*To the Sailor*): Did you get a letter by the supply ship, Seger?

SAILOR: Yes, Herr Commandant.

COMMANDER: Everything all right?

SAILOR (*Calmly*): They're starving, Herr Commandant.

COMMANDER (*To the Lieutenant*): *That's* how the English make war!

LIEUTENANT (*In a low voice*): And we retaliate by starving English women and children. That's our war, yours and mine.

COMMANDER: We have a job to do. We have to do it, not think. Besides, it's the best way. If we starve them, we shall get peace more quickly. Everyone at home is crying out for that:— *Peace with Honor!*

(*The Sailor smiles a bitter, sarcastic smile.*)

COMMANDER: Did you smile?

SAILOR: Yes, Herr Commandant.

COMMANDER: Anywhere else, you'd be court-martialed for that smile. But not on board my ship. Here we are all one. It was I who smiled. I am free to smile when I want to. (*Looks through the periscope*) Ship ahead. Seventy degrees. (*A pause*)

Norwegian flag, Norwegian markings.

LIEUTENANT: That fits.

COMMANDER: Apparently. (*Gives an order*) Eighty degrees.

SAILOR (*Repeating*): Eighty degrees. (*He turns the wheel.*)

LIEUTENANT: Günther, give them a chance. If they don't have time, they'll freeze to death in the boats. If they get that far.

COMMANDER: I don't trust the appearance of the ship. I daren't.

LIEUTENANT: Remember the child we shot in the lifeboat.

COMMANDER: What's the use of all this?

LIEUTENANT: I'm trying to save myself as a man.

COMMANDER: Poor Erwin! I'm better off. I am a dead man. Anyone who has gone through what I have is done for. He hasn't wife or children any more. I only recognize one thing,— *I am responsible for my people.* I daren't.

LIEUTENANT (*With sudden gentleness*): I understand you, Günther.

COMMANDER: Notice my words:—"dare not," "afraid," "frightened." They call me a brave man; it appears on my uniform; my Emperor has told me so; but I know only one law, and that I act upon—Fear.

(*Issues his order.*)

Stand by starboard torpedo tube!

A VOICE OFF STAGE: Stand by starboard torpedo tube.

COMMANDER: Ready.

VOICE: Ready.

Scene 3

(*The forecastle of the "Vargefjell." Alf is walking up and down the engine-room deck, wearing his life-jacket. The Swiller and Ingolf are sitting eating at the table. Henry is lying in his*

*bunk, reading old letters. Behind two bunk curtains we hear
the heavy breathing of sleeping men.*)

ALF (*Stopping*): I don't understand what you're thinking
of. You *are* supposed to wear life-jackets.

SWILLER: What good are they? If we go, we go.

ALF: But didn't you hear what I told you? Just now, when I
was on deck with the look-out—

SWILLER: It's the devil the way that chap tramps up there!
Even if he's fed up and cold, he might go away and tramp by
himself, on the starboard side, over the heads of the sailors—

ALF: We suddenly heard a bang down to the southeast, and
saw flames shoot up.

SWILLER: Now we've been on this run a month, and we'll get
through this evening as well. It may have been a mine, and no
one's going to strike that mine any more. If you really must
think, think of that. You're a good lad, Alf, really you are, but
you've been walking about on your farm *thinking* about the
sea,—thinking about being torpedoed, and thinking only makes
a chap nervous. Don't think of anything. Don't give a damn
for anything.

ALF: It was a U-boat, I'm sure.

SWILLER: Henry, did I ever tell you about that U-boat that
the Swedish serving-maid fixed? I met her myself in Newcastle.
They have serving-maids on board their boats—those damned
Swedes;—don't I wish I had one!! Well, the ship was sunk, and
they'd rowed off to the U-boat. Then up comes an English
destroyer tearing along at forty knots. The U-boat was making
to dive, but then that girl took the end of a plank that was
floating about, and shoved it down the escape hatch, so that
they couldn't shut it. Well, in the end the German got under,
but the destroyer came up at full speed and dropped a depth
charge.—All that came up was a few sailors' caps and a little oil.

HENRY: What a life that must be!

SWILLER: Yes, that's how it went.

(*Alf has sat down in the semi-darkness.*)

INGOLF: All right by me, if we copped it this evening.—So that I could get home. I only need one more torpedoing, and then I can start engineering school. I've saved up all the money we get when we lose our kit, and I figure that if I'm careful I shall manage all right when we're torpedoed for the fifth time.

SWILLER: So you're going to end up amidships?

INGOLF: That was my idea. I'll tell you one thing, Swiller. I remember the day my dad came home and had been sacked after he'd been forty years in Simonsen's warehouse on the Vaagsalmenning. They wanted younger people, they said. Dad died of it. That time I swore they shouldn't get *me;* I would get on and one day be a free man. Did you ever think of going to school, Swiller?

SWILLER: Oh, somehow I never got as far as that. You see, I was illegitimate and that's a funny thing. (*Lowering his voice so that Alf shall not hear.*) But you may get home sooner than you think. I was talking to the chief just now: in the English patrol boat that stopped us this afternoon, they thought there was plenty of U-boats ahead.

INGOLF: Good deal!

ALF (*Has got up and is listening*): Now the steps on deck have stopped. Did you hear? He's looking at something now.

SWILLER: I think you'd better sit down, Alf. How about a game of cards? It's not seven bells yet. Can't he stop walking if he likes. Expect he's standing thinking of his old woman.

ALF: Give us a tune.

SWILLER (*Reaching for his concertina in the bunk*): All right (*Plays and sings*).

Farewell, dear mother Norway, I'm sailing over sea,
But thanks for all the childhood days through which you
    nurtured me;
You were p'raps a trifle stingy with the humble toiler's food,
But what you give your scholars is both plentiful and good.

Now off to foreign countries like the swallow I must fly,

Right across the mighty ocean, where the waves roll broad
    and high;
We can make a living yonder if we only work, and so
Thank you kindly, old Columbus, since you showed us
    where to go.

Now the captain's on the bridge, and all the engines
    start to roar,
As we wave to our acquaintance, left behind upon the shore;
And I really must confess it, that I feel a trifle blue,
As behind the far horizon mother Norway sinks from view.
(*He puts down the concertina, and says to Alf*): Now you
can hear him again, tramping about up there, can't you?—What
are *you* lying thinking about, Henry?—As if I need to ask! It's
the devil that everyone must look so silly when they're thinking
about love. They get that idiotic light on their mugs, just like
people in the street at home, when the band goes by.
    HENRY: I suppose you've got somebody at home too—
    SWILLER: Why buy a cow when milk is so cheap?
    HENRY: But surely there's somebody different from the rest?
    SWILLER: Oh well, I did know one too. She worked in the
canning factory at Viken. But one day she sat on the belt in the
lunch break, and when the whistle blew she was carried off and
mashed. But there's a lot of nice lasses in the world. The half-
breeds in North Africa are good-hearted girls. They call 'em
Media-Medias. And what tempers they've got! If you take up
with one, and then one day take another, you can easily get
a knife in your back. Yes, they're good-hearted gals. But the
gals down in Montevideo, I like them too; we was down there
for four years—
    HENRY: I s'pose you've got a lot of kids down there, then.
    SWILLER: Oh, a few shoe shine boys maybe—
    ALF: What time d'you think we'll put in?
    SWILLER: Search me! (*Listens*)—We're strolling along at not
more than seven knots. Those landlubbers down there don't

keep steam up. Damned if it's more than 150 pounds. So *we'll* have the job, 'cos it's not going to be said of our watch that we can't keep up top steam.

INGOLF: We won't be in until tomorrow evening.

SWILLER: Just so it's before the whorehouses close! Then I'll meet my girl, Gabbi. She sticks to me all the time I'm in port. And she's so kind. Once when I'd ripped up my clothes, she fixed 'em for me; sat at it for several hours. (*Paternally, to Alf*)—This time I'll take you with me. You'll have such a rest, you'll be the better for it for a whole week.

INGOLF: They say there's a new order out. The houses are to be closed to everyone but soldiers from six to ten every evening, and the rest don't get in till later.

SWILLER (*Meditatively*): There's nothing wrong with that, I don't think. Remember where they're going!

HENRY (*Propping himself on his arm*): It's queer about those boys—working folk like us, nearly all of 'em. What they've gone through, day after day, these years! There's some as says men are all bad; I think they're something too big to grasp. Do you think it's anything for chaps like that, who've done what they have, to build a better world?—Pull everything down and build it up better again.—After the war, you'll see. Nothing's impossible when *they* come back. (*He adds gently*) Only— they don't come back.

ALF (*Repeats in a whisper*): Don't come back!

(*He gets up and walks up and down the engine-room, then sits down in his place in the shadow.*)

SWILLER (*In a low voice*): Henry, you mustn't talk about serious things like that. You know—Ingolf and I are grown-up men, but Alfie's so dreadfully nervous. I'll tell you one thing, and I know what I'm talking about. The only useful thing in a situation like this is to talk about women.

(*Alf has got to his feet again, and listens, trembling.*)

THE LOOKOUT (*Shouts from the deck overhead*): U-boat!

(*The steam siren blows, and continues for the remainder of the scene. Henry and two others fling themselves out of their bunks.*)

SWILLER: All right, we hear you!

THE LOOKOUT: Torpedo!

SWILLER: They're in a hell of a hurry this time, those guys! But if it's coming, it's coming—Hang on to me, Alfie.

(*An explosion. The lamp goes out. A shriek is heard.*)

HENRY (*In the dark*): Who was that?

SWILLER: Poor old Ingolf.

(*The shriek changes to a groaning, pitiful death cry. As the curtain falls, the orchestra strikes up a music-hall tune. An actor, full of health and high spirits, comes on quickly, and sings the topical song of the days of the boom—"Who goes there? Who goes there?" During the last verse he has with him six chorus girls, made up as jolly sailors.*)

Scene 4

(*Room reserved for a party in a restaurant. Ditlef, Freddy, Birger, and several others. Besides these, the Russian violinist Sascha Erdman. Konrad is sitting at the piano.*)

DITLEF: Gentlemen! Today we have the pleasure of seeing amongst us the world-famous pianist Mr. Konrad Heggland—

ALL: Hooray for Konrad! Get up and bow. (*Konrad bows.*)

DITLEF: In response to innumerable requests, he has consented to give us a rendering of the most moving of all the items in his repertoire which have enraptured the public everywhere:—"Old Man Noah."

ALL: Bravo!

DITLEF: As judge and umpire in this wager between Mr. Konrad Heggland and Mr. Birger Meyer, we have been fortunate enough to secure the services of the no less world-famous Russian violinist, the musical star—Herr Sascha Erdman!

BIRGER: Hair and all!

DITLEF: So now all of you keep quiet as mice. Are you ready, Konrad? One—two—three!

(*In dead silence, Konrad plays "Old Man Noah." Immediately afterwards, all start talking.*)

DITLEF (*Raising his hand*): Silence for Herr Erdman!

ERDMAN (*Smiling*) : Faultless, gentlemen!—A—What shall I call it—an inspired performance!

ALL: Konrad's done it!—Good old Konrad!

KONRAD (*Beaming with pleasure*) : Wasn't I good?

DITLEF: I should think you were! There's no one like Konrad! (*He conducts at a frantic pace—"For he's a jolly good fellow."*)

BIRGER (*Producing a bundle of notes*): Will you take it in thousands, Konrad?

KONRAD: I'm not particular, Birger. No one can call me that!

BIRGER (*Soured by his loss, to Freddy*): What the hell has Ditlef brought that Russian up here for? Just as if we couldn't manage it ourselves. Why should we pal up with mountebanks like that?

FREDDY: He's no ordinary mountebank, Birger. They say he makes good money.

DITLEF (*To Erdman*) : Maybe it strikes you as odd that we should let ourselves go like this. But you must remember the times we're going through.—Tension, responsibility, day and night. We need to relax our nerves.

ERDMAN (*Smiling*): In my country, people of a certain sort have been relaxing their nerves in this way for several hundred years.

BIRGER (*Petulantly, to Erdman*) : Maybe you think fifty thousand matter to me. Do you? Then I'll give you an example. Yesterday I bought a Tönsberg boat at eleven in the morning for three and a half million, and sold it at one o'clock for four. And how was I able to do it, do you think? Why, because there's something called individual initiative.

KONRAD: That's true.—Mud in your eye, Birger!

BIRGER: Look at old Ditlef, look at old Konrad! And look at old Freddy! Wasn't it his foresight, his adaptability, that made him buy such big holdings of flour in 14 that he could fix his own price?

FREDDY: Keep me out of it, Birger. I'd call your attention to the fact that our family fortune dates from the Crimean War.

THE SIX DANCING GIRLS (*Come dashing in*): Who won? Konrad? Hurrah for Konrad!

FIRST GIRL (*Seeing Konrad stuff his bill-fold into his pocket*) : Surely you can spare us a little of the money?

BIRGER: Yes, you shall have money—good Norwegian bank notes. But then we must have *value* for the money.

KONRAD: Did you hear that! That was good! (*Pinching a girl*) We shall get value, eh?

DITLEF: What shall we give these little girls to drink?

KONRAD: Nigger's blood, eh? Porter and champagne.

BIRGER: Yes, that'll make 'em tight sooner.

(*Konrad and Birger set to work with a huge silver bowl between them. It is foaming with alcohol.*)

FREDDY (*To Ditlef*): I'm not too keen on the sort of orgy that's starting now. I prefer something more intimate, apart from the fact that the new arrivals aren't my type.

DITLEF (*Indicating to Freddy with a nod the Second Girl, who is dazzlingly young*): An acquaintance of mine down below tells me she's what they call a virgin. Incredible as it sounds.

FREDDY: I'll devote my attention to her, Ditlef.

DITLEF (*Tasting, with deep appreciation*) : It don't taste bad. (*To Konrad*) I appoint you to look after the bowl. You're to bail out, Konrad.

(*Konrad starts doing so.*)

DITLEF (*To Erdman*) : I should like to show you some Russian icons I have. I got 'em originally through a business connection. You know, I started in earnest as long ago as the Russo-Japanese war. It would be nice to know what they may be worth.

A WAITRESS (*Entering*) : A telegram for Mr. Bang.

DITLEF: There's no peace to be had. Not even in the brief moments of rest when we try to get away from business.

(Exit with Erdman. Freddy stands in the background with the telegram. A dance orchestra begins playing in the next room.)

KONRAD: Now for a dance with you!

(He and Birger dance out with the girls in a grotesque dance. Ditlef reenters and steps forward with Freddy.)

FREDDY *(Sharply)*: A swindle! Our man in Rio wires that the whole streetcar scheme is a fraud. Marshes where we were promised building sites. Four hundred thousand from each of us gone down the drain!

DITLEF *(Bitterly)*: And the names on the prospectus were supposed to be from among our most prominent men.

FREDDY: The loss is quite serious, unless—

DITLEF: Unless what?

FREDDY: I've thought of a possibility—Konrad! Of course he's had some serious losses lately.

DITLEF *(Suddenly taking it seriously)*: So they'd cheat us—they would, would they? I'll tell you something, Freddy. I remember the time my father got into difficulties. I was only a child at the time, but I remember how it broke him up. They'd swindled him too, he always said so afterwards. And who was there ready to give him a helping hand? Not a soul! That taught me a bit about human nature! If you lose—they drop you; they'll have your blood. But if you're a winner, you can trample on their faces and they'll thank you for it!

I remember my dad's white face, as he lay dying: it was as if he wanted to say to me—*Ditlef: you must never be a loser!*

FREDDY: And there's another point. You've got your children to look after, Ditlef,—to make the future safe and happy for them.

DITLEF: Thank you for saying that. Besides—we mustn't forget, Freddy, a telegram like that may be over-hasty.

FREDDY: I think that's quite possible, **Ditlef.**

DITLEF: The shares may still turn out very profitable.

FREDDY: I entirely agree. Now I'll call Konrad in. (*In the doorway*) Konrad!

KONRAD (*Comes chasing two girls in, goes up to the bowl, and says to one of them*) : Afterwards I shall come up and bathe you—And dry you, what?

FIRST GIRL (*Holding out her glass*): I'd rather you bailed out. Bail away!

(*Freddy beckons Konrad to him: the Girls go off to the dance.*)

FREDDY: Would you like to come in on a pretty big thing, Konrad? Rio streetcars. Our leading names on the prospectus.

KONRAD: I'll tell you how it is. I've been drinking. And so I'm not keen about it. Was it streetcars you said? Do you remember what old Smit, who used to teach us Norwegian literature, used to tell us? How Ibsen—the author, you know—put all his money into trolley shares, and made a mint—

DITLEF: Smit? Should think I do remember him! We three often gave him a hell of a time, and you were the worst, Konrad. Do you know what we'll do—we'll send him a few thousand from the three of us—three old pupils! You'll want to be in on that, won't you, Konrad?

FREDDY: On second thought, I doubt if Konrad can manage to come into the Rio scheme, Ditlef. It's a matter of very considerable sums.

KONRAD (*Hurt*): How much?

FREDDY: Eight hundred thousand.

KONRAD: And you don't think old Konrad is good for eight hundred thousand!

FREDDY: You must really decide that for yourself, Konrad. I wouldn't press you in any way—

KONRAD: Come on with the papers, Freddy. (*Signs*) That settles it. I'm taking trolley shares—same as Ibsen!

SOME OF THE GIRLS (*Rushing in, to Ditlef*) : Oh, can't you get him to play? They say he's so wonderful! (*To Erdman, who has entered*) Do play!

DITLEF: You know, there'll be no trouble about a check.

ERDMAN (*Who has been feeling lonely and out of it*): Very well, I will play. I should like to give the money to children whose fathers have fallen in the war.

BIRGER: Just bluffing!

(*Erdman takes his violin and plays a melancholy Russian folk tune.*)

SECOND GIRL: How lovely thas was! (*All applaud.*)

KONRAD (*Feeling sentimental*): How good it is to be here, Ditlef.—Among friends.

BIRGER (*Growing more and more bad-tempered*): Ditlef, I think you're a rotten stoker. I'm freezing. Can't you put something in the stove?

DITLEF: What?—Freezing with all these little girls round you!

BIRGER: Yes, I'm freezing. (*Suddenly, to Erdman*) What is a violin like that worth?

ERDMAN: About two thousand pounds.

BIRGER (*Smashing the violin*): Here's something for you to build a fire with!

DITLEF: Dreadfully sorry, Herr Erdman; that was embarrassing.

FREDDY (*With a contemptuous jerk of his head towards Birger*): No breeding! (*All stand stock-still, looking at Erdman.*)

ERDMAN: There are many like you in the world: one day, I believe, you will all have the same fate! (*Exit.*)

BIRGER (*Pulling out his money*): Here's a good two thousand pounds!

DITLEF: He's gone.

FREDDY: Go over to his hotel tomorrow, Birger. He'll take the money and kiss your hand.

DITLEF: Well, now we must cheer things up a bit. We'll have a drink. You mustn't forget to keep bailing, Konrad.

KONRAD (*Who has fallen on the sofa with a girl*): I'm so tired.

BIRGER (*Slumping down in the same place with the bits of violin in his hand*) : Now we'll start stoking with Beethoven and Mozart and Schubert's unfinished—eh?

DITLEF: Stick to it, Konrad. It was you who were to bail, old fellow!

BIRGER (*Very drunk*) : Stick to it, I tell you! Bail, Konrad, Bail!

(*As the scene closes, the orchestra plays "The Sailor's Last Voyage," arranged as jazz. After a minute, it changes to the real tune, played with all its agonizing solemnity, and the light slowly dawns on the lifeboat at sea. The dead-drunk figures of the orgy receive a kind of echo from the men frozen to death in the boat.*)

Scene 5

(*The lifeboat at sea, with a rag of sail set. Three men are lying frozen to death. The Captain is steering. Henry is sitting beside the Swiller, who is bailing. Rough weather and high sea.*)

LAKSEVAAG (*A sailor, in the bottom of the boat*) : Bail! Bail!

CAPTAIN BERG: Now you must take a rest, Swiller. You've been bailing all the time.

SWILLER: Somebody's got to do it.

LAKSEVAAG: Gimme some water!

CAPTAIN BERG: We haven't any, Laksevaag.

LAKSEVAAG: Water!

CAPTAIN BERG: Now you must take your turn at bailing, Gustav.

GUSTAV: I can't.

SWILLER: Pull yourself together, or I'll let you have one!

GUSTAV: I can't.

SWILLER: Maybe you'd rather go the same way as the three stiffs frozen beside you?—Bail, you damned farmer! (*Gustav bails.*)

SWILLER (*To Laksevaag*) : Where does it feel worst?

LAKSEVAAG: In my chest. I'm so cold.

SWILLER: Here's my sweater. But, I tell you, be careful with it. (*To the Captain*) How far have we come now?

CAPTAIN BERG: I make it twenty miles from land.

SWILLER: And what time can we get in?

CAPTAIN BERG: Twenty-four hours, if we don't run into a head wind.

SWILLER: Twenty-four hours more!

CAPTAIN BERG: The "Vargefjell's" last voyage has turned out to be a sad one.

SWILLER: Yes, you said it! Of the stokers there's only me and Henry left. Just us two, Henry. But we won't give up. Will we, Henry? I'm thinking of Alfie—I knew he would drown 'cos he put on his life-jacket.—How are you feeling, Henry? (*Henry merely groans*) —Why don't you answer? Don't you know me, Henry?—It's me, the Swiller—We're in sight of land, Henry! We can see a boat that'll pick us up, Henry!—No, 'fraid he's a goner.

GUSTAV: I can't go on!

SWILLER: You damn well can!

GUSTAV: I'm so cold.

SWILLER: Aye, your pal Tromsö's not cold, if that's what you're thinking of! But we're nearly in now, Gustav. Think of that! Think about getting home!

GUSTAV: Sing then, Swiller. It was such a help when you sang just now.

SWILLER (*Singing as he bails*) :
"Oh Lina was my sweetheart and the best of friends to me,
From Market place to Custom House the fairest maid
                                                        was she.

And oh, what eyes my Lina had and oh, what lovely hair;
And if you've seen my Lina you can fancy my despair,
For I'll nevermore be coming back to Bergen!"
(*Bends down to Henry*) : What's that you're saying, Henry?

CAPTAIN BERG: He's delirious now.

HENRY: It's fine weather, all the same. The drums have struck up now. I'm carrying the flag. It's the Skutevik battalion. Thanks for the auriculas, Lillian. How happy everyone looks.—Don't leave me, don't leave me!

SWILLER: No, I'm not leaving you.

GUSTAV: You must sing, Swiller, or I can't do anything.

SWILLER (*Sings*):

But quickly, much too quickly, the days of childhood
        passed,
And we stood for confirmation in the parish church at last,
There was not a girl like Lina, so lovely and so smart,
And the smile that then she gave me warmed the cockles
        of my heart.
For—I'll nevermore be coming back to Bergen!

(*He takes Henry in his arms*): Henry! Henry! (*Pause*) Ah well, Henry. (*To the Captain*) Aye, now Henry's gone same way as the others.

LAKSEVAAG (*Groaning in the bottom of the boat*): Is it any good? Put a stop to it. Anything's better than this!

GUSTAV: Sing, Swiller, sing!

SWILLER: No, we won't give up yet.

SWILLER (*Sings into a squall which lashes the boat*):

So after many a weary year of toil and stress was o'er,
And nobody was left to write me letters any more,
One day I was torpedoed, and got home to Bergen town,
But then she'd wed another, so my happiness was flown.
So—I'll never more be coming back to Bergen!

(*The curtain begins to fall slowly at the beginning of this stanza.*)

ACT III

Scene 1

(*In front of the curtain. Ditlef and Freddy.*)

DITLEF: I must say, Freddy, I don't really like the spirit of the people. All these sinkings are getting on their nerves. And the agitators start their tricks at once. And who has to stand the gaff? Us.

FREDDY: I think the case against the spies has come up just at the psychological moment. It gives people something else to think about. I happened to be passing this morning when Olsen and the others were taken from the police van to the court. I really thought the crowd would tear them to pieces.

DITLEF: Do you know what shocks me almost more than anything? That they've sold themselves so *cheap*. (*Opens a paper*). One can't help agreeing with what the papers say. Listen to *The Way of the World*. "It is a measure of the meanness of the crime, that it has not even the faint semblance of justification which consists in a respectable payment." And *The Shipping News* says:—"One would have sworn that Norwegians would not have been attracted to this dirty work by the wretched German tips they got." And here's a man writing in *The News*:—"With no fellow feeling for the nation from which they were hewn, and in which they were fostered, they sell its life and property for—200 crowns a month!"

FREDDY: Two hundred crowns!

DITLEV (*Folding up the paper, with emotion*): And they call themselves Norwegians!

(*Enter Cummingham.*)

DITLEF: We were just talking about the spy case, Mr. Cummingham. Interesting to hear your view.

CUMMINGHAM: These people—what have they done? In this

case, practically nothing.

DITLEF: But haven't they reported the sailings of ships to the Germans? Haven't they sent innocent seamen to their deaths?

CUMMINGHAM: I know you'd like to think so, Mr. Mathiesen. But there's no evidence of it.

FREDDY: Then England isn't interested in this case?

CUMMINGHAM: On the contrary, she is. We're very glad to see an example made. Splendid that it should be emphasized that spying, even on a trivial scale, is wrong and criminal.— Except when it's done for us. (*He moves away.*)

DITLEF: He's not very sociable these days. But I think it would be right—even a public duty—Freddy, to write an article on the spies for the papers. We should mobilize all this whole-some indignation against them; we should demand the severest punishment; this is a point where all right-thinking persons can be united.

FREDDY: I think you've got something there, Ditlef.

Scene 2

(*A narrow alley, sloping down to the harbor. Outside the small houses are steps, where much of the action takes place. Slightly up the hill, the main street crosses.*)

ALMA (*Who is sitting talking to her father, Ludvigsen*): No! Things are *not* all right with me. You know Malvin was the kindest chap you could imagine. But since he came home you wouldn't know him again. It was something frightful— that last torpedoing. What a sight he was! Covered with blood, and with iron splinters in his head and all over. As long as he was ill, there was nothing against him. It's since he got well that he's been so utterly impossible.

LUDVIGSEN: I suppose he'll soon be off again, now?

ALMA: That's how it is. We'll soon have no money left. I

expect he'll set out again next week; there's no way out of it.
I think that is what has affected him so. Not that he's frightened,
but he's grown so bitter. Always brooding, hardly ever speaks
to me, believes I just want to have him away again—

FIRST BOY (*Entering with a large errand-basket*): Aunt
Alma—

ALMA: That you, John?—Aren't you at work?

FIRST BOY: Oh yes, but I had to come close by here with a
parcel. So I thought I might ask you if maybe you had a slice
of bread. I'm so hungry.

ALMA: But, Lord knows, I don't know where to turn, either.
Can't you come back tomorrow?

MALVIN (*Having come out*): Here's a few pennies for you,
John!

(*The boy thanks him and exits.*)

MALVIN (*Sharply*) He oughtn't to go away from us without
anything.

ALMA: Whatever I do is wrong, Malvin.

MALVIN: So you don't think I'm entitled to give him a few
pennies? You think I haven't earned enough lately?—Oh, well.
You won't be troubled with me long.

ALMA: Have I ever said so?

MALVIN: I understand you all right.

ALMA: You talk as if I almost wished—

MALVIN: You'd like to have had the twenty thousand that
the widows get! Don't you worry, Alma. Just wait a little!

ALMA: Why do you hurt me like that?

(*Malvin goes up the street. An angry man comes hurrying in.*)

LUDVIGSEN: What are you in such a hurry for, Siggy?

ANGRY MAN: I'm off to *The News* with an advertisement,
to say I'm no relation of the Olsen who's a spy.

LUDVIGSEN: Right you are, Siggy. (*The Angry Man hurries
off.*) Those spies ought to be hung head downwards by their
feet. Aye, you read what Ditlef Mathiesen thought.

LILLIAN (*Comes out on her step with her child on her arm.*

She stands listening): Do you hear? That fine, high note in the air. It's all the kids who are out with their hoops. They're running now along every street, all over the town. It's the spring. That's what Henry always was saying. It's spring, he'd say, just as much as the first bright leaves—that wonderful music of the hoops on an evening like this.—Do you hear that sound, baby?

LUDVIGSEN (*Bending over the child*): Give the man a smile!

ALMA (*Tenderly*): Yes, if we were all like you, there'd be no trouble.

LILLIAN: Isn't she sweet?—Do that with your little mouth. (*To Alma*) Did you see? How clever she is.—Henry said a queer thing when he was home; he says a lot of queer things—Henry does. At first, he said, when she was only a couple of months old, she *knew* much, much more. When she just lay and followed us with her blue eyes, there was nothing in the world hid from her, he said. Did you ever hear such a thing! But now, he said, she's grown more important to herself, she learns from day to day, she cries and forgets and smiles and gets impatient and then happy again; and one day she won't *know* anything any more, and then she'll be grown up like you and me, he said.—That Henry!

ALMA: Do you hear from him?

LILLIAN: He thinks he'll be back by the summer. (*To the child*) Shall we go with daddy and look for buttercups out at Hellen? Shall we, my precious, shall we?

(*The Pastor suddenly appears before the house. Lillian sees him.*)

PASTOR: Yes, it is you I am looking for. (*Tries to stroke the child's hair gently.*)

LILLIAN: Don't touch her!

PASTOR: I am the bearer of sad news.—The saddest.

LILLIAN (*In a monotonous, dull tone*): God, God!—There isn't a God when a thing like this can happen!

PASTOR: You mustn't say that. Perhaps God has a use for

young men in heaven.

Malvin (*Gravely*) : He's taken a lot of them to himself, these last years.

Pastor (*Sadly*) : Who dares to say he knows the will of God?

(*Lillian enters the house, followed by the Pastor.*)

Alma: No God, isn't there? Would Malvin have been safe with me, if God hadn't stopped him from going out? (*She clings to Malvin.*)

Malvin: Go in to Lillian!

(*Enter Aalesund and Johanne, his wife, coming down the street. After them a cabin boy and his mother Andrea. A low animal-like howling is heard from the house. All stop.*)

Aalesund: What's that?

Ludvigsen: It's the parson; he's going round.

Aalesund: What boat's been sunk?

Ludvigsen: The "Vargefjell."

Aalesund: Many lost?

Ludvigsen: I couldn't say.

Malvin: Are you leaving again this evening, Aalesund?

Aalesund: Yes, in "Blaaeggen." (*The Pastor comes out again.*)

Johanne: Did many go down with her?

Pastor: There were eight drowned when the ship went down: six froze to death, for they were in the boats five days in frost and stormy weather, before they reached land. Four were rescued. (*Looks at his list*) —Can anyone tell me where Number 6 Nöstesmuget is,—Berly Magnussen?

Aalesund: It's right down here.

Pastor: Thanks, thanks. (*He goes on.*)

Johanne: Oh God, is he going to Berly? (*She bursts into tears. Andrea cries too. The men stand pale and silent.*)

Skipper Meydell (*Has come out on his step. He is elderly, white-haired but vigorous. He suddenly shouts*) : It's the spies! The spies have done it! (*The people are fired by the words, as a smoldering fire by gasoline.*)

AALESUND: Yes, it's the spies!

JOHANNE: It's the fault of the spies!

MALVIN: Perhaps others are to blame, too.

AALESUND: Who?

MALVIN: The men who send us out.

MEYDELL (*Scornfully*): Don't you know that the ships *must* go out, to bring us our daily bread?

MALVIN: How many ships do you think there are that carry daily bread—corn and coal? It's not *that* trade our ships are in.

MEYDELL: We have to.

MALVIN: But they make money at it—*they* do. But us who do the job, what sort of life, what sort of hope do they give us?

LUDVIGSEN: Now don't be unreasonable, Malvin. The owners may be a poor lot, that's true enough. But just now we've nothing against 'em. I've grown old in the union. I remember all those years—how hard it was to fight our way to the least of our rights. But its different now. For instance, they never do you out of your overtime. You get what you earn. And they give you extras. You get two crowns a day for going into the danger zone.

MEYDELL (*Bitterly*): I don't know which of you's the worst. There's some things too big to bargain about. Two crowns here and there!—We didn't think that way when I was young. We thought it was grand to show our flag all round the world. I've been a skipper for five and thirty years, and I've seen people stand still in the ports from north to south, and what were they looking at? They were looking at our flag. That made me proud. That was enough for me!

MALVIN: I've seen the flag, too. One time I remember was not long ago, out in the Atlantic, a winter day. I was lying swimming among bits of wreckage, and then I saw the flag being sucked down, when the stern went under.—And I've seen the flag some other times as well. (*Slowly and menacingly*) P'raps it's not right for them to *use the flag against us*, beat us down with the flag, every time we demand more human treatment.—But one day we'll take our flag away from them. For it's *our* flag!

MEYDELL: You can save your breath; I understand you. You're soon going out again. I'm going to use an ugly word, but I'll use it all the same:—You're afraid, old man!

MALVIN (*Smiling*): I think you'd better go back to your pictures of sailing ships and your shipping shares that are rising so nicely. Afraid? Yes, I think we're right to be afraid of dying, when we think the thing we're to die for isn't right. But it takes something to get acquainted with that fear. And you needn't worry. I shall go out again.

ANDREA (*Quietly, with the calm of despair*) : There, you see. You're going out, yourself. What do you want the rest of us to do? I've lost two boys at sea in the last year, and now here's the youngest with me; he's to be cabin boy on "Blaaeggen."— What do you want us to do, Malvin?

MEYDELL: Kill the spies. Some have been caught, but there's plenty left. They say Olsen is directing them *from prison*. His wife is at large, and so is his son.

JOHANNE: They used the boy for everything—

FIRST BOY: I know 'im—

JOHANNE: He delivered telegrams, so that no one should suspect—

FIRST BOY: He got everything he wanted—a bike—

SECOND BOY: I'd rather have done without a bike, if I'd bin him.

MEYDELL: The spies keep track of everything; they've got radio stations. You can be sure there's a report gone out to all the U-boats that "Blaaeggen" sails tonight.

ANDREA: Oh, God!

MEYDELL: They know you're walking down the hill at this moment.

ANDREA: Can anything be done?

MEYDELL: We can hate them, punish them, clear them out. Put the fear of God into those that aren't caught yet. Hunt them back to their holes like rats!

(*Above, in the main street, Leif is seen stealing across by the house wall.*)

First Boy: There's that there Leif!

Johanne: The spy's son!

Meydell: The worst of them all.

Second Boy: He's got a letter in his hand.

Aalesund: He's after *us,* this time.

Second Boy: It was him that murdered old Sigurd.

Meydell: Stop him!

First Boy: Stone him.

Leif (*Shielding his pale face with his arm*): Don't! Don't! (*They throw stones at him.*)

First Boy: Did yer see? That hit him!

Malvin (*Throwing himself between them*): You're mad! Do you want to murder the boy?

(*Leif runs away down the main street.*)

Second Boy: Did yer see? He was bleedin'—

Aalesund (*Ashamed*): Is it better that he murder us?

(*Ditlef arrives, walking along the main street in the opposite direction.*)

Malvin: If you want to stone anybody, stone *him.*

Ludvigsen: How can you say a thing like that?

Andrea: Be fair, Malvin. I do sewing for Miss Berents, who works in his office. She says he's an uncommon good sort, a kind-hearted man, grand to his children.

Malvin: But he has a harder heart for us. What's the word?— A heart of gold.

Ditlef: I know there are some people among us who would like to protect the spies. That's their own affair. I'll only say that I'll fight to my last breath against the men who send our heroic seamen to the bottom.

Andrea: Thanks for wishing to help us.

Aalesund (*Respectfully*): Yes, we're grateful to you, sir, for speaking like a man!

Scene 3

(*Ditlef's home. Monumental and ornate.*)

DITLEF (*With feeling, looking at himself in the mirror, while he adjusts his Order of St. Olav*): Yes, you've been a good friend to Norway, Ditlef. (*Catches sight of Freddy*) Nice of you to help Augusta with the places, Freddy.

FREDDY: I must say the table looks very well.—Good taste.

DITLEF: And I've arranged the menu myself. I think you'll like it. We start with grilled oysters. I thought it would be pleasant to give a little party today. The papers were nice, eh?—Patriotism, social interest, culture.

FREDDY: But then, your gift was unique. A whole new hall in the Art Museum filled with French art! World-famous pictures, Ditlef!

DITLEF: I think I've been lucky.—Here's one I've kept for myself. Delicate, eh? Isn't that skin painted so that you'd like to bite it? (*With confidential satisfaction*) And one thing more. Monrad Henriksen, who ought to know, tells me I've got a bargain there. I think I've a *flair*—seen the right moment. There are a good many people down there who haven't the chance to live with such pictures nowadays.

FREDDY (*Approvingly*): But this Monrad Henriksen, isn't he the chap that writes on social art and paints all kinds of propaganda pictures against war?—Scenes in the trenches, with titles like "Gethsemane," "Golgotha," and so forth? Isn't he really against the present order?

DITLEF: I'm not keen on that sort of picture,—far from it. Isn't there misery and wretchedness enough in the world? I like the sort of artists who paint *flesh*. But even supposing he now and then paints rather anti-war, that doesn't matter. Who does he depend on, who is it that gives him commissions? Why, us! He comes like a shot at the merest hint from me, and so do all the other painters. Besides, there's no harm in them. They're decent chaps. And they're so good at singing after midnight suppers.

FREDDY: I think your gift, Ditlef, is particularly important at a time when there are so many revolutionary forces at work, both here and abroad. It stresses the fact that *culture* is on our side. It is the same idea that I am trying to follow logically, when, as you know, I open my doors to men of culture. And I'm delighted to be able to welcome them more than ever, now that Margrethe and I are married.

DITLEF: And you're still hitting it off well?

FREDDY: We are, Ditlef; in complete harmony. I'll tell you—there was one thing Margrethe has been afraid of all her life. Very natural for the daughter of such a rich man. She was afraid someone would take her for her money. Actually, I've often felt the same, as the years went by. My financial position was much the same. I venture to say that it was the certainty that money didn't come into it which threw Margrethe and me together. I've come into port, Ditlef. I think I can say I've matured through this marriage. The family feeling that was always strong in me has grown deeper. I feel it my duty to preserve and increase the values that have been entrusted to me.

DITLEF: We've got a big responsibility, Freddy.

FREDDY: But it shocks me to look at the conditions all round. Demands are increasing; wages are going up. Possibly we are still able to pay these sums. But bear one thing in mind, Ditlef. Every day the war lasts, thousands of young men become cripples. They get a small pension, but they'll be keen to look about for a job. At the same time, our modern machines have grown easy to handle. I need only think of my own. A cripple, a man without legs or short of an arm, could manage them splendidly. These men will be grateful for quite a small wage; they'll never dream of striking, of discontent, making demands. If we at home are to meet this competition, *wages must go down*. But do you think our Norwegian workers'll understand that?

DITLEF: They've no breadth of view, Freddy. Don't see the relationships.

FREDDY: I think the day will come when we shall be tempted to invest our resources in undertakings of this sort abroad. Concerns where there is peace, stability. With a labor supply of cheap war casualties, who will see where their interest lies.

DITLEF: Sounds like a good idea, Freddy. And it's attractive at the same time to be able to support these fellows who've been so hard hit.

MAID (*Entering*): Mr. Cummingham would like to speak to you, sir.

DITLEF: I hear he's grown so nervous.

FREDDY: They say he's trying to get out to the front.

DITLEF: That sounds incredible, with the soft job he's got here.

CUMMINGHAM (*Entering*): I've come to ask you to give all possible assistance to my successor, Mr. Edwards. He can be expected at any moment.

DITLEF: And what about you, Mr. Cummingham?

CUMMINGHAM: A destroyer is coming to fetch me. Perhaps today, perhaps tomorrow. It's safest not to know when.

FREDDY: We shall all miss you.

DITLEF: Hope you'll have nothing but pleasant recollections to take with you. It must have been an interesting time—plenty happening.

CUMMINGHAM (*Confidentially, in a low ominous voice*): It has been an interesting time. I've seen a lot. You two know what I've seen.

DITLEF (*Changing the subject*): You must have been intolerably overworked.

CUMMINGHAM (*Ignoring the remark*): And yet! You were outside it all. You had no obligation toward anyone—not to speak of. I looked on you as foreigners. But, as you know;— *my countrymen do business too.*

DITLEF (*Catching his calm, sinister matter-of-fact tone*):

You're thinking of the nickel exports?

CUMMINGHAM: Yes, I'm thinking how my countrymen are selling nickel, via Norway and Sweden, to keep the German ammunition factories going. And I think of our war graves in France, they're like children's graves;—tens of thousands of them! They earn a good profit, gentlemen!

DITLEF: Mr. Cummingham!

CUMMINGHAM (*Still in a quite level tone*): I knew a young man once. A friend of his wrote from the trenches to the boy's father, after he was killed:—"He was one of those who go out not to kill, but to be killed." And he added:—"There are a lot of them out here." I've gradually understood better what he meant.

DITLEF: You are overwrought now, Mr. Cummingham. One day you'll understand how very unnatural such an idea is. Self-preservation is a stronger instinct than anything else!

CUMMINGHAM: Don't you think one can sometimes see mankind in a way that makes the urge for self-preservation feel like something indecent?

(*He stands looking before him for a moment. Then he gives a sort of nod, and says*) Good evening!

(*And he is gone.*)

FREDDY: The man that's gone out of that door is finished.

(*Ditlef does not reply. A kind of shudder seems to run through him. The telephone rings.*)

DITLEF (*Takes it up and says in a low voice*): Very well. Thank You. (*Puts back the receiver*) That was "Blaaeggen." Been torpedoed. In the Channel.

FREDDY: Any casualties?

DITLEF: Only the cabin boy.

FREDDY: She was bought for four million?

DITLEF: Yes.

FREDDY: And insured for six?

DITLEF (*Almost in a whisper*): Yes.—I didn't like him: it was as if he was accusing us—

Voices of Children: Daddy, Daddy!

Ditlef: Good Lord, the kids!

(*His three small children come on in their night dresses,—charming, well-cared-for children.*)

Little Ditlef: Daddy, why haven't you been up to say good-night to us?

Lyder: Did you forget?

Little Ditlef: No, of course not.

Hannemor: Father's such a kind man.

Ditlef (*Lifts her up, much moved*): God bless you for those words, Hannemor. I don't think those blue eyes of yours can be mistaken. And you say Father's a kind man. Oh, you don't know what a joy children are, Freddy.—To sit up by the little white beds, when you come home in the evening. It gives you a new faith, a new courage.

So you think Father's kind, do you, Hannemor? How nice it feels to stroke your curls. All the nasty things they say about Father, all the troubles, I can just sort of stroke away, in this fair, silky hair of yours.

Little Ditlef: Mummy says you're going to make a speech. Can't you make it to us?

Lyder: Oh, do, Daddy!

Hannemor: Say yes, Father.

Ditlef: I can't refuse you anything. You shall hear the last bit. Very well then:—

Ladies and gentlemen:—The gentlemen are Uncle Freddy and Lyder and little Ditlef; and the lady is you, Hannemor.

Let us restore to this country, from which our ships go out, some of the good things we produce. Let us adorn our country with beauty, art, and culture. A new and more lovely Norway. A happier future. And, if the war goes on, I believe that we can look forward to such a future with confidence, trust, and hope.

Little Ditlef: How clever you were, Daddy!

Ditlef (*Delighted*): And now, off to bed with you! I'll

carry you, Hannemor. For there's a lot of people coming now, to thank Daddy for giving them the pictures.—*They* think Father's a kind man, too!

CURTAIN

EPILOGUE

Scene 1

(Immediately after the fall of the curtain on Act III, a gentleman rises in a private box.)

THE GENTLEMAN: Ladies and Gentlemen: I feel constrained to say a few words. The picture which we have been shown of the war years over here is a bitter and dark one. But let us be honest; there can hardly be many of us who recall that time with pleasure. We lost our heads at that time. We made profit out of the war, and perhaps we did not do what we should have done for the men who risked their lives under the Norwegian flag. But all that is past. Today we see the truth in its context, and we also feel gratitude. One thing is certain: there is no one nearer to our hearts than the Norwegian seaman. We are entitled to say to the unknown heroes of those days—*We have not forgotten you.* I feel, ladies and gentlemen, that we should all stand up as a tribute to those men.

(At this moment, the gong sounds, the date "1935" appears on the curtain, and it rises to reveal the lodging for homeless men. We see six beds, and get the impression of several more beyond. On the wall, in large letters, is the inscription—"Come unto me, all that are heavy laden, and I will give you rest."

Gustav is sitting on his bunk. Stavanger is in bed, as well as a Sick Man, who coughs violently at intervals. It is snowing outside. Enter Jappen, forty years old, with a pale thin face, and Ottar, twenty years old, bitter and sarcastic.)

JAPPEN (*To Gustav*): That friend of yours didn't get in. He was three pennies short.

GUSTAV: It's a blasted shame they won't let a guy in just because he's three pennies short.

JAPPEN: If you're half a penny short, you don't get in.

GUSTAV: I'll go down and fetch him.

Jappen: Can't he raise three pennies, then?

Gustav: I'd better go. He mustn't keep outside in this weather. But I ain't got more 'n a penny.

Stavanger: Here's half a penny.

A Voice (*From inside the room*): Here's the penny I've got.

Gustav: That's a good job. (*Collects the money and goes out.*)

Jappen: Roald didn't get in neither.

Ottar (*Sarcastically*): But he'll manage to get a roof over his head, no matter what.

Jappen (*Turning round towards the beds at the back*): It was Simonsen the shopkeeper that was after him. "Stop with me," he says, "I've drink in stock," he says, "You're such a nice-looking lad," he says. Ah well, there's more than one of 'em hanging around out here. There's Ole Lufter and that seedy Nilsen in Leppen. But Simonsen—he's the most reg'lar, he sticks to his beat on the quay.

Ottar: Becos he's sure to find someone there.

Jappen (*Bitterly*): Wot the hell's it matter if you does go home with him? You gets plenty to drink, and when he tries his tricks you can give him a good kick and clear out—

Ottar: Yes, so they say!

(*The wind whistles through the house. Enter Gustav and the Swiller.*)

Stavanger: So there you are. It's awful to stick outside, and it's awful to lie in here, but it's a good thing old Gustav found you.

Swiller (*Warming himself at the stove*): Yes,—talk about life! You're not allowed to fight. You're not allowed to steal. You're not allowed to kill yourself. There's no work. What's a chap to do?

Jappen: Wot's a man to do, you say. I can tell you one thing. Drink when you get the chance. That's wot you must do. And I think it's the right thing, too.

Do you think it's a good idea for us to walk about with

empty bellies broodin' on how we're treated? We get a bunk here and a bite of grub before we turn out. Then we get no food till next morning. It's out of the house by eight o'clock. Then it's tramping the streets, sloping into the warming-room to thaw out a bit, then it's tramp the streets again.—Hour after hour, till they open here in the evening.—Day after day,—year after year! Are you to carry on with that in mind. But, if you drink, maybe you'll reckerlect you was a man once, like other men. P'raps you're free to remember that!

SWILLER: To tell you the truth, Jappen, I sometimes drink myself, so's not to forget that I'm made in God's image. But if you're always drinking, with the scrap of grub we get, it don't do. Look at Oscar, who was here a fortnight ago. He finished where he had to. Down at the bend,—at Nevengaarden that was. (*Points at the sick man*) How's he?

STAVANGER: It's inflammation of the lungs. And, you know, he's not much strength to stand up to it.

SWILLER: Lars the Liar went pretty quick downhill too. You wasn't here yesterday, when he died. It was me and Emil found it out. We were pretty tight, both of us. Lights were out, we had some furniture polish with us, and we were shaking Jakob to wake him up. I had to go out, and then I see Liar-Lars stretched out so queer with his arms right down on the deck. Surely you're not dead, says I, ye old devil, for he was quite cold. You mustn't have any more truck with him, says Emil, surely you can see he's dead. And in the morning we saw he was.

GUSTAV: That's not the worst thing that can happen to you.

SWILLER: Oh yes, it is; absolutely the worst.—Dying. And that's been the way of it since the dawn of time, as they say.

GUSTAV: Oh, I don't know. Do you remember that time in the lifeboat, Swiller? You told us not to give in. Seems to me we're in the same boat now. Only it's worse this time. I've bin four years out of work, you've bin three. Only this time we shan't never get to land.

(*The whistle of a steamer is heard in the harbor.*)

SWILLER: Did you hear? Three longs. That's the Spanish line. The "Stromboli"!

JAPPEN: Ain't it the "Solferino" on that trip now?

SWILLER: No, it was the "Stromboli." I know her voice. If I've once heard a boat, I know her. Yes, now the "Stromboli" is off to the Mediterranean. I know one of the stokers aboard,—the Man-eater, they call him, 'cause he's always after women. If it was for women, he'd walk from Bergen to the Holy Sepulchre. He's on the 8 to 12 watch; now he'll be down in the engine room. (*Lies back in his bunk.*)

STAVANGER: Ah, if I was aboard there—

JAPPEN: Come down to a hot climate. Don't walk about coughing your guts up.

STAVANGER: I shouldn't be in such a hurry to get back!

GUSTAV: We'll never get out no more.

OTTAR (*Spitefully*): What are *you* grousing about? You've no work now, but you've had work one time. You've got something to remember, you've seen the sea, sat in the fo'csle together, come across women, you've bin in it. But I've never bin *in it*. I've never had a job, and never shall. *I never shall!* I'll never get a chance to prove myself. Never live!

SWILLER (*Raising himself in the bunk*): There's a lot can happen to you still. You're so young. Think of me, that's forty-five. That's a lot for a stoker. I'll tell you one thing:—It's not only ashes they heave out of the engine room and dump overboard.—How old are you? Twenty? Oh no. You needn't lose heart yet.

OTTAR (*Menacingly*): I've not lost heart. I think I'll live to see the day when there's enough of us to ask *those chaps*:—What have you done to us?

SWILLER: Mightn't be such a silly question.—You're like a fellow I knew when I was in the old "Lyderhorn." What was your father's name?

OTTAR: Malvin Monsen.

SWILLER: Yes, it was old Malvin. He went with the "Skuld"

in 1918, didn't he?

OTTAR: Yes.

GUSTAV: The war. Those were the days. I'd have no objection to their coming again. There was work then, and no one to do you down; then one man was as good as another.

SWILLER: You don't really mean that, Gustav. I remember some of your shipmates and mine, and then I'm sure you don't think so.

THE MANAGER (*Entering*) : Well, well, I must turn out the lights now. Good-night, all.

(*A hostile growl. He turns off the light and exit. The men go on talking in the semi-darkness.*)

SWILLER: If I was skipper of the craft where he was lieutenant, he'd be overboard before we got to Kvarven.

STAVANGER: I notice there's not much sleeping. You know how it is on an empty belly.

SWILLER: Day after tomorrow the "Dover Castle" gets in. Then we'll get a square meal for once. On the English boats—and the German too for that matter—there's folk as have seen the world; they know how life is. They know that if you come aboard at a time like this, there's no questions to be asked. They just trot out the dish of food at once.

OTTAR: I'm so hungry!

JAPPEN: That's the good thing about drinking. You lose your appetite.

(*He coughs violently. The sick man in bed groans.*)

SWILLER: Well, we must sleep now, chaps. *Remember, we've got to be at work first thing tomorrow!*

(*Stavanger laughs, followed by Ottar, finally all join in. But the laughter has an unpleasantly menacing sound.*)

Scene 2

(*In front of the curtain; a pale, eerie light. Ditlef and Freddy.*)

DITLEF: I don't understand any more. We wish well to everyone, and what has come of it? Unemployment, bitterness, hate. I can't sleep at night, Freddy. That's never happened to me before. I feel as if the earth was quaking under our feet, we're groping in the dark; what's it all leading to? I'm often tempted to say like little Ditlef—Haven't we got *one man?*

FREDDY: I've lost all the pleasure I had in my business. Control and planning everywhere. And continual demands, Ditlef.

DITLEF: And that at a time when all expenditure has to be cut. I only have to mention one word:—relief.

FREDDY: These sums are no longer high, Ditlef. They're astronomical.

DITLEF: What's the remedy?—I'm frightened, Freddy. I look with sympathy on the wave of religious revival which is sweeping over the world. I think the idea is right in itself; at a time like this we must leave nothing untried. We must let love of humanity have a place in our life (*Meditatively*) But is that anything to *build* on?

FREDDY: It leads nowhere, Ditlef. Believe me.

DITLEF: I took my morning walk round the harbor, today as usual, Freddy. One ship had come from having been laid up, she was lying alongside the quay: two of her crew were hanging over the side, clearing rust; it had a promising sound, it cheered me up, Freddy. But out in the harbor I saw all the ships laid up; they lay in rows, with their bows to sea. I felt they were longing for the sea—longing to hear life and bustle on board. But there they lay at anchor, and there they'll stay. After a lifetime's experience, I believe that if the situation is to improve, there is only one thing that must happen,—

(*Enter a Newsboy.*)

DITLEF (*Opening the paper*): Did you hear what I was saying, Freddy? There's only one thing that must happen. Here it is—"*Better Outlook for Shipping.*" "*Will There Be War in the East?*"

(*A wild, uncanny roll of drums starts. The curtain is torn aside, and the whole play seems to explode in an atmosphere of speculation and war. On a moving band, soldiers approach with steel helmets and bayonets. The whole scene is bathed in a gray-green, cadaverous light. On each side of the soldiers, two groups of persons are arranged. Left:—Ditlef, Freddy, Ludvigsen, Skipper Meydell, and a man with a cold, impersonal ghastliness about him. He symbolizes the Stock Exchange: he stands reading the tape which comes all the time from a ticker-tape machine. He stands highest in the group.*

To the right:—The Swiller, Ottar, a Young Workman, and a Woman who occupies the same position in this group as the Stock-Exchange creature in his. Between the two groups, there is a conventionalized iron structure, which is still in darkness.)

STOCK-EXCHANGE CREATURE (*Reading the tape*): The market is rising.

DITLEF: The ships are going out again.

FREDDY: The wheels are starting to turn.

THE YOUNG WORKMAN: It is our comrades in all countries who are going out to be killed.

LUDVIGSEN (*Persuasively*): The employers become so reasonable. Never cheat you of your overtime.

SWILLER: Do you want *us* to join up and keep the war going —*us* that remember?

DITLEF: New hands will get work. New mouths can be fed.

OTTAR (*Harshly*): But will the world never get better? Always the same, always outrage, oppression and blood?

MEYDELL: We'll show our flag on the seas, we are the men who venture forth.

YOUNG WORKMAN: No one will escape this time. If we don't do what we can to stop war, it will kill us.

ALL ON THE STOCK-EXCHANGE SIDE: There is an eternal instinct in human nature. Don't stop individual enterprise— personal initiative!

(*Two machine guns posted at the back of the hall open fire. Some soldiers fall. The rest march on, advancing eternally towards the audience.*)

OTTAR (*Shrieks*): No! (*The shooting stops; the soldiers march on*).

THE WOMAN: I am humanity. I am life. Within me I have growing stars. And other stars shall flow thither, and I shall give new life. I have growth to give, I have tenderness and strength; I must be perfected, with the perfection of which the corn dreams in the spring rain and the sunshine of summer.

I am a human being, and is not this the law?

STOCK-EXCHANGE CREATURE: Krupp, 300 per cent. Armstrong-Vickers, 400 per cent. Bethlehem Steel, 500.

ALL IN THE WOMAN's GROUP: THE GAS IS COMING!

STOCK-EXCHANGE CREATURE: Chemical Combine, 600.

THE WOMAN: But *we* in our land, surely we shall not be affected. For we know what *peace* is.

I have seen the eider duck swimming with her young where the channels shone in the evening light.

I have walked among the bright birch trees, deep in the heart of this country, and have clung to a silvery stem and wept with my longing for home, since I loved the country so much that I felt I could never come home.

Every flake of snow beneath the frosty stars on the mountains, every brown cluster of seaweed swaying in the ripples of the south wind, as far as the land extends, have taught us a single longing—for Peace.

STOCK-EXCHANGE CREATURE: Glittertind, 200 per cent. Kvittingsöy, 300 per cent. Tana River, 400.

(*The machine guns begin again. The soldiers fall. During the shooting, the light gradually increases on the iron structure between the two groups. We see that it is a conventionalized stern of a ship. With the Norwegian flag flapping in the breeze. Ottar, the Swiller, and the Young Workman are now standing on her deck. The shooting stops.*)

STOCK-EXCHANGE CREATURE: The market is looking brighter. Will there be war in the East?

THE MEN (*Answering with a shout*): NO!
(*At this moment, the factory whistles sound,—the sirens for
the general strike.*

CURTAIN

THE MAN WHO LIVED HIS LIFE OVER

A PLAY IN THREE ACTS BY
PÄR LAGERKVIST

TRANSLATED FROM THE SWEDISH BY

WALTER GUSTAFSSON

INTRODUCTION BY

ROBERT D. SPECTOR

INTRODUCTION

More than any other modern Swedish writer, Pär Lagerkvist
(b. 1891) has won his countrymen's admiration and affection.
With obvious delight those who have even momentarily pene-
trated his public mask of silence, his official reticence about his
work, repeat their tales of his simple dedication to his vocation
and his reluctance to yield to pressures that would turn him
from a writer into something of a literary celebrity or show-
man. He scoffs, they tell us, at promotional ventures in connection with such things as cinematic adaptations of his novels;
he refuses to write articles "to order" on special occasions.
Warm and at ease with friends, he nevertheless speaks envi-
ously of those medieval monks who were left entirely to the
pursuit of their labors. People who were with him when he won
the Nobel Prize in 1951 attest to his pride in the award, but
all who know him even slightly agree that he did not permit
even that honor to alter his attitude toward his artistic purpose,
which—in the Greek sense of the word for *poet*—is "to do" or
"to make."

He has continued to create, to shape his literary world, in
a variety of genres, so that in his "person and work," as Alrik
Gustafson remarks, "Swedish literature in the last half century
has its greatest and on the whole most representative figure."
Swedish readers can readily assent, for they are aware of his
influence and achievement in poetry, prose, and the drama.

In English-language countries, however, Lagerkvist's reputation comes almost entirely from his fiction—some of his short
stories and tales, particularly the collection in *The Eternal
Smile;* his masterful study of evil in *The Dwarf;* his probing
analysis of Christian faith and the meaning of existence in

Barabbas, The Sibyl, The Death of Ahasuerus, Pilgrim at Sea, The Holy Land, and *Herod and Mariamne.* These appeal to the modern temper, the search for values in an age when the old orthodoxies no longer satisfy. Despite their historical settings, his novels address themselves to the questions that contemporary man finds most intriguing, and Lagerkvist fits neatly into a cultural milieu which honors such French writers as Albert Camus and Jean-Paul Sartre.

Lagerkvist's poetry and drama, however, are relatively unknown in English-language nations. His poetry naturally suffers from the difficulties in translation, and out of his nine volumes of verse, published between 1916 and 1953, only a handful of lyrics is available in English. From these poems it is hardly possible to estimate either their impact on modern Swedish poetry or their intrinsic merits. Yet *Ångest,* his first book of poetry, with its startling new notes and sounds, has been described as a "pillar of modernism in Swedish literature," and *Aftonland,* his final volume, stands as a major achievement in his country's poetry. Having brought freshness and originality to his nation's traditional verse—dying in nineteenth-century conventions—Lagerkvist continued to produce a body of work noteworthy for its artistic, rather than merely historical, merits.

Although more available than his poetry in English, Lagerkvist's drama has suffered from a lack of translations, only now being brought into greater supply through the work of Thomas Buckman. The American-Scandinavian Foundation has published translations of *Let Man Live* and *The Man Without a Soul; Midsummer Dream in the Workhouse* appeared in England in 1953; and Buckman has made available the three one-act plays of *The Difficult Hour,* together with the important critical essay, *Modern Theater,* and has recently added translations of four other Lagerkvist dramas.

Like his poetry, Lagerkvist's dramas helped to shape the development of the genre in modern Sweden. Again like his poetry, his plays bear a strong thematic and tonal resemblance to his fiction, giving his work a remarkable degree of unity and allowing the reader to regard the whole as Lagerkvist's own created literary world.

Together with his poetry, Lagerkvist's dramas anteceded his interest in the novel, although not shorter fictional forms. Indeed, his original concern for the theater—related to his interest in modern painting—probably marked his earliest genuine literary involvement. It has been no casual involvement, producing as it has nine full-length and six shorter plays and covering, since his first drama in 1917, thirty-six years in his creative life.

For Lagerkvist the drama has never seemed as consequential as prose, toward which his attitude approaches the reverential. Nevertheless, he regarded it as significant enough to devote careful study to its forms and development and to write one of his few critical essays on the subject. In his years in Denmark during the First World War, he devoted considerable time to investigating medieval drama, which—together with his later exploration of classical and Indian theater, as well as an intense reading of Strindberg and the German expressionists—strongly influenced his own work.

What that work was to be was foreshadowed in great part by his essay *Modern Theater*, written in 1918. Attacking the decadence of the Swedish theater at that time, Lagerkvist cast his lot with Strindberg against the realistic and naturalistic Ibsenism that dominated the contemporary Swedish stage. On the positive side, he sought, as he himself wrote, "A theater which gives the imagination of both dramatist and actor greater freedom of movement and greater audacity, a simpler, more immediate, and more expressive form." How well he describes what proves to be his repeated dramatic method when he calls for a drama in which "everything is directed to one purpose— the liberation of a single mood, a single feeling whose intensity increasingly grows and grows. Everything irrelevant is excluded even if rather important to the continuity or to the faithfulness of representation. Everything which occurs is meaningful and of equal weight."

As Buckman has noted, Lagerkvist's drama—although later including modified forms of realism, lessening the early overwhelming expressionism—"never abandoned the basic tenets of his program [in *Modern Theater*]: the unity of artistic effect, the necessity for an inner compulsion to create, art as a way toward deeper personal realization and knowledge, the prerogative of the playwright to create freely and to imply in his work the full use of all the possibilities of the modern stage." These remain throughout. And yet, it is possible to show different stages in Lagerkvist's dramatic career, different interests reflecting the period, and, of course, different degrees of achievement.

In his earliest plays, Lagerkvist was finding his way, either guided too frequently by Strindberg or lost in an expressionistic maze. *The Last Man* (1917) deals with the perplexing dualities of love and hate—not unusual in his later work, but handled ineptly here. With *The Difficult Hour* (1918)—three one-act plays concerned with the experience of death—Lagerkvist at least, as Buckman notes, gave evidence of his dramatic ability, an ability that became quite apparent in *The Secret of Heaven* (1919), a drama which presents characters trying to "comprehend the meaning of existence through their own limited vision." For all of these plays, whatever their limitations, there is the great merit of attempted experimentation—a moving away from conventional plot and characterization, a forging of new forms that causes critics, as in *The Invisible One* (1923), to seek new descriptive labels, terms like "a series of ritual scenes" or "oratorio."

The Man Who Lived His Life Over (*Han som fick leva om sitt liv*, 1928), presented in this volume, marked a major transition in Lagerkvist's dramatic technique as well as a statement characteristic of his later philosophy. Alf Sjöberg, the great Swedish director, has called it the author's best drama for stage production. Here Lagerkvist combines the visionary elements of his earlier plays with a setting familiarly realistic. Using his detailed knowledge of Småland types in his characterization and setting, he provides a groundwork for the mystical power that formerly ran too wildly through his work. Whatever the metaphysical implications of the drama, his characters struggle with the very real problems of living in this world. Out of the action which presents a man whose life lived over proves no more successful than his original existence, Lagerkvist argues that man can only try to make the best of an existence over which he has little control.

The structure of the play—counterposing as it does Daniel's past and present life—seems ideally suited to Lagerkvist's theme of the dualities in man's nature and existence, that omnipresent need to find a balance between reason and emotion, that insistent awareness that good and evil are not separate entities but rather belong to one whole. In Daniel's first life he has yielded completely to his *id;* he has, in Jöran Mjöberg's words, "allowed his nature to claim its due without self-restraint." Daniel's second chance follows the dictates of the *super-ego,* an excessive moral code leading to destruction with the same inevitability wrought by unbridled passion. As Mjöberg has shown, Lagerkvist's play is strongly influenced by classical drama, and in his attempt to discover how "to reconcile the nether powers with the laws of the world," Lagerkvist displays the concern of the classical Greek playwrights.

By no means does this exhaust the thematic interests of a play which, like most of Lagerkvist's drama, closely parallels the form of a philosophical essay without yielding its dramatic intensity. Out of Daniel's struggle to make his second life more meaningful than the first, to truly exist rather than merely to live, evolves a second theme: man's relationship to the indifferent universe, which has the power to affect him but stands beyond his capacity to strike back. Against the miserableness of man's enforced existence, Daniel cries out for an opportunity to live his "real life," his "own life." It is the existentialist cry in the night that rings out through most of Lagerkvist's major work and, indeed, through much of contemporary literature. It is his particular achievement as an artist, however, that he does not let such philosophical preoccupations diminish his art as art.

In the following years Lagerkvist responded artistically to the catastrophe threatening civilization. Three plays in the 1930s reflect contemporary evils. Despite its historical setting, *The King* (1932) presents the brutality apparent in European political events; and however influenced by Sir James Frazer's *The Golden Bough,* with its ritualistic theories, *The Hangman* (1934) makes one of the earliest attacks directly on Hitler's barbarism. Both, of course, carry further Lagerkvist's combination of his old expressionism with a violent kind of realism. *The Man Without a Soul* (1936) —showing the effects of a political murder on the assassin—indicates how well Lagerkvist could deal with contemporary life without yielding to simple realistic or naturalistic techniques. Indeed, only *Victory in the Dark* (1939), a didactic drama, sacrifices artistic unconventionality for the sake of its theme.

Subsequent plays returned Lagerkvist to more purely dramatic purposes. In perhaps his finest blending of realism and fantasy, Lagerkvist allows the old man in *Midsummer Dream in the Workhouse* (1941) to create a dream world of hope for a young girl, turning at the same time his depressing surroundings into an enchanted dream of his own. *The Philosopher's Stone* (1947) seems a lesser drama, with a more conventional plot that sets science and religion against each other and shows the effects of each when pushed unreasonably to its extreme. In *Let Man Live* (1949), however, there is nothing conventional, as his characters, each with a tale of martyrdom, step forth on a barren stage to tell their tales of woe. How much Lagerkvist's play suggests how far ahead of his times he has been! How much of his technique has foreshadowed Sartre's existential drama and the theater of the absurd!

In 1953 Lagerkvist successfully adapted his novel *Barabbas* for the stage, and its popularity provides a reminder that his plays appeal to the public as well as to the critics. On Swedish radio and in provincial productions, as well as under the sophisticated direction of Per Lindberg, Olof Molander, and Alf Sjöberg, they have gained widespread audience approval, making Lagerkvist's career in the theater—as Buckman declares —one in which any playwright might take pride. With the possible exception of Hjalmar Bergman, he is the foremost dramatist in contemporary Sweden, and his dramatic work marks him as "one of the most important Northern playwrights after Ibsen and Strindberg."

ROBERT D. SPECTOR

Long Island University

THE MAN WHO LIVED HIS LIFE OVER

CHARACTERS

DANIEL
ANNA
AGNES
HUGO } THEIR CHILDREN
INGRID
ELOF
BOMAN, AN OLD MAN
KARLSON
THE PRISONER

ACT I

(*Darkness—An appealing, commanding voice*): Rise up! Your prayer is heard. You may live again!

(*A shaft of light breaks through from above.*)

DANIEL (*Steps into the light, stands as if possessed and bewildered. Raises his hands aloft*): I am alive! I am alive! . . . It is not true that I am dead! I am breathing . . . Feel, my heart beats now! Yes! Yes! I am alive! I can live my life over again . . . because I must . . . It couldn't be so—no, not so terrible . . . It wasn't me—it was really someone else . . . I can live my real life—my own life!—Yes, yes—it is true—I feel it—oh, my soul, you now can be alive—you are free, free—freed from all . . . You shall live now—you shall be victorious—A new life! A new life! (*It has become light. The scene is the workshop of a shoemaker. Tables with tools, half-finished shoes, lasts. A sewing machine. Large sheets of leather propped up against the wall. He notices that it has become light. Looks around*) What is this?—Where am I? —What strange place is this? (*Strokes his forehead*) Surely —Now I remember—This is my workroom—Here is the table where I sat and worked—Yes.—Surely . . . Oh, I have forgotten everything—Yes . . . I have been away . . . (*Walks around and looks*) Now I recognize . . . (*Stops at the table, handles the tools*) The hammer . . . and the awl . . . and the lasts . . .—Yes, yes . . . (*Walks again around the room. Stops. Walks around again. Exclaims*) Why am I here! Shall I sit there again! At that table and mend shoes! Shall I be locked in here again! In this room! . . . I will surely live! Live! No . . . Why do I flare up so . . . (*Stands and considers matters, becomes calm*) Why shouldn't I be a shoemaker . . . It was really not that . . . What was it? (*Puts his hand to his head*) What kind of thing was it? I don't remember . . . no, not clearly . . . Only that it was something terrible . . . Oh, God . . . Why shouldn't I sit here . . . do my . . . as before . . . Why shouldn't I . . . Of course I have a living soul! Yes it will live now—it's real life—for which it was intended—its true life, its own—Yes, free, free—freed from darkness and death—to exist—to be victorious, victorious . . .

KARLSON (*Comes in*): Good morning, shoemaker. Take a look at my boy's shoes. I need them for Saturday. Can it be done? Thick quality soles, mind you. No slipshod stuff. Can't you put on taps or some such reinforcement? He wears out his shoes so damned fast that it is a scandal. What a mess they are! And it's no more than a month since they were half-soled. No, it's a shame. I'll tell you, boys like that can't walk like decent folks, they drag their feet after them. And they are on the go all day with all the devilment they find to do. If they could begin to be useful some time and not wear out things so fast and begin to pay for themselves, that would help. Nothing like that nowadays. No, no, by jeepers. I can tell you. I had hardly reached thirteen when I began to work. And hard stiff work it was, I can tell you, to go from early morning to late at night. It was that. You had to learn to get ahead in the world or else. And that's how it ought to be. Isn't the inner leather about gone too? There's hardly enough to sew on. Isn't it a shame! Can you see? What do you say about that? Can you possibly put a sole on? Is there enough to sew to?

DANIEL: Yes. Yes, I think so.

KARLSON: Good . . . His mother says he needs them by Saturday. O.K.? And sew it together here in back too . . .

DANIEL: Yes . . . surely . . .

KARLSON: Oh Lord, how they are scuffed up. (*Tosses coins on the table*) Three and fifty down the drain. It really cuts in on the pay, I tell you. Three and fifty! Is that the price?

DANIEL: Yes, that's the price.

KARLSON: It hasn't come down? Now, how could I believe that? Have you ever seen a shoemaker whose prices come down? Not I anyway. But they go up. And they blame the leather for the higher prices. God damn it, they haven't used much leather as long as I remember. Once I read they were going down, but they didn't after all. Oh no, it doesn't work that way. Oh no, no, by jeepers. It's tough on a poor workman with five kids who wear out as much leather as they can, all of them from the time they get up until bedtime. The smallest one hasn't started yet but he will—as soon as he's able.

DANIEL (*Has gone away to the window*): No—see! . . . Is it true? (*Opens the windows*) The sun! And all the trees in the grove are in bloom . . . the horse chestnut . . . and the lindens . . . And the rosebushes! So wonderful . . . wonderful on the earth . . . O my God! I am alive! I am alive!

KARLSON: Sure, you're alive. Anybody can see that. Be a pity, otherwise.

DANIEL: See, how the sun shines! How bright it is! And the whole sky . . . pure and clear . . .

KARLSON: Yes, there's nothing wrong with the weather.

(*Daniel turns around, looks at him.*)

KARLSON: Fine weather.

DANIEL: But . . . is it true? See how bright it shines! The sun! The sun!

KARLSON: Sure it's sunny. You can say that again. Dangerous heat too. They say it's a wave. Heat and more heat. You feel it especially when you're loading hay. You sweat so you can't stand it. O.K. I'll be in on Saturday, then. So long. (*Goes.*)

DANIEL (*Stands alone in the sunlight—quietly to himself*): I am alive . . .

BOMAN (*An old man, has stepped into the door opening. Places with a thud his wooden leg inside the threshold*): True. True. There you said something. (*Comes in*) We live and we live every day that passes from morn to night, and never an hour for anything else. It's our trade and we are never free. So it's arranged. A truer word was never spoken! Young man, can you also tell us whence and why? Whence all this life? Whence all this strife, this tangle in which people are involved from the time they are born until they die? Whence? Why?

Tell me this and I will take you into my arms and never forget what you revealed to me. My trade is to live and—as I understand from your words—so is yours also. Do you love life? I don't. I wouldn't have chosen it except by compulsion, because every occupation binds the free spirit in the human breast. I carry it out but with moderation. I don't live any more than necessary. (*Sits down*) Look at my leg, the only one I have. And more than enough for me. In this life, which is without significance, I confine myself to the most essential. Oh yes, that's what I do, and that's how it is. Who are you, young man? You who are standing at the window and . . .

DANIEL: I? . . . I'm a shoemaker.

BOMAN: Shoemaker. I see that, yes . . . shoemaker. Nothing else?

DANIEL: No.

BOMAN: Oh, we are always a little something more . . . I am called Boman and am not the one I appear to be. Oh no, no, far from it. I've been running down hill a bit. But that's nothing, nothing at all! I'm so thankful for that!

(*Daniel looks at him, wondering.*)

BOMAN: It's me, yes. As I told you, I live no more than is necessary. I limit myself in every way and by all possible means. Yes, that I do. Only the most necessary. I am not like those who in their vanity desire everything. Look at my shoe. The only one I own and have owned as long as I remember. Isn't that enough? Do I need more? No, I need only one. Young friend, will you put a sole on this shoe for half the price ordinary mortals pay in their extravagance? Will you?

DANIEL: Well . . . I will do it . . . for you.

BOMAN: It's worn out, it's in rags . . . See, how it looks! And the trouser cuff is frayed . . . Oi, oi, oi! Yes, you leg, you are a constant sorrow to me because you are alive. You must have socks, you must have shoes which wear out, which waste away. Vanity of vanities . . . (*Strokes the wooden leg*) But you, my dead friend, my good faithful comrade, you have never given me any trouble. You never complain, nor have any material needs. Because you are dead, you are above that. For forty years you have served me, patient, subservient, though you know I'm far inferior to you, that I was never worthy of you. For forty years! And you are no more worn now than when, in my youth, you came to support this tottering body. You do not wear out; corruption has no power over you. Because you do not live. You will live after me because you are dead. You will help some other poor devil on his way through life, some-time, when I am lying in my grave . . . Yes, long after I am dust and mold you shall be found, as the house survives long after the boarder has moved far away for good . . . Remember me sometimes, I who for a little while was an impatient guest with you . . . Yes, yes, so it is, so it is . . . True, young friend?

(*Daniel looks at him. Shakes his head.*)

BOMAN: What do you say?

DANIEL: You don't speak so I can understand you.

BOMAN: I speak as a wise man. That's the reason. Yes. Yes. (*Sighs.*)

DANIEL: Isn't it then something great and beautiful to live?

BOMAN: Not at all. Not at all. Life is the heaviest burden the earth bears.

DANIEL: I don't believe that.

BOMAN: No? You are young.

DANIEL: Young?

BOMAN: Didn't I see you standing in the sunlight with your hands pressed against your breast, saying to yourself: I'm alive!

DANIEL: Yes . . . But for me everything is very different from what it is for others.

BOMAN: Yes. Yes, so most people think.

(*Daniel is silent.*)

BOMAN: How is your case different, if I may ask?

(*Daniel does not answer.*)

BOMAN: It's true. I have never seen a person who just stood and thought about being alive.

DANIEL: I guess most people don't . . .

BOMAN: Not any longer. But you, young man, stood in ecstasy, looking up to heaven and whispering in awe to yourself: I am alive . . . Who are you?

(*Daniel does not answer.*)

BOMAN: Who are you who speak so strangely in your loneliness? I would like to ask.

DANIEL: I?

BOMAN: Yes.

DANIEL: I have been dead and allowed to come back to life again.

BOMAN: You don't mean it! Poor fellow, you were dead and now you have to come back here again!

DANIEL: I had to . . .

BOMAN: I fully understand that you wouldn't do it willingly.

DANIEL: I had to . . . because I hadn't lived as I should have.

BOMAN (*Shows keen interest but is confused. Appears changed*) : As you should?

DANIEL: No, not the right life . . .

BOMAN: Right? Your right life? . . . (*Thoughtfully—after a moment*) You are strange . . . (*Is again silent*) Not your right life you said . . .

DANIEL: No . . . not my own . . . Now I will live it as it was meant to be, as I should have done. Yes, the real life for which I was intended. Not the one I was driven into—inflamed into—which was not mine. No, it couldn't be left that way! I had to live my life over—I had to, had to! . . . A new life!

BOMAN (*Looks at him. Looks away. Afterwards, curtly*) : It will be the same thing all over again.

DANIEL: No, it must not be so! It must not! For God's sake, don't say that!

BOMAN: What was it then . . .

DANIEL: I don't remember . . . it's strange . . . I'm not allowed to remember it, so it can be something different . . . yes, something new, something more perfect . . . Can't we change our lives? Can't we? Tell me!

BOMAN: Change it?

DANIEL: Yes! Make it into something perfect . . . something
. . . The time before, it wasn't me, it was someone else . . . Now
I will live for myself . . . Be the one I really am . . . As I wished
. . . as I ought to be . . . according to my true being . . . Haven't
we a life of our own?

BOMAN: Yes . . . that we have, of course.

DANIEL: Yes! . . . See the sun! How it shines! . . . It's like pure
light to walk in, live in, find a new existence . . .

BOMAN: So it appears.

DANIEL: O my soul, you shall live . . . be yourself . . . fulfill
that for which you were chosen . . . You must not be anything
else! No, no, it must not happen! It must not! Each one has
his own life!

BOMAN: His own . . .

DANIEL: Yes!

BOMAN: That would seem most natural.

DANIEL: Yes. A life we control, that is *like* us.

BOMAN: But, is my life—the life I've lived—really mine? I
don't know. It should be, but is it?

DANIEL: You aren't sure?

BOMAN: Well, yes. Life has dragged me along the whole
time. I'm Boman, the man with one leg. Perfectly correct, yes.
He who goes from place to place selling shoelaces. Because my
life is to sell shoelaces. My soul was elected for that. So the
answer is yes, my young friend.

(*Daniel looks at him, oppressed.*)

BOMAN: What I didn't know was that it was determined in
advance. You don't learn until it has happened. Once I thought
of being a great and distinguished man. I thought I should
accomplish many remarkable things. But then came this business with the leg. And so I became an old rummy instead. Quite
a difference, you might say. But it doesn't matter.

DANIEL: Doesn't matter!

BOMAN: No, there's no meaning. And it doesn't help to meddle in such matters. Things are going to happen as they must happen.

DANIEL: No meaning! If our life turns out entirely different from what it should, then we must . . . not pay any attention to it! Let it go any old way!

(*Boman doesn't answer.*)

DANIEL: And we have a responsibility!

BOMAN: Responsibility?

DANIEL: Yes! Shouldn't we pay attention to what life becomes?

BOMAN (*Angrily*): Does life pay attention to us? Why should we pay attention to it, then!

DANIEL: Doesn't it? . . . I don't know . . . doesn't it perhaps do that? But it certainly depends on ourselves. It must. If it didn't depend on us, what sense would there be in living?

BOMAN: I didn't decide to lose my leg. It was an accident.

DANIEL: Yes—certainly . . .

BOMAN: That's the way it was.

(*Daniel silent, oppressed.*)

BOMAN: Fate, as they call it.

DANIEL (*To himself, quaking in fear*): Fate . . !

BOMAN: Yes . . . it was in the cards that this should happen to me, I believe . . . I was fated to have only one leg.

DANIEL (*Anxiously*): Oh no!

BOMAN: That was the idea. And so it came about!

(*Daniel pulls away from him.*)

BOMAN: No, my young friend, it's as I say. One shouldn't nose about in such matters. It will be as it will be.

DANIEL (*Shouts excitedly*): No . . . don't say that! . . . for God's sake!

(*Boman notices how shaken he is. Is suddenly silent.*)

DANIEL (*Moves forward to the window. Stands with clasped hands, whispers quietly*): A new life . . .

(*Boman sits and looks at him for a long time. Stares. They are both silent.*)

DANIEL (*Moves his lips as if in prayer*) : . . . as I ought . . . as it should have been . . . Yes, yes . . .

BOMAN (*To himself*) : Yes . . . as it should . . . (*Looks at Daniel.*) It's a beautiful dream, that . . .

DANIEL: Dream?

BOMAN: To live your life over again. If we could do it . . . maybe things would be different . . .

DANIEL: Yes! Something else . . . Something entirely different!

BOMAN: But you can't tell . . . (*Pensively*) When you walk like this, limping your way through life . . . is it so strange that you begin to drink a little . . . Perfectly natural, I say. One thing leads to another . . .

DANIEL: Yes . . .

BOMAN: It's not so pleasant to think . . .

DANIEL: What?

BOMAN (*Doesn't answer. After a moment*): I meant . . . when I was young, I never thought it would be like this. No, not this way . . . But what happens the way you think it will? Not one day. Not one little hour. And one's life . . . One's life . . . ?

DANIEL: Doesn't it become . . . ? Never . . . ?

BOMAN: Don't ask me. What do I know—I'm only an old man who goes about selling shoelaces. And when I've sold them all, I drink up the money. But what's a man to do? He needs something in his body . . . and when he has it like this . . . Is it so strange?

DANIEL: No . . . But if it had never happened, the accident! If it . . . !

BOMAN: Well . . . no doubt something else would have happened instead. And it would have brought its troubles too. Who says it would have been any better? I don't know what would be best for me really . . . Or maybe I should say, I don't know it any more . . .

DANIEL: No . . . you've forgot it.

(*Boman nods in agreement*).

DANIEL: Yes, we forget! The one thing we are here for. I must not forget. I must not! Because I haven't lived as I should have!

BOMAN: As we should . . .

DANIEL: Not my own life! We live just *any* way, and then call it our own life!

BOMAN: Yes . . . it's true.

DANIEL: We live out something that was thrown to us . . . it doesn't matter what . . . anything . . .

BOMAN: Yes, so it is. So it is, young man. You are completely right . . . You must have given it some thought . . . But that life becomes ours in a way, you see. We get used to it. It becomes, as it were, us. So it goes. We can't escape it.

DANIEL (*Violently excited*): No . . . ! No . . . !

BOMAN: Yes, I tell you. Now I'm so used to my wooden leg . . . that I really believe I'd miss it . . . Yes, so it goes!

DANIEL (*Walks violently around the room*): No . . . ! God . . . ! What is this inside of me . . . burning like a fire! I'm afraid of myself!

BOMAN (*Terrified*): What is it, dear boy . . . !

DANIEL: I have the feeling I've done something dreadful! Something horrible!

BOMAN: But my dear fellow . . .

(*Daniel stops suddenly. Stands staring at his hands.*)

BOMAN: What . . . what's wrong with you?

DANIEL (*Tortured*): I don't know . . .

BOMAN: Then . . . calm yourself, young friend . . .

DANIEL: O God, what have I done, what have I done! (*Has an impulse to put his hands to his face, but checks himself and looks at them. They begin to shake.*)

BOMAN: So . . . so . . . don't be frightened . . . Are you afraid of life somehow, my child? You shouldn't be . . . Certainly it is difficult . . . yes, yes . . . it can be agonizing . . . And one doesn't know what is coming . . . what it is that lies in wait for us . . . But we live as best we can, we do our best. Yes, we ought to do that . . . You should too! And then no one can ask more of you . . . Yes, we live the best we can . . . this hard,

hard life . . . we put up with it . . . drag ourselves through it . . . day by day, year by year . . . as well as we are able . . . And we have our dreams, we have our dreams! Have you thought of that? And there is kindness, there *is* kindness . . . And we have our dreams . . . I'll tell you . . . When I've stretched out in a pasture for the night, loosened the straps to stop the chafing, then I lie and dream . . . lie there and look up at the stars which I know so well, which are with me everywhere . . . look at them until I see nothing else . . . And the wooden leg doesn't matter any more . . . It lies alongside me as if it were something else . . . but like a good friend. Yes, that's the way it is . . . and in the midst of my dreams I sleep away like a child . . . happy and secure, far away from the earth . . . yes, yes . . . far from everything . . . And afterwards, when I wake in the morning then I put on my leg again and limp into town to sell a bit. Hobble around the streets, stand at corners where people are sure to come . . . Things go well enough. But it's not old man Boman there. No, not him. For old man Boman is dreams, he is dreams . . . So are all of us. (*Looks at Daniel*) What do you say, young friend?

(*Daniel does not answer*).

BOMAN: Well, that's how it is . . . Remarkable . . . the weather we're having, you noticed? Yes, in summer it's beautiful and you don't need to freeze. And how bright it is! Even during the nights it is light—so it should be always! That's how I like it! Do you?

DANIEL: Well . . .

BOMAN: Just look! When it's like this, a man can't help being happy. I pay little attention to this life here. No, I think it's ugly. I repeat, it is ugly. But I accept it with contentment, you understand. I make allowances for it. And when everything looks so bright and friendly, as now, then I think: things may get better! Who knows! Perhaps life can get better! Yes, so warm and beautiful . . . Just look! Isn't it beautiful! And when you're young and alive with everything before you! Not as it is with an old stumbler like me. Oh no, no. But once I was a gay and lusty playboy, I can tell you. No troubles and no sorrows then. No, it was glorious to plan ahead . . . about everything, about how you would live! . . . Afterwards you slide back as you get old and stiff-jointed and the end is in sight . . . Oh yes, yes, yes—but I don't complain. No, no, I don't complain . . . Take a look! Yes, this is just the day for me to have my shoe half-soled. I don't need it, you see. Will you do it for me? That's nice. (*Takes off the shoe carefully . . . stands barefooted*) You seem to be looking at . . . Yes, I do have a sock. An A-1 sock, you'll see . . . (*Takes it out of his pocket*) Yes sir! Darned and everything. But that one I must have for the winter. I must lay it by. (*Folds it carefully and puts it back*) Yes, it's lovely in the summer . . . No need to freeze. And the sun shines on all of us . . . it forgets no one . . . It pays no special attention to anyone but then it forgets no one either . . . And flowers and such things fine and dandy . . . Isn't it wonderful? I like such things . . . Do you?

DANIEL: Yes . . .

BOMAN: Yes, yes . . . that's what I like . . . (*Sits and examines the shoe closely*) It's pretty badly worn, I should say. Takes a lot of punishment because I'm always on the go, you see. I seldom sit down to rest. You'll have to be careful when you work on it. What does a half-sole cost these days?

DANIEL: That would be . . . three and fifty . . .

BOMAN: Three and fifty! That's pretty steep. It must have gone up. That would make it one and seventy-five for a single shoe. (*Counts out the money*) Ten . . . fifteen . . . eighteen . . . No, it isn't enough. It isn't enough, young friend. I'm so poor lately. Business is bad. They must be buying, instead, at the shoemakers.

DANIEL: I'll do the job anyway.

BOMAN: Will you do it? Will you? As a colleague . . . yes, I mean . . . we are in the same line . . .

DANIEL: Of course I will.

BOMAN: Many thanks to you! Many thanks! (*Stands up and clasps his hand*) And now I go out into the sunlight a spell, and . . . it will be delicious . . . Such a day. Such a glorious day! Don't you agree?

DANIEL: Of course . . . of course . . .

BOMAN (*Goes out. Turns around at the door and looks at Daniel. Quietly to himself*): A new life . . . a new life . . . (*Goes out.*)

(*Daniel sits down at the work table. Looks over his tools, arranges everything as it should be. Begins to work.*)

ANNA (*Enters*): Hello there! I wonder if I can order a pair of shoes.

DANIEL: Yes—indeed.

ANNA (*Has seated herself. Takes off one shoe*): I want summer shoes. With ankle straps, I thought.

DANIEL (*Kneels down before her, takes measurements—looks up . . . as if far away. Draws his hand over his forehead. To himself*): Strange . . . it's as if I remembered something . . . a woman I met . . . (*Stands up*) Yes, yes! So it was . . . and then something horrible happened!

ANNA: What's the matter?

DANIEL: Oh . . . it's . . . nothing really . . .

ANNA: Was it something you dreamed?

DANIEL: Yes . . . I dreamed . . . I dreamed such a remarkable dream . . .

ANNA: About what? Not about me surely? (*Laughs merrily.*)

(*Daniel looks at her. A flicker of a smile plays over his face*).

ANNA: Yes, it's funny how you dream about something at night, and then it comes back to you in the daylight when you're thinking of something quite different. It feels so strange, doesn't it?

DANIEL: It does, that . . .

ANNA: To think that such things stay in the head. They seem crazy when you're completely awake. Don't I know!

DANIEL (*Looks at her*): Who are you?

ANNA: I? My name is Anna.

DANIEL: Anna?

ANNA: Don't you think that's an awful name? Everybody thinks so. It's nothing special, of course. But when you're given a name in baptism—then . . .

DANIEL: No, it's pretty . . . Anna . . . I think it's a beautiful name!

ANNA: Your name is Daniel. I saw it on your sign.

DANIEL: Yes, that's right.

ANNA: It's not so common.

DANIEL: No . . . How do you like it?

ANNA: Daniel? . . . Daniel? . . . Yes . . . yes indeed . . . (*He smiles. Anna blushes*) Did you get my measurements?

DANIEL: No, I forgot one of them. (*Takes the measurement.*)

ANNA: With ankle straps, as I said before. I want yellow kid, so they'll look chic. They're to be my best summer shoes, so do an especially good job with them. Remember.

DANIEL: Yes!

ANNA: But the heels mustn't be too high. I want to be able to walk in them easily. And yet they ought to be smart and nice looking, of course.

DANIEL: Yes, surely.

ANNA: They should be cut quite deep right here.

DANIEL: Yes. That can be done. I'll do my very best.

ANNA: Good . . . But what kind of dream was it really? You looked all shaken up. Was it something terrible?

DANIEL: No . . . no, it wasn't.

ANNA: Well, I think it was anyway. I could see it on your face. Usch, how horribly one can dream— But it doesn't make much difference what one dreams, you know. First when I wake up I think it's real. Because I awake in the midst of it. But I rub my eyes hard, and I'm happy. So happy! I have such creepy dreams too sometimes. I don't know where they come from because I don't have such thoughts. But I just don't pay attention to them. It isn't that way, I tell you.

DANIEL: How do you think it is, then?

ANNA: How is it? Yes . . . It is, of course, as if I were up and awake and took care of my duties, or as if I were out walking in the evening, and the weather is beautiful and I see the sun go down on Lake Ringboda—or something like that. That's the way it is, of course . . . isn't it?

DANIEL: Yes . . . But it can be very different . . . something else . . . that you never thought of . . . that you never could . . . !

ANNA: Yes . . . sometimes I dream so beautifully that I never want to awaken.

(*Daniel's face brightens, he stands looking at her. But afterwards his face becomes dark and troubled.*)

ANNA: How gloomy you look!

(*Daniel does not answer. Passes a troubled hand over his forehead.*)

ANNA: I understand . . . you poor man . . . Did you dream about her?

DANIEL: Dream? . . . about her? Whom?

ANNA: Her . . . Yes, her whom you met . . .

DANIEL: Yes . . . we met . . . I don't remember . . . but we met surely . . . while we lived . . . It's dangerous for people to meet, do you know that!

ANNA: Dangerous? What do you mean?

DANIEL: It *is* dangerous, I say!

ANNA: No . . . it can't be. If two people like each other? Then it's only right and beautiful. That is to say, if they have a strong affection for each other.

DANIEL: An affection? . . .

ANNA: Yes. If they love each other. Isn't that what you mean?

DANIEL (*Probes his memory, searches within*): Love? . . . Love?

ANNA: Yes, then it can't be anything else than . . .

DANIEL (*Looks at her*): There's so much goodness in your eyes. When I look into them I feel as if I could never do anything evil . . .

ANNA: Anything evil?

DANIEL: No, never.

ANNA: Have you done something evil?

DANIEL (*Cringes before her candid gaze. Presses his hand against his breast. After a while, in low voice*): No . . . it wasn't me. It was someone else.

ANNA: I feel so sorry for you. You have gone through something difficult. And that's why you have such terrible dreams.

DANIEL: Love? . . . (*Goes forward to her*) Is it possible to love so much that . . . that perhaps . . . I mean . . . so that one's life would be transformed?

ANNA: Yes, without a doubt.

DANIEL: You really think so?

ANNA: Yes, if one truly loves—that must change everything.

DANIEL: One's whole life, the whole . . . Do you believe that!

ANNA: Yes, I believe that.

DANIEL (*Walks around in deep thought. Stops*): But then he would have to be a truly good person . . .

ANNA: If he weren't good, he couldn't love.

(*Daniel looks away—then at her.*)

ANNA: But I've also heard that true love makes a person good. I can believe that.

DANIEL: Yes! One becomes it . . . one becomes a good person . . . if it is true love . . . as it ought to be . . .

ANNA: You know what? There's something I can't understand. I can't understand how love can be anything but true love. You hear so much talk. Can you make it out?

DANIEL (*Stands quietly engrossed in something. Afterward in a low voice*): No . . . I can't. (*As if happy*) I don't understand it at all. . . .

ANNA: I mean when you love you must love truly. You can't do it any other way. The lovers must want nothing but good for each other, only good, always! Isn't it so? I don't understand what you meant when you talked about "doing evil." Can you do that when you love? Can you do someone evil then? Can you really? Tell me!

DANIEL (*Slowly*): No . . . no, I don't understand . . . (*Goes up to her, joyous and still*) When you talk about it I can't understand how it could be possible either . . . (*They look at each other quietly.*)

ANNA: I don't know . . . But I firmly believe in what I say. What do you think?

DANIEL: I believe . . . ! I . . . (*Becomes quiet.*)

ANNA: Yes, if two people should meet . . . It means so much, so much . . . I don't know . . . But it can't be anything but good. They live for each other to make each other happy. They both desire the same thing, to make something beautiful . . . bright and beautiful, the two of them together. So they will be really happy! But they can't, if they do evil to each other.

DANIEL: No, no . . .

ANNA: I don't understand it. The idea is that they should help each other. It must be so, because life has so much grief in it. But you know that yourself . . . and there's so much trouble. But they must help each other, so that life can be what it ought to be. That's what I think!

DANIEL: Yes, as it ought to be! As it should!

ANNA: Oh, I know a good many . . . Do you know they live as if they really wished only to make trouble for each other. That's all they want, it seems. But that isn't love. They're only fooling themselves.

DANIEL: It's something else, it is . . .!

ANNA: Yes, what is it? Can you make it out? I don't fathom it. Why do they have anything to do with each other when they can't be good to each other! That is surely the real purpose of people living together.

DANIEL: Yes—so it is.

ANNA: Well, how we go on chatting! I completely forgot that I should be home and . . .

DANIEL: No, don't go . . . not just now . . . (*They smile at each other.*)

DANIEL: You have so much faith in life!

ANNA: Why shouldn't I?

DANIEL: I want to, too!

ANNA: It has never done any evil to me, not intentionally, anyhow. Otherwise it has, of course.

DANIEL: Has it? But why?

ANNA: Oh . . . I don't know . . . It wants to do well. Though it doesn't always happen that way.

DANIEL: You mean that it was your own fault?

ANNA: Oh, no . . . yes, maybe. Always a little, I guess.

DANIEL: Yes, do you know what I think? I think it depends on ourselves. We have the responsibility. Life is blamed for being so and so. But life is only ourselves! Don't you believe that, too?

ANNA: I guess so . . .

DANIEL: It depends on us how it comes out, only on us!

ANNA: Only? Yes . . . Yes, it depends, of course, on whether we try to do right or whether we want to be mean people. Some wish to be evil and things turn out bad for them. And as it goes very badly for them, they become even more wicked. But you feel sorry for lots of people too. You do! Many poor unfortunates are to be pitied. Yes, I can't figure out such things . . . I don't understand. I only want to believe the best.

DANIEL: Yes, yes . . . who can do more? Who understands? I think you understand a great deal anyway . . . To me it seems like a great deal . . . a great deal . . . How did you come to learn all this you are saying?

ANNA: But, dear man, is that so remarkable? Everybody knows that!

DANIEL: Everybody? . . . To think that you came here . . . Do you live nearby?

ANNA: Yes, I'm a maid at the Holmers'. Have you never seen me?

DANIEL: No never. I didn't know before this that you existed . . .

ANNA: Yes, indeed, I exist all right.

DANIEL: To think that you came . . . and today . . . came in here . . . Isn't it strange? How can I thank you for it . . .

ANNA: Oh, my dear, what do you mean . . . it was really a matter of the purest chance, that I needed these shoes.

DANIEL (*Happy, excited*): Yes! Chance—perhaps that's what it all is!

ANNA: Really it was a matter of chance all along because I didn't know what shoemaker to go to, that is until I heard how good you were.

DANIEL: Oh, that it was you who came, you who could say this to me, when I so much needed it. No one else . . .

ANNA: No, it might just as well have been another. I mean someone who didn't notice that you were troubled. Because you were, I saw that clearly . . . But you aren't anymore, are you?

DANIEL: No, not now.

ANNA: Then I'm happy.

DANIEL: May I see you again?

ANNA: Oh, I'll have to come for my shoes. (*Laughs.*)

DANIEL (*Smiles*): Yes, of course.

ANNA: When will that be?

DANIEL: Yes—if you'd look in the day after tomorrow perhaps? Or for that matter, tomorrow!

ANNA: Fine and dandy. I need them as soon as the work can be done. The weather is splendid, isn't it?

DANIEL: Yes, indeed! . . .

ANNA: Oh, it's glorious. In weather like this you don't know how happy I am. That's why I keep chattering so much! Now, promise to make them real nice!

DANIEL: I promise . . .

ANNA: Many thanks! That was nice. (*Stands up to go.*)

DANIEL (*Takes her hand, looks at her for a long time in silence*): Do you really believe it . . . what you said . . .

ANNA: What do you mean?

DANIEL: . . . that everything can be changed . . . if one wants it, if one wishes for it hard enough?

ANNA: Yes . . . without any doubt. I firmly believe it!

DANIEL: Remember that you said it to me.

ANNA: Yes . . . (*At the door.*) Good-by then!

DANIEL: Good-by!

(*Anna goes out.*)

DANIEL: A new life? . . . A new life? . . .

END OF ACT I

ACT II

(Daniel sits at his work in his cobbler's shop. The room reveals poverty, is poorly lighted. A table has been placed in the room and on it Anna is laying out the evening meal. As she comes in from the right, she closes the door carefully after her. Agnes and Hugo, their half-grown children, sit in one corner, somewhat apart from each other. A violent agonizing blast of wind is heard outside. The outer door breaks open, dry leaves and dust from the street are blown in.)

DANIEL: Close the door! Close the door, kids! *(Hugo and Agnes jump up to close it)* What hellish weather it is!

ANNA: Please, Daniel. The children . . .

DANIEL: The children! What about them?

(Anna makes a quieting gesture.)

DANIEL: They don't have enough sense to close the door!

ANNA: It's closed now. *(Arranges things on the table. Agnes helps.)*

DANIEL *(Stops work. Listens)*: What a blast of wind, it . . .

ANNA: Yes, it's nasty weather.

DANIEL *(After a pause)*: How could the door blow open!

ANNA: It wasn't properly latched.

DANIEL: Not latched? I closed it myself. It was *(After a wait)* It's suffocating too . . . isn't it, Anna?

ANNA: No, I don't feel it.

DANIEL: You don't feel it! To me it seems as if I couldn't breathe . . .

ANNA *(Comes forward to him)*: You're certainly restless tonight, my dear.

DANIEL: Restless?

ANNA: Yes. Perhaps it's this eternal wind that keeps blowing.

DANIEL: What difference does that make?

ANNA: None, perhaps, since we are indoors . . . Yes, it's nice to have a home . . . And we're going to eat pretty soon.

(Daniel puts away his work. Gets up to walk back and forth.)
(Anna goes out to bring in food, returns with a dish.)

DANIEL: Why must we eat here in the shop! Is it necessary?

ANNA: My dear, the little ones . . . We must keep it dark where they're sleeping.

(Daniel doesn't answer. They sit down to the table, serve themselves, and eat. All are silent.)

DANIEL: I can't eat. *(Gets up.)*

ANNA: Now what's the trouble with you tonight, Daniel!

DANIEL: Tonight!

ANNA: What's the matter with you?

DANIEL: Nothing, as far as I know.

ANNA: You're not like yourself . . . Has anything happened?

DANIEL: Happened? Happened! Anything happened!

ANNA: Well?

DANIEL: You ought to know that nothing has happened! What would it be. Haven't you seen that I've been sitting here all day long, mending shoes. Like every day, of course. Has something happened!

ANNA: No, it's been as usual. But you have been a bit different, I think . . . I don't understand . . . *(She and the children continue to eat.)*

DANIEL: Happened!

ANNA: No, it hasn't . . . it's nothing . . . We have it so quiet and cozy . . . and such good food . . . My dear, come and eat and be a good boy . . . I've prepared potato cakes which you are so fond of.

(Daniel refusing.)

ANNA: My dear . . . You don't act this way . . . you aren't like yourself.

DANIEL: Like myself!

ANNA: No . . . Come now . . .

DANIEL *(Paces back and forth)*: *You* eat! *(As they sit and look at him)* Go on, eat!

ANNA: Children, do you want some more? *(Serves them. They*

are all quiet for some time.)

DANIEL (*Stops*): I must get out!

ANNA: But my dear, when the wind is so terrible . . .

DANIEL: What's the difference! Do you think it's dangerous?

ANNA: No, but . . . what would you do outside?

DANIEL: Do? . . . Nothing . . . But why should I be locked in here?

ANNA (*Rises. Takes a few steps towards him*) : Tell me what is on your mind . . .

DANIEL: To sit here from morning till night . . . day after day . . . until a man . . . (*Holds his breast convulsively to control himself*) Why shouldn't I go out!

ANNA: Dear Daniel . . . Yes, I understand so well that you are tired. You sit here all the time and toil early and late to lay by for us . . . The same drudgery, always the same. Never anything else. But life is that way. It must be so.

DANIEL: Life . . .

ANNA: Yes . . .

DANIEL: Is this it!

ANNA: It's the same for all . . .

DANIEL (*After a pause*) : You don't know what it's like for me!

ANNA: No . . . you don't have much to say . . . I'm the only one who does the talking in this house and soon I'll have little enough to say . . . You never tell me anything.

DANIEL: I don't have anything to tell.

ANNA: No . . .

(*Daniel walks back and forth.*)

ANNA: So that's that.

DANIEL: What *should* I say!

ANNA: I don't know . . . (*One of the children starts crying in the next room. She hurries out.*)

DANIEL (*Back and forth excited. Sometimes stops and listens to the gale. Anna comes back, closing the door quietly after herself*): What are they screaming about!

ANNA: Daniel . . . No one was screaming. Little Elof was crying. He usually wakes up at night and cries, and then I have to hold his hand a little while.

DANIEL: Hold his hand!

ANNA: Yes.

DANIEL: Is that necessary?

ANNA (*With firmness*): Yes!

DANIEL: No one used to hold my hand.

ANNA: No, you had no mother . . .

DANIEL: No! What was the need of that!

ANNA: Daniel . . . How you . . .

DANIEL: I was only born! Isn't that enough!

ANNA: Yes, for you perhaps—hard as you are.

DANIEL: Hard! The main thing is to be born, so one can live! Isn't that the truth!

(*Anna doesn't answer.*)

DANIEL: Just to live!—All these bonds . . . till at last a man can't move! Everything is mixed up, tangled in everything else, so you can't separate one thing from another. Life's supposed to be one's own! It ought to be a question of *me* sometimes! Me myself!

ANNA: You and always you.

DANIEL: Yes! Now it's a question of me! Now! For I am alive! *I!* Do you hear it—I!

(*Anna recoils from his wild look. The children crawl back against the wall.*)

DANIEL: What a hellish blast of wind that is! (*Paces back and forth in the room, like an animal, violently excited*) Everything hinders a man—puts bonds on him—closes him in!—Why do I sit here imprisoned? What kind of life is this! It isn't mine! Mine . . . It could be anybody's! Just so somebody sits here at the last . . . just lives . . . one day after another—does what is required—just lives! From morning to night . . . year after year . . . the same . . . And a man has to have children, so life will go on, go on . . . But where does it end? When does it come to something? When will man really live? He himself as he really it! Yes, as I am, I say! *As I am!* I who should have lived so differently . . . something else! I know it! What have I to do with all this? Nothing! I'm not to be hemmed in! Bound hand and foot! But I will break free! I will! By all the devils! . . . I don't know what you want!—But no one will strangle me— You think so—Fence in a living person! But I'll break out. Tear open the cage!—Nor be suffocated to death either—I won't be suffocated!—Do you hear? I'm a man! I must live, live!—I!— myself!

(*A man rips open the door, though there is no sound except that of the wind. He resembles Daniel, has the same clothes. His eyes are wildly open, full of horror. He stands motionless, after closing the door. He is panting violently without being heard. He totters a few steps into the room. Looks at what he holds in his hand, a knife dripping with blood. Thrusts it quickly down into his pocket. Stares at his bloody hands, which begin to shake, quiver. Staggers to the workbench and dries the knife on a rag lying there. Hurries back to the door. Pulls up his collar. Looks anxiously around in the room everywhere, at everything. Smuggles himself out again into the night.*)

DANIEL (*Who has followed him with a fevered look, recoils in insane fear. The others have only seen the father. He continues to hold his arms up over his head as if to protect himself*) : No—No!—What have I done!—What have I done! (*Looks at his hands, stares at them intently. They begin to tremble*) What have I done! No!—It isn't true! It isn't true! Not now; No, no, not now Anna—my beloved—And my children—my dear children—It isn't true!—not now! (*Forward to Anna, embraces her, hides himself in her arms*) My beloved, you—

ANNA: Poor Daniel, you are really sick . . . you are feverish . . . Your mind is wandering!—You are seeing things. What was it!

DANIEL: No, it isn't true!—Not now!—My beloved—and my children—Come . . . come close to me . . . Dear children, are you afraid . . . are you afraid of me—Don't you recognize me . . . —your father! O God . . . my God . . . (*Staggers, as if he were about to collapse.*)

ANNA (*Leads him to the sofa to lie down*): Poor, poor Daniel, you are really sick . . . (*Arranges things for him, covers him up.*)

DANIEL (*After a brief pause. Pulls himself up*): What a night this is—the wind . . .I . . .! God, my God . . . What have I done!

ANNA: Dear Daniel, your mind is wandering . . . You don't know what you are saying . . . —Dear, dear Daniel . . . Why do you talk this way . . .

DANIEL: No, it isn't true!—It's something else . . . yes, yes, something new, something else . . . Now, I have you—beloved . . . I have you . . . —And you my children . . . Come close to me . . . Stay here near me . . . (*Draws them up to him*) —Yes, yes, something else . . . bright . . . happy . . . as it ought to be . . .And you, Anna . . . beloved . . . (*Grips her hand hard*) You must promise me . . . promise me that it will be different . . . bright . . . As you know it should be . . . as you know . . .

ANNA: Yes, yes! . . .

DANIEL: You must promise me . . .

ANNA: What, love . . .

DANIEL: That I will be the one I ought to be . . . That I will be Daniel . . . the true Daniel . . . —your Daniel, my beloved . . .

ANNA: Yes, I'll be so good to you, I'll be so good to you . . .

DANIEL: But I'll be the true Daniel, do you hear, your Daniel . . .

ANNA: Yes, yes, I'll be so good to you . . .

DANIEL: And help me! So I can live my right life . . . as it was meant to be . . .

ANNA: Yes, I will help you . . . always be with you . . . here at your side . . .

DANIEL: I must never do anything evil, never, do you hear!

ANNA: No, no . . .

DANIEL: You must promise me . . .

ANNA: But love . . . You have never done anything evil . . . You have always been so good to us . . . Dear Daniel . . . you are the best man I know in the whole world . . . You fly into a rage sometimes, yes, you do . . . Then you can be horribly violent, you must admit. Real fearful! Then I don't recognize you.

DANIEL: We must be human beings. Good, honest men . . .

ANNA: But otherwise you are so good, so good always . . .

DANIEL: We must overcome ourselves . . . resist . . . In order to be calm . . . calm . . . We must be like you . . . beloved . . . like you . . .

ANNA: Do you say that? (*Smiles*)—Oh not like me, dear Daniel. That can't be. I'm too simple a person!

DANIEL: Yes, like you . . . like you . . .

ANNA: It's all right for me, but not for others, I'm afraid.

DANIEL: Pure in heart, like you . . . good and quiet like you . . . Yes, as quiet and faithful as you are, beloved . . . —So that there will be peace . . . peace . . .

ANNA (*Gets down on her knees by the bed, fondles him*): Oh my dear, my dear . . . so you say . . . and so you used to say when we first met . . . —And you've said it since, though not so often of course . . .

DANIEL: Now I'll say it often . . . and not forget it . . . never . . .

ANNA: My darling . . . (*She lies caressing him for some time; he strokes her hair, draws her to him.*)

ANNA (*Looks up at him, radiantly happy*): Now at last I know . . .

DANIEL: What . . . what do you know?

ANNA: Know a little about you . . . What you are, what you are thinking about . . . your worries, how you go about in anguish . . .

DANIEL: Yes . . .

ANNA (*Kisses him as if to thank him*): Do you know, I feel as if I've found you now really . . . at last . . . as you really are . . .

My Daniel . . . Yes, as you say! My Daniel!

DANIEL: Yes, yours, yours.

ANNA: I go about thinking of you so often . . . especially when you are depressed and restless . . . Then I sometimes feel it's so sad you didn't have a mother . . . never any home . . . Then it can't be right . . . One's so alone . . . torn away from everything . . .

DANIEL: Yes, yes.

ANNA: But now you have me . . . Don't you?

DANIEL: Yes, now it's entirely different . . . Now I have you.

ANNA: And we have our home . . .

DANIEL: Yes, our dear home . . .

ANNA: Aren't you happy about that!

DANIEL: Yes, so happy and thankful, beloved . . . I can't say how thankful . . .

ANNA: So good . . . (*Embraces him*) Think how we have worked to make it ours!

DANIEL: Yes, *ours* . . .

ANNA: But now it's ours, Daniel! Now it's really ours.

DANIEL: Yes, yes . . . It's *ours*. We will go on living here . . . you and I . . . for each other . . . and for our children, so that they will grow up to be good . . .

ANNA: Yes, Daniel . . .

DANIEL: We must be good . . . truly good . . . we who belong together . . . we who love each other . . .

ANNA: Yes. Yes . . . I love to hear you say it . . .

DANIEL: We must be like you . . . quiet like you . . . So that there will be peace . . .

ANNA: Yes, peace . . .

DANIEL (*Draws her up close to himself*): My beloved . . . (*They lie long in each other's arms.*)

ANNA (*Raises herself. Strokes his forehead caressingly*): So, sweetheart . . . Now you must rest. Lie here and be happy. You aren't cold?

DANIEL: No.

ANNA (*Tucks him in better, arranges the pillow. Kisses him. Leaves. To the children, in a low voice*) : Father is ill; he is going to rest . . . Now we must be very quiet . . . (*She stacks the dishes noiselessly. Folds the tablecloth. Withdraws to tidy up the room. Finds the cloth rag on the work table. Surprised, terrified*) No! . . . What is it! Blood!—Where did it come from!

(*Daniel pulls himself up. Looks in that direction, full of anguish.*)

HUGO AND AGNES (*Come up to look*) : Blood!—Blood! . . .

END OF ACT II

ACT III

(*Daniel, now old and gray, sits at his work as before. On the other side of the table sits Elof helping at the trade. Each is occupied with his own work. Nothing is said.*)

ANNA (*Comes in through the door at the right. She is a white-haired old woman*) : How goes it now?

DANIEL: Oh, so, so.

ANNA: And you, Elof?

(*Elof nods in silence without looking up.*)

ANNA: You look a bit pale, I think. (*Lays her hand on her son's head*) That's because you sit in here all the time.

DANIEL: What difference does that make? He's a full grown man.

ANNA: Yes, of course. That may be. But he's become so pale lately, he certainly has. And doesn't say anything. Just like his father. No one knows what you think about, you two. This is a tight-lipped family, that's certain. The men especially! We women folk, though, we have our little say-so, thank God.

DANIEL: Yes, keep it up, Anna. We are happy to listen.

ANNA: You don't say!

(*Daniel nods in agreement and smiles.*)

ANNA: We just got a letter from Agnes in the mail.

DANIEL: So? How are they?

ANNA: Oh, fine . . .

DANIEL: And the little ones are healthy?

ANNA: Growing and flourishing. The baby has a bit of a cough, but it's nothing.

DANIEL: Oh no, he can take it.

ANNA: She writes that Hugo drops in on them sometimes.

DANIEL: Naturally.

ANNA: Can you imagine, he's had a raise in pay. Twenty crowns more a month.

DANIEL: What do you know! That's not bad.

ANNA: No, now he'll be on easy street. He ought to write to us himself, but she says it'll be a while before he does, so she felt she should tell us.

DANIEL: That's nice, mother. Yes, Hugo can take care of himself. It's plain enough, or he wouldn't have got a raise in pay so soon.

ANNA: No, he's only been there a short time. The dear boy. If only they weren't so far away. I don't know why that has to be.

DANIEL: Is the letter in there?

ANNA: You can read it yourself later.

DANIEL: Yes, surely. Yes, it's gone well for the children, you have to admit that.

ANNA: That's true. We have much to thank God for.

DANIEL: They've gone out into the world and become decent people, able to take care of themselves. We've tried to bring them up right. I believe one can say they've grown up in a good home, though it's been hard going many times. They've taken with them what was needed to make a success in life.

(*Anna steps over to him, lays her hand tenderly on his shoulder.*)

DANIEL: It's you they have to thank most of all, mother.

ANNA: No, my dear, what would have become of them if you hadn't kept striving and toiling for us all your life through. And been such a good and loving father to them.

DANIEL: Oh, I've done only what any father would.

ANNA: It's easy to say, but not so easy to do.

DANIEL (*Looks at her*): But that's the way it should be, mother.

ANNA: And now we sit here, old and almost alone, only the youngest left. But Ingrid doesn't seem so far away. The blessed little life! It's a great joy to see her. If only everything goes well when the time comes.

DANIEL: That we must hope for.

ANNA: Yes, yes. One never knows.

DANIEL: Oh, it'll be all right.

ANNA (*Walks about, arranging things*) : It seems strange to have almost all the children away. Don't you think so, Daniel? We hardly ever see them any more.

DANIEL: Oh, they must fly out of the nest when they grow up. That's to be expected. Otherwise they wouldn't amount to anything. It's as if they were near us anyway. They let us know as soon as anything happens.

ANNA: Yes.—Yes, God bless all of them and keep them from evil . . . (*Walks over to Elof and strokes his hair*) How is it with you, Elof?

(*Elof looks at her. Takes hold of her hand gently and pushes it away.*)

INGRID (*In from the street. Blonde, bareheaded, in a white dress*) : Hello there! Hello!

ANNA: No! Is it really you, Ingrid dear! How nice! (*Ingrid greets all of them*) We were just talking about you!

INGRID: Really?

ANNA: Yes, you said you were coming but I didn't expect you so soon. How are you? How do you feel?

INGRID: Good, of course.

ANNA: Of course. You take it all for granted.

INGRID: Why sure!

ANNA: Oh, just wait, that will come. But God be praised that you get around in such fine shape.

INGRID: Oh mother, how you talk. It's nothing. Anyhow it's a long time off.

ANNA: Yes, I know.

INGRID: I brought along a few baby things. And I need to ask you some questions, mother.

ANNA: Yes, surely. Let's see!

(*Ingrid opens the package on the table in the room.*)

ANNA: No, how sweet they are!

INGRID: Yes, aren't they!

ANNA (*Holds out a pair of knitted socks*) : Have you seen, daddy? Look, Elof!

INGRID: Now, what does the shoemaker have to say?

DANIEL: You've put them together pretty well.

INGRID: I finished them last night, you know. And then I showed them to Hilding. He didn't even dare to touch them.

DANIEL: I wouldn't either.

INGRID: And he thought it was *wonderful* I could make something like that. You must get it from your dad, he said.

DANIEL: Maybe so—

ANNA (*Puts them back carefully*): Oh, oh, what small feet!

INGRID (*At the table*): And this . . . for sweaters!

ANNA: It looks like flannel. That's nice.

INGRID: And think, I got it cheap. It was on sale.

ANNA: How lucky! You should cut it in a single piece, you know. I'll show you how. And you have a shirt already sewed.

INGRID: Yes!

ANNA: Hm.—But you've got the seams inside.

INGRID: Why . . .

ANNA: They should be outside.

INGRID: No! Should they really?

ANNA: Babies have such tender skins. That's the reason, you see. The seams should be sewn outside, or they'll chafe.

INGRID: Is that so! Live and learn!

ANNA: Yes, that's right.

DANIEL: Mother knows about these things. All you have to do is ask.

ANNA: You can tell by your own, my child. Just copy it. Here it's done right. You wore this as a child. And Elof also . . . Yes, so it goes. Eh, Daniel?

(*Daniel nods in agreement.*)

ANNA: And you must prepare swaddling clothes.

INGRID: But do they use such things nowadays, mother?

ANNA: Oh, dear child, do you think everything changes? What would happen? Of course, one doesn't bind them up as in the old days.

INGRID: Of course not—You know, Hilding thinks it's strange, all this. When he comes home he rummages about in my things to see if I've made anything new. He isn't supposed to, because I want to show them to him—But it doesn't matter. And then we sit and chatter away and chatter away. Oh Lord, how we chatter . . .

ANNA: What in the world about?

INGRID: Oh . . . we talk about . . . about all this . . . He thinks it's thrilling.

ANNA: Thrilling! Yes, the men . . .

INGRID: And I think it's thrilling too . . .

ANNA: You do?

INGRID: I mean . . . You can *say* that . . . although you don't exactly mean it, mother dear.

ANNA: I understand . . . Yes, you lucky children. How is your man doing? He's always welcome here.

INGRID: Of course!—Can you imagine, last night after they had got their pay he came home with flowers, four tulips in a pot, wrapped in the finest silk paper. And it was for me! Can you imagine! I almost cried . . . He had gone and bought them! And we can't afford it.

ANNA: It was sweet of him! He's really kind.

INGRID: Oh, he is so good that sometimes when I sit and think of him, I get tears in my eyes.

(*Elof looks at his sister. Continues to look at her intently.*)

ANNA (*Pats her on her arm*): It was fine that you got each other.

INGRID: It was meant that we should!

ANNA: It was, that.

INGRID: Where there is love, two people should have each other.

ANNA: Yes, certainly.

INGRID: Especially when they are as much in love as Hilding and I are.

(*Anna nods in agreement.*)

INGRID: And now, I have the flowers alongside me on the

table . . . They're very nice, you see . . . Such good company.

ANNA: Yes, surely. Yes, yes, dear child . . . (*Pats her a little.*)

INGRID: But later I'll have a terrific lot to do!

ANNA: Yes, you can be sure of that.

INGRID: Yes, that'll be good. Because one can't always sit and think about things. The whole of life through maybe.

ANNA: No, there won't be any time for that, darling. You'll have enough to do, you'll see.

INGRID: But it'll be only fun. When it's for ourselves all the time! And it'll go like a ball!

ANNA: Yes, surely.

INGRID: Come, mother, let's go in and have a little chat by ourselves . . . there was something I wanted to ask . . .

ANNA: Yes. Yes . . . Let's sit in the kitchen. It's cozy there . . . And then you can look at what I've been doing (*They go out.*) And we've had a letter from Agnes, which you must read. They've a lot of good news to tell.

INGRID: I must hear about it . . . (*Out to the right.*)

(*Daniel and Elof are alone. They are quiet.*)

(*Elof gets up and walks restlessly around the room.*)

DANIEL: What's the matter?

(*Elof doesn't answer.*)

DANIEL: Get to work!

ELOF: I can't!

DANIEL: You can!

(*Elof shakes his head, goes back and forth.*)

DANIEL: Are you up to that again! Do your work, and you won't have time for your crazy ideas. (*After a wait*) What a son you are!

(*Elof stops and looks at him.*)

DANIEL: Yes! I said it! It's shameful!

ELOF: What's shameful?

DANIEL: To run after a woman like that!

ELOF: What's it to do with you?

DANIEL: You answer your father like that!

ELOF: Let me be then. Just let me be.

DANIEL: Don't you know I want to help you?

ELOF: Dad . . . do it, then . . . No . . . No one wants to help me . . . and no one can . . . Just let me alone . . .

DANIEL: But you know, Elof. She isn't worthy of you.

ELOF: I love her.

DANIEL: Love?

ELOF: Yes. That's the whole story.

DANIEL: Love! You call that love! Boy, you don't know what love is.

ELOF: What is it, then? What do I know, then? Why am I this way? Tell me! If you know so much! Do you think I care what it is? That I go around thinking about it? No. I . . . I'm in love, that's all. It has nothing to do with the mind . . . Nothing . . .

DANIEL: At any rate, you're always thinking of her.

ELOF (*Covers his eyes with his hands, groans*): No . . . oh no . . .

DANIEL: Poor boy . . . —Elof, I'll tell you. I know life. I know how hard it is. We must be strong. When such things come to pass we must resist, fight as hard as we can. Or it will go badly! Believe me. I know it.—Are you happy? Does this business make you even a little bit happy? You aren't yourself any more!

(*Elof shakes his head.*)

DANIEL: No, we become something else. Not ourselves! Everything goes to pieces, for all of us. Shame and misery and humiliation, nothing else comes of it. But don't think that these things should have such power over us. It isn't necessary, I tell you. Certainly not. When it's all over, it will seem no more than a slight vapor. When the dust has settled, it will be as before. Oh, it seems so important . . . We feel that it means life itself!—And afterwards when it's over, we can't understand how we took it so hard. Then we realize how it really is . . . It isn't at all as we thought. Nor are we either.

ELOF: Why do you tell me all this, dad.

DANIEL: Why? So you'll understand . . .

ELOF: I don't understand such things.

DANIEL: No, I know you don't. That's why I tell you about them.

ELOF: Yes, yes . . .

DANIEL: We all have many sides to our nature, I tell you, and much that can be pretty dangerous. But we must control ourselves a little, not let everything loose, as you do. We must be strong, Elof. We must have the ability to withstand. Hold up under temptation. That we must do.

ELOF: Strong? . . .

DANIEL: Yes! Exactly!

ELOF: I'm not strong . . .

DANIEL: No, you aren't. And more's the pity.

ELOF: Oh, father . . . why . . . What's the use of talking . . .

DANIEL: None, when you don't listen, when you don't care . . .

ELOF: You can't say *that.*

DANIEL (*Looks up at him*): Can't I?

(*Elof shakes his head.*)

DANIEL (*After a pause.*) Elof . . . You shall have a very different kind of woman some day. Believe me. You are a serious-minded, inward youngster. I know you. Yes, I understand you, I think I can say. And she . . . she's empty and superficial . . . not to say . . .

ELOF: Why do you talk about her.—Oh don't do it . . . —not about her . . . —

DANIEL: But she's not worthy of you! You know that yourself! Isn't she . . .

ELOF (*Helpless*): But how does it happen I love her then . . . —Father . . . How can it be?

DANIEL: Love . . . What do you mean by love?

(*Elof doesn't answer.*)

DANIEL: How does it feel? Can you . . .

ELOF: It's . . . it's like rushing out into the night, screaming and screaming!

DANIEL: Screaming? . . .

ELOF: Yes!—I don't know . . . I can't say it . . . What's the use of talking . . .

DANIEL: But child . . . you must use your common sense . . . you musn't go overboard this way, must be sensible . . . —You understand, you can never find happiness this way . . .

ELOF: Happiness? . . .

DANIEL: No, you don't think about that. Nor where you are bound! That's plain to see!

ELOF: Happiness . . . No, I don't think about that . . . —And why should I? I don't know what kind of happiness you mean.

DANIEL: Well, I'll tell you. To live a life in peace and joy together, in a quiet home that is truly blessed, where everything is love and understanding and goodness, so that you mean everything to each other. Have everything in common. That's true happiness, my son.

ELOF: But, father, one doesn't love just to be happy . . . at least that way.

(*Daniel is silent.*)

ELOF (*Walks around quietly. To himself*) : I don't care . . . It's not worth so much . . .

DANIEL: Worth? Don't you think it's worth something? The happiness your father and mother have had, that you've seen since childhood, grown up in. Haven't you noticed it? Like the rest of us here. If only when we sat around the table evenings and chatted and no one had anything but good to say to the others, never a hard word. Peace and warmth and goodness. Isn't that something?

(*Elof oppressed. Doesn't answer.*)

DANIEL: And Ingrid's happiness . . . you have only to look at her to feel it. Isn't that something? . . .

ELOF (*Helpless*): I can't . . .

DANIEL: You can! But not with that woman. Not with a woman who has no regard for your welfare, who never can . . .

Elof: Oh, why . . .

Daniel: Yes, Elof, I understand . . . I understand how it hurts you . . . That's why you're so desperate. But put it all away from you. Break it off and make an end of it. Don't bring disgrace on us all. And misfortune on yourself! You don't want to bring such sorrow on your old parents . . .

Don't you want to live an honorable life, become a good man who takes care of himself and does his duty . . . so that some day, when the time comes, you'll find a woman you really can love because she deserves it, because you suit each other, someone to bring you true happiness . . . —So, use a little sense . . .

Elof: Sense ! . . .

Daniel: Yes! A little of it might come in handy!

Elof (*Smiles*): Sense . . .

Daniel (*Exclaims*): If you have no self-control, let me help you! Think! To lay your life in ruins! Throw yourself away on a person like that! . . . Such a . . . slut!

Elof: Stop! . . .

Daniel: Isn't it true?

Elof: No! She isn't that!

Daniel: But . . .

Elof: She isn't that! She's . . .

Daniel: Everybody knows. They come and tell me the kind of woman my boy is going out with. No better than a slut, I tell you!

Elof: What difference does it make?

Daniel: Difference!

Elof: What she is, what she . . . —What does it matter!

Daniel: Oh, dear God . . .

Elof (*After a pause*): I don't care what they say, all their gossip . . .

Daniel: But . . . are you out of your mind . . .

Elof (*Draws away. Stands quietly. Then*): To me she's no slut. I've only held her hand . . .

DANIEL: Yes, I can believe.

ELOF: What?

DANIEL: Held her hand.

ELOF: Yes. I love her though.

DANIEL: Love! And you think she's worth that?

ELOF: Worth! My love makes her worthy. Otherwise I wouldn't need to love her!

DANIEL (*Looks at him, baffled but smiling. Then*) : And you don't care what she is!

(*Elof doesn't answer.*)

DANIEL: You don't care!

ELOF: She's the one I love anyway.

DANIEL: Don't let me hear such foolish talk! How can you love such a person! It's only lust, I tell you.

ELOF: Lust . . . But I've never . . .

DANIEL: Never what?

ELOF (*Walks back and forth covering his face with his hands*) : Oh, why does it have to be this way? Why? . . . Why? (*He bursts into tears.*)

DANIEL: But what is really troubling you, if you don't care what kind of woman she is?

(*Elof is silent.*)

DANIEL: You ought to be very much satisfied with everything. (*Elof doesn't answer.*)

DANIEL: Well?

ELOF: She doesn't care a thing about me, father . . .

DANIEL: What are you saying? She doesn't care? And yet you run after her! Such a one! . . . A laughing stock to the town! Doesn't care about you! (*Breaks into laughter*)—That's a fine thing! I call that love! True love! I've never heard anything like it! (*When he has quieted down*) So that's how it is. She doesn't care at all for you! So . . . Thank God for that . . . Thank God! God be praised . . .

ELOF: She doesn't think I'm worth anything.

DANIEL: Worth! Anything to her!

Elof: No. Or she'd love me as I do her.

Daniel: She! She's the one who's worth something!

Elof: Oh, what's the use of talking . . .

Daniel: You are mad. Completely mad!

(*Elof shakes his head.*)

Daniel: My boy, my boy . . . calm yourself . . . come to your senses. You have a little reason left. You aren't yet . . .

Elof: I'm only tired, tired . . . Oh, father, why does it have to be this way?

Daniel: This way? What do you mean?

Elof: Why is the world like this?

Daniel: Well . . . it isn't quite what you expect it to be.

Elof: Why can't we love each other . . .

Daniel: You tell me. But sometimes it's not so bad.

Elof: How can you say it? Is it a good thing that we can't love each other! What kind of hell is this?

Daniel: I don't know . . .

Elof: Only to keep wanting, wanting so much . . . and no one comes, no one cares . . . So it is! And so it must be! Oh, God . . . I won't have it! I won't have it!

Daniel: There, there . . . Everything will be all right again. You'll see. It isn't worth getting excited about. You are so young, that's why, you see. Things aren't as desperate as you think. Oh no! There's much to be happy about in this life, though it's not easy sometimes. Oh, everything will be different . . . You'll have to pull yourself together though. And not behave this way!—Learn your trade, dedicate yourself to it, assume responsibility . . . Become a first-class workman. You'll see, it will go fine!

Elof: But nothing matters anymore, father . . . nothing . . .

Daniel: No! That's all too clear! You seem to be going completely to pieces!

Elof: I can't help it . . .

Daniel: Nonsense! To lose your mind over a slut who doesn't give a nickel for you. I never heard the like.

ELOF: I don't want . . .

DANIEL: What is it you don't want?

ELOF: I don't want it this way, father . . .

DANIEL: Here in the world? No, you may be right.

ELOF: I can't stand it . . .

DANIEL: But it is what it is, my boy. Whether we like it or not.

ELOF: I can't stand it . . .

DANIEL: Well, change it then.

ELOF: I? I?—Oh God . . . (*Walks around in despair. Stops. Stands and looks at something far off*): For me she's everything.

DANIEL: Everything! . . . It's madness!

ELOF: Nothing can change that, nothing . . .

DANIEL: Then let me tell you this! If you don't stop running after her, I'll drive you out of the house! Did you hear me?

ELOF (*Looks at him. After a pause, calmly*) : I can go away myself, father.

DANIEL: Now you know it, anyway!

(*Elof goes forward and stands at the window.*)

DANIEL: Are you standing there, looking for her to come with . . .

ELOF (*Shakes his head in denial. Afterwards*) : I was just looking . . . It's strange how beautiful it is . . . That it can be so beautiful . . .

DANIEL: So, get down to work then!

ELOF (*Walks slowly through the room. Answers calmly and quietly*) : No.

DANIEL: Get to work, I say. Do your duty! We have a lot to do today, you know. Do you hear!

ELOF: No.

DANIEL: Don't you listen to what I say? It's strange . . . Won't you obey when your father . . .!

ELOF: No. (*Goes out to the right.*)

(*Daniel looks after him, wondering. Bends over his work.*)

(*A man comes in, with no sound from the door. He is dressed in prison garb, his head closely cropped. Gray, old. He resembles*

Daniel, but his face is heavily etched with passion and suffering. Comes forward to the shoemaker's work table. When he walks, no steps are heard.)

(Daniel becomes violently agitated.)

THE PRISONER *(Looks at Daniel. Then)* : I escaped!

(Daniel shrinks from him.)

THE PRISONER: They put me behind bars! I who did what was right! I who am right.

DANIEL: You . . . —Who are you . . .

THE PRISONER *(After a pause)* : Don't you recognize me?

(Daniel stares at him in horror.)

THE PRISONER *(Forward to the table)*: Why are you sitting here?

DANIEL *(Looks at the table and then at him anxiously)* : What do you want! . . . Why . . . —Why did you come . . .!

(The Prisoner merely stands and looks at him, for a long time. A shot is heard from the room to the right. He listens, tense).

DANIEL *(Springs to his feet)* : What was that!

THE PRISONER *(Wildly screams)* : Blood! Blood!

(Daniel stands as if turned to stone.)

(The screams of Anna and Ingrid are heard from inside): God in Heaven . . .! He's shot himself! . . . —Elof!

(Daniel rushes out.)

(The Prisoner is alone. Walks slowly forward, to the table. Takes up the tools in his hands. Looks at them. Flings them on the floor. Moves to the center of the room, looks around. Comes forward to the table near the sofa, on which are some flowers. Seizes them and looks at them. Is about to fling them away, but hesitates and replaces them as his mind seems to wander away. The lamenting of the women is heard within. He listens. Stands and smiles. Begins to walk around in the room, with his head down, taking the same number of steps in each direction.)

(Daniel comes back. Sinks in a heap at the workshop table.)

THE PRISONER *(Comes forward to him)* : They locked me up!

I who am right! (*Stands over him*) Didn't I do right!

DANIEL: Elof! . . . —Elof! . . .

THE PRISONER: I rushed after her! . . . out into the night . . . caught up with her . . . stuck the knife in her, so she—! Yes!— (*Walks around the other*) Because I loved her!—Don't you remember?—I loved her! (*Stands over him, gasping. Whispers*) I sneaked back to the place . . . afterwards . . . —Lay there caressing her, when they came . . . Don't you remember . . .—don't you remember . . . No. (*Draws away from him a little.*)

DANIEL: Elof! . . . —my poor, poor child! . . .

THE PRISONER (*Comes back*): You drove him to his death! It was you! You are a murderer! Yes! *You!* (*Continues to pace*) I . . . all I did was love . . . nothing more than love . . . I'm innocent. (*Goes back to him. With intense emotion*) Well! Was it wrong? That's what you'd say! You who sit here withering away in all your common sense! What do you know about it? What do you understand? You! Do you know how it is when it breaks loose . . . (*Paces violently around the room.*) You put us behind bars! Shut us up! Lock us in! But we break out! Nothing can prevent it! Even if you walled us in, shackled me fast so I couldn't move a muscle! I'd break out anyway!

DANIEL: Elof . . . Elof . . . How could you do it?

THE PRISONER: The fire has to be suppressed! That's what you think! With all the rubbish you can throw on it! It has to be choked, for God's sake! But no! I say it must burn! That's the thing! Once it's glowing all over then the fire must break out sometime. Do you understand! So you can see what it's like! It's beautiful when it flames up! Then you can see how life is all about you! How it really looks! Do you hear me? It's beautiful . . . nothing but beautiful . . . —Something great and glorious . . . something wonderful . . . (*On hearing the lamentation of the women within*) What are they shrieking about? When the prison walls collapse . . . and the prisoners escape . . . stand looking at the fire, which was their prison . . .—all made of fire! Oh, it's magnificent!—Isn't it! Answer me. Say something!

DANIEL (*Rocks back and forth, holding his head in his hands*) : No, no . . . we must not . . .

THE PRISONER: Must not! Must not love? Just go on being shoemakers, you think. Just sitting there—like you. We're alive, aren't we? Why shouldn't we be what we are? So be it.

DANIEL: No, no . . .

THE PRISONER: I loved, loved, with body and soul, with my whole being, with everything I had!—And she. She did nothing but evil to me! You know that! Nothing but evil, day by day, year after year, never anything but evil. Drove me to misery, anguish, madness . . . Do you hear me? And I, I loved—only loved—loved and loved her until I didn't know what to do with myself, or what to do with all this inside of me! I did right! Only what I should! Do you hear me! Oh, it was beautiful to draw blood!—Don't you remember? . . .

(*Daniel shudders. Draws back from him.*)

THE PRISONER: That evening when it came over me, when it broke out—the wind—do you remember—the eternal blast of wind—it was enough to drive a man crazy—Oh, it was glorious to be free, free! To break out! At last . . . after all the suffering . . . all the anguish and woe . . . —I was in agony. I was in agony! What could I do!—In the moment of release—when the fetters loosen, fall off—When all is laid bare—just as it is. I'm innocent! Innocent, I tell you! I haven't done anything. Nothing. Only what was right. What I had to do.

DANIEL: That's horrible . . .

THE PRISONER: Horrible? It was my life. Can I help it! The only one I had. (*Forward to the other person*) And you! What have you done with yours! What have you been living for? Tell me! Answer me. What have you to say?

DANIEL: I have tried to be a man, as well as I was able . . .

THE PRISONER: You! Been a man! Sitting here? Pursuing your work, drudging away, doing your so-called duty? And when he came here out of the misery of his heart, with his pain, his agonies, you didn't understand what he was talking about. And you say you've been a man!

(*Daniel hides his face in his hands.*)

THE PRISONER: You drove him to his death! You became a murderer, you too!

DANIEL: No, no . . . I didn't mean to . . .

THE PRISONER (*Looks at him for a long time. Becomes changed. Says slowly*) : No . . . you didn't mean to . . . We never mean to . . . Not *that*. We don't intend to do what we do—no, something else, something else . . .

I longed for something great and pure . . . that it should be made over, everything . . . that it shouldn't be so . . . No, no longer so . . . after release, release . . . It would be something great, that I felt, something wonderful . . . And so I ended up a beast! Nothing more . . . Haven't I a living soul, the soul of a human being within me? When will it show itself, make itself known? Tell me! When! Answer me!

(*Daniel sits, sunk in brooding thoughts.*)

THE PRISONER: Control ourselves! . . . Our passions! What's the good of them then? How can we live with them? We must do that! Damn the life that gives us passions—only to be suffocated! To think we must be consumed by them in order to live— to be what we are . . . You held him back! And what was the gain? You drove him to his death!

DANIEL: No, no, I didn't mean to . . .

THE PRISONER: Nor I either when I rushed out into the night . . . —I didn't mean to!

DANIEL: God, oh God, how shall we be men, how shall we be what you want us to be . . .

THE PRISONER (*Quietly*) : Yes . . . How shall we be men? Our lives . . . when shall we begin to live them? (*Walks about, deep in thought.*) And he! Now he lies there like a soulless animal, besmirched and bloody from wallowing in desires which he hadn't yet understood! Inflamed like an animal! Like an animal inflamed.

DANIEL: No . . . It was not so! It was something else . . . He sacrificed himself to bear witness for love, for the soul of man. I understand that now.

THE PRISONER: Blood, always blood . . .

DANIEL: And when I saw . . . He was calm and beautiful in death . . . lay as if he were dreaming about something . . . What are you dreaming about, my child . . .

THE PRISONER (*Anxious, tormented from within. Then*): But he had to die! He wasn't permitted to live!

DANIEL: He wasn't like us . . . He went ahead, as if to show the way. And now he is out of sight. (*Stands up. Stands and stares ahead of him in brooding and sorrow*) I have lived and become gray and tried to be a good and righteous man . . . and tried to understand life . . . And yet I didn't understand him . . . That which filled me once, my whole soul—I didn't understand . . . —I drove him to death . . . My own child . . . when he needed me . . . when he called me . . . (*Breaks into tears.*)

THE PRISONER: Twilight falls upon the eyes, the eyes of us all, and we go astray . . . —You. And I. All astray. Roads leading everywhere, but no single one in the right direction . . . And one which leads out into emptiness . . .

DANIEL: Emptiness?—No.

THE PRISONER: I don't know . . . Perhaps not. But who are we who must wander out there . . . limitless throngs endlessly marching . . . You and I . . . and he . . . all of us . . . all . . . throng after throng . . . after having lived in this world, crowded together in love and hate, with our instincts and desires . . . I see only life and more life, but what am I in all this? And you? What are we?

I am preparing myself to go—like him. Because the prison walls are rent apart and my soul is free. Free?—Free? (*Looks around in the room at everything in it, as if he were looking far off*) No. A man's own life. It's something he never has a chance to live. (*As he moves slowly to the door.*) No.—No.—No. (*Goes out.*)

(Anna and Ingrid come in. The old woman is tottering, broken by sorrow.)

(Daniel embraces her for a long time and then the daughter.)

ANNA: Oh my God, how hard you are, how hard you are! . . . What have I done that you must strike me such a dreadful blow, take away from me my beloved son whom you, yourself, gave to me and whom I have fostered and protected from all evil from the time he was small. What sorrows you have loaded on him which he was unable to bear, poor child, which you saw he didn't have the strength to bear . . . My poor defenseless child . . . And I who watched over him, my smallest, so that nothing should happen to him . . . got up at night to lay a cover over him . . . —And you, you strike him down bloody with thy hand of destiny!

What have we done that you must punish us so!—What have we done?—My God, my God . . .

Yes, I know we must die. But why did he never have a chance to live? Why wasn't he allowed that? Isn't that your purpose with us?—Why do you destroy what you yourself have planted? Why do you harvest in the spring, you who have, out of your wisdom, prescribed the course of nature.

Yes, I talk too much . . . What do I, a poor old woman, understand when you act, you who are so great and terrible . . . What can I say about that.

He lay and cried so often in the night when he was little, I had to sit and hold his hand . . . yet why shouldn't we cry, cry . . . maybe he was never meant to be happy?

What do I know? . . . Only you know and you say nothing, never anything . . . And so we never get to know.—What do I understand of your judgments, I, an old woman . . . For sixty-three years I have wandered on this earth and still I know nothing . . . Now I am tired . . . You, stern God, whom I've talked with every day, to whom I've prayed for my children and for us all, that we might wander on the right path, do you wonder that I'm tired . . . Take me home to you . . . as you have taken my beloved son . . . And let us know thy purpose with us . . .

Yes, yes, you have a purpose in everything . . . But we don't understand you because we aren't like you . . . We don't understand when you take from us the most precious thing you gave . . . —And let our poor innocent children come to such a death . . . !

(*Ingrid breaks into violent weeping.*)

ANNA: No, no, little Ingrid, you must not . . . (*Goes up to Daniel*) Daniel, dear . . . Do you understand . . .

(*Daniel draws her close.*)

ANNA: Do you understand God's purpose in this?

(*Daniel shakes his head.*)

ANNA (*To her daughter*): No, my dear child, you mustn't cry . . . it's for you to . . . yet what else could you do . . .

Poor woman, you who need to be quiet and happy . . . —we women, we must bear children . . . we, weak, fragile, creatures . . . who must bring children into the world . . . (*Caresses her to quiet her*)

INGRID: No, little mother . . . I'm not . . . I'm thinking about Elof . . . I know why he . . . —I understand him so well . . . everything so well . . . I know love too . . . —Oh God, that life could be so cruel!

ANNA (*Sinks in a heap on a chair*): My own child . . . And without saying anything . . . If only I could make out why . . . why . . .

DANIEL (*Comes forward and strokes her hair gently*): Maybe he went away to live the life he longed for here.

ANNA: Longed for. Why must we long for so much here? I don't understand . . . I, a simple woman, only a poor mother, who has born my children and watched over them so that they might become good people, as I know God willed, that at last they be allowed to enter into his kingdom, into his great peace . . . But I've not longed. I've always only believed. And then you strike me so hard . . . (*Sinks in a heap over the table.*

Daniel and Ingrid walk around quietly. She raises her head. Sees the baby clothes lying beside her. Picks them up) You poor little one who must come into this world . . . this world of sorrow . . . to weep and wail . . . to try the pitiful lot of mankind . . . (*She dries her eyes. Folds the garments carefully together, smoothes them out*) Poor little one . . . God help you and keep you and give you peace, peace . . .

CURTAIN